GUITAR GEAR

GUITAR GEAR

Edited by John Brosh
From the pages of **Guitar Player Magazine**

Quill/A Guitar Player Book
New York

Art Director/Designer
Dominic Milano

General Manager
Judie Eremo

Associate Designer
Victoria Ann Philp

Darkroom
Cheryl Matthews (Director), Paul Haggard,
Mark Medalie

Typesetting
Leslie K. Bartz (Director), Birgit Byrd,
Leanne Milano

Proofreading
Helen Casabona, Jake Hunter, Jerry Martin,
Steve Sorensen

Editor: Guitar Player Magazine
Tom Wheeler

President/Publisher: GPI Publications
Jim Crockett

Associate Publisher: GPI Publications
Don Menn

Director: GPI Books
Alan Rinzler

For their invaluable assistance in putting this book together, special thanks to Craig Anderton, Tom Mulhern, Keith Reinegger, and especially Tom Wheeler for the use of so many photos from his *The Guitar Book* and *American Guitars* (Harper & Row).

Library of Congress Catalog Card Number: 84-62774

ISBN: 0-688-03108-0

Printed in the United States of America

GUITAR GEAR PHOTO CREDITS

Pages 9, 12, 16-19, 23-31, 48, 55, 67-68, 69 right, 70 top, 79, 82, 84 left, 85, 87-88, 107, 134, 140, 154 right, 161, 170-183, 186-191, 197 top three, 206, 219-235, 239, 241-242, 245 left, 246 right, 247, 249, 250-251, 252 left: courtesy of the manufacturers; 13: Jim Hatlo; 16: top right, Jon Sievert; 33: top, *American Guitars*, Tom Wheeler, published by Harper & Row; bottom, Chip Schofield; 34-45: Chip Schofield; 47: Sweethaws Wood Photographics; 49: Jon Sievert; 50: top, *American Guitars*, bottom right, *The Guitar Book*, Tom Wheeler, published by Harper & Row; 51: Jon Sievert; 52: Jim Santana; 53: Sweethaws Wood Photographics; 56: Jon Sievert; 57: John W. Paterson; 59: Sweethaws Wood Photographics; 63: courtesy of George Gruhn; 64: George Gruhn; 69: left, *American Guitars*; 70 bottom, Paul Natkin/Photo Reserve; 71: Sweethaws Wood Photographics; 72: left, Jon Sievert; right, Andy Caufield; 73: Sweethaws Wood Photographics; 76: top, Jon Sievert; bottom right, *The Guitar Book*; bottom left, courtesy of John Carruthers; 77: both, *American Guitars*; 80: *The Guitar Book*; 81: middle right, bottom left and right, *The Guitar Book*; 83: *The Guitar Book*; 84: right, *The Guitar Book*; 86: top left, Stars Guitars; top right, bottom left, *The Guitar Book*; 89: *The Guitar Book*; 90: Robert Buccovio; 91: *American Guitars*; 92: *The Guitar Book*; 95: *The Guitar Book*; 96: *The Guitar Book*; 98: *American Guitars*; 99: *The Guitar Book*; 101: *The Guitar Book*; 103: *The Guitar Book*; 104: *The Guitar Book*; 118-125: Jon Sievert; 127-129: courtesy of John Carruthers; 130-131: Jon Kiesel; 136-139: courtesy of John Carruthers; 142-143: courtesy of John Carruthers; 145: Dawn Torres; 146: Neil Zlozower; 147-152: Dawn Torres; 154: left, Jon Sievert; 157: Jon Sievert; 163-168: Jon Sievert; 184: Jon Sievert; 195 top, *American Guitars*; bottom, Neil Zlozower; 197: bottom, Neil Zlozower; 207-215: Jon Sievert; 217: Jonathan E. Sa'adah; 236-237: Sweethaws Wood Photographics; 240: Sweethaws Wood Photographics; 243: Sweethaws Wood Photographics; 245: right, courtesy of George Gruhn; 246: left, Jim Hatlo; 248: Jim Hatlo; 252: right, Jon Sievert.

INTRODUCTION

Today's guitar player can choose from a great variety of basic and sophisticated music equipment with which to create a broad spectrum of sound. A dazzling array of instruments, accessories, gadgets, and electronic devices has become crucial to the practice and performance and creative fulfillment of millions of guitar players—both professional and amateur alike—throughout the world.

This book introduces and explains the most essential and useful components of today's guitar gear. Written, edited, and designed by the staff of *Guitar Player* Magazine, it describes, analyzes, and offers advice about all this musical hardware.

Guitar Player Magazine has always made it a policy to publish information, inspiration, and advice from working professional musicians. Consequently some of the world's finest guitar players, guitar teachers, and guitar makers have written for *Guitar Player* Magazine creating the valuable legacy that follows.

Please note the original publication dates as listed with each article. Some go back as far as 1973. But all present basic principles and classic examples that are timely and valuable today.

CONTENTS

Introduction, 5

1. HOW GUITARS WORK
Acoustic Theory, 11
Acoustic Guitar Sound, 12
A Primer On Pickups, 14

2. HOW GUITARS ARE MADE
Guitar Research Engineers, 23
Gibson Factory Tour, 33
The Business Of Lutherie, 46

3. BUYING A GUITAR
Steel-Strings For Different
    Styles, 63
Choosing An Electric Guitar
    Body, 66
Necks, Fingerboards, Frets &
    Inlays, 71
Neck/Body Joints, Pegheads &
    Tuning Keys, 75
Pickups And Electronics, 79
Bridges And Tailpieces, 84
The Vintage Guitar Market, 91

4. GUITAR CARE AND REPAIR
Guitar Maintenance, 109
Intonation, 112
Tuning Devices And
    Intonation, 115
Intonation And Truss Rods, 126
Bridge Adjustments For
    Acoustics, 118
Bridge Adjustments For
    Electrics, 120
Action Height At The Nut, 121

String Length Adjustments On
   Acoustics, 122
String Length Adjustments On
   Electrics, 124
Finish Maintenance, 126

5. BUILDING AND CUSTOMIZING YOUR OWN GUITAR

Building A Kit Guitar, 133
Guitar Kits And Replacement
   Parts, 145
Electric Guitar Replacement
   Parts: Tips For The Buyer, 150
Understanding Onboard
   Preamps, 153
Building An Onboard
   Preamp/EQ, 156

6. ELECTRONIC EFFECTS AND ACCESSORIES

The Guitar Cord, 163
Effects Devices, 169
Chorus Lines, 175
Graphic Versus Parametric
   EQ, 177
Handbook Of Multiple
   Effects, 179
Building A Pedalboard, 182
Multi-Effects And
   Programmers, 185

7. AMP SYSTEMS

All About Amps, 193
Applications Of An Electric
   Guitar Amplifier, 198
Amp Glossary, 202
Tubes: Mechanics &
   Mystique, 205
Mesa/Boogie Factory Tour, 208

8. GUITAR SYNTHESIZERS

A Guided Tour Of The Guitar
   Synthesizer, 219
Guitar Synthesizer Update, 225
Guitar Synthesis: The Roland
   GR-300 And G-808, 230
Guitar Synthesizer
   Applications, 232

9. RECENT DEVELOPMENTS IN GUITAR EQUIPMENT

Radical Acoustics, 239
Alternative Electrics, 247

About The Authors, 254

1. HOW GUITARS WORK

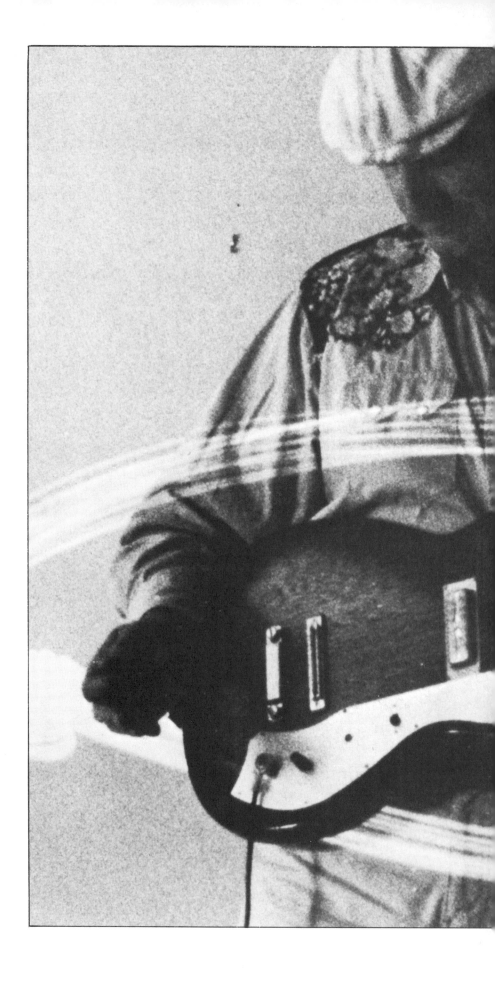

INTRODUCTION

In this chapter, special consideration is given to the fundamental nature of sound—how it's produced, how it's transmitted and shaped, and how it's perceived—with special emphasis on the needs of the guitarist. Esteemed guitar collector/designer George Gruhn explains the basis of sound, addressing such often misunderstood topics as where sound comes from, how tone is produced, and why no two guitars sound alike. The second part explores the particularly strong relationship between acoustic guitar construction and tone, why f-holes, flat tops, and specific finishes are as important to the sound as to the beauty, and the importance of good strings and proper maintenance. In the third section, the genealogy and function of pickups is clearly laid out, tracing their evolution from simple single-coils in the 1920s through the emergence of humbuckers and the ultimate hotrodding of both types. Everything from why certain pickups sound certain ways to how you should choose the right pickup for your guitar is included.

ACOUSTIC THEORY

February 1977. One of the surest ways to get into an argument with any musician or instrument collector is to introduce the topic of acoustical theory. As it is currently understood by most musicians and, unfortunately, as it is applied by most musical instrument makers, acoustics consists primarily of a mixture of voodoo magic and patent medicine with a very small sprinkling of scientific knowledge. Everyone seems willing enough to agree that some instruments sound better than others. However, hardly any two people seem to agree on what constitutes good versus bad tone or in what manner musical instrument construction is related to sound.

There are many different types of music and as many different opinions as to what constitutes good tone. It is ultimately no more possible to answer the question, "Do Fender Stratocasters sound better than Telecasters?" or "Do Martin Ds sound better than Martin 000s?" than it would be to determine whether Jimi Hendrix was a better musician than Les Paul or Johnny Smith. Clearly they are different, but a direct comparison is almost impossible. It is perfectly possible for a guitar to have an extremely fine fingerpicking sound and a relatively poor tone for flatpicking, or vice versa. The ideal bluegrass guitar may be a dreadful blues guitar. There really is no such thing as a guitar which is uniformly excellent for all types of music. Just as there are many different kinds of music, guitars are made in a wide variety of structural types and offer many different sounds. The only guitars which are equally usable for all kinds of music are those which are of such poor quality as to be equally *useless*, no matter what kind of music one plays.

An immediate problem encountered in any discussion of musical sound is the enormous difficulty of verbally describing sounds. Words simply are not capable of conveying a complete impression of an auditory experience. There are, however, a number of terms which are frequently encountered when musicians discuss tone. Some instruments seem to have a "woody sound" while others may sound "metallic." Musicians frequently speak of an instrument as having a "full" or "fat" sound versus a "thin" sound, or they may refer to an instrument as being "mellow" or "harsh." While these terms do not in themselves adequately describe a sound, their common usage does indicate that there is at least some agreement among musicians concerning different types of tone.

Sound waves are airborne vibratory patterns which may vary both in amplitude and frequency. Changes in amplitude (strength of vibration) are interpreted by the brain as changes in volume, while changes in frequency (number of vibrations per second) are interpreted as changes in pitch. Very few musical tones consist of a pure note of a single amplitude and frequency, but are instead a complex pattern consisting of a dominant amplitude and frequency and many subordinate overtones and harmonic frequencies. This complex pattern is interpreted by the brain as "tonal color." If one plays the same piece of music on a guitar and on a banjo, the result is quite different although the notes on the paper may be exactly the same. This is largely due to the markedly different tonal color of the two instruments. On a more subtle level, no two guitars (even of the same model) produce exactly the same sound. These differences are measurable and the characteristics of any particular instrument are as distinctive as a fingerprint.

While quality of sound is ultimately a subjective judgment, it is at least possible to objectively measure the sound output of different instruments and to compare them. On the most elementary level, the sound of a guitar may be analyzed by the response graph for a single note. For example, the open A string. An oscilloscope recording of one note is capable of providing considerable information about the tonal color of a particular instrument. However, for the musician there are many other properties of equal importance which require analysis. While the various types of guitars are tuned the same and have the same range of notes on the fingerboard, the response patterns of different guitars vary markedly. A compre-

hensive profile of the sound of any one guitar should involve the following four measurements of each note on the fingerboard:

1. Volume at standard playing pressure. This measurement would involve a recording of the decibel volume of each note on the fingerboard when striking the string for that note with the same degree of force. Due to their construction, both electric and acoustic guitars are uniquely sensitive to varying frequencies and therefore amplify different notes to a greater or lesser degree. An instrument may amplify low notes more than high notes and therefore have a bass-oriented sound or vice versa. In addition, most instruments are more responsive to some notes in the scale than others and may respond better in one key than another. Graphs plotting volume of each note on a fingerboard demonstrate that no guitar amplifies all notes equally well. However, some instruments provide a more even response than others. To a large extent, what a listener hears as "tonal balance" is a function of an instrument's ability to amplify both bass and treble equally. Most jazz players prefer instruments with what they call "even response," whereas many country and bluegrass players prefer guitars which offer a booming bass response and a somewhat weaker treble.

2. Frequency response. "Tone color" at standard playing pressure. This measurement would involve a recording of the frequency response "tone color" of each note on the fingerboard. Just as instruments differ in their ability to amplify notes, thereby producing notes varying in volume, guitars also differ markedly in their response to overtones and harmonic frequencies of different notes. It is possible, for example, for a guitar to produce bass notes with a "rich" sound and a wide variety of harmonic frequencies and overtones, while it produces "thin" sounding treble notes with fewer overtones and harmonics. What the ear interprets as "tonal balance" of a guitar is, therefore, a function not only of the volume of bass and treble, but of the "tonal color" of those bass and treble notes.

3. Dynamic range (tonal range of the volume capable with varying pressure and frequency response at different volumes). This measurement would involve a decibel recording of

the volume produced with varying pick pressure from that point at which the first sound is produced until the point at which further pick pressure does not result in an increased volume. It would also involve a measurement of the frequency response in "tone color" at these varying volumes. Guitars differ from each other very greatly in their dynamic range. Some instruments sound very good at low volume but are not capable of being played at high volume. Others are just the opposite. It is a rare guitar, indeed, which sounds equally good at both low and high volume. Typically most instruments, when played very softly, produce a somewhat "thin sound" and lack some of the overtones and harmonics present when they are played at what we have previously called a standard playing pressure. It should be noted that this "standard playing pressure" is a rather loosely defined term which will differ on each instrument. However, most guitars do have a response pattern that sounds best at a certain pick pressure. Most acoustic guitar players are well aware of the fact that different instruments have their own charac-

teristic "feel" and respond to the pick quite differently from one another. The upper limit of a guitar's dynamic range is determined by two factors: (1) that point at which further pick pressure does not result in an increase in volume; and (2) that point at which further pick pressure produces "tonal distortion." Distortion occurs when a string is hit with sufficient force that overtones and harmonics conflicting with the fundamental note are produced. Some guitars are considerably more efficient than others at converting string vibration into sound waves, and these instruments have a greater dynamic range than those which are less efficient.

4. Sustain. This is a measurement of the time duration of the note produced when a string is struck at standard playing pressure. Guitars vary enormously in their sustaining characteristics and musicians differ in their opinions as to what amount of sustain is desirable. Ultimately, it is a matter of personal preference and the type of music one plays.

Musicians frequently speak of one guitar as having a greater "carrying

power" or "cutting tone" than another. Some guitars seem to record better than others, and it is frequently noted that a guitar which may sound terrific when one sits down and plays a solo alone at home may not sound nearly as good onstage with a band or vice versa. Many musicians use different guitars onstage and in the studio for this reason. Such differences between instruments are a function of the factors we have begun to examine. It is quite obvious that when a musician is playing in a band, high volume is desirable, whereas in a studio recording situation volume is much less critical. High-and low-frequency sounds differ in their ability to travel over distance and in their "penetrating power" or ability to cut through noise. Therefore, two notes, while they may be the same on the musical staff, if they are of differing tonal color, may be very different in their "cutting power." In addition, both the human ear and microphones are differentially sensitive to varying frequencies, a distinction which is of obvious importance in any discussion of music, since that which is not heard is musically irrelevant.

George Gruhn

ACOUSTIC GUITAR SOUND

April, May 1977. Acoustic guitars have traditionally been made in several structural types: arch-top f-hole, flat-top steel-string, classical, and flamenco. These instruments differ from each other in construction and in the type of sound they produce. Typical arch-top guitar construction is similar to a violin with a carved top and back, the strings fastened to the body by a tailpiece, and the bridge held in place by downward string pressure. In contrast, flat-top steel-string guitars, classical guitars, and flamenco guitars each feature a flat top with a round soundhole, a flat back, and a bridge which is securely glued to the top with the strings fastened directly to it. String tension on a flat-top produces an upward stress on the top of the instrument.

Arch-top and flat-top guitars differ so radically from each other they are difficult to directly compare with each other. There are, however, a number of structural variables which, while poorly understood, appear to be highly significant in their effect upon the sound of any type of acoustic guitar.

While most musical instruments are made in standard sizes, there has been little agreement on what should be a "standard" guitar size. Modern makers have produced guitars varying in size from 12" to 19" at the widest point on the lower bout of the body. The size of the body is directly related to the volume of the air chamber. Each different size and shape air chamber is characterized by its own particular resonating frequency, which of necessity alters

Left: Bob Benedetto's Cremona model arch-top cutaway is especially suited to jazz and exemplifies traditional acoustic styling. Note the elaborate inlay on the unusual ebony tailpiece. Opposite: A Gibson F-25 flat-top steel-string acoustic with slotted headstock most commonly associated with classical guitars.

the sound of the instrument as a whole.

In addition to the resonating frequency of the air chamber, the guitar body itself has a resonant frequency which may be observed by tapping on the instrument. The note produced might be called the *wood resonance* of the guitar, as opposed to the *air chamber resonance* we have previously discussed. The wood resonance is derived from a complex interaction of factors, such as type and thickness of wood, bracing, finish, and assembly technique. The top and back of the guitar have distinctive *tap tones* which can best be determined by tapping upon these parts before the body is assembled. While I am not aware of any documented research concerning the relationship of tap tones to the tone of the final guitar, the problem has been studied for years by violin makers, many of whom go to great pains to actually tune the top and back to particular notes.

The tops of most acoustic guitars are made from spruce or closely related woods. It is generally agreed that each particular species of tree produces wood which differs from other species in its acoustical properties. Straightness of grain, width of annual growth rings, and density of wood are directly related to growing conditions of the tree. Most guitar makers prefer spruce with relatively straight, close grain and high den-

sity. Wood with these properties is the product of slow growing trees.

Most of the better quality classical guitars have rosewood backs and sides, whereas flamenco guitars have traditionally been made of cypress. Arch-top models generally have maple backs and sides, whereas the better flat-tops utilize rosewood or maple. The C.F. Martin Organization has used rosewood on its better guitars to the exclusion of maple, while other companies such as Guild and Gibson have produced many of their best models with maple backs and sides. Mahogany backs and sides have been reserved by most makers for their "lesser" student models. It is frequently found in studio recording that a mahogany guitar will have a better tonal balance than a similar rosewood instrument.

Thickness and gradation of wood (backs and tops) are equally important as the type of wood used. In addition, the bracing pattern—as well as the type of wood used for the braces and the gradation of the braces—greatly alters the response characteristics of both the top and the back. As a rule of thumb, thin wood responds well to low frequencies thus giving good bass tones, while thicker wood has a higher frequency response and a more trebly sound. Acoustic guitar construction usually involves a delicate compromise between gradation of wood and brac-

ing for acoustical properties versus the need for structural stability and durability.

While the finish on a guitar obviously enhances the instrument's beauty and increases its durability, it also alters the guitar's tonal characteristics, because each different type of finish will affect the guitar's tone in varying ways. Many older guitars, especially those made before the turn of the century, had either spirit varnish or oil varnish finishes. However, the most common finish used prior to the 1930s was shellac-based French polish. Today most high-quality guitars are finished with lacquer, often artificial lacquers instead of the more expensive and difficult to procure natural lacquers. The less expensive models employ acrylic finishes which are exceedingly hard and durable (though their tonal merits are debatable), but cosmetic repairs on this type of finish are difficult at best. The chemical composition of most finishes changes over a number of years, undergoing prolonged, slow drying so a thirty-year-old finish is not directly comparable with a newer one of the same material.

The neck and bridge, in addition to their obvious structural functions, influence the sound of the guitar. String vibration is conveyed to the soundboard primarily via the bridge, and to some extent the neck. The total mass of the neck, as well its density and composition definitely alter the guitar's tone. The size and shape of the bridge and saddle and the material they're made of also appear to be very important.

There has been considerable debate among makers and musicians as to what effect, if any, ornamentation and binding have on guitar tone. It is entirely illogical to assume that any inlay or binding on the neck would alter the sound. There is, however, little doubt that a large, thick pickguard glued onto the top of a flat-top will affect tone. Arch-top models normally have an elevated pickguard which is not directly fastened to the top of the instrument; however, a large pickguard will sometimes partially cover one of the f-holes. Many rhythm players prefer to remove the pickguard and claim that the resulting volume is greater.

Most binding and ornamental inlay on tops, back, and sides of guitars are restricted to the edges of instruments. These are not freely vibrating surfaces, as they are located over the rigid interior structural banding. Therefore, it is wrong to assume that ornamental edge trim greatly changes the sound of a guitar. But, as a rule, most makers utilize more ornamentation on their better, more expensive models, so these guitars may sound better, even though their tone is derived from excellence of construction rather than the ornamentation itself. Inlay has seldom been used on vibrating surfaces (such as tops and backs), and it can be expected that extensive inlay work on these areas would hamper the instrument's sound.

No guitar will sound its best unless it is properly set up and in good condition. Cracks, warpage, loose braces, refinishing, poor intonation, etc., can greatly hinder the tone of an otherwise excellent instrument. When shopping for a guitar, it is critical to understand that poor tone can be the result of either a poor setup or repair work. While it is relatively easy to compare two properly set-up instruments and determine which one is most suitable for your needs, it is a real art to be able to examine a guitar which is not in playable condition and to determine its ultimate potential.

While good strings are relatively inexpensive, they do profoundly influence the sound and responsiveness of a guitar. The gauge of the string, as well as the type of metal and matter of construction, profoundly influence string vibration and the resulting sound of the guitar.

No two acoustic guitars sound exactly the same; each one is as individual as a fingerprint and has its own particular feel. Of equal importance is the fact that no two musicians seem to have exactly the same technique; each one has his particular touch in playing a guitar. It is quite possible for two equally fine musicians to play the same guitar, and for one of them to be very pleased with the instrument while the other finds it poorly suited to his needs. Guitars and musicians are both such temperamental animals that finding the right match is often difficult. Any good musician has his "up" days when he feels especially creative and his "down" days when nothing he plays really seems to sound right. While guitars obviously are not really alive, they are so sensitive to environmental conditions—like temperature, humidity, and other external factors such as how much they have been played recently—that they, too, seem to have personalities and "up" and "down" days of their own.

George Gruhn

A PRIMER ON PICKUPS

February 1978. Perhaps because of its combination of technology and sheer flash, the electric guitar has generated some astonishingly inaccurate hearsay. Among various sources of prize-winning rumors, the topic of pickups is a formidable one, spawning some true champs. It has caused much disagreement among manufacturers, engineers, and dealers, who debate with relish the attributes of their various products while waving about charts of electromagnetic phenomena. Unfortunately, when all of the information hits the fan, the consumer (who only wants to sound like Eric Clapton on Cream's second album and couldn't possibly care less about resonant peaks) is often bewildered. However, despite the jive, a basic understanding of pickups is worth pursuing—and simpler than it first appears.

Gibson's most distinguished designer, Lloyd Loar, had built an electric double bass way back in the '20s. When Gibson rejected the instrument, Loar resigned and founded the Vivi-Tone company, which eventually folded; the public was not yet ready for electric instruments. In the mid '30s, Gibson introduced a pickup which soon acquired the nickname "Charlie Christian." Most of the electric instruments of the time were lap steels, such as Rickenbacker's Frying Pan and Gibson's EH-150. However, the electric Spanish guitar became a favorite in big bands, especially after World War II, and Gibson featured the Christian pickup on several models. Epiphones were also immensely popular at the time. The advent of Fender established the solid-body as a commercial reality in the late '40s and early '50s. Since then, the variety of products remained stable until the past few years, when pickups caused a tremendous amount of interest among consumers and manufacturers alike.

Transducers convert energy from one form into another. A pickup, or electromechanical transducer, is a device that converts the tones produced by string vibrations into impulses of electricity. Ideally, the frequency of each impulse corresponds to the pitch of the vibrating string. Most pickups consist of a permanent magnet (or six magnetically charged polepieces) surrounded by a coil of fine wire. Vibrating strings generate variable currents of electricity in the coil's magnetic field.

What does the pickup pick up? String vibrations. The vibration patterns may be quite complex, involving the interaction of many variables. However, when discussing pickups it helps to think of the string vibrating in a single elliptical pattern, or loop. Near the center arc, the longer waves produce lower (bass) frequencies, while at either end (nut and bridge) the tautness of the string causes shorter wavelengths, or treble frequencies. Typically, there is no

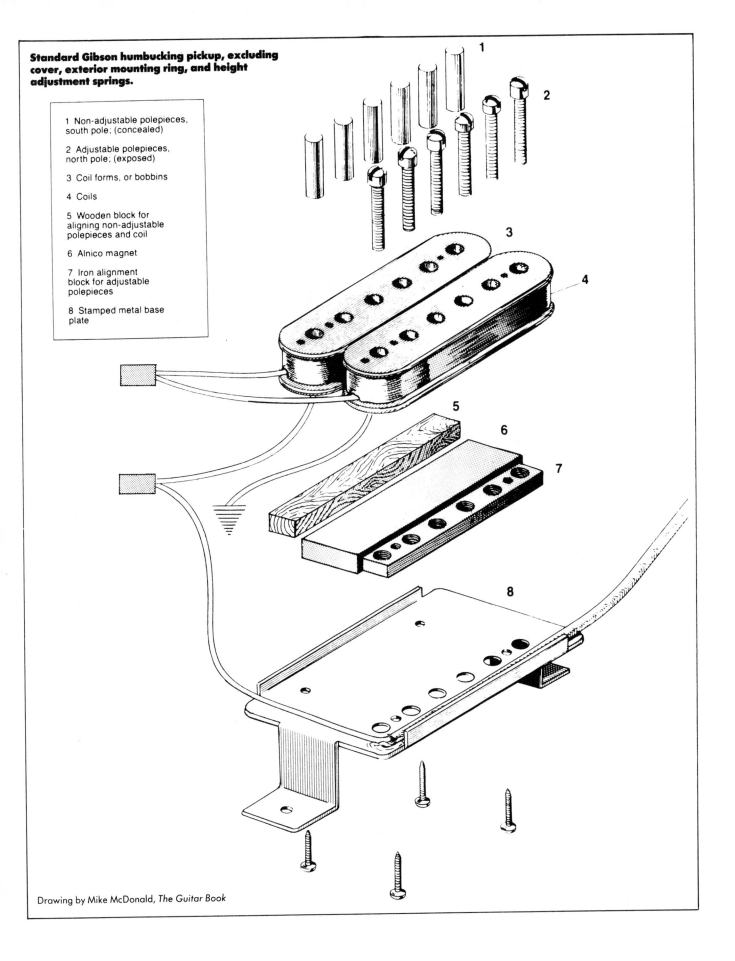

Standard Gibson humbucking pickup, excluding cover, exterior mounting ring, and height adjustment springs.

1 Non-adjustable polepieces, south pole; (concealed)

2 Adjustable polepieces, north pole; (exposed)

3 Coil forms, or bobbins

4 Coils

5 Wooden block for aligning non-adjustable polepieces and coil

6 Alnico magnet

7 Iron alignment block for adjustable polepieces

8 Stamped metal base plate

Drawing by Mike McDonald, *The Guitar Book*

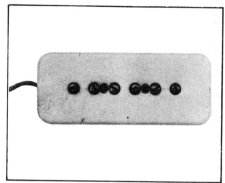

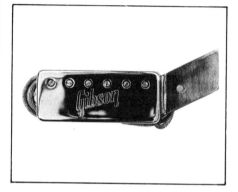

Clockwise from top right: Gibson single-coil "soap bar" pickup from a 1953 Gibson Les Paul; Gibson Crest (Johnny Smith-type) pickup; Bartolini Hi-A pickup mounted in an acoustic guitar's soundhole; Rowe-DeArmond's Model 220-C tripod-mount humbucker designed for soundhole placement. Opposite: Three Seymour Duncan humbuckers with combinations of black and white coil bobbins.

difference between a guitar's bass and treble pickups except in their location along the string length—bass pickup near the center, treble near the bridge.

Single-coil pickups and humbuckings. Practically all pickups have either one or two coils of wire, and since performance varies substantially depending upon the number of coils, it is useful to simply divide all pickups into two groups: single-coil, and humbuckings (double-coil). The first group is older; for decades, its most popular examples have been Fender's Telecaster and (since '54) Stratocaster pickups. By far the most significant and most imitated humbucking is Gibson's original version.

Among engineers, one of several topics of argument is the ideal number of wraps in the coil. Generally, the more wraps, the stronger the output. However, more wraps cause increased inductance (the property by which an electromotive force is induced by a change of current), and when inductance gets too high, the pickup suffers a loss of treble. Thus, balancing the considerations of output and frequency response is one of the compromises faced by a pickup designer.

The humbucking was originally intended to reduce or eliminate extraneous noise, and it works remarkably well. Its two coils are wired in series; that is, current passes through one, then the other. They are also wired out of phase, so that noise in one coil is ideally cancelled by a corresponding signal flowing in the opposite direction through the other coil. If the two coils could physically occupy the same space, noise-free operation could theoretically result; of course, the coils can only be placed side by side, and cancellation, while not total, is nevertheless substantial.

Humbuckers have a distinctive tone—broad, or "fat." The inductance of the coils' many turns causes some loss of highs as compared to, say, a super-bright, single-coil Fender pickup with fewer turns. Another reason for the humbucker's thicker sound is that its two coils sample frequencies from a wider length of string compared to a narrow single-coil pickup, and some cancella-

tion occurs when a vibration over one coil is offset by an equal and opposite vibration over the adjacent coil. The coils are right next to each other, so it is the shortest wavelengths—the highest frequencies—that cancel; thus, the tone suffers somewhat at the treble end of the spectrum.

Seth Lover was the engineer who designed Gibson's humbucking pickup. Gibson applied for a patent on June 22, 1955, and from that time until the patent was awarded (July 28, 1959), each pickup bore a "patent-applied-for" label. Later "patent-number" humbuckings have slightly smaller magnets and other minor changes in design. Although the tones of the two types can be distinguished by a discriminating listener, there are mechanical and electronic inconsistencies among pickups in both categories that make it difficult to generalize about their differences in sound. Patent-applied-for Gibsons are considered by many collectors and some rock stars to be the hippest possible pickups; as is often the case with other guitar gear, this popularity is due to a mixture of performance and sheer snob appeal.

The bobbins (coil forms) of a patent-applied-for may be black, off-white, or one of each. Since pickups with particular electronic characteristics and distinctive tones may have been assembled during a period when bobbins of a certain color were available, rumors have

sprouted that associate a pickup's tone with the color of the bobbins. In fact, the color alone has no effect upon sound.

Fender's humbucker—also designed by Mr. Lover—was developed several years ago and is stock equipment on the Telecaster Deluxe and Telecaster Custom.

Magnets and polepieces. Electric guitar pickups typically use one of two types of magnets: Alnico (iron plus ALuminum, NIckel, and CObalt) or ceramic. Ceramic magnets (identified by the letters "ox"—Arnox, Indox, etc.) are made from a clay impregnated with ferrous particles and subjected to intense pressure and high temperatures. Both ceramics and Alnicos are available in various grades; for example, Alnico 5 has for years been an industry standard.

Other factors remaining equal, ceramic magnets are substantially cheaper and much more resistant to demagnetization than Alnico magnets. They're more powerful as well. The Hot Rod kit by Alembic (45 Foley St., Santa Rosa, CA 95401), for example, is simply a set of ceramic replacement magnets. When substituted for stock Alnicos, output is doubled. (Note: Tone is also changed.)

Gibson's standard humbucking has one magnet, located underneath and between the coils. Its poles are found on the long edges, not at both ends. The

row of polepieces near the north-pole edge has a north-pole charge; the other polepieces are south-pole. Sometimes the engineer will specify supplementary magnets for additional strength. One example, found on Gibson's L6-S, is the Super Humbucking, which has a pair of extra magnets running parallel to the center magnet and located between the polepieces and the outside edges of the pickup.

Certain units have a row of six cylinders that protrude through the pickup cover. On some (e.g., Gibson humbucking), these are polepieces that conduct magnetism from an internal magnet to the string area. On others (e.g., Telecaster), the cylinders are actual magnets. Technically, polepieces are not magnets, but most manufacturers ignore precise nomenclature and call them polepieces anyway.

Polepieces are often threaded like screws in order to provide individual adjustment of the pickup's magnetic response to each string. Magnetic response increases as the polepiece is moved closer to the string. However, if the polepiece (or entire pickup) is set *too* close, or if the magnet itself is too powerful, the excessive magnetism will actually exert a pull upon the string, hampering vibration and possibly resulting in false harmonics, a loss of treble, or impaired sustain. The signal increases as magnetic force increases (up to the point of magnetic saturation).

While the versatility of individual adjustment is considered a definite plus, there is a negative aspect which, at least in the opinion of some pickup designers, more than outweighs the advantages: the absence of an intense concentration of magnetic energy

between the polepieces. Since each string is aligned directly over its respective polepiece, a loss of signal occurs when the string is bent and moved away from the polepiece into an area of reduced magnetism. One solution has been the replacement of each row of polepieces with a single fin, or blade, that spans the long axis of the pickup. The current trend is away from individually adjustable polepieces. Examples of pickups with either blade-type or unexposed polepieces include: Travis Bean, Alembic, Dirty Works, Bill Lawrence, Bartolini Hi-A, Peavey, and Gibson's S-1 and Super Humbucking.

Impedance. An object's resistance to AC current flow—its impedance—is measured in ohms. A primary determinant of this characteristic in pickups is the number of wraps in the coil(s). Abbreviated "Z," impedance also depends upon inductance, DC resistance, and the signal's frequency. Pickups are usually rated either low-impedance (generally, below 600 ohms) or high-impedance (generally, over 8,000 ohms); the overwhelming majority is high-impedance.

Low-impedance units have a cleaner sound, flatter frequency response, and an adaptability to long guitar cables. (High-impedance pickups, when used with long cables, suffer electrical interference and/or loss of treble.) Low-impedance pickups also require fewer wraps in the coil, therefore producing less inductance; this causes less capacitance (the property that, in certain systems, permits the storage of electrical energy), which in turn allows a brighter sound. Furthermore, standard pickups usually entail a noticeable sacrifice of treble when the volume knob is turned down; on low-impedance devices, the problem is reduced. Ovation installs low-impedance pickups on several models, and over the past few years Gibson has introduced a whole line of low-impedance pickups.

Resonant peaks. Most pickups can transduce the mechanical energy of vibrating strings into electrical impulses with a reasonable degree of accuracy—but only up to a certain point on the frequency response graph. This point depends upon the pickup's impedance, which, as previously noted, depends upon several variables. Beyond this level, frequency response declines considerably. Just *before* the fall-off point, there is a slight *gain* in output. The pickup responds most efficiently to this narrow band of frequencies, or reso-

Above: Two EMG humbucking pickups with built-in active circuitry in a Gibson Les Paul. Opposite: A trio of DiMarzio single-coils in classic Stratocaster configuration.

nant peak. Represented by a slight bump at the apex of the frequency response curve, the resonant peak is the most important determinant of a pickup's sound. Lesser factors include the magnetic properties, composition, and gauge of the strings.

Shielding. Household wiring, special effects devices, the transformer(s) in your amplifier, and florescent or neon lighting are all electrostactic or electromagnetic sources of unwanted noise. Proper grounding and the use of low-noise pickups can reduce the buzzing. Another important method—one that is too often ignored—is shielding. *All* electrical components—pickups, potentiometers, jacks, plugs, wires, and cords—should be adequately shielded, not only to alleviate noise, but to insure safety. Shocks that result from the careless use of high-powered systems can be dangerous, even fatal.

While too little shielding permits noise, too much of it can increase capacitance to the point where treble tone is lost. Some of America's major manufacturers, failing to strike a proper balance among the considerations of performance, noise-free operation, and safety, have for years produced guitars with unsatisfactory shielding. It is difficult to justify the shortcoming, since there are several available approaches to achieving optimum shielding. One is to surround the compartment containing electrical parts with a sheet of aluminum foil. Another is to enclose the pots with separate cans while shielding internal cables with a protective outer layer. Some companies apply a pure silver conductive paint. (Note: Only persons experienced with electronics should attempt to shield their instruments.)

Pickup volume. Unless a preamp is used, the level of signal leaving the pickup depends primarily upon the magnet's force and the number of wraps in the coil(s). (The wire's diameter is a less important factor; most companies use from 40 to 44 gauge.) "The hotter, the better" is a false assumption which, taken to its logical extreme, dictates that fantastic pickups could be built with those giant electromagnets that are used in junkyards to lift old car bodies. While such pickups would absolutely guarantee you a featured role on any stage, the tone would win no prizes. When comparing pickups for output, be sure to note the differences in tone as well. Building a hot (loud) pickup is easy; building a hot pickup with a wide frequency response is tricky, since some methods of increasing output can also cause increased capacitance, which, if excessive, can produce a mushy sound. On the other hand, a hot pickup with reasonable capacitance may provide precisely the sound you are looking for.

Out of phase. "Phase" refers to the time synchronization of electronic signals or sound waves. As previously mentioned, certain frequencies can be canceled when a string's vibrations over one coil are offset by equal and opposite vibrations over the other coil. Similarly, when both pickups are activated, the vibrations are again slightly out of phase simply because the pickups are positioned at different places under the strings. The resulting cancellations produce a sweet, somewhat thin tone.

A phase switch—a simple, double-throw, bipolar switch—intensifies this phenomenon by *electrically* reversing two pickups' phase relationship. The tone suggests that it could lapse into a squeak without warning—perfect for raunchy funk, snarling blues, or for finger-popping a few country-style chicken clucks on a Telecaster. Considering the increased versatility and low cost, the phase switch is a bargain among sound modifiers. It is easily installed by a repairman, and it is offered as a stock item on some models by Guild, B.C.

Rich, Peavey, Ibanez, and several others.

Buying a pickup. Choosing a pickup used to be easy: What'll it be—Gibson or Fender? But with the emergence of the replacement pickup industry and the growth of new guitar manufacturers, the range of choices has increased considerably. The music business is characterized by, among other things, the technical complexities of various products, the inexperience of many consumers, the mystery and emotionalism of the music itself, and the factual shortcomings of some advertisements. It all adds up to some rather dazzling rumors, and while the public is fortunately becoming more informed, intelligent discussion is still too often lost beneath an avalanche of hype.

Pickup design is a process of compromise. As previously noted, there are advantages to having only a few turns in the coil, other advantages to having many. The design of a pickup requires several such trade-offs, because a concentration upon one attribute may necessitate the sacrifice of another, just as the car with the greatest acceleration is unlikely to be the most economical.

Though confronted by identical laws of physics, engineers clearly differ in philosophy about where to draw lines between opposing factors. As a result, pickups vary substantially in performance. Despite all the graphs and specs, the best way to choose among pickups is simply to listen to them. When an advertisement promises that the product looks a certain way when charted on a graph or a scope, it is helpful only if the consumer appreciates the effect upon the *sound*. Among such ads, distinguish between those that clearly specify testing procedures and those that don't. It's as easy for an advertiser to make a pickup "sound" good on paper as it is to make a hair spray appear crucial to your sex life. Don't be intimidated by all the technical lingo and conflicting ads. Remember that aside from the considerations involved with *any* purchase—cost, guarantee, durability, etc.—the one valid criterion for choosing a pickup is simple: What sounds good to you?

Tom Wheeler

2. HOW GUITARS ARE MADE

INTRODUCTION

Behind every great-sounding instrument is a lot of research, countless hours of hard work, high-quality materials, and especially in the case of guitars, a bit of magic. Such aspects as treble/bass balance, tonal brilliance, and proper projection are the age-old concerns of luthiers; pickup impedance, sustain, and myriad complexities introduced by high technology—especially in the electric guitar—have mandated that builders and musicians alike understand the fundamentals of such diverse fields as acoustics, electronics, and woodworking. Profiled in the first section of Chapter Two, *Guitar Player*'s Guitar Research Engineers, are the movers and shakers in the guitar design realm, the masterminds who must stay one step ahead of the competition while creating a product that will appeal to the guitar buyer. The decisions and details of guitar creation are revealed through intimate discussions with the top R&D men at Fender, Gibson, Gretsch, Ibanez, Ovation, and Peavey. Once the designs are chosen, the instruments must be built, and the pictorial tour of the massive Gibson factory in Nashville shows how it's done on a grand scale. The chapter's final section, The Business Of Lutherie, demonstrates that for every major manufacturer, there are dozens of luthiers working independently or in small shops. A round-table discussion by a dozen of the top American luthiers addresses all aspects of guitar making and repair from the small businessman's standpoint.

Fender guitar research engineers Freddie Tavares and Greg Wilson: Input from musicians is vital to creating new designs.

GUITAR RESEARCH ENGINEERS

July 1979. Everyone knows what an electric guitar is, although there might be some disagreement among guitarists about which of the scores of new and used instruments currently available provides the best sound for any given playing situation, or which guitar seems to be the most adaptable to the ever-widening range of stylistic directions many musicians are currently exploring.

Besides musical considerations, guitarists often take a number of other factors into account before purchasing an instrument, including the unit's pickup and control configuration, its scale length, physical makeup (including shape, weight, color, types of wood and/or synthetics used, etc.), warranty, and, of course, its cost. After weighing

both musical and aesthetic criteria and after putting the guitar to the ultimate test, by playing it, the buyer is then ready to make the important financial and artistic commitment.

But have you ever wondered why there are so many electric guitars to choose from, and just who is responsible for designing them? For instance, what's the reason for one company offering a dozen models while another only manufactures two or three? How were the instrument's shape, electronic configuration, fretboard length, material composition, finish, and price determined? And who are the guitar designers? How did they get their jobs—which, in many ways, greatly affect the future of electrified music? And what kinds of personal

and professional experiences are necessary for someone to become a guitar research engineer?

These and other questions were asked of a number of instrument design representatives and consultants for some of the oldest and newest electric guitar manufacturing concerns: Fender, Gibson, Gretsch, Ibanez, Ovation, and Peavey. Their responses describe many of the subjective and objective realities faced when designing and building guitars. And while each person knows guitars inside and out, they all possess expertise in other areas of instrument manufacturing as well, such as marketing and merchandising, public relations, electronics, and creative design.

You'll also discover that these designers aren't ivory tower dwellers. They need input from a variety of sources—professional and amateur musicians, trade publications, marketing departments, instrument dealers, machine shops, wood supply warehouses, co-workers, etc.—before their creations ever leave the drawing board. And gathering this information takes many of them away from their workbenches and onto the road, discovering firsthand what features players and dealers want in a guitar.

It has been said that the difference between plagiarism, or blatantly copying another's work, and originality is a matter of semantics. If you copy one person's work, that's plagiarism, while emulating two or more is research. Few guitars are unique. While many manufacturers produce instruments of differing body shapes, scale lengths, electronic configurations, and material compositions, which of their creations is truly *the* guitar? Is a solidbody more of a guitar than a hollowbody? Do active or passive electronics determine whether an instrument is to be called a guitar or not? And what about shape, or color, or species of wood and/or synthetics used: Does an aluminum neck make a guitar not a guitar? The research engineers in this story make some interesting comments about what they consider a guitar to be.

So whether you're playing a solidbody, semi-solid, or hollowbody electric guitar with active or passive electronics; a single- or double-cutaway; one, two, or three pickups; a natural, sunburst, or other color finish; one of these guitar research and design engineers may well have either conceived or modified it. And while none of them could be too specific about what's coming in the future from their respective companies, the enthusiasm, dedication, and knowledge about the instrument displayed by each of them in their comments about what research and development (R&D) is all about portends nothing less than a new and exciting era for the electric guitar and its players.

Bill Kaman, OVATION

Although 27-year-old Bill Kaman is the son of Ovation's president, he earned his stripes as a guitar research designer on his own merit. Bill has been working on and off at the Ovation factory in Connecticut for the last 13 years, and from that experience has gained valuable insights into many facets of instrument construction. "I'd be in the detail shop one summer, after school was out," he says, "while the next I'd work in the top shop." But his big move into the company occurred in 1974 when he, still a senior in college, volunteered his services to the production of what became the Applause and Matrix acoustic guitars.

"The aerospace division of Kaman was tackling the project of building a good guitar that would be sold at a lower price than our other Ovations," he recalls. "While they have far more knowledge than I concerning materials,

construction and tooling methods, and the like, if you don't know what a guitar is supposed to look and feel like, you don't get too far. So for two weeks in January of '74, I made the 200-mile trip to the factory to help out. It was the middle of winter; so, of course, the heater in my car broke. But it was lots of fun, and when I graduated from college I decided to come on here full-time."

Realism is a fundamental principle in Bill's philosophy of guitar manufacturing. "You have to know what other guitars are available," he says. "Most all companies make a good product, and once you reach a certain level, they're all good. So it just becomes a subjective question of what you personally want." If this is true, how do you make your guitar a winner? "First," Bill says, "you do it by talking to professionals who make their living by playing instruments and get input from them as to what they like and don't like in a guitar, and what they feel is lacking in present-day instruments. Also, it helps if you play yourself and have a circle of friends who play, because from just talking with them you get another valuable perspective concerning what a guitar should look and sound like."

After the research engineer collects various opinions, the process of designing and building guitars begins. "In the case of our electrics," Bill says, "we wanted them to be unique. So we built the Deacon and the Breadwinner with some interesting features like active electronics. And after they were out for a while, we decided to expand the line a bit more and offer instruments with a more conventional shape and without active electronics. And the result was the Preacher and the Viper.

"A lot of people liked the active electronics, but they didn't like the shape of either the Deacon or the Breadwinner; so then came the Preacher Deluxe. What I am getting at is we start with a guitar that we know is good and we work from there. If there's enough demand for a modification or a completely revamped unit, we'll build it."

Even when there is a great demand for a certain type of guitar, building it often presents its own special set of problems for the designer. "I have to be concerned about making a design that will meet the instrument's targeted price," Bill says. "And there are some things, you know, that take time to change, and the wait can be frustrating. For instance, you have to first decide that the modification is necessary, and then you think about what's the best

Ovation Glen Campbell 12-string.

way to do it. Sometimes you need to retool, or get a new casting, and from the time you want to do it until it actually gets done might be a year or so.

"Designs are also greatly affected by cost factors. The original design may be quite good, but when you actually get down to building it, the instrument or component part may be very difficult to tool as originally designed. But if we did it a little bit differently, maybe changed the shape somewhat, then it would be a lot easier to tool. And the end result of all this is that we would reduce our costs—and be able to offer the guitar at a lower retail price—without affecting the quality of the product or radically changing the initial concept and design features that made us build the guitar in the first place."

Many of Bill's ideas eventually find their way onto an Ovation guitar, and he is modest about his role as a research designer. "I've designed some instruments based on many of my own conceptions about what a guitar should be." he says, "but if one person thinks he or she is going to design the whole thing—and that's going to be it—then you can bet that that person is going to miss the mark. Guitar designing to me is not an ego thing. You want to have a good instrument that's going to be popular enough to sell.

"I'll design a guitar, then present it to a number of players and other people involved with instrument production. Sometimes they suggest changes, and if they make sense, we'll do it. Even if I don't personally like the modifications, if I think they're valid, well, it's done. And while I can say honestly that I've never had a design turned down cold, I just don't go creating for the sake of creating either. If there's a need, you build something to fit that need. And the way I originally envision a guitar, and the way it finally comes out, well, sometimes it's quite different, and sometimes not."

Bill lists his requirements for someone who wants to become a guitar research and development engineer as knowledge and experience in guitar playing and repair as well as management experience. "When you're running an R&D department," he says, "you need to be able to understand budgets, cost estimates, and people. Also, some knowledge of machinery and tooling would be helpful. You might come up with an idea, but if there's no way to make it, it's not going to go. And if you can take some mechanical engineering courses, so you understand layouts, graphics, etc., those would be valuable. But the most important thing to me is an understanding of what a guitar is all about and a love for the instrument. You probably won't go far in the business if your heart isn't in it."

Jeff Hasselberger

Jeff Hasselberger's conception of what guitar design engineering is all about reflects very well the opinion of most of his peers: "Guitar research and development might sound like a romantic job, but in fact it's a lot of legwork, comparative data, prototypes, blind alleys, failures, and, once in a great while, a pretty satisfying success or two." The 32-year-old head of R&D and marketing director for Ibanez has, in the six short years he's worked for the Japanese instrument manufacturer, helped to firmly establish Ibanez guitars as the choice of many professional and amateur U.S. guitarists.

Jeff's past personal and professional activities before concentrating all of his time and energies designing and promoting Ibanez's guitar line include training as a mechanical engineer (although he received his college degree in English), journalist, and advertising writer; gigging in many rock and roll bands; racing automobiles; running his own advertising agency; and working in a retail music store as a salesperson and as a guitar repair person. His affiliation with Ibanez came about quite by chance. "I was sort of in the right place at the right time," he says. "I'd built guitars for myself and did repair work for other people. When Ibanez first wanted to enter the U.S. market, they needed someone who could help them out both with designing guitars as well as with promoting and advertising them. With my background, everything just fell into place."

When designing a guitar, Jeff pays special attention to what all musicians, from the beginner to the serious professional, want. "I try to get a cross section of input from virtually everyone," he says, "from players like George Benson right down to the people just starting out. If you don't approach guitar designing that way, it's very easy to slip into one way of thinking and, eventually, your product line begins to reflect that narrow vision.

"I strive to maintain as broad a perspective as I can when designing instruments. For instance, if advanced players are requesting certain features, I try to put them into two or three very advanced guitars. And those things that are important to beginners, I incorporate into several simple models. We work very closely with many big name players, not only because their endorsements are valuable, but because they are often slightly ahead of the majority of guitar players in 'sensitivity level.' In many ways, professional guitarists remind me of the race car drivers I used to work with. They hang their equipment out on the ragged edge of its capability. It takes someone whose total commitment is to musical expression to take any instrument to its creative and technical limits."

Yet even with all this information, it is almost impossible to guarantee the success of a new guitar model. "Sometimes," Jeff admits, "it's difficult to determine whether a product succeeds because of itself, or in spite of itself." Ibanez first entered the U.S. guitar market with many copies of American models. And while they were not the first company in the history of guitar manufacturing to do a bit of "creative borrowing" from the competition, it could be said that they were one of the best in the business of building replicas. "We didn't just want to follow everybody else," Jeff says, "but at the time we were in the process of learning—everything from instrument construction to marketing strategies—from our competition. But later, we started to promote our Artist series very heavily. Then, after having a bit of court trouble about one of our copies—which, actually, we settled some time ago—we accelerated our production efforts of totally original instruments. So rather than plan what came to be known as Musician and Performer Series guitars over a period of a few years, they just happened in six months."

Jeff's approach to guitar designing reflects both a sensitivity to and awareness of popular musical trends as well as a sound knowledge of successful merchandizing. "All the legitimate manufacturers are trying to market instruments that have a wide appeal and application," he says. "So to meet these criteria, I design in features that

Ibanez Lee Ritenour model electric.

will appeal to a broad base of players. Some people labor under the misconception that this approach to guitar designing involves some sort of compromise, or 'what's best versus what's saleable.' The real fact is, what's best usually *is* what's saleable.

"A guitar should be evaluated according to two criteria: utility and aesthetics. What importance should be placed on each may be subject to debate, but for my money, I'll take about 70% utility and 30% aesthetics. The bottom line, however, is always 'What's its cost?' To build a guitar for one person, where money is no object, isn't really hard to do. Building a guitar that gives a lot of people something substantial to work with is quite another story, especially when you have to make it affordable. You can draw a parallel between guitar building and music. To come up with unusual music—without any form—is pretty elementary. But to work within an existing format and come up with a new insight is, to me, where true art lies."

But even with what seems to be a very logical aproach to guitar design and manufacturing, Jeff occasionally comes up with a loser or two. "Sometimes I'll come up with a design that I love," he admits, "and I scrap it because someone was able to demonstrate to me that it was rotten. Actually, something might look great in its two-dimensional blueprint stage, but when a prototype is built, you look at it again, shake your head a few times in disbelief wondering how you could have ever thought something like that was decent, and yell, 'Ugh! That's terrible!'"

For people interested in getting into guitar research and development, Jeff has some humorous yet honest advice. "It's a perfect job for a guitar freak," he says, "but there just aren't that many positions available that I'm aware of. Probably there are less than 50 R&D jobs in the entire country, and short of assassination, there's no easy way to get one of them." Jeff feels that his mechanical engineering and guitar building experience helped him a great deal. And, he would be quick to add; so did his journalism and humanities training, since they fostered in him a feeling for and an ability to communicate with people.

If Jeff were to hire someone, and he says he receives quite a few letters concerning this, "I'd first look for someone who is humble. The last thing I need is some bozo who thinks he or she knows all there's to know about guitars. If you've got very strong ideas about gui-

tar design and are not willing to compromise, because you think you've discovered the ultimate instrument, then I heartily recommend that you start your own guitar company."
[Ed. Note: Jeff has since left Ibanez.]

Bob Monday

Bob Monday chairs the 15-member product committee at Gretsch. When he's not meeting with marketing, manufacturing, financial, guitar product, and engineering experts, or contemplating new designs, he's on the road demonstrating guitar prototypes to dealers and musicians: "I already know what I think, but I need to know what's happening with the players—what they want—before I try to develop new ideas."

As with many other people involved with designing and marketing guitars, Bob spends equal amounts of time in the workshop and with reams of technical data. "All information concerning guitar products is filtered through me," he says. "If an idea comes in, I have to formalize it, do all the legwork and research on it, and present it to the committee. If I feel a drawing will be sufficient to explain my point, then that's what I'll use.

"If, on the other hand, it takes a working prototype, I'll go down to our engineering department and often work hand-in-hand with them. Sometimes it may be something very simple, like a change on a specific model's neck, so I'll send a request to our factory to build a neck to these specifications for comparison purposes. We'll spend a great deal of time and money just trying to work out little details, but often it's these little things that make all the difference."

Bob has been a guitarist for 16 years, and was on the road with a rock band for much of that time: so in many ways he's an expert concerning what professional musicians want in an instrument. In addition to his playing experience, he was involved in sales and advertising as well as having 10 years of background in repair work tinkering with "everything from a mandolin to a digital synthesizer," he says.

Current musical trends and customer demand play equally important roles in Bob's R&D work, as do other guitar manufacturers' products. "If you walk around with blinders on," he admits, "and don't look at your competitors, then you don't learn what successes— and failures—they might have had that can in some ways affect your own

designs. While we're interested in what's happening to them, however, that doesn't mean we're doing the same things they are. We're looking to be different, yet still appealing to the broad spectrum of guitar players. And in taking a mass-marketing approach, it's a matter of incorporating the correct playability and cosmetic features at the right price."

Gretsch is currently in the midst of great change. Bob says: "We're making an all-out effort to become a major consideration in the rock guitar market. While we'll always be in the country market, our engineering staff is working feverishly on new designs, and not just guitars. We're going to be coming out with more solidbody electrics with what we feel are hotter and more progressive pickups in the not-too-distant future."

How does Bob Monday avoid designing financial lemons—guitars that might look good but which would never appeal to the general public? "Oftentimes our marketing people will say that this isn't what's going on right now and the consumer isn't looking for that particular kind of instrument at the moment," he says. "But that doesn't

Gretsch 1959-'60-style White Falcon.

mean we can't say, 'Hey, this is a new idea—we're just jumping into a new frontier here—so let's build it.' When this happens, I usually hit the road and 'fly the friendly skies.' I'll go to Chicago, New York, Atlanta, and most major cities in the U.S. to find the answer.

"Then I walk into a music store, and there's some person sitting there wearing a flannel shirt and jeans, and I'll hand him or her a guitar and say, 'What do you think about this?' If they say that it's great, that's fine. If I'm told the guitar is lousy, that's fine, too. I have to know what the public thinks before the instrument is built and marketed. If they want it, great; if they don't want it, fine; I'll put it on a shelf."

But guitar designing and construction, unfortunately, is not as easy as settling on what players want and then building an instrument. "Some of the problems involve other than compiling information and making sure your formalization truly reflects a broad cross section of player opinions," Bob says. "They have to do with basic communication problems and materials acquisition. Our purchasing department has many sleepless nights trying to make sure we have the parts supplied to our factory so that they can meet their production schedules. We'll also have problems like writing final inspections to make sure that everything on the guitar is correct."

"If I hear we have a problem somewhere, I get together with all the people involved and we sit down and figure out just what the trouble is and how we can make it better. It's a matter of constant change and communication. We have to know what each other is doing, and that's tough to do; because sometimes you get so busy just trying to keep up with things and then, all of a sudden, you have to make even more time to get back to the problems and take care of this or that immediately. It's tough to keep it rolling smoothly."

Bob has three major requirements for anyone who's interested in pursuing a career as a guitar research engineer: repair, sales, and playing experience. "It's very nice if you can be an engineer, a luthier, and a crack sales and marketing expert. All those things are great, but it's very hard to do it all. So I'd look for someone who has a basic understanding of all three, although the most important thing is to know the guitar and how it works. If somebody tells you they don't like the instrument for some reason—if you sit down and play, it has this problem or if you stand up and play, it has that problem—you have to

be able to relate to what they're saying.

"But the product manager is not the whole ball game. He or she works closely with many other people who are experts in their particular field. Although I don't know all the answers, and there's not one person here at Gretsch who claims to, together we're going to make sure we know as much as humanly possible before proceeding."

Chip Todd

Chip Todd hails from Beaumont, Texas, and he has been a guitar design engineer with Peavey Electronics since 1975. Before joining the R&D staff of the Meridian, Mississippi-based firm, however, he involved himself with a wide variety of other professional activities: he raced automobiles professionally, managed the advertising department for high-performance auto parts builder Mickey Thompson, owned a guitar repair company in Houston, designed monorails, and earned two college degrees—a Bachelor of Science in mechanical engineering and a Master of Fine Arts in commercial design. "When I first came to work at Peavey," Chip recalls, "I helped get the guitar factory going. I designed some of the machinery and set up the production line. But now I'm doing strictly guitar design work as well as running our service and quality control departments.

The name Peavey has long been known for its high quality line of amplifiers, mixers, graphic equalizers, speaker enclosures, and electronic components. Hartley Peavey, the company's president, turned his longtime dream of building an electric guitar into a reality, the T-60 solidbody, with Chip Todd's help. Briefly what happened was that Hartley asked Chip to analyze the then-current guitar market, discover which features on existing instruments were the most popular with players, and then collate all that information with what both men knew *they* wanted a guitar to look and sound like. "One of the major aspects of our guitar that has made it so successful," Chip believes, "is its wiring setup, which was designed by Red Rhodes. The T-60 achieves what we feel to be a remarkably wide tone range, and it doesn't need batteries or a built-in preamp to do so."

Most guitars—at least, successful models—usually aren't created in a vacuum. Chip, like many other guitar research engineers, relies heavily both on his own knowledge of instrument design technology as well as feedback from players and dealers when he

Peavey T-60 solidbody electric.

refines an existing model or contemplates building an entirely new guitar. One very interesting component of his personal commitment to the Peavey guitar is the monthly technical seminar he holds for dealers. "We'll get quite a few people down to Meridian each month," he says, "and often they'll grill me about the how's and why's of our product."

When first designing the T-60, Chip had to confront a problem common to all guitar research engineers who build instruments for mass production: How do you create a decent guitar that won't cost the consumer an arm and a leg? For instance, while there is some current debate as to the availability, or lack thereof, of certain wood species traditionally used in guitar manufacturing, the fact remains that wood is becoming increasingly more expensive. "But we're not going to let this affect the quality of our guitar," Chip says. "For example, ebony has been the standard material used for fingerboards over the years, but walnut also has a high degree of acid resistance and re-siliency, while being less expensive. So we steer clear of ebony because of its cost versus what good it does."

In addition to restrictions placed on Chip because of material costs, he must also contend with his boss' own personal attitude when designing an instrument. "The main restriction Hartley places on all his people," he says, "is the question, 'Would you buy it yourself?'" He stresses what Chip refers to as value engineering. "If you can do something for $1.50 instead of $5.00," he says, "and it doesn't bother the customer or affect the instrument's overall performance, then we do it."

While the T-60 solidbody and its companion model, the T-40 bass, have sold quite well, not all of Chip's ideas have become guitars. "There are a number of things that would be really great on an instrument," he admits, "but if you'd put them on one, it probably would make the guitar unmarketable. For instance, there's a great deal to be said about a headless guitar, where you do all the tuning on the butt end of the instrument. But guitarists, in general, are unbelievably conservative creatures; not in dress, or language, or lifestyle, particularly, but in what they want a guitar to be. Sometimes they'll buy tradition for its own sake, instead of trying out a new instrument whose quality may be first-rate and whose price may be much lower than the older company's product."

Peavey has no ambition to market scores of different guitar models. "We would rather concentrate on building a few good, versatile instruments," Chip says, "and do a better job on those, than to water down our efforts by building a whole bunch of models. I'm currently designing some new guitars with a few of the other folks we have around here—loudspeaker and electronics engineers. We're always open to new ideas, and it's quite conceivable that we'll be presenting a new guitar or two very soon. Also, I'm working on some modifications, you could call them optional extras, for the T-60."

While the transition Chip has made from his past professional activities to his current duties as a guitar research engineer wasn't a particularly difficult one, there was a time early on with

Peavey that posed some interesting problems. "When I was working on the monorail," he recalls, "I had to do a lot of tolerancing, draft angles, and new materials evaluation scientifically, not just by trial-and-error. On the first guitar I worked on here we drew up plans like a designer, not an engineer, would; and when our vendors came back before they did the tooling, we had to get together with them and figure out the draft angles we could live with and the tolerances here and there and yonder. So I learned right off to take a much more scientific rather than purely aesthetic approach to designing."

Chip considers his experiences and training in mechanical engineering to have been the most helpful in preparing him for his current job. "But it really helps if you also know how to play the guitar," he adds. "You have to be able to understand where a musician is coming from when he or she tells you what's good or bad about your product. And probably the most important thing is to always be inquisitive. If someone says something, I want to know why."
[Ed. Note: Chip now works for Fender.]

Abraham Wechter

Currently a working apprentice with guitar research and design engineer Richard Schneider and a consultant for Gibson, Abraham Wechter has a background that is well-suited to instrument design. Beginning with a job in a Seattle music store, he then went into partnership with another luthier and began building his own acoustic guitars and mandolins. While his business was quite successful, Abe still felt that he needed further study; so after a visit to the Society of Classical Guitar in New York seeking names of professional luthiers, he moved to Detroit to study the acoustical bracing systems and design philosophies of Dr. Michael Kasha and Schneider. And when Rick moved to Kalamazoo, Michigan, as a consultant for Gibson, Abe went with him and eventually found his way into Gibson's R&D department as a prototype builder. "When I first came to Gibson," Abe recalls, "I did a lot of work with different bracing patterns and other components of acoustic guitars. But more recently I've been getting into things applicable to electric guitars, such as wood impregnation and design work."

Wechter's definition of what his job responsibilities are reflects his own eclectic approach to R&D. "My primary responsibility," he says, "is to develop

products that suit the musical requirements of our clients. This includes exploration to expand our conception of musical possibilities as well as preserving traditional forms. We are constantly in touch with the playing public through direct personal contact, our clinics, and other channels. Relying on this information to help us set basic guidelines, we then target model introduction and changes that, at this point, are still relatively flexible."

Gibson produces more guitar models than any other manufacturer. And as a result, its R&D team is quite large. Coordination between designers, marketing specialists, manufacturers, and other components of the team is handled by R&D head Bruce Bolen. When a new model has tentatively been decided upon, a number of precise steps are followed by Abe and the other design engineers. "First, we specify the details," Abe says. "Perhaps preliminary sketches of the instrument are required. At this point, we are working within basic price guidelines set by the marketing department.

"Responsibilities for developing various aspects of the guitar are then assigned to different members of our team. One person may work on pickups, while another designs a new peghead inlay. After each person has finished their respective assignment, we collate parts and build prototypes. These instruments are reviewed, any necessary corrections made, and then we build the show models."

While all this might sound rather restrictive and mechanical, Abe feels that there still remains a great deal of creativity. "On an individual basis," he says, "every different assignment will have its own special requirements. Sometimes you'll need to do quite a bit of experimentation. One project I'm currently working on has turned my workbench into a small laboratory. And at other times you may hit upon an idea, file it in the back of your mind for a few weeks, and then sit down at the drawing board one day and it pops right out."

Every guitar manufacturer has a person or committee who gives final approval to all designs. At Gibson, it's Bruce Bolen. But even though Bruce has the power to accept or to reject a proposed guitar model, Abe feels that he is a benevolent dictator. "Even after the guitar has been designed and priced out," Abe says, "there may be small details that are handled more informally. For example, I was carving down a prototype a few days ago and realized that there wasn't anything in the specifications that either called for or didn't call for a heel cap. I thought it should have one, so I asked a few folks working with me about it. And when I called our foreman at White Wood—that's what we call the place where our guitar bodies and necks are assembled—he gave me his opinion of whether or not it would be difficult to place a heel cap on that particular model. The final decision to include it was then relayed to Bruce, who agreed to it."

When Abe designs a guitar, he has to be aware of various cost and production factors that are out of his direct control. "Two very important things I keep in mind when designing a guitar are to make it cost-effective and simple—streamline the design. Because the cost of re-tooling and new machinery is so expensive, I always try to consider using existing tooling and fixtures as much as the design will permit. In addition, you must know the limitations of your materials. For example, abalone is quite a bit more fragile than pearl, and knowing this might influence the intricacy of my inlay design. And if you're routing pockets for electronics in solidbody, you have to know how close you can get to the edge before risking eventual cracking problems in a certain species of wood."

Like most other guitar designers, Abe has had a few of his ideas modified. Some of the reasons he cites are cost and time restrictions. "You might wake up one morning with a great idea," he says, "get it down in some preliminary sketches, show them around, and discover that it would cost too much to do. And sometimes your idea is modified to the point where it no longer resembles your original conception—although this *can* be a real improvement. But most often, there just

Gibson updates a classic: Flying V's with custom finishes.

simply isn't any time to pursue an idea, because of other research work that has a higher priority at that moment."

While he admits that the number of guitar models Gibson manufactures is mostly a marketing department decision, Abe is personally an advocate of producing many different instrument types. "I feel that in offering a wide variety of models," he says, "we provide players with a full range of instrument types and formats." And for someone who wants to enter the field of guitar research and design, Abe outlines what he'd look for in a potential co-worker: "The person would have to be a tinkerer. And while an academic background is useful, a sense of pride and craftsmanship and an attention to fine detail is absolutely essential. Also, he or she should have an artistic nature. This is not easy to teach someone: There are many excellent craftspersons who lack originality, and these people would not fit in at Gibson very well. At the same time, you have to have a level head, because often there is quite a bit of pressure to get your job done on time. And you really have to enjoy your work if you are going to do well at it."

Fred Tavares

There have been few electric guitars in the history of the instrument that are still as popular as the Fender Stratocaster, and there are few R&D people as knowledgeable about the business as is 66-year-old Freddie Tavares. Once head of Fender's guitar research department, Freddie now occupies the role of consultant to the new R&D head, Gregg Wilson [see accompanying story]. It was Freddie and company founder Leo Fender who designed the first Strat. "When I came to work for Leo in 1953," he recalls, "besides doing odd jobs, I helped him lay out the Stratocaster on the drawing board.

"I remember that we had a piece of paper with lines drawn on it: six lines for the strings, and two crosslines for the nut and the bridge. Then we drew a body on it, erasing here and there until we got the shape we liked. Remember, at that time Leo was the total owner of the place, which had some peculiar advantages. There was no stalling around when it was time to get something done. Leo would say, 'That's the shape I like,' or, 'Let's put in three pickups—two is good, but three will kill them,' and it would get done."

Originally from Hawaii, Freddie came to the U.S. to live during the late '40s. An accomplished steel guitar player and self-taught in the field of electronics and audio amplification ("I was at the mercy of radiomen fixing my amplifier: They'd charge you any price they wanted"), Tavares also worked as a freelance studio musician until Leo Fender asked him to be an assistant in R&D.

Freddie recalls how he used to design instruments. "When it was just Leo and me," he says, "we did what we pleased. In other words, Leo did what he pleased, and I was his assistant. We didn't worry about things like distributors or the sales department telling us what to do; we listened to the musicians directly. But this is an enormous corporation now, and we must do things the proper way. We listen like crazy to what marketing wants."

Freddie has some definite ideas about what a guitar is supposed to look and sound like, and his beliefs are consistent with those expressed by most younger guitar research engineers. And while he strives to maintain an objective perspective when it comes to popular music trends, he finds it difficult at times to accept the modern vocabulary of electronics. "I still call capacitors condensers," he says, "and I still resent them changing the name. I hate to say 'Hertz,' even. If you ask somebody what it means, they'll tell you cycles per second. So why say 'Hertz?'"

Because Fender doesn't offer as wide a variety of guitar models as do other manufacturers, Freddie's major concern has been to modify the existing line, adding refinements when and if called for. But it isn't always easy to do. "There were some improvements we wanted to make on the Stratocaster," he admits. "However, marketing's attitude was not to fool with success. But we were pressured at one time to change from a three-position to a five-position switch on the Stratocaster, which we did. The unit's the same—it does the same job electrically—as the three position unit, except the contacts are longer and there are detents that lock the switch in two extra positions. And many musicians used to do the very same thing on the old three-position switch by carefully setting it and holding their breath hoping not to bump it."

When new models were introduced into the Fender catalog, it wasn't always the direct result of what musicians wanted. "Some of it was just Leo and I, too, you know," Freddie says. "For instance, when we built the Stratocaster, we thought that was the world's greatest guitar. Then we said, 'Let's make something even better.' So we built the Jazzmaster. It was great: It had a rhythm switch so you could preset the rhythm pickup. And if you only had one guitar in your band you didn't have to fool with the volume control all the time for leads or for comping. But no one would buy it in the quantities that they bought the Telecasters and Strats."

Large volume sales can mean decreased quality control in order to produce enough instruments to meet demands. And while Fender, like all the other companies who gear production to a mass-marketing philosophy, cannot boast that all of their guitars leave the factory in perfect working order, when an error is discovered, it is dealt with immediately. "We've had some problems at times," Freddie admits, "because someone was in too big of a hurry to get things through, or some production outfit, who had a quota to make, would try to circumvent quality control. But whenever we catch something, which more often than not we do, we'd rip the whole mess out of finished goods, take them out of the package, and fix every last one."

Freddie takes a very practical stance on an instrument's cost effectiveness versus what it will do. "You can design certain wonderful features that might need a lot of machine work," he says, "and that can be really expensive. The problem is, if you have something and there's a $5.00 labor charge per unit—and you make 2,000,000 units—well, that's $10,000,000. Whereas, if you buy a $100,000. machine that can do the job, you have no more charges after the one initial expense." And what are Freddie's feelings about wood shortages? "We don't have any trouble getting good wood, as far as I know," he says. "We pay through the nose and take it on the chin like good soldiers."

For those interested in some day working in Fender's R&D department, Freddie Tavares offers some sage advice: "We would consider him or her as primarily a project engineer, a guitar designer, so you always like to have somebody who plays the darn thing. That doesn't mean you couldn't have a good person in the job who didn't play, but it's much better if he or she does, because then they're simpatico, you know.

"Second, the person has to show some ability, such as, 'Hey, I made this guitar when I was 18.' And, finally, he or she should be creative, maybe with a background in commercial design. But we don't need just a competent person, we want one who has that certain spark: that combination of ability and

potential to grow with us. And, of course, it doesn't hurt if that person knows our product."

Gregg Wilson

Fender's new manager of guitar design, 31-year-old Gregg Wilson, came to the company in 1977. Before that time he played in a rock band, did freelance photography, and studied mechanical engineering at the University of Colorado. While at the university, he became involved with retail music sales, and later moved to the West Coast to work for a wholesale instrument and supply firm before joining Fender's R&D team.

Like many other guitar manufacturers, Fender employs specialists in marketing whose job it is to gather and update information about what the playing public wants in a guitar. But for Gregg, this informational source is not the only one he relies on when thinking about new designs or modifications. "By the time this feedback reaches me in R&D," he says, "it has come from the musicians and has been filtered through the retail music dealers, or salespeople, sales management, and marketing. In effect, I get fifth-hand information, and I don't like that.

"To compensate for this, I have a list of about 12 dealers and 30 working players who are scattered all over the country and overseas that I contact directly. Every month I'll spend half a day on the phone to ask them personally what's going on in the world. I need street-level information like this when I design. So as a result, the research and design I do is oriented to the user—who is the playing musician, either professional, semi-pro, or strictly amateur—and to what he or she needs at the time."

Not only do the comments from musicians influence his designs, but the guitars of other manufacturers get serious consideration as well. "The point at which I start to pay strong attention to what other people are doing," he says, "other than looking at the physical and electronic parameters inherent in their designs, is when information starts coming back from the field that their guitar is selling like

crazy. If the instrument is doing that well, then it's doing exactly what it was designed to do: reach a market. So we will either figure out what we can do that will put one of our existing products into closer competitive range with that specific model, or we'll design a new animal and make it competitive."

But whether Gregg designs a guitar in hopes of making Fender competitive in an existing market or builds one that establishes its own unique appeal among players, compelling other manufacturers to take notice, the final approval for any and all instruments comes from the marketing department. "But here's the trick," Gregg adds. "Marketing will not approve a design unless they have strong assurances from our customers, who are the Fender dealers and users who field-test an instrument in its final configuration. In addition, they must get a go-ahead from manufacturing, who says they can build the thing the way it's designed, and from me. I have to be happy with it. If any one of those components says no—obviously, our customers are the most important—we just go back and change the thing.''

As with all guitar research engineers, Gregg also confronts design restrictions often predicated on simple economic considerations. "The restrictions on me are twofold," he says. "The first is a cost factor. Under normal circumstances, I'm shooting for a target price. If we're going to sell an instrument on the street for $500.00, then I've got to be able to bring that instrument in for a certain number of dollars in our manufacturing facility for us to sell it to the dealer at his discount while still making a profit for us.

"The second restriction is based on what we are capable of building in quantity, in time to be able to match this market. The bigger a company gets, the slower it usually is to change. So, let's suppose that I would come out with something completely new and different that we don't have machinery for. If we have to buy a new machine, normally the quickest we'll see it is two months—that's if we were to place a purchase order for it the same day. On the other hand, that same machine may take us up to two years to get in. So the design restrictions I'm getting from that standpoint center around the fact that my designing often has to be geared around our existing production capabilities.

"As far as wild projects go, I have, for all intents and purposes, no limitations. Fender is totally committed to R&D. I have been known to say, 'Let's build this, because it ought to be the best guitar in the history of the universe.' And when I got down to it, sure enough it was. But we learned some things and got good test data from it, and we know that at this particular point in time there's no way in the world that we can build or sell the thing. But it's always there for future reference.''

Some of the older guitar manufacturing concerns have reissued a few of their once-standard models because of current strong demands for them. But Gregg explains why he, and Fender, are reluctant to follow suit. "If I had the choice between playing, let's say, a '54 Strat or a '79 Strat onstage, I'd take the new one every time. That instrument, in the time period that it's been in existence, has gone through lots of changes: some of which are visible, but many more of which are not. And the difficulties we discovered with the Strat as time progressed, plus our increased abilities in manufacturing technology allow us to produce a substantially better instrument for a relatively smaller amount of money to the customer.

"You see, in the time that the Strat's been out, the price has more than doubled. But the price on just about any comparable guitar is up much more than that. What we're looking at here is a situation where we could go back and build Strats exactly as they were built in 1954, but what you'd end up with is an instrument that's not as good as a modern one, and it would cost us a bloody fortune to do. There's a running joke around the company that goes, 'We don't build them like we used to, and we *never* did.'''

Anyone thinking about sending their resume to Fender in hopes of joining their R&D team should listen to what Gregg would be looking for in a potential candidate. "If I were going to hire a new guitar designer tomorrow," he says, "first of all, the person would have to be an engineer. I don't care whether he or she did it by going to school, or on the job, or whether they literally reinvented the laws of physics on their own. The second thing is that you must be a guitar player and know guitars backwards and forwards. This company, and I'm sure many others, has hired someone who came in with magnificent credentials but didn't know the guitar, and it turned into a national disaster for everyone concerned.

"A person should also have some real world intelligence and understand, for example, how business works. You must be aware of the fact that saying 'wouldn't it be nice' is not going to get it done. And he or she must be able to relate design work to every other facet of the music industry as it involves the company. Last but not least, you've got to remember that you'll be working with other people, and we here in R&D have little room for egos. Whether or not I become well-known in the guitar design industry doesn't particularly matter to me. The fact that my designs create inherently good instruments, and the fact that I get to have fun doing them, are what make the job worthwhile.''

Jim Schwartz

GIBSON FACTORY TOUR

Gibson's namesake Orville Gibson.

May 1982. Five miles east of Music City, U.S.A.—Nashville, Tennessee—lies Gibson's main guitar manufacturing facility. With 72,000 square feet of space, this modern woodworking factory, which features centralized heating, air conditioning, and dust collecting, has been the point of origin for most of the company's electrics since it opened its doors in 1975. Meanwhile, Gibson's larger, older plant in Kalamazoo, Michigan, continues its 65-year-old heritage of production for banjos, mandolins, acoustic guitars, and custom carved-top guitars (for example, the L-5CES, Johnny Smith, Super 400, and Byrdland); it also serves as the center for their research, design, and development, as well as customer and artist relations. The Nashville facility produces the bulk of the company's output: Les Pauls (including The Paul, Custom, Standard, Standard 80, Standard 80 Elite, Deluxe, and XR II), the semi-solidbodies (ES-347, ES-335T, ES-335TD, ES Artist, and ES-335 DOT), The SG and SG Standard, ES-335 S Deluxe, Victory Standard and Victory Artist Basses, Victory MV II and MV X guitars, Sonex Deluxe and Artist models, GGC 700, and Chet Atkins Classic Electric.

The following pictorial tour of the Gibson Nashville facility takes you through the plant, and shows the many processes involved in producing an electric guitar today. Plant Manager Whitey Morrison and guitar builder/repairman Ron Armstrong offer explanations of the processes pictured, in the same order as they were performed, starting with raw wood and ending in professional-quality electrics. The following chart illustrates the many steps that occur in the creation of a guitar at the Nashville plant. They are numbered in chronological order, and are grouped according to department.

Tom Mulhern and Whitey Morrison

Inside Gibson's Nashville facility.

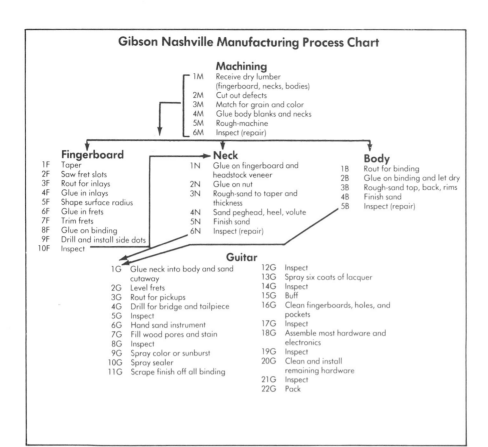

Gibson Nashville Manufacturing Process Chart

Machining

1M	Receive dry lumber (fingerboard, necks, bodies)
2M	Cut out defects
3M	Match for grain and color
4M	Glue body blanks and necks
5M	Rough-machine
6M	Inspect (repair)

Fingerboard

1F	Taper
2F	Saw fret slots
3F	Rout for inlays
4F	Glue in inlays
5F	Shape surface radius
6F	Glue in frets
7F	Trim frets
8F	Glue on binding
9F	Drill and install side dots
10F	Inspect

Neck

1N	Glue on fingerboard and headstock veneer
2N	Glue on nut
3N	Rough-sand to taper and thickness
4N	Sand peghead, heel, volute
5N	Finish sand
6N	Inspect (repair)

Body

1B	Rout for binding
2B	Glue on binding and let dry
3B	Rough-sand top, back, rims
4B	Finish sand
5B	Inspect (repair)

Guitar

1G	Glue neck into body and sand cutaway
2G	Level frets
3G	Rout for pickups
4G	Drill for bridge and tailpiece
5G	Inspect
6G	Hand sand instrument
7G	Fill wood pores and stain
8G	Inspect
9G	Spray color or sunburst
10G	Spray sealer
11G	Scrape finish off all binding
12G	Inspect
13G	Spray six coats of lacquer
14G	Inspect
15G	Buff
16G	Clean fingerboards, holes, and pockets
17G	Inspect
18G	Assemble most hardware and electronics
19G	Inspect
20G	Clean and install remaining hardware
21G	Inspect
22G	Pack

Machining the wood: **1.** Quality control manager Alf Fiddler inspecting dry Honduras mahogany just received. **2.** Curly—or fiddle-back—maple, which will be used for Les Paul Standard 80 tops. **3.** A Tylor glue press is used in gluing The Paul body blanks and Les Paul neck blanks.

1.

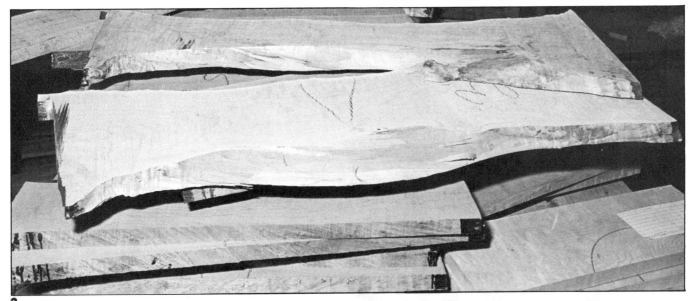

2.

3.

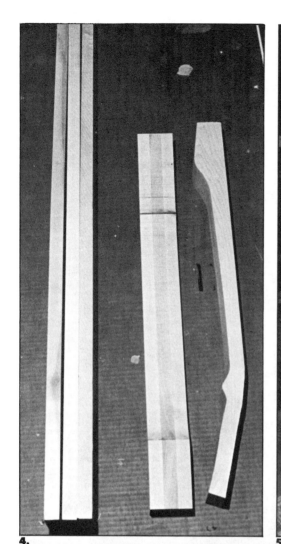

4.

5.

6.

Machining the wood: **4.** Members of solid maple are matched for grain and color and used for Les Paul necks. **5.** This vertical hydraulic press glues maple tops to mahogany backs for making Les Paul body blanks. **6.** The contour of a Les Paul neck is created using this rotary profile shaper. **7.** The profile shaper bits in the foreground are for shaping the Gibson trademark scroll peghead (the curves in the cutter coincide with the final shape at the end of the headstock) and the shape of the neck, while the shaper bit in the background is for rough-cutting the sides of the neck. **8.** The neck of a Victory Bass is held by a special jig against a vertical cutting head (which rotates at a speed of 7,200 rpm) for hand-shaping. **9.** This stack of rough-machined Les Paul neck blanks awaits transit to their next operation.

7.

8.

9.

Machining the wood: **10.** This machine carves four Les Paul bodies at a time, forming the traditional arch in their tops. **11.** Victory Bass bodies are rough-machined by a numerically controlled router, which follows a computer program to cut the outer profile, control cavity, and pickup wells. **12.** Les Paul bodies await inspection (note cavities routed for pickup selector switch and controls). Body: **13.** While a clamp holds this Les Paul Standard body in position, a worker glues the binding in place. **14.** Cloth straps secure the binding while the glue dries. The bodies will be rough-sanded, then finish-sanded.

10.

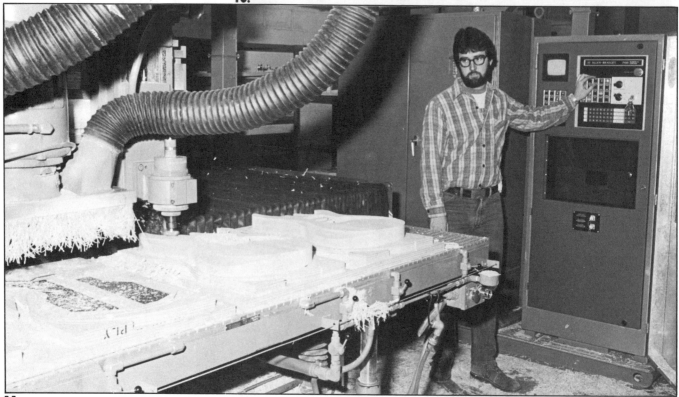

11.

12.

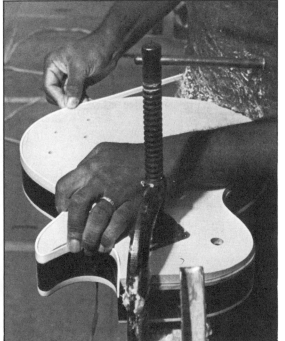

13.

14.

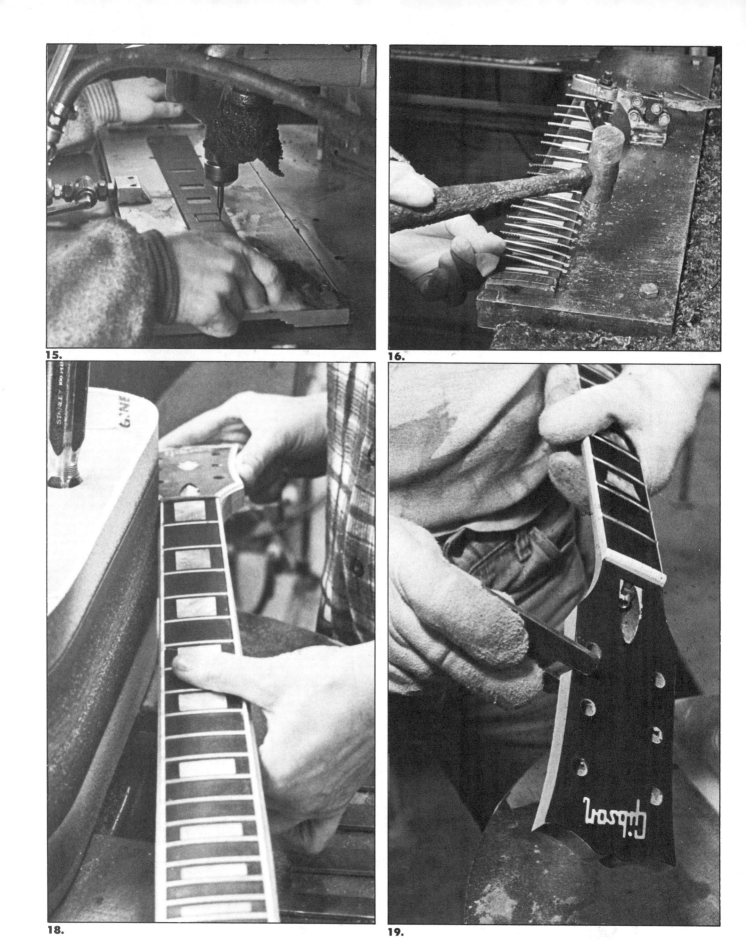

15.

16.

18.

19.

17.

20.

Fingerboard, neck, and body: **15.** Routing slots for inlays in a Les Paul Custom fingerboard. **16.** Seating the frets with a mallet; glue is applied to the fret slots, and a hydraulic press then pushes the frets into the fingerboard. **17.** Inspecting a Les Paul Deluxe neck after gluing on the fingerboard; note truss rod adjusting nut and binding that protrudes into the fingerboard for additional holding strength. **18.** Using a belt sander, a Nashville factory worker completes the final machining/sanding of an ES-347 peghead. **19.** Using a special gauge to inspect the peghead thickness of a Les Paul Deluxe. Assembling the guitars: **20.** Fitting a Les Paul Custom neck into the specially machined slot in the body.
21. Large C-clamps hold the necks in place while the glue dries.

21.

22.

23.

24.

25.

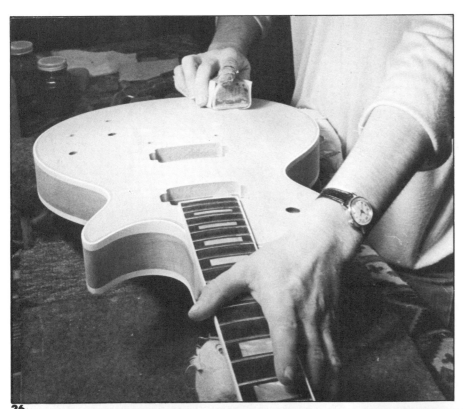

26.

Assembling the guitars: **22.** Sanding the cutaway of the body flush with the neck. **23.** A mask is placed over the body for protection as the frets are checked for levelness and dressed. **24.** Pickup wells are routed into a Les Paul Custom body; note protector screen to deflect wood chips away from operator. **25.** A template aids in inspection of bridge-hole alignment on an MV X Victory Guitar. **26.** Hand-sanding a Les Paul custom before finishing. **27.** Victory and ES models are transferred by a hanging conveyor to be finished.

27.

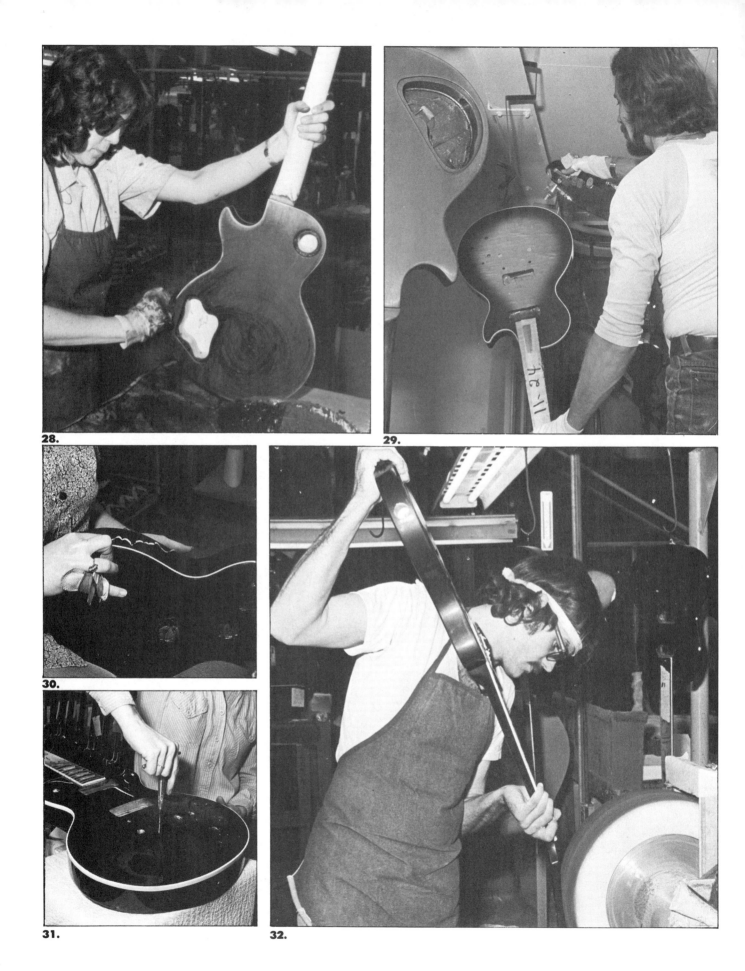

28.

29.

30.

31.

32.

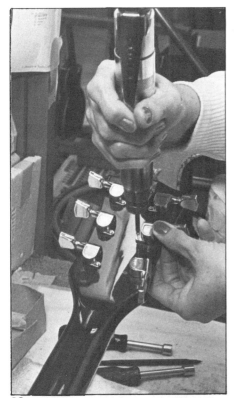

33.

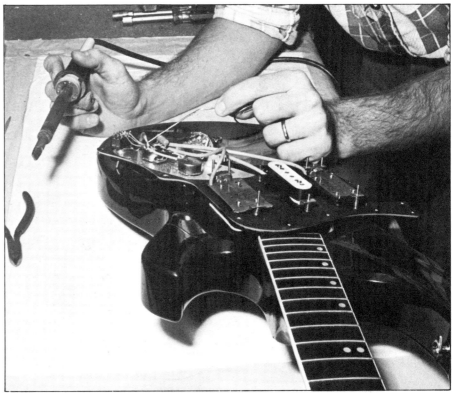

34.

35.

Assembling the guitars: **28.** A sealing and staining material is worked into the mahogany back of a Les Paul custom to make the surface smoother and more attractive. **29.** After filling, the sunburst color is sprayed on. **30.** Hand-scraping the coloring off the binding; the worker wears a leather cover to protect her little finger from the sharp blade. **31.** Cleaning holes after buffing a Les Paul Deluxe. **32.** Buffing the peghead. **33.** Installing Schaller tuning machines on a Les Paul Custom using a pneumatic power screwdriver. **34.** The active control plate assembly of an MV X Victory Guitar is installed. **35.** A Sonex Active receives final inspection before packing.

THE BUSINESS OF LUTHERIE

February 1981. Just as the guitar movement has expanded in the last 20 years, so has the demand also burgeoned for high-quality instruments that match the ever-increasing abilities of the players. But while most players can find something well suited to their needs from the extensive product lines of large companies, there are some guitarists who want special instruments—those unlike any others. There's a small cadre of people, called luthiers, dedicated to making these instruments. It is interesting to examine some of the different approaches they take and the problems they face in pursuing their craft, such as meeting customers' individual needs, maintaining a business, and obtaining materials.

Lutherie is an unusual occupation in today's production-line oriented society, harking back to a tradition of individual craftsmanship hundreds of years old. And although lutherie has been around since man first decided to make devices with musical qualities, the last 10 to 15 years have seen one of the greatest increases in the number of people actively involved with building their own instruments.

Several luthiers cite the social upheaval of the '60s as a factor that made it possible for them to get started in what most people would perceive as an alternative lifestyle. Indeed, those dedicated to the art of guitar building usually see themselves as having different values than those who work nine-to-five jobs. These values are not always compatible with those necessary for survival in the business world, and the conflict between the demands of art and business, and how to resolve that conflict, spawns myriad approaches and solutions.

There are broad differences among builders regarding methods of construction, training, marketing strategies, business practices, and even the definition of a luthier or a hand-built guitar. Therefore, the following article makes no attempt to endorse or promote any one approach; what works for one person may be totally wrong for another. The ideas and opinions included here were taken from many sources, includ-ing interviews with nine different luthiers, several dozen questionnaires, and a round table discussion on "The Business Of Lutherie" held in July, 1980, at the Seventh Annual Guild of American Luthiers Convention in San Francisco. The Guild was formed in 1972 as an organization dedicated to sharing information among musical instrument builders. According to Tim Olsen, one of the co-founders of the Guild, membership numbers about 1,500, and the majority have been building for less than ten years.

Responses by the following luthiers were gathered through various discussions; they are opinions expressed by individuals, and are not necessarily the views of the Guild of American Luthiers.

George Gruhn
Gruhn Guitars
410 Broadway
Nashville, TN 37203

R.E. Brune
R.E. Brune, Luthier
800 Greenwood St.
Evanston, IL 60201

Phil Petillo
Petillo Guitars
1206 Herbert Ave.
Ocean, NJ 07712

Tim Olsen
Olsen Lutherie
8222 S. Park Ave.
Tacoma, WA 98408

Rick Turner
Turner Guitars
24 E. Commercial
Ignacio, CA 94947

Robert Lundberg
6532 S.E. 71st Ave.
Portland, OR 97206

Steve Klein
Klein Custom Guitars
22522 Burndale Rd.
Sonoma, CA 95476

Max Krimmel
Salina Star Rt.
Boulder, CO 80302

Ervin Somogyi
3052 Telegraph Ave.
Berkeley, CA 94705

Lane Moller
Lane Moller Guitars
Box 4131
Chico, CA 95927

Robert L. Venn
Roberto-Venn School
5445 E. Washington
Phoenix, AZ 85034

David Russell Young
Wampeter Works
20448 Enadia Way
Canoga Park,
CA 91306

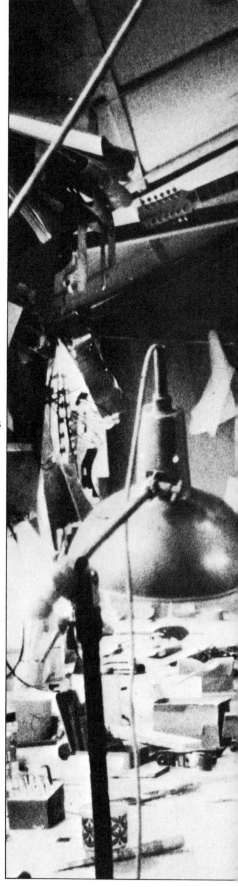

Inside a luthier's shop: Guitars in all stages of completion or repair hang on the walls; hand and power tools, some homemade, fill the room.

San Francisco's cavernous Palace of Fine Arts was the site for the Guild's Seventh Annual Convention. In past years, the convention has been held in several locations (including Tacoma, Washington; Evanston, Illinois; Boston, Massachusetts; and Winfield, Kansas), in an attempt to reach luthiers who could not otherwise travel long distances from their homes to participate. This year's event featured lectures, concerts, and a display of instruments from 100 makers. A broad range of participants attended, from those who build only a few instruments a year in their spare time to small-scale manufacturers.

There were many types and styles of acoustic and electric stringed instruments represented, from tradtional dreadnought steel-string designs to wild-looking custom creations. The common denominator throughout the proceedings was the sense of dedication demonstrated by everyone involved. Steve Klein, a luthier of 13 years, spoke of the progress made by the lutherie movement in expanding the level of craftsmanship: "The quality of the average guitar in this room, compared to ten years ago, is phenomenal. The craftsmen in here are incredible. Just as woodworkers alone—if nothing else—they make the average carpenter look like a hack. And on top of that, their intuitive, creative, and acoustical sense of how to go about building not only a fine-looking but also a playable and structurally stable instrument is real good, too."

Attendance at a Guild convention provides a valuable chance for luthiers to see what their contemporaries in other regions are doing. Participants discuss different approaches to common problems, thereby gaining insight into aspects of instrument construction that they might not have considered. The opportunity to compare one's work to that of fellow luthiers can also help a builder develop higher standards for his own workmanship.

Part of the convention's speaking program was the presentation of lecture demonstrations by respected Guild members covering various aspects of lutherie. Among the topics included were "Fretted Stringed Instrument Acoustics" by Bill Lewis, "Lute Construction" by Robert Lundberg, "State-Of-The-Art Electronic Guitars" by Rick Turner, and "Experimental Steel-String Guitar Construction" by Steve Klein. The nighttime concerts by various artists, including dulcimer players Robert Force and Albert d'Ossche, guitarists Alex de Grassi and David Tannenbaum, and mandolinist David Grisman's Quintet, were also well attended.

On the minds of many builders at the convention was the question of how to improve their chances for economic survival. This topic was dealt with on the opening night of the convention in a round table panel discussion entitled "The Business of Lutherie." The participants were Steve Klein, George Gruhn, Max Krimmel, Robert Lundberg, and R.E. Brune. Each spoke on how to cope with the difficulties of running their own enterprises.

The need for such a discussion indicates the dichotomy that plagues many luthiers: They want to build instruments to the highest level of quality and individuality, but they also need to produce and sell enough of them to survive. At the crux of the problem is time: It generally requires a great deal of work to build even one instrument, let alone enough of them to keep a luthier fed, clothed, housed, and provided with the materials and tools he needs to keep going. "The problem," explains George Gruhn, "is that a dealer such as myself can sell a guitar in five minutes that a luthier slaved on for three months, and I make perhaps as much or more on it as the luthier does. Whether it's fair or not, that's the way business works. And so, as far as I'm concerned, it is virtually impossible to have the standard of living which I prefer by personally hand-making instruments one at a time, with no help."

There are a number of ways to deal with this dilemma. One of them is to adjust to a lower material standard of living. "Luthiers are poor people," says Tim Olsen. "They always have been, and they're always going to be, because they choose to be poor people." But is this necessarily true? R.E. Brune states, "It is realistic that a person can make a living from building." It is a matter of somehow learning to build instruments faster. Once a luthier decides to accelerate his pace, many questions are raised, ranging from the almost philosophical ("At what point does a luthier become a manufacturer?") to the strictly practical ("How do you cater to the needs of individual customers and still maintain cost-effective production?").

Defining lutherie. What distinguishes a luthier from a manufacturer? Every luthier has his own definition, but many feel that the work could be loosely considered manufacturing when one

instrument is like another. And because so many of the builders create on a custom-order basis, they generally feel that their pursuit would amount to little more than assembly line production if it didn't make any difference who was going to be playing the instrument.

While he doesn't believe that guitars produced to a standard design are inherently bad, Olsen feels that it is the ability to tailor a guitar to a particular individual's playing style and tastes that is the essence of true lutherie. Phil Petillo agrees: "My philosophy is that 'custom-made' should mean just that. We get mail from a lot of different guitar makers trying to sell something, and they always have three or four models,

Above: Luthier William Eaton showing his harp guitar at the 1980 Guild of American Luthiers show. Opposite: Andrew Manson fitting a temporary gluing brace into an acoustic's body in a mold.

for instance, and you pick one of the four. Well, I think that's crazy. I have a brochure, and we have information that we send out, and we refer to these as examples, not as, 'This is what you're gonna get.' We design instruments around people's needs and wants."

Naturally, there are varying degrees of individuality, because there's an incredibly broad range of choice in the design, materials, and ornamentation of a guitar. Some builders are best equipped to handle certain types of

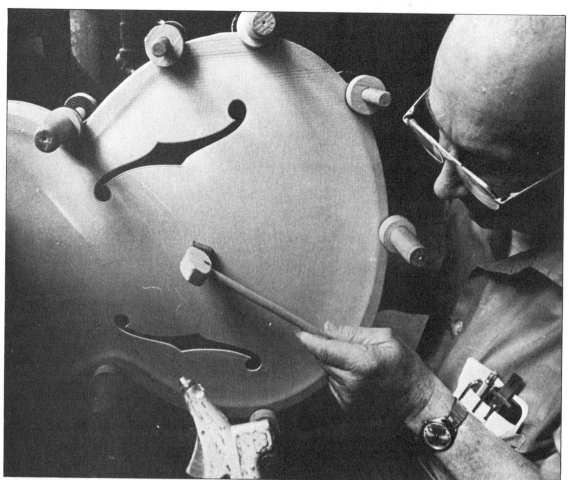

Left: A technician taps a carved top with a piano mallet, using the sound to guide him in sanding the internal braces. Below, left: Dressing the frets with fine sandpaper. Below, right: Binding is glued and held in place with elastic straps. Opposite: Ornate peghead of Larrivee steel-string acoustic.

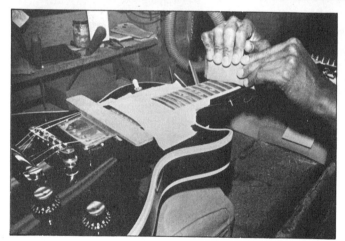

requests, depending on their own inclinations and abilities, their shop facilities, and the availability of materials. Whereas builder A may let the customer specify everything from the shape of the peghead to the type of wood used in the back and sides, builder B may only be willing to work with a certain type of wood, although he will let the buyer dictate other features, such as the scale length or neck shape. Often an important factor is the builder's own

preference for certain designs or materials. For example, one very well-known luthier thinks rosewood is completely unsuitable for guitars, whereas Lane Moller believes Brazilian rosewood to be the ultimate tone wood, and uses it extensively in his acoustics.

The reputation of the builder for constructing a guitar with particular features or a certain tone is often a deciding factor when a player conceives his dream instrument. Brune

points out, "I don't really get people coming to me for a specific sound. What I get now is people who are familiar with my instruments, and who have shopped around. They will come in and say they really love the sound of my instruments, and tell me that they want one. So it's a matter of which goes first—the cart or the horse."

Some builders don't accept commissions from specific customers at all; they would rather build something that pleases themselves, rather than let the customer determine the outcome of the instrument. One such man is David Russell Young. "My basic interest," he explains, "is continuing research and development. That has a lot to recommend against it, as far as an economic strategy goes, because it's a very inefficient way to build instruments. But I do feel like I've been able to make steady improvements and still see room for a lot of improvement. And that's really what makes building exciting for me. I'm not that enthusiastic about sitting down and stamping out 500 identical instruments like cookie cutters just to make a buck."

Although Young's philosophy has taken him out on a rather shaky financial limb, he, like Brune, has established enough of a reputation for building excellent guitars that he is able to sell whatever he builds. Nevertheless, the problem remains to build enough of them to the same high standards to enable him to move to a more stable economic footing.

Speeding production: Lutherie or manufacturing? There are several ways for a builder to increase production speed. One method is to simply organize his work efficiently and improve the level of skill through prac-

tice. With regard to organizing the work, Brune points out that, contrary to popular belief, it's sometimes good to be lazy. "I think one of the outstanding qualities that any luthier can have is a patina of laziness, because this is going to force you to think every operation through," he explains. "You'll find out how you can do it a little bit easier and a little bit faster, and therefore increase your production."

Steve Klein agrees that some operations lend themselves to a production-oriented approach. "Whenever I'm cutting out neck blanks, or anything like that, I don't cut out just one," he says. "So now I've got more neck blanks on hand than I've ever made guitars, and eventually I'll be able to go in there and start grabbing pieces. Then things will happen much faster."

Another way to speed production is to replace hand labor with machine labor, where feasible. For instance, the cutting and shaping of the guitar parts are time-consuming operations if done by hand. A carving machine, however, can give consistent results in much less time. This approach is often difficult for the luthier to accept; it seems to go against what he is trying to achieve by spending a lot of time with each project he builds. Because of the variations in each piece of wood and the different combinations of design features and decorative adornments, especially in acoustic guitars, many builders deem it inadvisable to tool up. They claim that the instrument becomes too standardized; one turns out just like another.

This is not to say that the quality necessarily goes down, however. Rick Turner contends that just the opposite is true: "The basic processes in woodworking are selective destruction of the wood, and what's left over is your product. If a neck can be carved in four minutes on a shaper, or in a half hour by hand, I'll take the shaper every time. And I find that in most instances, in the production mode, the quality of the woodworking goes up." The logic behind this is that a machine can be set up to produce a consistently good product every time, whereas a human hand is more prone to error. Lane Moller points out: "When I first started, I was bending the sides by hand. And that's nowhere near as accurate as using a mold that a machinist has made for you."

When mechanization is introduced, the individuality of the instrument may be on the line. What if the customer wants a neck tapered a bit differently to suit particular requirements? Turner

has an answer to that, too: "If you work it out ahead ot time, a lot ot the jigging and fixturing can be flexible enough to enable you to make quick changeovers that will meet your customer's specs, especially in things like neck width and thickness. The basic tooling remains the same, but you just make an adjustment here or there, and you still have the advantage of guiding your pieces of wood through the machine, rather than doing it all by hand."

If a machine can perform some operation as well as or better than a luthier can do it by hand, while retaining the flexibility for the builder to accommodate different customers' requests, why will a luthier claim that his handmade products are better than those produced in a factory? Perhaps the issue of "handmade" or "machine-made" hinges on just *how many* hands are involved in the making of an instrument. "To my mind," says Steve Klein, "a handmade guitar is a guitar that was made by one set of hands. One mind and one set of hands carried that guitar to completion, and was involved in all aspects of building it. So, when the builder got to one stage, he wasn't relying on the guy last in the assembly line, who glued on the last piece, to have done his job right. I'll put the bracing on a guitar face, carve it, and shape it to a point where I think, 'Okay, it looks good.' Then I'll glue it on to the sides, and I'll stop again, and almost always go back in, cut some more, shape some more. That doesn't happen in a factory setup."

Lane Moller explains why he thinks this procedure usually produces a better guitar: "As opposed to a factory, where a guitar would just come out nearly identical every time, a luthier is able to work with the wood. Every guitar top is a little bit different, depending on the cross-silking in the top, the grains per inch, and the stiffness of the top. Now, I work with each top individually when I brace it. So what that nets you is a guitar that's going to sound the best for that particular wood. It's going to maximize your results."

Pricing. The guitar builder who can introduce production techniques and tooling into the construction of an instrument, while still retaining a high level of quality, has a distinct financial advantage over the luthier who performs every operation by hand: He can keep operation costs down. If a maker can reduce the amount of time spent on each instrument, he can produce more instruments. And if he can do that, he can afford to sell them for less money, making them affordable to a greater share of the guitar-buying market. This becomes especially important when you consider that a typical starting price for a handmade guitar ranges between $700 and $1,500. That immediately puts the small-scale and relatively unknown luthier's guitars in direct competition with some fine models from large, well-known guitar companies who spend a lot to promote their products. And if a customer wants an instrument loaded with options that require more work, he can wind up paying almost as much for his new guitar as he would for a modestly priced small car.

How does a luthier determine what to charge? Not surprisingly, there is a broad variety of approaches. The more business-oriented ones have an accurate idea of how much time they've put into each guitar, how much the materials cost, how much shop overhead they have, what type of clientele they're selling to, and what the going market price is for an equivalent instrument. They take all these factors into consideration when setting prices, while other builders have only vague notions about such cost factors and usually suffer as a result.

R.E. Brune typifies the businesslike approach to pricing: "My philosophy of pricing has been to produce an item which is equal to or superior to what could be obtained somewhere else, at a price equal to or less than what someone would have to pay somewhere else." Other builders, though, are not quite so objective. Steve Klein points out: "I'm not totally relying on what I get for my instruments as an income, and in that case you don't have to sit down and develop a realistic price in terms of hours and materials and the like. Because of my experimentation and the extra time I put into my guitars, that would make the instruments totally unreasonable in today's market. Since I build so few of them, and since they are unique, I always try to ask a little more than the average. I think I've made my own market, and people put up with that."

Klein is able to follow this approach and survive partly because he decided from the very beginning on an unusual and risky marketing strategy. Rather than try to compete with companies like Martin and Gibson by producing traditional guitars in the $700 to $1,500 price range, he decided to build an

Opposite: Inspecting an Alembic's sculpted body and intricate fingerboard inlay. Right: Luthier Ian Sheffner carving a neck.

Luthier Steve Klein (R) and guitarist John Cippolina. Opposite: Handmade wooden clamps secure fan braces while the glue sets up.

unusual design and try to sell his instruments to well-known—and well-off—recording stars. He explains, "You're selling, first of all, to a customer who is using the instrument as a tool in his business, which means he can write it off [for tax purposes]. Out of all the money that's coming in, he probably has an account especially for investing in instruments—and that could be anything from electrics to acoustics. In the recent past, I've noticed a definite slowdown, but usually a musician wants to spend the money. He *has* to spend the money—it's senseless to sit on it—so he's looking around. Having spent large amounts of money on guitars in the past, he won't hesitate nearly as much as the average person. As soon as you start asking two grand, you're in a little different league."

Survival for Klein has come about as the result of a combination of talent, hard work, persistence, promotional ability, and a willingness to sacrifice a comfortable standard of living and maintain a low overhead. It's not a formula that would work for everybody, as Rick Turner points out: "I'm very, very glad that I made the decision to start off

in the under-$1,500 price range. Some production guitars now list at $2,500 and up, and if I had come out on the market with something in that price range I wouldn't be in business right now. Now I'm trying to get under $1,000, because that is where the money is, and that also is an area that is extremely difficult for individual luthiers to crack into."

A large number of instrument builders don't have to worry about the price or the quantity of instruments they build, for the simple reason that they have no intention of making a living from lutherie. Tim Olsen says that a surprisingly large proportion of the Guild's membership is composed of retired people who build instruments as a hobby. They have a pension or some other source of income, so they don't have to worry about whether they make any money from their avocation.

Some luthiers simply feel entitled to receive a high price for their hand-built instruments because they believe that their guitars are better than anything available from the large companies. But there may be some discrepancy between what the luthier feels his instrument is worth, given the time involved in building it and the level of skill he brings to his craft, and what the existing market is willing or able to pay. George Gruhn explains, "Say you want to build the ultimate dulcimer. If you

find that the market for dulcimers is such that people are willing to spend anywhere from $75 to as much as $300, and you can build a dulcimer that's the finest dulcimer the world ever saw for $2,500, you might have a really rough time of it. There *are* things that you could do that might well be the best ever, and the public still wouldn't buy it. And it might be an honest value for the labor you put into it."

Of course, when the customer comes in with a design in mind and asks the luthier to build it, then the two can work out a price in advance. Thus, having set a price agreeable to both parties the builder has a guaranteed sale—*maybe*.

Keeping the customer satisfied.
What is the contractual relationship between builder and buyer? Is a person obligated to pay for a custom-built guitar if it turns out to be different from what he expected it to be? Isn't it risky to agree to pay for something you haven't even seen? Brune says, "My way of doing business generally entails taking 20 percent down when the person orders the instrument, with the balance due when the instrument is delivered; and this is subject to the customer's satisfaction. Since they're buying something that doesn't yet exist, I don't expect them to accept full responsibility until they've had the option of rejecting the instrument—which so far nobody's done—but they have that option." Buyers of Brune guitars have a good idea of what to expect, however, since Brune feels it is important to build a consistent product. Like many other luthiers he has worked hard to establish a reputation for doing so.

A one-off builder sometimes approaches the issue differently, as David Russell Young explains: "Like most custom builders, I used to work on commission, where details such as what kind of woods, special neck dimensions, inlays, and so forth, would be specified. I don't take commissions anymore, because I discovered that in some instances you can have a problem where you are caught between what your instrument is and what the customer's fantasy of your instrument might be. That can lead to misunderstandings and stress, so what I'm doing now is just building the instruments that are most interesting to me, and they come up for sale after they're finished.

Max Krimmel agrees that the approach of building first and selling later has definite advantages for both parties. He tries to encourage this practice by charging less for guitars he's already built than for a custom-ordered job. "I want to encourage people to buy what's there," he comments. "That way you save them from having to wait; you don't hear, 'Well, gosh, I didn't think it was going to sound like that!'"

Attracting customers. Obviously, it's up to the luthier to decide whether he wants to be locked into a certain style by accepting commissions years in advance. Some may not feel stifled by this at all, but rather grateful for being assured a steady income from their work. However, most don't have the problem in the first place. They must still get enough prospective customers to come to them, which means they must develop ways to promote themselves. "You're going to have a lot of trouble reaching a market," R.E. Brune comments. "When you're starting out, it's going to be rough no matter what you do, because your instruments aren't known, your style is not really set, and you're constantly changing, and so you don't even have a really identifiable product."

The typical luthier usually relies on word of mouth to spread news of his guitar-building ability. Although slow, more often than not it's the only course he has open to him. By performing repairs one can broaden his potential clientele. "Repair work is one very excellent way for a luthier to introduce himself to his own local area and at least get a start someplace—people will always come to you with repairs," explains Brune. "And I have found in my

own analysis of my business that many people who were satisfied with my work ordered instruments."

Independent luthiers, whether just starting off or established for years, usually rely on ways of promoting themselves that don't cost money. They simply don't have the capital to spend on advertising or promotional gimmickry. Their efforts must be directed toward obtaining free or relatively inexpensive exposure. The Guild of American Luthiers conventions are a valuable opportunity for them, since the events provide a chance to exhibit instruments to an audience that has demonstrated an interest in guitars simply by attending. Also, the Guild purposely tries to hold down the booth costs to the luthiers to enable them to participate. Other exhibitions, such as the Smithsonian Institution's Renwick Gallery exhibit on "The Harmonious Craft" are also helpful to the luthier, as are magazine and newspaper articles and educational films.

Another reason why some luthiers don't rely on expensive promotions is that they don't want to become caught up in what they perceive as mass-media hype. It's one thing to claim in a splashy ad that your product is the best, but they would rather convince people by letting their work speak for itself: The effect of an ad can't compare with the effect of strumming a chord on a newly completed, beautifully finished guitar.

Luthiers' attitudes and approaches. In general, luthiers love what they're doing, as opposed to doing it for the sake of fame or fortune. Brune explains why: "You have to love it to begin with, or else you won't stick with it. There are many other things you could do and make more money at. And eventually if you don't really love it, you won't stick with it no matter how profitable it is, because it is a heck of a lot of work even when you handle it efficiently."

How people relate to the business of lutherie is another matter altogether. Some, like Phil Petillo, don't want to be bothered by business at all. But not all are lucky enough to have his solution. "I have been very fortunate," he explains, "because my wife, Lucille, runs our business. I don't have to get involved in that like most people. There was a time when I was involved in it, and I suffered physically and mentally by trying to be Mr. Know-It-All. Once my wife took it over, it relieved a huge burden."

Ervin Somogyi has also found it difficult to adjust to the exigencies of the business world: "I never had business

experience before in the sense that running a business entails responsibilities, and one of them is to keep regular hours. And that was really hard for me to do, because sometimes I just didn't feel like coming in at whatever the sign on the door said. And when you make an agreement with yourself and your customer that the repairs will be done around a certain date, you can't have them wait two or three months. That was something I had to learn, and it's an important lesson."

Of course, if you don't have a retail operation, you don't have to keep regular hours. However, one must still put the time into the business. Steve Klein admits that he's rarely in his shop before 11:00 A.M., but points out that on many occasions he's worked until four in the morning. He feels that the flexibility and self-satisfaction he's derived from having his own business help make up for the financial insecurity he's had to adjust to. He explains: "Say you've got to work four or five months before you get a vacation. When you get home, you don't want to think about the business, and then you've got to get up in the morning to get there and punch in on time. Not having to look at life and deal with it on that level is, to me, a real bonus, especially when you're trying to be creative, when you're trying to attain and sustain the concentration needed to build an instrument to the quality of the average guitar at the Guild convention."

Perhaps more than any other aspect, it is the opportunity for self-expression that hooks people on lutherie. After all, these products are tangible manifestations of their makers' own unique talents and abilities, and completing an instrument provides a thrill and a sense of satisfaction hard to find in other fields of endeavor. Ervin Somogyi reflects on how he decided to build his first guitar: "It goes back to about 1969 or '70, when a friend of mine built a guitar, which I thought was just fantastic—a real, live person whom I knew, who actually had made something. My background is academic—I just went to school for a long time—and it seemed to me that everything that I had done was on paper, whereas this friend of mine had actually manufactured a real, live object. And I just couldn't get over that. Also I've been playing guitar for over 20 years now. Anyway, I decided to go out and build a guitar of my own."

Satisfaction comes in all different forms. Some, like R.E. Brune, develop a very pragmatic attitude towards themselves and their calling. Brune says, "Building serially, as instrument makers do, you're constructing almost the same thing, over and over. You're not really an artist, per se, although you can call yourself that. It's a matter of self-conception, I suppose, but I don't view myself too differently from anyone else producing a product. And I try to build the best instrument I know how to, at a price that's as good as or better than anyone else's. And therein I find my challenge—reconciling those two."

Not all luthiers have such an unassuming attitude. Many think, justifiably, that there's more than a little art involved in their approach to building; many also feel that scientific theory is important. "I consider this to be an art and a science," claims Phil Petillo, and several others expressed a similar sentiment. Certainly, both disciplines are called upon in designing, building, and decorating a guitar. Petillo explains: "The technology available today will work, if properly understood. Things like curing material, adhesives, stress and strain, structural analysis, and others, are important to know about." Petillo is a licensed mechanical engineer, and says that much of the information he's found by reading engineering journals has helped him in his work.

David Russell Young has used information published by the Catgut Acoustical Society [112 Essex Ave., Montclair, NJ 07042] to help him design and adjust the braces on his guitars' tops. "The Catgut Acoustical Society has been trying to evolve a science of musical instrument construction," he says. "They have been to the science of musical instruments and the academic and musical communities what the Guild of American Luthiers has been to the dissemination of the technology of instrument making."

Yet another person interested in the the possibilities of using scientific analysis to improve the guitar's tone is Tim White, an acoustician and guitar maker. He recently launched a publication called the *Journal of Guitar Acoustics* [4543 Page Ave., Michigan Center, MI 49254], which is "designed to provide an open forum for the presentation and discussion of matters relating to fretted stringed instrument tone, tone production, and tonal perception," according to White's introductory literature. A sampling of topics to be covered in future issues includes "Long Time Average Spectroscopy Of Guitar And Dulcimer Tones," "Harmonic Patterns Of A Dead Guitar String," and "Basic Sound Production And Percep-

tion," among others. His publication should be of considerable interest to luthiers who want to understand more about the sound of their instruments.

Although the scientific approach has its benefits, Steve Klein suspects that there are still relatively few luthiers extensively incorporating scientific research into their building techniques. The availability of such information is growing, but Klein thinks there's a limited number of builders who have the educational background to really understand it or the technical building skills to apply it effectively. For this reason, he doesn't particularly emphasize a knowledge of acoustic theory as a vital attribute. "The scientific and theoretical aspect of the instrument should not be totally overworked," he says. "Theory is just that—theory. Theory and actuality work like this: They start to mesh, but there's a point where they don't quite jibe, and you need that subtle balance between structure, acoustics, and aesthetics to be successful. A good intuitive instrument maker can make even a square box sound phenomenal."

Lane Moller agrees that a builder can develop an intuitive sense to guide him in making decisions on the structure and sound of his guitars. "From a lot of the things I've read," he explains, "some theoreticians think that a round soundhole for guitars is superior. Now I've gone into an oval soundhole that runs parallel with the strings on my OOM-style guitars, and it was more the result of intuition and to create a certain look for the instrument. And I've found that that's given me an incredible increase in tone and volume—more bass, more of everything. So I really would say that intuition enters into it because if I had only gone by what I was told and what I had read, my guitars would never have evolved an oval hole."

While science and intuition enter in the *design* and *construction* of a guitar, an artistic sensitivity is also needed when determining its appearance. Many luthiers add ornate inlay or marquetry work, or sometimes adorn the guitar with intricate carvings. The decoration, if done tastefully, adds considerably to the beauty of the instrument, but Rick Turner thinks it's possible to carry a good thing too far: "I feel that there are far too many luthiers whose primary function is to decorate, and far too few whose primary function is to design true musical tools."

Education and training. Most luthiers are self-taught, simply because they became interested when there were few

people to learn from and few sources of printed information. Says David Russell Young, "When I started, the only book that was out was the little A.P. Sharpe *Make Your Own Spanish Guitar* book—32 pages [Clifford Essex Pub., 20 Earlham St., Cambridge Circus, London, WC2, England]." That was 1965. By the early '70s, another book had come out, Irving Sloane's *Classic Guitar Construction* [E.P. Dutton, 201 Park Ave. South, New York, NY 10003]. Known informally among luthiers as "The Bible," the text is credited by Young as the first book that included enough reasonable information for a person to turn out an acceptable guitar.

A number of books have come out since then, including Young's own *The Steel-String Guitar, Construction And Repair* [Chilton Books, Chilton Way, Radnor, PA 19089], making it much easier for an aspiring luthier to get started now than it was ten years ago. The Guild of American Luthiers also publishes a quarterly newsletter and Data Sheets that provide technical information on lutherie-related topics. In addition, there are now several schools of lutherie with curriculums based on having the student build one or more guitars from scratch. A number of individual luthiers also offer private instruction or small classes on instrument construction.

There are varying opinions on the value of attending a lutherie school. While some see formal education as an important step, others feel that it's the wrong approach. Tim Olsen says, "I get calls all the time from people who ask, 'What school should I go to?' I tell them, 'Don't go to school. Take the money that you would spend on the school, get yourself some wood and tools, and start. If you've got six months to go to school, and if you've got $5,000, then you've got all you need to teach yourself.' You see, when you get out of school, you've got someone else's theories piled up in your head. You've got your money spent, your time is gone, you still don't have a shop, and you haven't done any work on your own. So I think it's a waste. I think people should have more confidence in themselves, because if they're not self-starters, lutherie is never going to be a means for them to make a living."

As can be expected, people who run guitar-building schools have different viewpoints than that expressed by Olsen. Charles Fox, who founded Vermont's Guitar Research and Design Center (now known as the American School of Lutherie), explained his school's approach to teaching. "The first task the students are put to is pattern making," Fox says. "We don't hand out anything in kit form, so their initial experience with the craft is on a fairly creative level. At the same time, none of them come here equipped to make basic decisions about changes of designs in guitars, so we hold the first guitar to a very strict set of rules. The point of their whole experience here is that it should serve as a really sound basis for a creative life as a craftsman. If they get very far out on this first instrument, they really don't have anything sound to refer to. On one hand, we're teaching them techniques and encouraging them to be future parts of the evolution of the instrument; at the same time we hold them down real tight in the kinds of liberties they can presume to take in this first guitar. And that's confusing for some people. Some of them come here with less than realistic notions of what it's all about, and they are more concerned with going home with some wing-ding instrument than they are with laying the basis for a career. We're trying to prepare them to be extremely creative—but responsibly."

Self-taught builders like Brune, Young, Somogyi, and Klein admit that they made a lot of mistakes when they were first starting out, and that they would have benefited from some type of instruction. Klein points out: "Probably my biggest downfall is the fact that I was never trained as a traditional woodworker. I never even took a high school woodshop class, since I was always oriented toward the art classes, such as drawing, painting, and sculpture. At this point I do regret that, and [lute maker] Robert Lundberg is a good example of someone who has got the woodworking thing *down*."

Robert Lundberg is unusual in that he was able to be an apprentice for about three years with two different European-trained master violin makers. From them he learned woodworking techniques and gained knowledge that he was then able to apply to building lutes.

Other makers who have also had the opportunity to serve an apprenticeship in the European tradition also sing the praises of this approach. Petillo originally worked for a family of Italian violin makers, and later was associated for many years with Jimmy DiSerio, who was a long-time helper to master archtop builder John D'Angelico. "Europe is a whole different scene," Petillo says. "When I was a young boy, I used to pick

a piece of wood up off the floor and they'd tell me what it was, where it came from, what part of the tree it was from, and why it was laying on the floor. And you learn a lot from things like that."

Even if a person can't find a European-trained craftsman to study under, it helps to find someone knowledgeable enough to guide him through the first few instruments he makes. Lane Moller points out: "There are just some things that you have to know. There are some different methods, and these basics have to be understood. From there a person can go on and develop their own theories. But understand the basics, or define one method that works for someone, and then go on. That, I think is essential."

The experienced luthiers interviewed agreed that it takes a long time and a serious commitment for a person to develop into a well-rounded instrument builder. Unfortunately, many people going into the craft have unrealistic expectations. "An awful lot of people have this romantic notion of the art of it all," says Rick Turner. "They're extremely impatient to become master craftsmen in less time than it takes to get through college. They do not understand the value received from someone who teaches, either in a formal situation—like a lutherie school—or in a less formal apprenticeship thing. I believe very strongly in the archaic, European form of apprenticeship—indentured servitude, if you will. I think that if somebody really wants to become a good luthier, they should be prepared to get into it before they're 25—preferably before they're 20—and work at pitifully low wages for at least four or five years, and not resent it. Unfortunately, that's not the way it is."

Charles Fox also recognizes that, be it good or bad, people often are not willing to wait as long for the fruits of their labor as they once were. His lutherie courses span a period of only six weeks. "This seems to be quite in sync with the needs of contemporary student craftsmen—American instant-type people," Fox explains. "There is really no way that the kind of traditional apprentice-master relationship that stretches over the years could find a place today in this country. We seemed to hit the format that works. There has never been any presumption that six weeks is sufficient time for somebody to be introduced to the art *and* to master it. We figured people have the rest of their lives to master it— if they are introduced to the proper

techniques and aren't knocking their heads against a wall trying to figure out how to do it. That's been our secret."

The future. Although one can argue the pros and cons of schools, their existence and growth indicates that interest in lutherie is continuing to broaden. But will the market for handmade guitars absorb an increasing number of instruments? Luthiers generally agree that theirs is a limited market. The people who buy their guitars are pros, semi-pros, or serious amateurs with a willingness to spend more money than the average guitarist to obtain a special instrument. For this reason, one-off instrument builders don't see themselves as competitors to large guitar companies. Klein points out: "If a company perceives that 90 percent of the people want X and 10 percent of the people want something else, they make only X. And there's 10 percent of the people who want something that's different. Take lutes, for example. Lutes are something that the mass market doesn't want, but the people who do want lutes want them badly, and they have no place to go."

George Gruhn believes that the number of luthiers is small enough that the demand for their instruments, although limited, still exceeds the supply. Speaking at the 1980 Guild of American Luthiers convention, he said, "If custom guitars were demanded by only five percent of all guitarists, that would still be a heck of a lot more people than all of us sitting up here together probably could produce

John McLaughlin's ornate doubleneck built by Rex Bogue.

instruments for. We can't fill that market. We're small enough that we can deliberately cater to a minority and still do well, whereas the big boys *must* cater to the majority."

Brune believes that current economic forces are, however, crimping the buying power of American consumers, as well as making it increasingly difficult for the luthier to get by: "My clientele are people who are all in the same situation that we're in, insofar as they're in a world where the dollar is worth less and less each day and the amount of money they spend on personal necessities is a much larger percentage of their paycheck. So their disposable income is dwindling, and at the same time the expenses of running the shop are increasing for us. We're being squeezed from two ends."

Many builders feel the pinch, and the problem is especially acute for those just starting out. "The beginning maker is up against a lot of things," Brune continues. "There are a lot of very good instruments in the $1,000 to $1,200 range, which is about the maximum price you can charge. And when you're beginning, that's when you're least efficient, so you're probably struggling to make one or two guitars a month. I need to make two guitars a month just to break even, and that's with an average price of $1,500 to $1,700. Plus I've got my tools and wood all paid for."

Often the difficulties of a neophyte luthier are overwhelming. Phil Petillo says: "I've met a lot of people that have gone into this business, bought material, had a suitable means of storage and a suitable place to work, suitable equipment, and found out what it was like. After they went through all this trouble thinking that the business was all peaches and cream, they found that it wasn't: it was a tremendous amount of work. A lot of them sold out."

But despite the difficulties, Petillo thinks the future could be good for the small, independent luthier—if he or she goes into it with the right attitude. "I think the future is bright for the small guy," he says. "The overhead on big companies is enormous, so their prices are going to reflect that. The little guy can work out of a cellar if he wants to, making ten instruments a year, and as long as he's got the proper materials and good construction techniques, he probably could make a living. But I think a lot of people have a big misconception about this business. Many think it's a glamorous business, or that there's a gold mine to be made. Well, I hate to disillusion them, but glamor is an ego thing, and you've got to separate egotism from common sense. A big mistake people make is they see it as a way to associate with someone, or they see only the finished product without realizing the amount of knowledge, hard work, materials, experience, and money that went into making it."

Rick Turner points out that the entrepreneurial approach might not be the only way to get into lutherie. "I don't see how anyone could get into lutherie and make a living at it without doing some repair work, unless one went to work for another maker and was content with that. I think that there's a good spot in the field for people who want to learn guitar-making, who are interested in working hard in woodworking, and who don't necessarily have the ambition or the masochism to run their own shops. And if they do want to run their own places, then they damn well ought to take some business courses at a junior college or something like that, or get their knowledge some other way. Hard knocks was my way, and I don't necessarily recommend it."

Modern luthiers may seem like throwbacks to a former time, ill-fated to be living in a world in which it is easier to survive by driving a truck or even collecting garbage than by being an artisan. However, Ervin Somogyi perhaps best exemplifies the attitude that will ensure the continuation of lutherie for years to come: "What makes the most sense to me, intuitively, is just to realize that I have enough. I build a few guitars, and I sell a few guitars, and that's okay for me. A lot of people in this aren't in it for business reasons. A friend of mine who went to the convention and talked to a lot of the luthiers said that everybody there liked what they were doing, and she was very impressed with that, because you don't often find a roomful of people who like what they're doing. I think that's really important."

John Brosh

3. BUYING A GUITAR

INTRODUCTION

Whether you've owned dozens of guitars or are contemplating your first purchase, a little guidance can help you choose the instrument that best suits your needs—and your budget. Beginning with the first segment of this chapter, Steel Strings For Different Styles, you can become well versed in what makes certain acoustics right for you, including their size, shape, interior structure, overall tone, and combinations of woods. Five sections under the heading of *Guitar Player*'s Choosing An Electric Guitar are devoted to the complex and often overwhelming details of choosing an electric guitar. Bodies, necks, fingerboards, inlays, neck/body joints, tuning machines, pickups, electronics, bridges, and tailpieces are scrutinized. Through concise explanations, the terminology of each component is detailed, as well as how each part interacts with the others to produce an electric's characteristic timbre. The final section, The Vintage Guitar Market, shows that while new guitars appeal to a lot of people, the lure of vintage guitars leads many on a quest for that "great old sound." Buyer beware! Just because a guitar is old doesn't mean it's necessarily valuable, and without a bit of savvy, you can get burned on what may seem an appealing deal. Tom Wheeler explains the difference between collectible and merely elderly instruments, picking the brains of the experts in the vintage field to guide you toward the right guitar.

STEEL-STRINGS FOR DIFFERENT STYLES

March, April 1979. The acoustic steel-string guitar is a remarkably versatile instrument. It can be flatpicked, finger-picked, or played with a bottleneck or slide and sound good in almost any kind of music from bluegrass to pop. Many acoustic guitarists today play several different styles, and these folks frequently ask me what kind of guitar will suit everything they do. Unfortunately, I don't know of any steel-string that works equally well for a wide variety of styles and techniques. In my opinion, at least, a single guitar that's genuinely all-purpose simply doesn't exist, although builders and manufacturers have made numerous attempts to develop such an instrument. The individual who plans to buy a steel-string should bear this in mind and select the type that best meets the requirements of his or her particular repertoire.

Some players will find that they need two or more different kinds of guitars to get the most out of the styles they play. We'll take a look at several kinds of music and the demands they make on a guitar. We'll also see how various features of construction—size, shape, type of wood, etc.—affect a guitar's ability to meet these demands.

For bluegrass and acoustic country-style playing, the general consensus of opinion seems to be that Martin D, or dreadnought, models work best. Bluegrass rhythm or backup usually consists of bass runs played in the first position using many open strings, and a capo is generally employed to obtain the open-string sound in any key. For this style (which is often underestimated and is far more difficult than it appears), you need a guitar with four very powerful, good sounding bottom strings. The sound of the *B* and high *E* strings isn't terribly important, and the guitar's action and intonation beyond the 5th fret are almost irrelevant.

For bluegrass rhythm most people prefer guitars with rosewood backs and sides (like the Martin D-28) because they tend to have a booming, resonant bass. On the other hand, people who play complex bluegrass and country leads such as Tony Rice and Doc Watson often like Mahogany guitars like the Martin D-18, because they tend to produce a somewhat thinner, clearer tone with more treble response than rosewood guitars.

Although Martin dreadnoughts are widely recognized as excellent sounding bluegrass and acoustic country guitars, many people today complain that they're difficult to play. Martin necks were designed for traditional first-position country rhythm playing and often don't suit modern hot lead players who demand comfortable action and precise intonation anywhere on the fingerboard. This is undoubtedly one reason why a growing number of bluegrass and country players are switching from Martins to guitars of similar design with more up-to-date necks. Many good quality guitars of this type are currently available and are gaining considerable acceptance, even among hard-core traditionalists. (The readers should bear in mind that a guitar should not be judged by how well it's set up; the action and intonation of many guitars can be vastly improved when they're set up properly or have needed repairs such as neck sets.)

Blues playing encompasses so many styles that no single guitar could be ideal for all of them. Generally speaking, blues players want a guitar with a strong treble even at the expense of bass, but beyond this their requirements vary widely. A number of Gibson flat-tops from the small LG models to the dreadnought-size J-45 and J-50 on up to the extra large J-200 are probably the most popular guitars for blues, but many players use Epiphones, Guilds, or Martins of various sizes.

A few people have discovered the little-known Maurer guitars made in Chicago around the turn of the century through the early '40s, which are fantastic blues instruments. For Delta blues, particularly bottleneck, many players want a funky sounding guitar and prefer some of the old Stellas to any Gibson or Martin. It's rather ironic that many excellent blues musicians want a sound that's almost diametrically opposed to what most luthiers spend their lives trying to achieve; this points up the fact that evaluating tone is a highly subjective matter.

Guitarists such as Stefan Grossman who play a variety of fingerpicking styles usually want a guitar with good tonal balance between the bass and treble, good volume, and good action and intonation all the way up the neck. Many of these folks use instruments smaller than dreadnoughts, such as the Martin OOO and OO models. Maurer guitars, which I mentioned previously, and those produced by Maurer under

Previous page: Four Martin steel-strings (L-R): a 1936 00-42, a 1937 000-18, a 1954 D-28, and a 1937 D-45 12-fret custom guitar. Right: Late-'30s Gibson Super 400 arch-top steel-string acoustic.

different names such as Euphonon, are among the finest fingerpicking guitars ever made. Although they're quite rare and can be fairly expensive, they're well worth the fingerpicker's attention.

Acoustic steel-string guitar has so many applications in jazz—from playing rhythm in a big band to playing solo in a club—that instruments that sound very different may be considered equally good for jazz. Almost all the most popular jazz guitars are carved arch-tops braced with only a bass bar and treble bar. These tend to have considerable volume and power with very little sustain. Their "barking" chord sound makes them especially good for orchestral rhythm playing.

Strombergs are considered to be some of the finest orchestral rhythm guitars ever built. The larger models in particular, such as the Master 400 (which is 19" across), are loud enough to cut through a 12-piece brass band, but they are often bass-heavy and can sound almost irritating when played softly by themselves. They are designed for rhythm playing, and in my opinion they are usually not too good for soloing or recording. The best Strombergs were made in the late '40s and '50s and have only one diagonal brace on the underside of the top, while earlier models from the '30s have a bass bar, treble bar, and several transverse braces.

Some arch-tops such as the Gibson L-10s, L-5s, and Super 400s from the mid to late '30s, the Gibson Johnny Smith models, and most of D'Angelico's later guitars built during the '40s and '50s all have X bracing. (Unlike X-braced flat-tops, which feature a main X and multiple smaller braces, X-braced arch-tops simply have two braces.) Arch-tops with X bracing tend to have less power but more sustain and flatter or more equal response than those with other types of bracing. D'Angelicos, for example, usually have extremely good balance with very even response from the nut to the last fret. While they may not be particularly loud, they have a very smooth, mellow sound and usually record especially well.

Ever since Crosby, Stills, Nash, & Young appeared onstage, acoustic guitar has been used fairly often by contemporary rock and pop players. Since playing styles vary so widely, it's hard to generalize about the ideal acoustic for pop or rock. I can say, however, that most rockers I deal with want acoustic guitars with considerable sustain as well as good balance and intonation. Sustain is a quality that can be described fairly well in physical terms. A guitar

produces a certain amount of string vibration that can be drained quickly or slowly depending on how it's built. The faster the string vibration is drained, the more volume and less sustain a guitar will have. When string vibration is drained more slowly, the sound will be sustained for a longer period; there will be less volume, however, since less energy is being converted to sound at any one time. As a general rule, therefore, acoustic guitars with good sustain aren't quite as loud as those that produce one short burst.

It's worth noting that a guitar can actually have too much sustain, especially for styles such as bluegrass and orchestral rhythm. The right balance of volume and sustain for the type of music to be played is an important consideration in selecting an acoustic instrument.

As we've seen, different playing styles make different demands on a guitar, and acoustic steel-strings of similar quality can have vastly different playing characteristics. It may be helpful to take a brief look at how some of the major structural features of a guitar affect qualities such as tone, volume, balance, and sustain.

Body size and shape. The Martin dreadnought body is so popular today that there almost seems to be a "dreadnought conspiracy" among acoustic guitar players. However, in my opinion the Martin D body size has certain deficiencies for playing styles that require a strong treble and maximum projection of the notes played at the higher frets. I think that this is due to its depth, which is 4⅞" on 14-fret models. In general, the deeper a guitar is, the more mellow and boomy it will be. Since the Martin dreadnought was designed for playing bass runs, the deep body works very well. But if a strong clear treble is desired, I don't think a guitar should be much deeper than four inches. Fortunately, there are some excellent alternatives to the D size body, such as the Martin O, OO, OOO, and M sizes, which I'll describe briefly. These are convenient examples, but the reader should bear in mind that there are other good body sizes and shapes available. Some of these are produced by guitar companies, ad others are original designs by independent makers.

The Martin 0 size guitars are 13½" wide and 4¼" deep. They tend to have good treble and work well for fingerpicking. Occasionally, they're a bit weak in the bass, but the 12-fret models with slightly longer bodies have surprisingly good bass. While they're not as

loud as the D's, the O's can still produce considerable volume.

The OO is 14-5/16" wide and 4⅛" deep and tends to be a bit more balanced than the O. The 12-fret models in particular frequently have very strong bass for their size. These guitars are excellent for fingerpicking and can also work well for some types of flatpicking.

The OOO, which is 15" across and 4⅛" deep (12-fret models are 4-1/16" deep) is one of the most versatile Martins ever made. This guitar cuts extraordinarily well and is excellent for flatpicking as well as fingerpicking. The bottom E string is a bit weak on some of them, but overall I think that the Martin OOOs—especially those built between 1934 and '38—come closer than anything to being the perfect all-purpose guitar.

The style M is a flat-top version of the pre-War Martin style F, an arch-top f-hole guitar. The M has the same shape as the OOO, but is 16" wide. These guitars are also highly versatile, with strong treble, good bass, and considerable volume.

Wood. There are a number of factors that affect a guitar's tone; the most significant one is the instrument's top. Most steel-strings have tops of spruce; there are several varieties—Adirondack, Canadian, American Sitka, and German alpine spruce. Each has a different type of tone. Martin guitars made prior to 1946 have Adirondack spruce tops; those made afterwards have Sitka spruce tops. I have compared many Martins whose construction is similar except for the wood in the tops, and to my ear, at least, there is a significant difference. Those with Adirondack spruce tops had a crisper tone and better treble response than those with Sitka spruce tops. (Martin continued to make a few guitars with Adirondack spruce tops on a random basis through the '50s and on into the '60s. These are easily recognized since Adirondack spruce ages to a yellow color, whereas Sitka spruce has a different grain and ages to a reddish brown or orange color.) In my opinion, German alpine spruce tends to be similar in tone to Adirondack spruce.

Most flat-top guitars have backs and sides of mahogany or various types of rosewood. The great classical guitar maker Torres once constructed a guitar with a back and sides of papier-mache and a top of very fine spruce. This instrument had excellent tone quality, although it lacked the power and projection of an all-wood guitar.

While Torres' classic experiment

demonstrated that good tone is primarily the result of the top, there's no doubt that a guitar derives some of its tonal character (as well as volume and power) from the back and sides. Rosewood and mahogany guitars certainly sound very different. Of course, tone quality is almost entirely subjective, but to my ear a hard, dense wood like Brazilian rosewood works best for rhythm guitar, while mahogany seems to work better for lead playing, where strong treble and maximum clarity are required. Due to trade restrictions, Martin and other large manufacturers have used Indian rather than Brazilian rosewood since late 1969. However, most older rosewood guitars are of the Brazilian variety, and many people feel that it is prettier than the Indian; some prefer the sound also. Brazilian rosewood is still used today by some independent builders who make small numbers of guitars.

Braces and bracing patterns. Martins made prior to 1944 have scalloped braces which provide structural strength with a minimal amount of mass. These guitars seem to be more responsive than those with the heavier, conventional struts, and in recent years many people have had the braces in their instruments shaved to achieve this effect—with varying degrees of success. Martin took

notice of the public's interest in the pre-War scalloped braces and reintroduced this feature on their herringbone HD-28 and M-38 models. Today, scalloped bracing is offered on several other Martin models as well as on custom instruments.

In contrast to Martins, many pre-War Gibsons such as the advance jumbos and some of the Nick Lucas models and J-35s have triangular cross section braces that look rather crude but are lightweight and achieve a remarkably fine result. Maurer guitars built as early as 1910 have unique laminated braces constructed like a sandwich with ebony or rosewood in the center. These guitars have excellent treble and sustain and are extremely durable. I've rarely seen a Maurer with this type of bracing that had the top pulled up or needed a neck set. This is remarkable when you consider that Martins were not even braced for steel strings until the late '20s and rarely hold up as well as steel-string Maurers made many years earlier.

Obviously, the bracing pattern is significant in determining the sound and structural stability of a steel-string guitar, but there has been little experimentation in this area. Most steel-string flat-tops have the familiar "X" bracing pattern, although the transverse or simple straight-across type is seen on some cheaper guitars.

Over the years, many tests have been conducted to determine how much difference listeners can detect in guitars of various sizes, shapes, woods, etc.; these experiments have shown that the ear tends to be very adaptable and have a short memory. Guitars may have astoundingly great differences in tone, but the members of an audience won't necessarily hear them. This is particularly true today, when very few people use the guitar in purely acoustical applications onstage. Played through a microphone and a modern PA system with EQ, almost any guitar can sound good for all practical purposes. The subtleties of a guitar's unamplified acoustic tone and other sound qualities really don't carry over 30 feet and may be irrelevant to an audience; still, they can be highly evident to the player.

In my opinion, the most important feature of a guitar is what it does for the guitarist who plays it. Some models have definite personalities that are stirring, and certain guitars have even inspired pieces of music or playing styles that would never have come into being if the instruments hadn't existed. In my view, it should be the goal of every guitar maker to produce instruments that will be inspirational to those who play them. Ideally, the musicians will in turn convey some of these qualities to their audiences.

George Gruhn

CHOOSING AN ELECTRIC GUITAR BODY

March 1982. Irresistible instruments are everywhere, and in just about any music store there is an electric guitar that *makes* you play it. Each note you pick seems to say, "Buy it." Often countering those urges is a little voice that warns, "You can't afford it." So, the guitar goes back on the rack, you leave the store, and it's the end of what might have been a beautiful love affair.

Fortunately, at one time or another many guitarists save up enough money

to buy that dream instrument. And yet despite the expense, the importance of selecting the right guitar, and the excitement of making the long-awaited purchase, they often do the wrong thing: They rush out and buy the item that's the newest, flashiest, or most popular—without spending the time to thoroughly familiarize themselves with the object of all that attention and all those dollars. While those qualities of newness, flash, and popularity may well

be assets, depending on your tastes, there are many other criteria that must be considered if you are to make a wise investment. As you read further, we'll address some of the fine points worthy of your scrutiny when deciding on the best sound and the best deal.

We fill focus mainly on the physical attributes of electric guitars, so general guidelines concerning where to buy them, pricing, variations in age, and country of origin will not be covered. First, we'll look at a part of the electric guitar that not only contributes to the sound, but in many cases is also its most important visual aspect: the body.

Throughout the electric guitar's evolution, there have emerged three basic body styles: the hollowbody, the semi-solidbody, and the solidbody. The first was the hollowbody, since early electrics were f-hole arch-tops with pickups added. The hollowbody type is the most susceptible to feedback. Because of its large size, open cavity, and basically thin shell (all of which initially con-

tributed to its function as an acoustic instrument), it resonates easily at moderate to high volumes and relatively low frequencies. However, recent advances such as graphic and parametric equalizers allow the guitarist to tame feedback to varying degrees by filtering out some of the offending resonant frequencies. If you like the comparatively mellow tone of an electric hollowbody—the instrument traditionally associated with mainstream jazz artists—be sure to try it out at the volume you estimate to be your usual playing level (perhaps even a little louder). Also, try it at many different tone settings: Its tendency to feed back depends on tone as well as volume.

Hollowbodies can be a few inches thick, and consequently may feel awkard to some guitarists (especially those used to comparatively thin solidbodies). Try playing one while standing up and while sitting down—a good test of any guitar's comfort.

If your preferences for tone run between the mellow and bright extremes, or your preference for instrument size runs between the large acoustic models and the compact solidbodies, perhaps a semi-solidbody is more up your alley. You can often obtain the sounds associated with solidbodies *and* hollowbodies with a semi-solid—without feeling as if you're hefting a piano under your arm.

Hollowbodies and semi-solidbodies are frequently constructed of *laminated* wood: this is, a type of plywood. Some arch-tops, including many of the world's finest models, have tops and backs carved from solid wood. They're often costly, and aren't generally as durable as laminates, since splits running the length of the grain can occur (in a laminate, each thin layer's grain pattern runs perpendicular to that of the adjacent layer, thus helping to prevent long cracks).

Although semi-solidbodies may look like thin hollowbodies, they are usually quite different in their construction. For instance, an arch-top typically has an internal bracing structure that adds rigidity and contributes somewhat to the tone; structurally, this makes hollowbody electrics more akin to acoustic guitars than to solidbodies. Most semi-solidbodies, on the other hand, have little or no bracing, and instead have a solid block of wood running through the full or partial length of the body (it can be viewed as an extension of the neck). This contributes a great deal to the structural integrity of the guitar, while greatly enhancing sustain and treble response.

There's one thing you must do when considering any semi-solidbody or hollowbody: Check the seams and joints for poor gluing or rough edges. Tap the body and listen for any buzzing—loose bracing or poorly joined components can be quite an expensive headache. The plastic or wood strips that often run along the guitar's edges are called *binding*. On any guitar, regardless of body type, look for loose binding.

Solidbodies are the most durable of all electrics. Often an inch or more thick, they are difficult to crack (unless you're Pete Townshend), widely available, and offered in just about every price range. Such woods as mahogany, alder, maple, koa, and ash are the traditional choices for guitar makers, although in the last half decade manufacturers have come to offer exotic hardwoods such as zebrawood, padauk, rosewood, and walnut. Extremely hard types of wood can increase the sustain in solidbodies, and raise the resonant frequency so high

that feedback via the wood is almost nonexistent (pickups, however, are a different story; they will be explored later). Guitars of Plexiglas, marble, aluminum, and graphite-epoxy substances have also been made in the quest for more sustain.

With the exception of their necks, solidbodies can be made of a single piece of wood, although it is standard practice to use two or three pieces of wood glued together. Many pieces can be used side by side to produce aesthetically pleasing montages of color and grain; they do not necessarily add to or detract from the sustaining characteristics of an instrument, unless they are of widely varying densities. Laminates of the latter type are commonly, but not exclusively, employed on guitars with neck-through-body designs.

In the case of solidbodies with natural finishes, it may be aesthetically pleasing to have as few pieces of wood as possible comprising the body. Consistency of the grain is another factor: If the pieces are too dissimilar, you may have a hard time should you ever try to sell the guitar to a potential buyer who really cares about looks. Bookmatching (splitting a single piece of wood and

then laying the halves side by side) creates a symmetrical grain pattern that radiates from the middle of the guitar, and also enhances cross patterns such as tiger striping. Sometimes two or more pieces of one type of wood will be laminated to form a core, and these will be covered by a one- or two-piece cap of another type. The purpose isn't to cover up anything; rather, it allows the manufacturer to combine woods with different properties, perhaps to balance considerations of weight, aesthetics, and sustain. Note: A cap is generally contoured, and may therefore increase the instrument's cost.

Solidbodies are too heavy for some guitarists. If you're used to another type of instrument, the weight of your first solidbody may well take some getting used to. At the very least, try one while standing up for a little while, using a comfortable strap. While you're at it, check to see if the neck is too heavy (let the instrument hang freely, using a well-secured strap). Even though the body may weigh quite a bit, the guitar might not be properly balanced. Also, if you ordinarily sit down playing, road test the guitar in that position.

Another potential pitfall of solid-

Left: Ampeg Super Stud and Heavy Stud dual- and single-cutaways. Right: Clearbody Ampeg/Dan Armstrong with removable pickup; Gibson Super V CES hollowbody, a variation on the classic L-5.

bodies concerns their sometimes alien shapes: Designers occasionally come up with a model that knocks you out but can't be held comfortably. On the other hand, an unusual shape may result from a desire for *increased* comfort; it's a matter of good design. At any rate, make sure the guitar feels comfortable. A weird shape may make it difficult for you to find a compatible guitar stand, or a case other than the one offered by the manufacturer. Also, watch out for pointed ends and long, thin horns at cutaways; they can jab you or your fellow musicians. But, if you like a guitar's *look* enough, you may ignore any discomfort; at least make sure you like the way such an instrument sounds and plays, and be sure that the quality is worth the price.

Regardless of what style of electric you want, you will often have the option

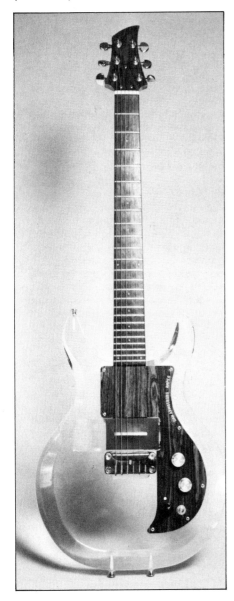

16th fret. A second cutaway is generally less crucial, but it does increase fretboard accessibility and may enhance the guitar's overall visual appeal.

Almost all solidbodies have some sort of contouring to increase the player's comfort; a scooped-out back, a beveled lower bout, gently sloping edges at a cutaway, etc. Make sure that the guitar you choose accommodates your needs—three or four hours of practice or performing can really magnify discomfort. Also, check where the strap buttons are located. Particularly on strange-shaped solidbodies, they may be in awkward places that make your strap twist in an uncomfortable manner. Such a problem can often be remedied simply be relocating the buttons. Be aware, though, that if you have any kind of vintage or limited-production guitar, the new holes drilled and the old ones left behind may devalue your instrument in the collector's market.

While electrics have traditionally featured clear lacquer finishes (sometimes over stain) that add depth to the wood grain's appearance, since the mid-'50s some manufacturers have offered a broad choice of colors. Paints of exotic colors may often have equally exotic chemical structures, and some epoxies and plastic or polyester types are extremely durable, even with the worst treatment. However, these types of finishes are often applied more heavily than lacquers and therefore lend themselves to opaqueness or translucence. Natural finishes and sunbursts, generally created using lacquer, can discolor with age. This is also true of some older white finishes (smoke, mildew, and sweat are the main culprits). If you're rough on guitars, get one with a durable finish. Most manufacturers are proud of their paint jobs, and will detail in their brochures what kind is used.

Lacquer can chip much more easily than most plastic types of finishes, simply because it is inherently more brittle (it gets more glassy with age), and because it is usually applied in many thin layers rather than a single heavy one. If you plan to play lots of gigs in cold weather, you may want to forego a lacquer finish—rapid temperature changes can cause tiny spiderweb cracks known as *checking*. While they don't harm the sound or structure of a guitar, these little cracks can look pretty bad.

So far we have explored the physical attributes of electric guitar bodies. Next we'll examine the neck, headstock, and other features of electrics.

Tom Mulhern

Top: This guitar has been contoured for extra comfort. Bottom: Tommy Shaw holds the striking Gibson Explorer, a mixture of comfort and cosmetic appeal.

of a single or double *cutaway*—an area of the body removed near the top of the neck. If you're planning to do stratospheric runs, make sure that you can get to the notes. Without at least one cutaway on the treble side, a guitar can frustrate any attempt to reach about the

NECKS, FINGERBOARDS, FRETS & INLAYS

April 1982. Distinguishing one guitar from another is often simply a matter of feeling. Many guitarists don't even have to see an instrument to identify it—or at least to decide whether they like it. Perhaps the most identifiable trait of a guitar's feel is the neck's shape. If it doesn't feel right, well . . . then it just doesn't feel right. Even if a guitarist likes the sound of an instrument, he may find it awfully hard to fall in love with a neck that feels like either a toothpick or a baseball bat.

When you pick up a new guitar and start noodling around, you immediately formulate an opinion: You like it or you don't. And the longer you have been playing, the faster you'll make the decision. The most striking features of a neck's feel have to do with its width, thickness, and radius. It's no secret that a classical guitar has a wider neck than most electrics. However, the variations in width from one electric to another can be quite noticeable.

There is no "best" width—only the optimum one for you. Analyze your playing style. Do you play primarily rhythm or lead? When testing a new guitar, play something with which you're familiar. A factor that enters here is the neck's taper. For instance, it

may be only 1¾" wide at the nut, but at the body joint it may be 2" wide. On the other hand, there may be little or no apparent taper at all. One look from a few feet away will usually be sufficient for you to check for taper. (Note: Bass guitars' necks often have the most radical tapers.)

Exact measurements of width aren't as important as the neck's feel. A neck may be slightly wider or narrower than what you're used to, but if it feels comfortable, then you don't need to know the measurements. Width alone, however, doesn't account for all of the feel. The thickness from the front of the fretboard to the back of the neck is also important. In many cases this is a function of the neck's radius—how circular it is, and to what size circle the neck is patterned after. If you were to saw the neck off of a typical guitar, you could see from the end that it is modeled after a circle. Therefore, the center of the neck's back will generally be the thickest part, whereas the sides approaching the fingerboard are much thinner.

The radius itself won't determine the neck's thickness. If, for instance, a circle with a 1" radius is sliced in half, the result will be a 1" thick half-circle. However, if the same circle is sliced *tangentially* (between two points not necessarily the greatest distance apart on the circle), the result will be a thinner

Above: The cut of a neck radius can be shallow or deep, greatly affecting playing comfort. Right: Detailed inlays add to a guitar's beauty and expense.

Neck materials and profiles affect player comfort. Above: Modulus Graphite's 6-string bass. Right: B.C. Rich guitars after neck carving.

neck, even though the radius is the same.

Some neck cross-sections appear oval, and still others are thicker at one side and taper to the other side. Naturally, the amount of comfort you derive from any of these neck shapes is purely subjective. Nonetheless, ask yourself this question when choosing the neck shape best suited to your needs. "Do I place my thumb right on the center of the neck's back, or do I wrap the thumb completely around the neck?" If

you wrap your hand around and have short fingers, you may want a thinner, narrower neck. Guitarists with longer fingers probably don't need a thin neck regardless of their grip. Be certain of your needs: play barre chords up and down the neck; try some lead licks; and play standing as well as sitting.

Another significant factor in neck comfort is the finish—or lack thereof. We've already discussed body finishes, and because so many guitars have the same finish on their necks as on their bodies, discussion of finish types will be foregone. Suffice it to say, if you want a lacquered, painted, or otherwise covered neck, make sure your hand can

move freely along its surface. Check for pits and rough areas. Durability is another good trait in a neck's finish. If you sweat extensively, a plastic-based finish such as polyurethane is a good choice. Sometimes no finish is preferable; although guitarists will rarely expose their necks to the harshness of sweat and finger oils. If nothing covers the wood, expect the neck to look fairly grungy and to possibly suffer a certain amount of decay. Some necks, like some bodies, have a rubbed oil finish. Such treatments require periodic replenishment with special wood finishing oil. If you consider a guitar with this type of coating, make sure you aren't allergic

to oils. If you are sensitive to oily or petroleum-based products, your skin may react similarly to the oil finish.

Let's examine the types of materials used to make a neck. There are basically four types of necks: one-piece wood, multiple-piece wood laminates, graphite-epoxy, and aluminum. Arguments in favor of and against each type have raged among guitar makers, and even now there is no clear *best* type. Each has its distinct qualities, though. For instance, a one-piece wood neck is handsome and if the wood is inherently straight, there should be little problem with twisting or warping.

Because not all wood tends to stay straight, some guitar builders will use two or more pieces of wood glued together, following the theory that a few different pieces of wood will have different properties. Accordingly, if one piece tries to warp, one of the other pieces will remain stable, or shift in an opposing direction; this cancels warpage and twisting. Exotic hardwoods may be used to give a stripey effect, but it's quite common for pieces of one kind of wood to be employed in a lamination.

Aluminum-neck guitars have been

available since the early '70s, and have been manufactured in a couple of different forms. The general construction consists of a neck molded from a single piece of aluminum. The metal is rigid, and unlike steel, not terribly heavy. Because many guitarists shunned the idea of a metal neck, commercial manufacturers either inlaid wood into slots running the length of the neck, or used the aluminum as the center of a laminated wood neck; some simply covered the aluminum with wood. Aluminum-neck guitars are fairly uncommon, and like instruments with graphite-epoxy necks, have often been maligned simply because of the non-wood materials used.

A product of recent work with satellite technology, graphite-epoxy is now molded for some necks. Its manufacturers say that it has the greatest stiffness-to-weight ratio of any substance, and although it isn't lighter than wood, it does make for a stiff neck that needs no truss rod.

Variations in the types of fingerboards can be summed up in two categories: material and contour. Fingerboards are commonly made of a hardwood such as maple, rosewood,

and ebony. In recent years, other exotic hardwoods (padauk, zebrawood, etc.) have been employed on some custom models. The three common woods—maple, rosewood, and ebony—have long been the mainstays of the guitar industry not only because of their great strength, but because of their color. Maple is generally very light colored, ranging from blonde to white, and can be highly figured with swirls or "bird's eyes." Rosewood is red to brown in color, and commonly has some vertical grain running throughout. Ebony is generally black, although it can sometimes have streaks of light brown or even white running through it.

Some fingerboards are not really fingerboards at all. Instead, they are simply the front of the neck smoothed into the form of a fingerboard with frets inlaid directly into the neck's face. A fingerboard can be either flat or slightly convex (i.e., higher in the middle). Depending on the amount of curvature and the height of the frets, bending of strings can be impeded on a curved fingerboard, because the string may "bot-

Aluminum necks, such as this Kramer bass', contribute to sustain and stability.

duced LEDs (light-emitting diodes) or fiber optics in their instruments to act as luminous position markers. LEDs must have electric wiring in the neck, and if one such light should prove defective (they're generally rated for a life of a few hundred years, but occasionally a bad one makes it past quality control), the fingerboard must be removed to facilitate replacement.

Fiber optics is a technique of using a clear solid plastic string to transmit light from a common source, and therefore eliminates the need for electrical wiring under the fingerboard. A light in the guitar's body provides all the necessary luminescence; if a bulb burns out, it's easy to replace. Both types of illumination can be quite helpful to the guitarist who plays in dark places or where lighting is inconsistent.

Binding, the thin strips of plastic, celluloid, or veneer that act as molding along the edges of the fingerboard, not only looks good, but in some cases can improve the overall feel of the neck. However, like the LEDs, fiber optics, and fancy inlays, it is only natural that such spiffy features will cost more. So, unless, you really *need* them, you may want to choose a model with simpler markers or no binding in favor of better pickups or tuning machines. In many cases, you won't have to choose between different amenities, and often a model is available only one way (take it or leave it). Nevertheless, be prepared in some cases to decide between cosmetics, comfort, and sound quality.

All but a few fingerboards have frets, and the majority of fretless electric instruments are basses. There are a few basic types of frets: regular, jumbo, and triangular. Regular frets by and large are fairly narrow, whereas jumbos have larger, rounder beads (tops). Triangular frets, designed by luthier Phil Petillo, look like a triangle from the side. Rather than availing a broad surface to the string for contact, they allow the string only one place to touch; in theory, the accuracy of the intonation is improved. At the opposite end of the spectrum is a fret milled down so low as to be almost inconsequential. When placed on a flat fingerboard, it can make string bending difficult for some because the string drags along the wood.

Regardless of the type of frets, you must check that they are smooth and evenly filed. Grooves and nicks are bad news for string life and intonation. Also, improper fret placement can mess up the intonation. If you're trying out an electric, ask the dealer if the intonation at the bridge is correct. If it is, and the

strings are good (new ones have the greatest chance of being easily tuned), the guitar should play in tune at every fret. If it doesn't, the cause may be a bad string, so check the intonation with all strings. If you still encounter problems, inaccurate fret placement may be indicated; ask the dealer to check it with a strobe tuner or similar device.

Don't feel as if you're putting him out: If you are to make an investment in a guitar, you'll only be throwing good money away if everything doesn't check out *before* you buy. If a fret is displaced by a few millimeters, having the situation rectified can be an expensive hassle. A guitar with such problems is best left behind, unless you're in love with that particular one. However, beware that in severe cases of fret displacement, an entire new fingerboard may be necessary.

The number of frets may be important to you, depending on how much lead work you do and how much range you want. Frets have long been put on electrics in numbers ranging from 16 to 22, with 21 and 22 being about the norm for solidbodies. In recent years, though, 24-fret fingerboards have become fairly common. These afford two entire octaves of range per string. A few guitars have 36-fret, three-octave fingerboards, but after the 24th they're spaced so close together that they're impractical for many guitarists.

The distance between frets is directly proportional to the sounding length of the string. The longer the scale length, the wider the frets will be spaced apart. If you have short fingers, you may want a guitar with a shorter scale length, but if your fingers are fat, then you may want a guitar with the frets slightly farther apart—especially if you plan to play above the 12th fret often.

The number of frets will also determine the overall length of the fingerboard in relation to the sounding length of the entire string (e.g., on a scale of, say, 22", a 20-fret board will be much shorter than a 24-fret one). This difference in the number of frets may affect the placement of the bass pickup on a multiple-pickup guitar (or one with only a single pickup positioned near the neck).

One part of the guitar that has received a lot of attention in recent years is the nut—the little piece through which the strings pass from the fretboard to the tuning machines. Traditionally, nuts have been made of bone, ivory (now rare because of endangered species sanctions protecting elephants), ebony, and plastic. In the last decade-

tom-out''—snag on the wood as it is moved laterally along the frets.

A fingerboard is not only functional; it can be quite handsome, with a number of possible appointments. These include mother-of-pearl, metal (such as silver or brass), or contrasting wood inlays, which are set into the front and side of the fingerboard. They can be shaped as dots, squares, hexagons, parallelograms, or other designs such as birds, celestial bodies, etc.

A few manufacturers have intro-

and-a-half, metal nuts, such as those made of aluminum, steel, and brass, have appeared. Proponents of metal nuts claim that they increase sustain in the instrument. Detractors say that metals such as aluminum and brass are too soft, and therefore receive ever-deepening grooves as a result of retuning, which rubs the strings back and forth in the nut slots.

Almost all types of nuts cause problems for people with vibrato tailpieces. As the string's tension is relaxed, the string moves one way through the nut; when the tension is recovered, the string moves the other way. Often there is enough friction in the nut to grab the string slightly, causing it to not return to its original tension (which in turn causes out-of-tuneness). Lubricants such as graphite can be helpful, but some luthiers have another solution: small rollers for the strings to pass over. Another solution is a clamp, which holds the strings firmly at the nut.

Serving a dual function as both fret and nut is what's called a *zero fret*. It is a fret placed where the nut ordinarily is placed. The nut is then moved closer to the tuning machines. The purpose of a zero fret is simply to create an accurate breakover point for the strings so that intonation will be correct. In general, when a nut's grooves are filed correctly, the intonation will be fine. But wear in the slots or inaccurate grooving by the maker can cause problems. The zero fret effectively takes the responsibility for intonation away from the nut, and leaves only the chore of separating the strings. While in some cases zero frets can improve intonation, it should be noted that they are subject to the same wear and tear as any other fret.

Next we'll look at the headstock, tuning machines, bridges, and tailpieces. Before reading further, examine your guitar and see just how familiar you are with your instrument and your needs.

Tom Mulhern

NECK/BODY JOINTS, PEGHEADS, & TUNING KEYS

June 1982. Unless you know exactly what you need and want before you buy an electric guitar, you may find yourself the proud owner of a lemon—or at least something you're not completely satisfied with. Familiarity with the features and flaws of an instrument is your best defense against such disappointment. We've examined body types, materials, finishes, the neck, fingerboard, frets, and inlays. Now, we'll look at the design and function of the neck/body connection, truss rod, headstock, and tuning machines.

Neck/body connection. The connection of a neck to a body would seem like a simple matter, but in fact it is the source of much controversy. There are three basic types of necks: those that pass through the entire body, those that are glued on, and those that are bolted on. Each has its positive points as well as its pitfalls.

Necks that pass through the body are claimed by some luthiers to make for the best sustain because the neck and tailpiece act essentially as one piece, thus allowing the vibrations of the strings to be emphasized tremendously. However, in general a solid connection between any neck and body can ensure a great deal of sustain. The major drawback of the neck-through-body design lies in the difficulty of repair: If the neck is severely damaged, and must be detached from the body, the job is compounded in many cases by the extremely strong glue used to hold the sections together. In fact, the glue will often be stronger than the wood itself, making neck replacement difficult.

Some necks are glued onto the body. But there's more to it than just shooting glue on a neck and sticking it to a big piece of wood. The end of a glued-on neck is usually cut into the form of a dovetail. A matching notch is cut into the body, and the two parts mate solidly. The glue ensures a snug and lasting fit. The drawback to this method is similar to that of a neck-through-body configuration. However, it's easier to replace a glued-on neck, because it's just a matter of knocking, drilling, or chiseling out the dovetail, rather than trying to tear apart huge chunks of wood.

The bolt-on neck is the Henry Ford interchangeable parts approach to guitar building. In theory, any neck of a certain model can be placed on any body of the same model. Generally, three or four screws or bolts are used to attach the two parts. Repairs are quite easy—no glue, no power tools. However, if you take a bolt-on neck off and put it back on frequently, the screw threads in the neck can become stripped, and the neck won't hold on correctly. Also, if the body's slot doesn't match the shape of the neck's end, a sloppy, loose fit can result, causing the neck to be wobbly. Always make sure that a bolt-on neck does fit the slot correctly. Shims can be used to improve the fit.

Because strings exert a pull on the neck, it has a tendency to bow forward. The rigidity of a neck and the gauge of strings are factors in this. Some necks are so solid that they can resist the pull of strings. However, most can't do it alone (wood is fairly flexible), and a *truss rod* must be placed in the neck. A truss rod is generally a cylindrical steel rod (often wrapped in a plastic sheath) with a net on one end, imbedded in the neck. It helps shore up the neck against the strain of the strings. In fact, by turning the nut on the end of a truss rod, you can compensate for string tension to varying degrees. Truss rods are usually single pieces of steel, although a few manufacturers use two rods or a twisted pair; some have even created rods that look like a "T" or an "X" in cross-section. All serve basically the same function.

Some truss-rod adjusting nuts are located at the headstock under a small plate, while others are found at the base of the neck. A variety of adjusters is offered, ranging from screw types to standard nuts and Allen-type nuts. When checking out a guitar, find out how difficult it is to adjust the truss rod, and ask if a wrench for this purpose is included. Most rods require little

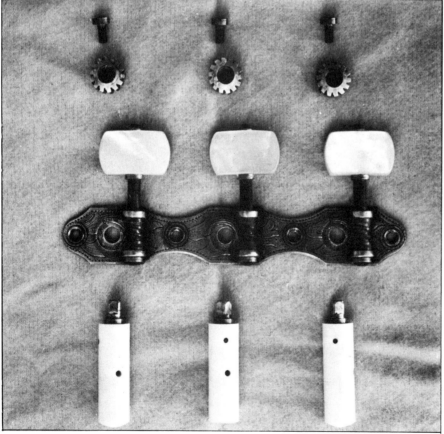

Headstocks and tuning machines come in all shapes and sizes. Top: Gibson's Victory Bass uses sleek 4-on-a-side Schaller tuners to hold its large strings. Left: These classical guitar tuners, shown disassembled, come three on a plate. Above: While some tuners have holes drilled through their barrels, others such as this one have slotted tops for quicker restringing. Opposite: Epiphone's Triumph headstock features three tuners on each side, while all six are aligned on one side of the Fender Jazzmaster's.

adjustment, provided you don't change from one string gauge to another constantly.

Headstocks and tuning machines.

Many guitarists and manufacturers think of the headstock only as a place to locate tuning machines and a string nut. However, its visual appeal is not to be underestimated: A striking body style can be rendered useless if the headstock looks wrong (e.g., a sharp, angular body with a blocky, boxy headstock). The reverse is true as well: A great-looking headstock usually won't save a poor body design.

There are several instantly recognizable headstock silhouettes—Fender, Gibson, Ovation, and Dean, to name a few—and their visual appeal has been due to balanced design between the headstock and the body. Behind the beauty in most cases is functional construction; a designer will often try to balance visual aesthetics with a configuration that is solid and dependable. No matter how good a guitar looks, if it performs poorly, it probably won't last long in the marketplace.

Although there are many different headstock shapes (each manufacturer often chooses one as its mainstay), there are essentially only two configurations: All six tuning machines on one side, or two parallel rows of three machines each. From time to time, there are deviations (Music Man's bass, for instance, has three tuning machines on one side and one on the other; some guitars and basses have tuning machines located on the body, making the headstock an optional decoration).

Traditionally, the tuning machines of a guitar have been arranged in two rows, with three per row. This is a throwback to the classical guitar, mandolin, and other earlier string instruments. It allows more space between the tuning knobs, and also spreads out the tension from the strings to both sides of the headstock. Unfortunately, with three tuners on one side and three on the other, tuning can be awkward. The guitarist must turn the three low-string tuners one way, and then reach under the neck to turn the treble tuners the other way. There is a tradeoff, though, in placing all the machines on one side. With six tuners in a row, the knobs are much closer together, and the string tension can cause neck twisting if the wood isn't very strong. However, on a good-quality guitar, the wood will likely be strong enough.

When properly arranged, six tuners on one side allow the strings to pass through the nut without then veering off toward the tuning machine. This alleviates some of the string *sticking* in the string nut as it passes through. If the string doesn't pass straight through the nut (especially one made of a soft material such as brass), the windings can dig in. The result is this: when tuning up or down, there is a delayed movement of the string. After you tune to the proper pitch, the string may let go of its grip on the nut and slip slightly (you usually hear a "ping"), causing the string to go sharp. Lubricating the nut can often prevent this to a certain extent, but if the guitar has a hand vibrato (which changes the tuning of a string by varying the string tension), the problem can be acute.

Related to this situation is the angle at which the headstock meets the neck of the guitar. Many manufacturers design headstocks that meet the neck at a fairly shallow angle, which causes the strings to press down a bit into the nut. This generally increases sustain and keeps the strings from flopping around in the nut slots. However, too much of an angle between headstock and neck can be a source of problems: The joint between the two parts can be under too much strain, and therefore prone to snapping; the string can be forced to drag too much through the nut, slowing sawing through the nut every time the guitar is retuned.

Tuning machines are available in a variety of types and sizes. Each guitar manufacturer often has a primary type, and may offer other models. The basic configuration consists of a worm-gear (which looks something like a screw) attached to the knob that meshes with a second gear that is attached to the post (or barrel) around which the string is wound. In general, you should look for one with a fairly large gear ratio, which is expressed in fractional terms such as 12:1 or 15:1 (the latter is the larger ratio). This means that for the post to turn once, the tuning knob must be turned 12 or 15 times. Small increments such as these are desirable, because they help in countering any tuner slip-

page caused by string tension. However, the design of the overall tuner must be considered as well.

Try this test on a tuning machine: Tune a string up, and then turn the knob the other way. Does the knob feel like it goes through a slack zone in which it has no effect on the post turning or the string's tuning? Most tuning machines have a small amount of *backlash*, but if there is too much free play, and the gear ratio is too small, you may want a better tuning machine.

If you really like a guitar, but find the tuning machines to be its weak point, try another guitar of the same model—the one you tried first may have a defective gear in one of its tuners. Then if you find the second guitar's tuning machines unacceptable, ask the proprietor if the guitar is available with better tuners as an option. You may

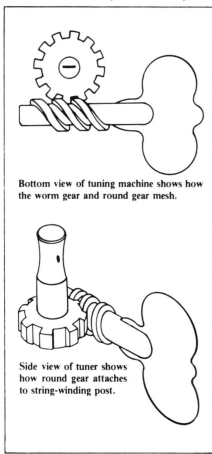

Bottom view of tuning machine shows how the worm gear and round gear mesh.

Side view of tuner shows how round gear attaches to string-winding post.

have to spend more, but after all, if the guitar isn't 100% up to snuff, you're not getting your money's worth at any price. And remember: All tuning machines wear with age. If they start out with problems, they'll only get worse.

Another aspect of tuning machines is how their gears are housed. A sealed, permanently lubricated tuner is preferable to an open one, or one that needs lubrication. Because it is completely enclosed, contamination from dust, oxidation, and finger grime is precluded. Gears that need lubrication are often not accompanied with instructions telling you what kind of lubrication is necessary—graphite, oil, WD-40, etc. If you guess incorrectly, and add, say, 3-In-1 oil to graphite, you'll wind up with pretty gummy gears.

This doesn't mean that tuners with exposed gears or which need periodic lubrication are *bad*. You simply must be aware of their care and feeding. Always ask your music dealer or a repairman. Don't pass up a perfectly good instrument because you don't know how to maintain a portion of it.

Often overlooked by guitarists is the type of knob on a tuning machine. In its most basic form, a tuning knob is just that: a simple knob of metal or plastic. There are literally dozens of variations on the tuning knob employed by various manufacturers, and each has its merits. Some are designed as much for cosmetic appeal as for their utility, and may feature ornate shapes or carvings. Others are made of plastic of one kind or another. Many are made of metal and are plated with nickel, chrome, or gold.

First of all, be sure that a tuning knob feels comfortable to you. If it feels like a modern art sculpture in your hand, it probably isn't your best choice. A plain shape (perhaps with an indent for gripping) may be your best bet. Also, make sure that you can get to the knob easily (the size of the knobs will be very important in deciding this, regardless of whether there are three or six tuners in a row).

Don't think plastic knobs are necessarily less durable than metal ones. They

usually last as long; in fact, the gears usually wear out before the knobs fall off. Some plastic ones can look like onyx or other stones, and metal has the distinct disadvantage of corroding. Nickel and chrome plating are fairly durable, but if you sweat a lot, even they won't protect the metal forever. And gold plating, which is very expensive (although it is sharp-looking), generally wears off very easily in time.

You'll find that the majority of good-quality tuners have metal knobs, but remember that good knobs don't always mean good gears. Keep in mind, too, that not all of the plastic or wood devices for winding strings fit all tuning machine knobs. If you have more than one guitar (especially if you have a double-neck or a 12-string), and change strings fairly often, this can be an important consideration. Another way around this is the new tuning machine with a built-in crank that folds out of the end (currently available only from Gibson).

Make sure that the posts of the tuning machines (around which the strings are wrapped) aren't too tall for your guitar. Some guitarists think that by adding very expensive tuners they're truly upgrading their instrument. However, they may put on tuners with too-tall posts, and this in turn affects the angle at which the string passes over the nut. If the angle is too shallow, string trees (little metal "T"s) or knobs are necessary on the headstock to pull the string down, in order to prevent buzz or loss of sustain.

Also, how the string attaches to the post is important. Some tuning machines have holes drilled through their posts, while others have a slot through them that is open at the top. Although there is no "best" in this department, you may want to try putting strings on both. Some guitarists find that the string keeps springing out of the slot while they are winding it for the first time. Others find that the hole in the spindle is hard to locate in a hurry. Try putting a string on both types. You may find that it makes little difference to you whether there is a slot or a hole in the the post.

Tom Mulhern

PICKUPS AND ELECTRONICS

August 1982. Alexander Graham Bell had no way of knowing back in 1876 that his invention of the telephone would have such a profound effect on the guitar a century later. However, the basis of his creation was a magnet and a wire coil, through which electrical impulses could either be collected or transferred into sound. In effect, he made the first pickup. We're now going to focus on the electronics—the pickups, pots, switches, and associated parts—which give the electric guitar its punch, tone, and overall character. The more knowledgeable you are concerning these parts, the better off you'll be in the marketplace. You'll be able to zero in on what you want and need without weeding through undesirable features, and nobody will be able to snow you into paying for features you have no interest in.

In the past century, man has invented the automobile, traveled into space, split the atom, and shuffled genes; however, today's guitar pickup is still basically very similar to Bell's crude lab prototype, and only slightly removed from the first single-coil models of the '20s and '30s. That's not to say the apparent lack of progress is *bad*. Baseball is still pretty much the same, light bulbs still follow Edison's basic design, and bicycles haven't gone out of style. A good idea is hard to top, and for the most part great inventions such as the pickup or the bicycle tend to be refined or revised more often than supplanted.

Let's look at the heart of the electric guitar: the pickup. In general it consists of a bobbin of insulating material (often ABS plastic) with several thousand turns of wire wrapped around it. Generally speaking, the more turns of wire on a bobbin, the higher the output voltage (translation: more wire, hotter pickup). Note, however, that as the number wire wraps is increased, there is in many cases a correspondingly greater loss of treble. Therefore, if you're interested in

Shielded wire between tone and volume control pots helps to keep stray signals from interfering with the instrument's sound. Metal cases over the pots contribute additional shielding.

a high-powered output and a full tonal range, you may have to make concessions and choose between optimum output and optimum tone.

Magnets are placed in proximity to the coil of wire (often in the center of the bobbin). When a string is struck, it disturbs the normal flow of magnetism (called flux) through the coil, and a corresponding current is produced. The current is then sent to the amp, where it is converted back into sound.

Polepieces. In order to focus the magnetism on the strings, *polepieces*— little cylindrical studs, screws, or Allen bolts— often extend up from the magnet to a point below each string. Some are height-adjustable, which allows the guitarist to balance the pickup's response to the strings (e.g., make the G string less prominent, or the low *E* more boomy). Adjusting polepieces too close to the strings can cause the magnetism to dampen their vibrations, resulting in a loss of sustain.

Unfortunately, when a string is bent, it may be moved off axis from the polepiece, resulting in a loss of magnetism and corresponding signal. In order to alleviate this proximity effect, some manufacturers use extra polepieces or a bar extending the width of the pickup,

instead of just six individual polepieces. Still other pickups are designed so that their magnets don't have exposed polepieces, and therefore no adjustment is possible (in many cases, you'll find that no adjustment is necessary).

When you try electric guitars, bend the strings as much as you normally would; in fact, bend a little extra. Some guitarists find the proximity effect annoying, while others are scarcely bothered by it. Polepieces or magnetic bars alone aren't the only way to adjust the distance between the pickup and the strings. Often either two or three screws hold the entire pickup in place, and allow for tilting of the pickups to optimize their effectiveness. Check to determine how many kinds of adjustment options are offered.

Coils. The first pickups were single-coils, and many guitars still feature them. They tend to have a bright sound, and therefore are good for full fidelity from the picking attack to the highest harmonics. Unfortunately, simple single-coils have a great tendency to pick up hum and stray noise caused by such electrical devices as motors, transformers, and fluorescent lights. The humbucking pickup, as its name implies, bucks the hum by connecting two coils in series (one wired into the next). The two coils are electrically out-of-phase, and according to theory, when one of two identical signals (such as noise) is inverted and combined with its non-inverted counterpart, they cancel each other.

Now, if both coils of a humbucker were to occupy the same space, they would not only cancel the noise, but the

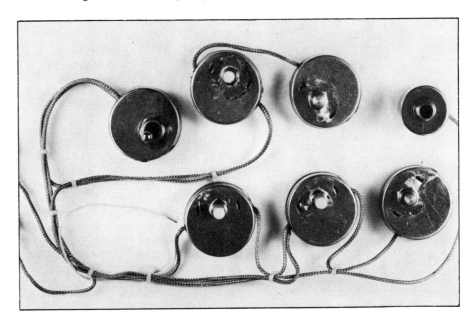

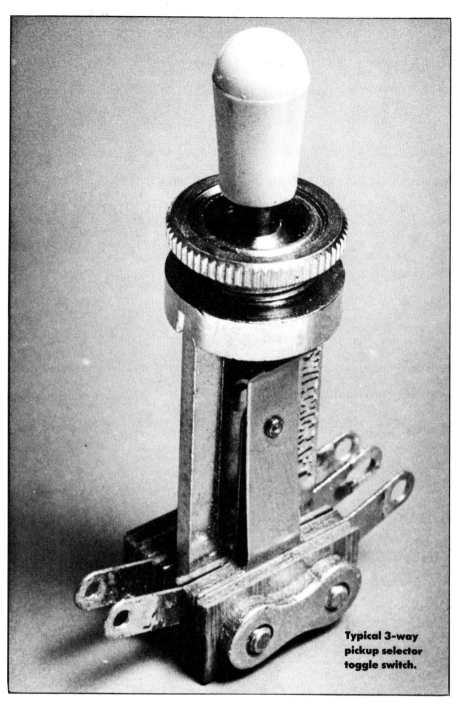

Typical 3-way pickup selector toggle switch.

placed on the treble response is responsible for their "fatter" sound. When you try out an electric, play in your normal style, and listen to the overall sound. Check for buzz (most music stores have fluorescent lights). Remember, in general, single-coils are more susceptible to buzz and hum pick-up. Make sure you're using a good cord—a poor one can let a surprising amount of noise into your signal chain.

Impedance. There are many variations on both types of pickups. The most common attribute of many pickups is their high impedance. This means that they have a high resistance to AC current flow, often due to the number of wraps of wire around their core. Other contributors to this phenomenon are inductance, DC resistance, and the frequency of the signal. Without getting into a discussion of the electrical ins and outs, let's just say that high-impedance circuits are generally more susceptible than low-impedance ones to noise and treble loss when coupled with long cords. Low-impedance pickups are fairly unusual, but they often have a flatter frequency response, and have fewer windings of wire (which means that they can be much brighter sounding than high-impedance ones).

Coil tapping and splitting. Other variances in pickup design include tapped outputs from each coil, coil splitting (we'll get into these later), and dummy pickups or dummy coils, which help to reduce hum and noise without entering into the actual pickup circuit (this allows for the humbucking effect without the associated loss of treble). Also some pickups have adjustable polepieces on both coils of their humbuckers. To a certain extent, this allows the guitarist to taper the frequency response, loudness, and humbucking characteristics of each string.

For the first 25 or so years electric guitars almost always had a single-coil pickup, a volume knob, and a tone knob. If the instrument had two pickups, a 3-way switch for pickup selection and additional tone and volume knobs were included. Such a simple configuration was in effect the industry standard, and today many guitarists covet vintage instruments for their simplicity of operation as well as their tonal qualities.

In the last two decades, the search for more sounds from electric guitars has led to many changes in the basic format, and now a mind-boggling variety of knobs and switches graces some instruments.

signal from the string as well. As it is, though, the coils are generally placed side-by-side, and the small distance between the two coils allows them to sense a different portion of the vibrating string. So, instead of both coils receiving the same signal, they "see" slightly different portions of the wave produced by the string, and therefore don't cancel each other out.

That's the blanket theory of the humbucking principle. In reality, high frequencies have very short wavelengths, and therefore at some frequen-cies a wave produced by a vibrating string will repeat in a short enough distance of the string's length so that both coils receive identical signals. Thus, there is some cancellation of the string's vibration. And since this phenomenon occurs primarily at high frequencies, the treble response can be limited. The same phase cancellation effect can be produced to varying degrees with multiple pickups—single-coil or humbucking.

This hasn't stopped people from using humbuckers. In fact, the limitation

Volume and tone controls. Some new twists have been added to these old standards. Try a stock instrument that has a pickup or two and corresponding volume and tone controls. It's pretty straightforward. Notice, though, that as you turn the volume down, there is usually a pronounced change in tone as well. A few manufacturers have found a way out of this (short of active circuitry, which we will discuss soon): Wire the volume pot with a capacitor. A capacitor acts as a selective filter, and since the pot rolls off the higher frequencies as it is turned down, a capacitor can be used to retain some highs. This, of course, is a simplified explanation, but suffice it to say that this approach allows the volume to be turned down without drastically affecting the tone.

Now, a tone control is generally a simple filter composed of a pot and a capacitor, and it is designed to take highs out of the signal by an amount determined by the setting of the tone pot. However, it doesn't add bass or treble; it can only subtract highs. This poses a couple of problems: First, if the treble is just right, but there isn't enough bass, you're out of luck. Second, if there's plenty of bass and not enough treble, you're also out of luck.

Active circuitry. Here's where active circuitry comes in. By including a small circuit—often a preamp with tone controls—it is possible to not only increase treble or bass, but to do so individually (the terms "boost" and "cut" enter in here). With such a circuit you can have glass-shattering highs while also having growly lows—or anything in between. The preamp portion allows you to boost the guitar's volume; like passive tone controls, passive volume pots can only *subtract* signals.

Try a guitar with an active preamp and compare it to a passive instrument. Some guitarists find the added frequency response desirable, while others find it too sterile or brittle. In any event, a preamp of this sort needs power— either in the form of a battery (or two) or an external power supply. If you consider an active model, remember: High-technology electronics can act strangely if abused. However, you can minimize the possibility of something ruining your performance. Thanks to the tremendous advances in microelectronics in recent years, preamps built into guitars can be extremely reliable and quiet.

You must be careful, though, to always check your batteries or power supply. Dead batteries are one of the

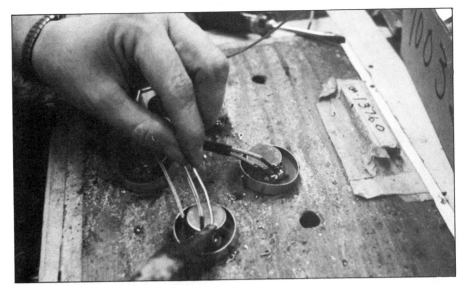

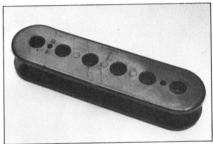

Clockwise from top: Soldering volume and tone potentiometers; a coil form, or bobbin, which is wrapped with wire (polepieces pass through the six large holes); rear view of a humbucker showing potting, a plastic or wax compound that seals the unit and prevents vibration-induced feedback; long-spring-tensioned screws allow for pickup height adjustment; a humbucker with Allen-screw adjustable polepieces.

biggest bugaboos a guitarist has in this age of multiple effects and hi-tech guitars. Some active guitars are designed so that you can bypass the active circuitry and use the guitar as a standard instrument. This can be quite comforting when you're halfway through a concert and you realize that you haven't changed the battery in your guitar in three months (so *that's* why it sounds so grungy).

A spinoff of synthesizer technology is the parametric equalizer, and a simple parametric can be included in some gui-

tars featuring active circuitry. Rather than simply being a treble or bass control, a parametric often consists of a few knobs. One determines the frequency center that you wish to affect; another determines the amount of boost or cut of that band; and another may be included for regeneration (also called "Q" or resonance). A parametric EQ circuit is sometimes tricky to work with, and can cause a severe "honk" or feedback in the frequency spectrum selected by the guitarist. Other filter options include lowpass, bandpass, and

Hamer's custom 12-string bass features knobs for adjusting each string's volume and tone, as well as knobs for master volume and tone.

high pass filters. As their names imply, they allow (respectively) lows, a selected frequency band, or highs to be passed, while other frequencies outside their domain are attenuated. Like parametrics, these unconventional controls can prove troublesome to the guitarist who is used to simply turning his tone control up or down. If favor of such circuits is their ability to drastically alter the timbre of a guitar, focus feedback into a predictible range, and give tones such as that derived from a backed-off wah-wah without tying up external effects. Greater flexibility is offered, but it is almost invariably at the expense of simplicity, and the more that is included in a guitar, the more you're likely to pay for it.

Coil splitting, phasing, tapping, series/parallel connection. Various pickup enhancements are quite popular now. These include in-phase/out-of-phase selection, coil splitting, series/parallel connection, and tapped pickup

outputs. Each is a variation on either a single-coil or a humbucker, and may involve more than one pickup. One of the oldest of these enhancements is in-phase/out-of-phase selection. This pertains primarily to a two-pickup guitar. When the outputs from the two pickups are mixed for the final output to the amp, they can be combined in two ways: in-phase or out-of-phase.

When the pickups are wired in-phase, both of their signals are combined in a way that there are few cancellations of frequencies, in fact, the signals tend to be reinforced as a result of in-phase waveforms being combined (remember from the explanation of humbuckers that each pickup "sees" the vibrations in only a small portion of a string; if two pickups detect the same wave in the same way, the waves are said to be in-phase). This can produce a bright sound. If the pickups are wired out-of-phase, many frequencies tend to be cancelled, creating a thinner, sweeter sound. The best way to illustrate this effect is to try a guitar with phase switching; note that its greatest effect is when both pickups' volume controls are at equal settings.

Phase switching requires only a double-pole/double-throw switch and no pickup modifications. Therefore, it is cheap and effective. Slightly more complex is *coil splitting*. Humbucking pickups are generally configured so that the two coils are wired in series. Coil splitting is achieved when a switch is included for selecting either coil separately, creating a brighter, single-coil sound (and in some cases, more noise). Some pickups are wired so that you can place them in single-coil, humbucking, or parallel wiring configurations. Try a guitar with these appointments if you're looking for a lot of variation. Be sure to weigh the flexibility of sound against the added price, too.

More complex than coil splitting is coil *tapping*. A normal pickup coil consists of a wire wound around a bobbin with each end being an electrical lead for connecting to selectors and other controls. A tapped pickup is wound part of the way, has a lead connected, and then is wound the rest of the way. By using a switch it's possible to tap into the pickup at different points, deriving different tones (the effect will depend on where the tap point lies, and whether the pickup is a humbucker or a single-coil). A few manufacturers have multiple coil taps on a single pickup, although they often recommend that you select the configuration you want and then solder jumper wires accordingly. Many commercially available guitars won't offer such flexibility; for most guitarists, though, a single tap is plenty (after the first dozen or so switches, the front of the guitar starts to get a bit cramped).

In an effort to give guitarists maximum flexibility, and perhaps lure them with lots of "extras," manufacturers will sometimes use some or all of the aforementioned options in combination on their guitars. And since many switches can be employed, a few companies now offer push/pull switches built into the volume and tone controls. For example, rather than flipping a toggle switch to place the pickups in phase, you simply pull on one of the knobs.

Knob and switch placement. The convenience factors involved in the number and placement of the knobs and switches is worthy of consideration. A clearly laid out guitar face can be a tremendous asset, and can mean the difference between a usable guitar with numerous features and a mind-boggling conversation piece that makes your life miserable. A volume knob placed where a guitarist can easily get his little finger around it can be the most important facet of a guitar's controls. (In fact, a few guitar companies design their instruments with only one volume knob and no other knobs or switches.) For others, the placement of the pickup selector is of utmost importance. Appraise and prioritize these features for yourself:

1. How easy is it to make quick tone and volume changes? Do you have to put much concentration into each change, or are the controls laid out in a logical way so that you can rely primarily on instinct to guide you to the correct ones? Are the controls grouped by their function (i.e., neck pickup's volume, tone, and coil-tap switches placed together, etc.)?
2. Do the toggle switches flip in the direction that's easiest to deal with? That is, when you activate a switch, does its handle move parallel or perpendicular to the strings?
3. Are any of the switches or knobs in annoying places? Check to see if you bump into them while playing rhythm *and* lead. Also, check to see if any of the switch handles or knobs are too long or short, or of so many different sizes as to make it hard for you to execute changes just by feel.

Output jacks and shielding. Output jacks pose few problems—until you trip over your cord. Then you may find out how durable or fragile it is. Make sure that the output jack is securely attached to the guitar. Some guitars have plates that hold the jack, while others simply

have a hole in the body to accommodate it. The only real oddball jack configuration is the slant-mounted Stratocaster type, which only allows you to use a cord with a straight plug. It should pose no problems unless you try to use effects or headphone amps that are designed to plug directly into a guitar.

An often overlooked feature—both by manufacturers and buyers—is shielding. In general, shielding consists of a conductive paint coating or a metal encasement or foil covering for the control and pickup cavities. Such shielding is grounded, and prevents a large percentage of extraneous electrical noise from entering the signal path inside the instrument. If you're not sure if a guitar is shielded, ask. If the salesperson isn't sure, ask them to take the cover plate off the control cavity so that you can see if there is shielding.

The most common types of shielding consist of a black carbon or copper conductive paint, copper or aluminum foil, or a form-fitted metal can that fits the entire cavity. Shielding in switch cavities (such as those holding pickup selectors), the pickup mounting holes, and around the output jack is desirable. Some guitars have small metal cans in which the pots, switches, and output jacks are individually placed. These can be found particularly on some hollow-body and semi-hollowbody models, where there is more space to accommodate them. If a guitar isn't completely shielded, don't worry, though: After-market shielding kits are available. Additionally, some guitar makers employ proper grounding techniques

and are able to circumvent a lot of problems without extensive shielding.

It's worthwhile to check for a ground wire between the bridge or tailpiece and the control cavity's ground point. This approach, which employs the guitarist's body as a capacitor in order to get rid of some extraneous interference, has been standard practice for many years, and is a potentially dangerous one. For instance, if you are touching the strings on such a guitar, and simultaneously touch another piece of equipment with its electrical polarity opposite from your amp's—completing the circuit—you can get a good shock or even be electrocuted. When you look inside the control cavity to check for shielding, check for a ground wire leading to the bridge or tailpiece as well. Repairmen can often eliminate this wire, add proper shielding, and maintain the guitar's low-noise characteristics. Otherwise, you may risk getting zapped. Of course, a wireless transmitter can be used to isolate you and the guitar from the live current.

Make sure that the pickup, tone, volume, and switching features offered on a guitar are what you want and need—not just extras to wow your friends and fans. If the effect of a certain control is too subtle and doesn't really appeal to you, find out if that same model of guitar is available without it. You may be able to save some money by forgoing features that you simply don't need.

Next we'll look at the bridge, tailpiece, and peripheral parts.

Tom Mulhern

Far left: A three-pickup configuration can be wired to either a 3-way or 5-way pickup selector. Left: Two humbuckers, each with separate tone and volume controls and a 3-way toggle selector.

BRIDGES AND TAILPIECES

December 1982. Like the rubber band, a guitar string is stretched between two points: the nut and the bridge. Although the ends of the strings actually terminate at the tuning machines and tailpiece, it is the distance between the nut and bridge that is of principal concern when producing and controlling the sound of the instrument. Let's examine the relationship between the bridge and tailpiece, the types of bridges and tailpieces, and other attributes of these parts.

Trapeze-style tailpieces. When the electric guitar evolved from the arch-top acoustic, the use of a separate bridge and tailpiece remained the standard for many years. In fact, today many arch-tops, semi-solidbodies, and even a few solidbodies sport separate bridges and trapeze-style tailpieces. (The trapeze design is so named because it looks much like a circus trapeze; its cross bar holds the strings and the two thin bars connect it to the lower rim of the body.) Despite their early

Below left: The Kaftan tailpiece is designed to raise or lower the pitch of pre-selected strings. Below right: The Fender Stratocaster bridge/tailpiece has six individual height- and intonation-adjustable saddles. Opposite: Framus bass bridge/tailpiece.

origins, though, they are neither obsolete nor inferior to the stop tailpiece or combination tailpiece/bridge units in use mainly on solidbodies and some semi-solidbodies for decades.

Often, the inclusion of a separate tailpiece and bridge arises out of necessity. In the case of hollowbody guitars, it is impractical to terminate the strings at the bridge; there is sufficient tension to pull the bridge off the top, causing extensive damage. Also, the type of bridge most commonly employed on arch-tops acts to couple the string vibration with the top, and so is essential to the tone and sustain (the tailpiece merely holds the ends of the strings). The top is allowed to resonate freely. This resonance often contributes to feedback. But even though hollowbodies are prone to feedback at higher volumes, many guitarists still prefer their full, acoustic tone.

Stop tailpieces. Stop, or stud, tailpieces and similarly designed bridge/tailpiece combinations demand a solid mooring of thick wood, metal, plastic, etc., whereas acoustic tops measure in the sixteenths of an inch in thickness—hopelessly insufficient to hold the metal studs on which the stop bridge and tailpiece rest. Thus a thick body is abso-

lutely necessary to anchor the string firmly.

Here is where design philosophies concerning the function of the bridge, tailpiece, body, and pickups split. For many who prefer the acoustic properties of the arch-tops and other hollowbodies, amplification is just that: making the instrument louder. Therefore, the basic tone of the guitar is of serious consequence. Solidbodies, on the other hand, are often designed to have relatively little resonance—at least in the audible spectrum—and in turn may contribute little to the overall sound (although it can have a great bearing, depending on the type of wood, pickups, and construction used). Instead, the pickups and strings work as a team to create a sound.

The semi-hollowbody has features of the solidbody and the hollowbody, since there is a solid wood block running the length of the body's inside. Because it is solid, studs or other moorings can be worked into it, giving the guitar an opportunity to be treated as a solidbody or a hollowbody insofar as the bridge and tailpiece are concerned. Because the rest of the guitar's body remains open cavities, some of the attributes of a hollowbody (a mellower tone, for instance) can be exploited.

Diverse bridge functions. Now, there must be some reason for the many types of bridges. Naturally. Besides the difference in feedback potential, there is the difference in string tension on the guitar. When a string passes over the bridge, it must "break" at an angle toward the bridge. It can't pass straight over the bridge because it would buzz

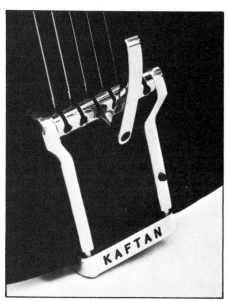

or slide around on its top. Its *down angle* is determined by the distance of the bridge to the tailpiece and how high the tailpiece is in relation to the bridge. A trapeze-style tailpiece, no matter how rigid, will have a lot of tension exerted on it by the strings, causing it to pull up a bit, and in turn creating a relatively shallow down angle. And because it is most often anchored to the lower end of the guitar (usually near the strap button), there is quite a potential for the strings to pull it up like a long lever. This may reduce the angle at which the string passes over the bridge, and thereby lessen sustain.

The stop tailpiece and the combination bridge/tailpiece are most often anchored into the top of a guitar with screws or large studs. (In order to add sustain, some manufacturers will place a heavy *sustain block*—a large piece of metal, often brass, which is intended to increase the bridge's apparent mass—in the body to better couple vibrations.) Strings can either pass through six holes in the tailpiece and have their ball ends held firmly at the back, or on some tailpieces their ball ends can slip into slots in the top of the bridge (the latter facilitates quick changes). In the case of separate bridges and tailpieces, the two can be height-adjusted separately, making the down angle of the string adjustable as well.

Down angle and sustain. How does the down angle affect the guitar's performance? It influences the sustain. (The down angle of the strings between the nut and the tuning machines will also have an effect.) The shallower the down angle, the less downward tension of the bridge. A deeper (more acute) down angle creates greater pressure on the bridge, and in turn adds to sustain and a particularly noticeable increase in the transmission of highs. This is, of course, a greatly simplified explanation, but it illustrates quickly how the bridge's position relative to the tailpiece's affects sustain.

If you're checking into an electric guitar, try playing instruments with both types of bridge and tailpiece configurations. The more similar the guitars are in every other respect (pickups, electronics, neck and body materials, etc.), the easier it will be to determine which one sounds and feels better to you as a result of its bridge/tailpiece format. Remember: A semi-solidbody or solidbody's trapeze-style tailpiece can often be replaced with a stud-type (provided that a center block is present). However, the mounting screws of the original tail-

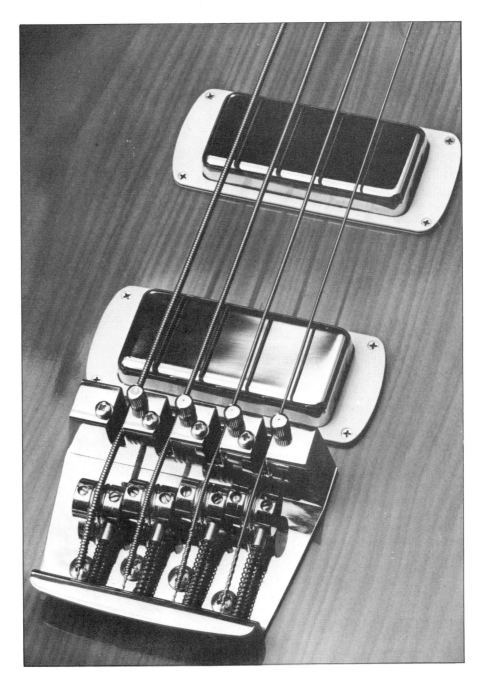

piece will leave holes in the lower end of the instrument. Conversely, if you decide to switch from a stop-style to a trapeze-style assembly, the stud mounting holes are generally quite large (on the order of about 1/2", and when filled will leave good-sized scars.

Electric guitars with acoustic-style bridges. Bridges on many arch-tops are made of wood or wood and metal. The base of the bridge is often a hardwood such as ebony or rosewood, and the saddle may be of the same material or metal. In some cases, the saddle is supported by adjusting screws which allow

you to set the appropriate string height. In addition, the saddle portion may be a single, angled piece designed for fixed approximate intonation. Alternatively, it may have small individual cuts in its top to intonate each string (this approach is commonly employed in acoustic steel-strings, and can work rather well, provided that one gauge of string is used consistently). Then there's the "tune-o-matic" type, which has adjustable individual saddles for each string.

If your primary interest is a hollow-body or semi-solidbody with a separate bridge and tailpiece, you may find that the tune-o-matic type is preferable,

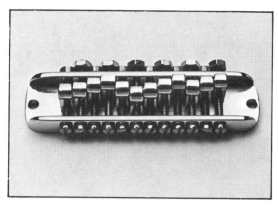

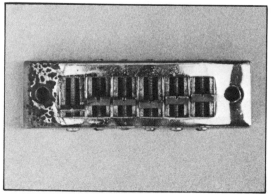

Clockwise from top left: Stars Guitars' all-brass 12-string tune-o-matic bridge; Gibson stop tailpiece and its mounting studs (the sleeves are set into the guitar's body and act as anchors for the screw-in studs; when a bridge's plating corrodes, exposing the metal beneath, acids and moisture from sweat continue to take their toll; Gibson's pioneering tune-o-matic design featured and adjustable saddle for each string. Below: This drawing illustrates the difference between single- and dual-screw tune-o-matic bridge saddles.

simply because it allows you to experiment with various types and gauges of strings. A fixed saddle or one cut with specific intonation doesn't afford the same amount of flexibility. However, don't necessarily rule out these types. They have been around for many, many years, and they do indeed contribute to the tone. Metal tends to transmit more highs than most woods, and therefore metal saddles can lend a brittle edge to the sound; also, adjusting screws between the bridge's base and the saddle structure act to alter the tone somewhat, because as sound passes from one material to another it refracts (bends much like light passing through a piece of glass), resulting in a distortion or alteration of the tone. Such a phenomenon is generally a concern of luthiers and acoustic researchers rather than guitarists. The overall sound of the instrument is often designed around such quirks.

The evolution of stop tailpieces and adjustable bridges. In one of its earliest and most basic forms, the stop tailpiece consisted of a cast or machined heavy piece of metal which had notches in its back to accomodate the termination of the strings, an integral saddle (canted and notched to provide a certain degree of intonation), and two holes or slots to allow it to rest on a pair

of large studs screwed into the body. This was an approach employed on Gibson solidbodies in the mid-50's. Gibson also introduced a tune-o-matic bridge, which was separate from the tailpiece and offered individual intonation adjustment of each string. The height of each string was not easily altered: saddles had to be filed or the bridge could be tilted (offering only limited relative degrees of height change). Although several variations of this bridge design have sprouted up over the past three decades, the basic concept remains intact: The bridge has two holes or slots for mounting it on a pair of studs. A slot is cut in the bridge and six saddles fit in. Each saddle is transversed by a screw, which when turned, moves the saddle, thereby adjusting the intonation.

Among the many variations on the tune-o-matic today are some that have saddles loaded with springs (to keep the tension on the saddles) and with screw adjusters that pass only through the front or back of the bridge base. A complaint with these is that the saddles pop out when strings are changed. Although this type is becoming increasingly rare, be sure to examine the bridge closely for this. The majority simply have either a slot cut in the bridge to accomodate these, or the bridge itself is a "U" channel (actually

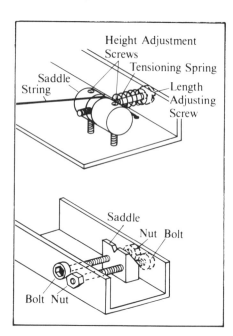

two 90-degree angles forming a base, a common front, and a back). Some companies have gone to a design that doesn't employ studs. Instead, the bridge is screwed or bolted directly to the body or a sustain block. A possible drawback to this approach is that in some designs, the height of the saddles is only adjustable in one way; through replacement. Some bridges are mounted on sustain blocks (as well as

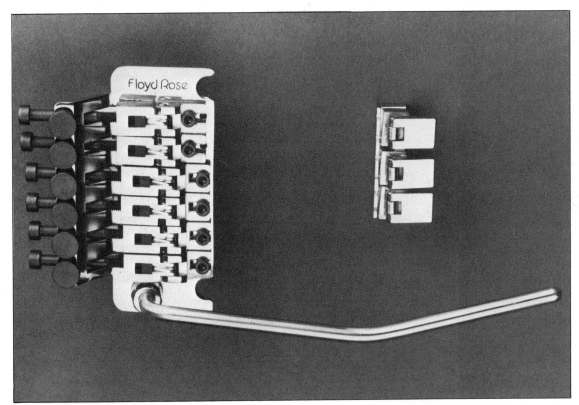

right in the body) using screw-type height adjusters. These facilitate raising or lowering the entire bridge.

Yet another kind has two screws passing through each saddle; one from each direction. The idea here is to loosen one screw, and then tighten the first one (alternatively, both screws can be adjusted at once, and then tightened concurrently). This helps to ensure that the saddle doesn't wobble (a single screw can sometimes act as an axle upon which a saddle rotates slightly), and some manufacturers believe that this helps to couple the string vibrations better through the more solid integration of the bridge and saddles.

While the tune-o-matic and other forms of stop bridges and tailpieces were being designed, Fender pursued an alternate bridge design that allowed for a certain degree of independent intonation and height adjustment, employing three saddles, each of which accommodated two strings. This type was common to the early Telecasters, and is still available on some today (Fender also has a bridge with six separate saddles). It allowed for intonation of two strings at a time by adjusting a screw attached to the bridge plate and the saddle. Some saddles have screw threads running around them; these act as string guides, and allow the string spacing to be adjusted. Two

screws in each saddle act as small legs, and regulate the height. Different companies have created variations on this design (including Fender, who makes a fully adjustable bridge/tailpiece with six individually intonation- and height-adjustable saddles), employing various metals, finishes, and shapes. (Gretsch had a bridge with a feature called Space Control, which consisted of a threaded axle with six round saddles with matching internal screw threads. They could be moved closer or farther apart by turning them.)

There are certainly less parts and less adjustments for intonation on a bridge with only three saddles than on a standard tune-o-matic type, but there is a tradeoff, since, for instance, the high *E* and *B* strings must be intonated as a unit. With this type of bridge one must also make sure that the springs tensioning the saddles are fairly tight; loose ones can rattle. On some models following this design, there is potential for side-to-side movement of the saddles. To minimize this action, some companies machine furrows in the bridge/tailpiece plate that keep the height adjustment screws in check.

Rattling parts. With this and all other types of bridges, always check for rattling. Belt a few really hard chords, fingerpick, bend strings, and use just about

every technique you can think of while testing a guitar. Listen closely for rattles and buzzes in the bridge. Play with an amp as well as without. Some noises caused by the bridge may not be apparent when you're noodling around without amplification, but when that guitar's cranked up, you may experience surprising and unpalatable sounds. If you hear something peculiar, try a similar guitar—it may simply be a misadjustment creating the gremlin.

If the problem persists, ask a repairman or salesperson to check it out. They may know how to rectify it. Otherwise, try a different model. While bridges aren't the most expensive part of a guitar, replacements can be somewhat costly and potentially difficult to install correctly. And there's no reason why you should have to accept a new guitar knowing that the bridge is unsuitable.

Fine tuning adjusters. In recent years, an added feature has come into play on some tune-o-matic bridges and tailpieces: fine-tuning adjusters. Long employed on violins, where tuning is absolutely critical due to the shortness of their scale, the fine tuner only made its way to the guitar in the past few years. After tuning the strings with the machines located on the headstock, a player can zero-in on the correct pitch as the strings stretch or as they go out of

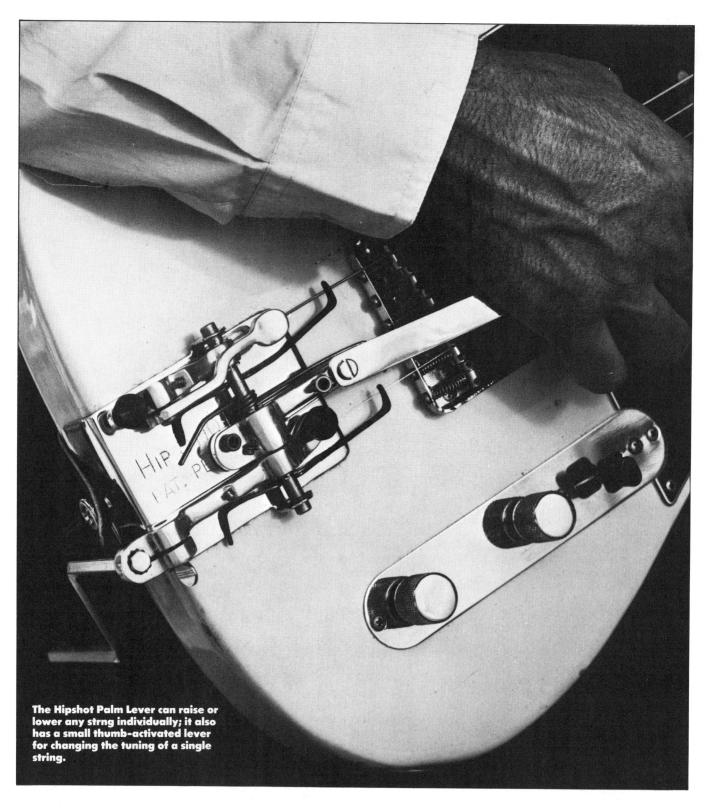

The Hipshot Palm Lever can raise or lower any strng individually; it also has a small thumb-activated lever for changing the tuning of a single string.

tune from use. The advantage to the fine tuner is that it can be operated with the picking hand. So, when you're playing a chord or a lead and you hear an out-of-tune string, you can reach down, adjust the tension, and keep on playing without missing a beat.

Some tune-o-matic bridge/tailpieces can cause problems after a while, especially if heavy strings are preferred. Because tune-o-matics are mounted on studs, those that act as a bridge and tailpiece have the strings terminate at their back. Studs can sometimes slowly tilt forward or be bent slightly after a while. If you prefer heavy strings, you may want to make sure that the studs are heavy-duty and that the body wood is very hard. As usual, if you're in doubt, ask the salesman or a repairman.

Tune-o-matic adjustability. On all tune-o-matics, a matter of major concern is the amount that the saddles can be adjusted. If their travel length is short, this may pose no problems *if* the bridge is already intonated and if you are willing to use the gauge of strings that the guitar is strung with. Ideally, the saddles should be somewhere around the middle of their travel length when the guitar is intonated. This ensures enough room for adjustment in case you decide to use strings of a different gauge, plus it helps to prevent the bridge from tilting (if all the saddles are near the end of their travel on the bridge's end nearest the pickups, there may be some tilting).

Saddles and sustain. The saddles themselves can be made of several materials: steel, brass, plastic, graphite, etc. When sound passes from one material to another, some filtering of harmonics may occur (naturally, the effect varies depending on how similar or dissimilar the materials are). This may or may not be a major point, depending on what kind of tone you prefer, but you may want to try similar guitars with different bridges—or at least different types of saddles—to see if there is a significant difference. If a saddle is wobbly or soft, it may prove troublesome and have an adverse effect on your guitar's sustain.

An alternative concept in gaining sustain calls for the strings to pass through holes in the body to terminate at the back. Some builders use this technique to couple the string vibration directly to the wood of the body. Heavy tailpieces bolted right to the top are also intended for this purpose.

The density of the materials used will also play a part in the transmission of sound and the creation of sustain. Some bridges are cast of soft alloys—occasionally indeterminate mixtures of zinc, iron, and other metals. This isn't necessarily undesirable of itself, but machined bridges are often made of a harder, denser alloy, such as brass, bronze, steel, etc. This allows vibrations to travel through more easily (the effect is most noticeable for highs).

Corrosion. One characteristic of metal has little to do with the sound, but plenty to do with aesthetics: corrosion. Most metal is prone to erosion by salt, acid, and moisture contained in sweat. In order to thwart the nasty effects of normal use, manufacturers often plate their bridges and tailpieces with chrome or nickel. Gold is another common plat-

This early Gibson stop tailpiece/bridge for solidbody electrics made no provisions for individual intonation adjustment.

ing; however, it is not only expensive, but it also lacks the durability of the other two: It is soft and therefore wears off with relative ease. Bare stainless steel holds up fairly well—with some rust, depending on the alloy used, but untreated brass gets pretty cruddy. Black and green tarnish accumulates wherever the brass is exposed.

Many parts makers now treat their brass hardware with a special epoxy or similarly durable material. The clear finish allows the full lustre of the metal to show through—impervious to the harshness of sweat. When you're checking out a guitar's bridge and tailpiece, ask what material it is made from. Also ask whether it is plated, coated, or otherwise treated. A particularly vulnerable combination is a cast bridge of fairly soft metals (zinc, for example). Once the protective plating wears off, corrosion runs rampant, pitting and etching the part.

A good wax can sometimes add protection, but your best insurance is to wipe any accumulated soil from the part regularly. Again, remember that gold is beautiful but easily scratched. If you're pretty rough to a guitar or sweat like crazy, select a more enduring plating or coating.

Tremolo bridges. Tremolo units have been around longer than the electric guitar—Doc Kauffman's earliest banjo model was made in 1929—yet even the most sophisticated models have one thing in common: they all bend the strings and alter the pitch. There have been some radical offshoots of the

tremolo, but by and large its concept is basic: move a lever, change the pitch.

One of the biggest drawbacks to tremolos, historically, has been their inability to *always* come back to tune. Some are pretty successful, but this success is measured in degrees. The most common form for the tremolo is that employed by Fender in its Stratocasters. A large metal block through which the strings pass and terminate has a lever on top and springs on the bottom. (Six individually height- and intonation-adjustable saddles are poised on top.) The springs provide offset tension to counteract the pull of the strings. The steel bar sets into the block, and by rocking the bar, one can change the tension and the corresponding pitch of the strings. This type of tremolo is often emulated, sometimes quite successfully.

Another type of tremolo has its roots in the Bigsby style of the '50s and '60s: The unit is fastened to the face of the guitar, and a large arm mounted on a tensioning spring governs an axle with six holes through which pass the strings. As the arm is depressed, turning the axle, the tension and pitch of the strings is lowered. Variations on this format have recently popped up—some with axles that turn, others with tailpieces that slant forward.

Which style is better? Naturally life would be too simple if that could be answered easily. Try both types. Some guitarists find the latter style too stiff for their liking, while others feel that the former goes out of tune too easily. Test them in this way: Tune the guitar. Play a chord and lower the pitch by depressing

The Bigsby tailpiece contains a single large spring; the strings pass through a rotating axle, which turns and lowers their pitch when the lever is depressed.

the arm. Now let the arm return. Is the guitar still in tune? If not, how close is it? Note that proper retuning is the result of many complex things occurring: The strings must not grab in the nut's slots or on the bridge saddles, the breaking angle of the string over the nut must be correct, and so forth. If you experience problems with a tremolo you try out, ask a repairman if he can remedy the situation. Lots of guitarists find ways around tuning problems (going light on the tremolo, using it only on the last song of a set, adjusting the balance of the strings and the springs, etc.), and some manufacturers employ features such as rollers for saddles and nuts to decrease the likelihood of strings catching in them.

In the last few years, a couple of locking mechanisms have been introduced on the tremolo. The Floyd Rose, Kramer, and Rockinger models all feature locking bridge saddles and locking nuts. These are available as stock equipment on some guitars. They all require patient initial tuning and can keep a guitar in tune during a lot of abuse. Some tremolos are also available with different string spacings, so check carefully. If you prefer your strings a certain distance apart or from the edges of the fingerboard, pay close attention while sizing up a tremolo.

When checking out a guitar, always give great scrutiny to the bridge and tailpiece. Organize your priorities. For instance, ask yourself such questions as: Do you want a tremolo? Does brass look better than stainless steel or chrome-plate? Can I adjust the intonation easily? Don't rush. Check each guitar carefully, and most important, ask questions. Your hard-earned money is on the line. Make that money work for you.
Tom Mulhern

THE VINTAGE GUITAR MARKET

Sunburst Les Paul, mint: $8,500. Maple-neck Strats, $2,500 and up. Flying V's slashed to $2,500: cash only. Will trade Explorer for late-model Oldsmobile.

* * * *

July 1979. One thing that all the old guitars in this hypothetical advertisement have in common is that they used to list for about $250. What's going on? Why does someone trade in an armload of new guitars for a single old one? Why do some Les Pauls have virtually no pure "collector's value" while others are worth 20 times their original price? Are old instruments really better? Which ones? Why, and why not? Is the dusty old guitar under your bed a potential gold mine, or just a dusty old guitar?

What follows will answer some of these questions, present opinions on others, and examine the interactions of buyers and sellers, instruments and prices, fads and trends. Some topics are avoided: There is no attempt to see who the biggest dealers are, no effort is made to duplicate the contents of various books on guitar history, and there is no comprehensive investment guide.

What does "vintage" mean? Larry Henrikson grew up around the music business, has had much experience, and now has over 500 old guitars—some of them very rare—at his store, Ax In Hand, in DeKalb, Illinois. He recalls, "I started shopping for used guitars in the late '60s, and somewhere between 1969 and 1974, 'used' guitars became 'vintage.' People use the word to describe

one-of-a-kind collector's guitars, but they also use it incorrectly when they're trying to attach some importance to a plain old used guitar."

The vintage guitar market is a system of *laissez-faire* commerce, a function of both the finite nature of its resources and the classic factors of supply and demand. But, as we'll see, its routine business aspects are compounded by fads and fiction, rumors and romance, greed and glamour. The rare instrument scene is populated mostly by knowledgeable musicians-turned-dealers who sell the instruments, the much less knowledgeable but increasingly aware amateur and professional players who buy them, as well as the collectors who buy, sell, and trade them on a regular basis. Out on the fringes is a menagerie of secretive eccentrics, hoarders, counterfeiters, and non-musician investors.

The rock star/collectors range from suckers who pretend to know a lot about guitars and regularly get taken to the cleaners by sellers, to people like Cheap Trick's Rick Nielsen, a shrewd shopper whose command of facts rivals that of many full-time dealers, and Steve Howe, a guitar connoisseur with a

This Danelectro Longhorn bass, built around 1960, features concentric tone and volume knobs, lipstick tube pickups, and a 24-fret fingerboard.

Maple-neck Stratocasters are among the most valuable Fenders.

huge collection.

The market recirculates hundreds of thousands of dollars every week, and it is changing in several important respects. Prices on many items are soaring, and the high value of popular guitars sometimes causes inordinately steep prices to be stuck on the turkeys. Customers are more aware than before, though ignorance or misconceptions still affect the particulars of many transactions. Regionalism is a major factor in pricing. On the East and West Coasts, vintage guitars generally bring substantially more money than in middle America (while the situation regarding new guitars is often the opposite). Danny Thorpe, of Austin's Heart Of Texas Music, guesses that a dotneck Gibson ES-335 may be worth $500 more in L.A. than in Texas: "Take Strats—I can sometimes get prices selling to East Coast *dealers*, who are going to resell, that are just as high as the ones that I get selling to local customers."

The sellers are changing, too. While there are still part-time traders out there in parking lots doing a little business from their station wagons, there are also full-time vintage instrument dealers and collectors who open specialty shops, hold well-attended expositions, publish catalogs, install vaults in their homes, deal through the mail in both domestic and international markets, and sock away dozens, or even hundreds, of rare collector's items.

Fewer treasures are turning up in attics. Many are already accounted for—they're "in circulation" among collectors and dealers. It is common for a particular "piece," as they are sometimes called, to go through the hands of one dealer several times over a period of years.

Instruments and prices. While there are many collectible guitars, only three brand names and a handful of models account for most of the reservoir of cash that percolates through the market's various commercial tributaries. The companies are Gibson, Fender, and Martin.

Most collectible Gibsons are electrics. Of these, the most important models are solidbodies made in the late '50s and very early '60s, including Les Pauls, SG/Les Pauls, Flying V's and Explorers; plus the '63-'65 reverse-body Firebird guitars and Thunderbird basses; as well as the original semi-hollow thin-line guitars such as the ES-355, ES-345, and especially the ES-335 dot-neck (so nick named because its small circular fingerboard position markers are easily distinguished from later block markers).

Among Les Pauls, the ultimate primo model is the '58-'60 sunburst finish Standard; in fact, it is currently the hottest collector's guitar among electrics. Almost invariably called a sunburst by dealers, it is certainly one of the most beautiful factory-stock solidbodies ever made, one for which Gibson should be eternally proud. The "flame" or "tiger stripe" pattern of the maple top—which varies considerably—is its most obvious feature. And depending on the nature of this pattern, the aging characteristics and color of the finish, and the overall condition of the guitar, a sunburst can now bring an easy three grand, maybe four, and according to recent reports, even five. In 1960 you could buy a new one for $265.00, without case.

Other popular single-cutaway Les Pauls include the various gold-tops and both two-pickup ('54-'57) and three-pickup ('57 and later) Customs. The Les Pauls from the same period that cost less to begin with are still functional, collectible guitars, though worth only a fraction of the others. These include Specials, TVs, and Juniors. When Gibson first changed the Les Paul to the sharp "horns" and double cutaway currently associated with the SG models, the instrument still bore the Les Paul name; these SG/Les Pauls, including Standards and Customs, are prized items. SGs, various arch-top acoustics and electrics, and a few flat-top models (e.g., J-200, J-185, Everly Brothers) are some of the Gibsons that appeal to more specialized groups of collectors.

Gibson's korina-body Flying V's and Explorers were bringing $3,500 and up a couple of years ago, although they have recently come down. Dot-neck 335s have radically increased in the past year or two and are expected by practically everyone to continue their rise in value. At the Greater Southwest Guitar Show, held in Dallas, March 31st-April 1st, 1979, there were several mint dot-necks with price tags (not necessarily the selling price) of $1,700 and over. The sunburst dot-necks cost $279.50 in 1960.

Important Fenders include pre-1965 Stratocasters, especially the older, maple-neck models (one especially lusted-after Strat is a white maple-neck with gold-plated parts). Larry Henrikson comments, "If the day hasn't arrived already when a truly mint '54 Strat is worth $2,000, it will soon." Any Broadcaster (the immediate predecessor to the Telecaster, and the Fender company's first instrument) is highly prized. Most Telecasters manufactured prior

to Fender's acquisition by CBS are worth at least twice their original list prices—maybe eight to ten times as much. All pre-CBS Precision Basses, or P-Basses, are prized, especially the '50s models; in general, the older the better, though the late '50s models with gold anodized pickguards are among the most valuable basses on the market.

The brand name and model are only part of the equation that collectors formulate when sizing up an instrument's worth. Condition, obviously, matters very much, but the age of the guitar—at least the period, and in some cases the actual year—is critical. There are plenty of Stratocasters, Les Pauls, Telecasters, and Precision Basses that have virtually no collector's value whatever on the present market; that is, their worth rests solely on their practical merits as musical instruments.

The magic of collectible electrics sometimes extends to pickups. An original Gibson patent-applied-for humbucking pickup, or PAF, can sell for $100 to $250 or more depending upon the colors of the two coils. Double blacks, according to Danny Thorpe, are at the low end, followed by split-coils—one white (cream), one black—followed by the scarce double whites.

The great majority of collectible steel-strings are Martins. Of those, the most highly desired models are the pre-War D-45s, which can sell for $6,000 to $8,000, and D-28 Herringbones, which can go for under $3,000 to over $5,000. Some of the others include various O, OO, and OOO models and certain D models (or dreadnoughts). Brazilian rosewood, no longer used by Martin, generally increases the instrument's value.

This is not to say that guitar buffs care about only three brands of instruments. Rather, it refers only to the fact that considering the immense variety of American guitars, most of the cash changes hands over a remarkably small number of models—Les Pauls, Strats, Teles, Precision Basses, various Martins, and a few others.

But across America there are handfuls of Rickenbacker freaks, Gretsch diehards, National and Dobro fanatics, and devotees of other brands: Mosrites are especially popular among Japanese buyers and eternal surfers. Hard-core bluegrassers care about Martins, Washburns, Lloyd Loar Gibson mandolins, a few arch-tops, various brands of banjos and other items, but in general their interest in vintage electrics is right around the vicinity of zero.

Older buffs (and a few younger ones

as well) sometimes get seriously into jazz era arch-tops, and for these folks a mint D'Angelico, Stromberg, Gibson, or Epiphone is where the world of guitar begins and ends.

In fact, you can pick practically any guitar—a custom DuPont Duco Jaguar, a Switchmaster with single-coils, a Gretsch Rancher with the triangular soundhole, whatever—and chances are, somewhere out there is a freak who cares about little else and has three of them stashed in a padlocked closet.

There are also certain Holy Grails, a few sacred White Buffaloes. These would include Gibson's korina Moderne, a bizarre solidbody so scarce that even experienced dealers hardly ever report sightings. While it's fun to speculate on the worth of such items, and while their existence is historically noteworthy, they have almost nothing to do with day-to-day vintage guitar trading for the simple reason that hardly anyone ever sees them.

There have been hundreds of models of guitars manufactured by scores of companies, and these models often change from year to year. Many people know that there's money to be made in old guitars, yet few have taken the time to investigate the details. As a result, a specific price is often too high or too low when compared to the instrument's general market worth. Tom Wittrock, of Third Eye Music in Springfield, Missouri, says, "A guy can get any old Martin and ask $800 or $900 and get it if the buyer doesn't know any better—even if it's just a OO-17 or something—just because it's old and a Martin. Certain things sell for way too much money. An instrument can be in the hard-to-get-rid-of category and yet still bring a lot of money from the guy who just wants a Gibson or whatever and doesn't really know anything. Very seldom does a guy who's looking for a sunburst have any inkling of what it will cost him."

Dave Wintz, of Houston's Rockin' Robin, agrees: "You know the old saying, 'a little knowledge is dangerous.' Well, a lot of people with old instruments think they have more than they do, and this has a lot to do with the market going bananas. The word 'old' is going around, and everyone thinks that anything that's old is worth millions of dollars, and people are paranoid and afraid that they're going to get ripped off if they don't charge a high price.

"Sometimes a dealer is just as unaware as the buyer, so he puts a $2,000 tag on a refinished Strat, and the kid walks in—he doesn't know otherwise, and so it reinforces this whole con-

sciousness of overpricing guitars, treating them like old violins and stuff. Plus, you've got guys in big rock groups saying in magazines that they play a '51 Strat or something, and of course they don't exist. It just goes on like that."

Vintage guitars have in recent years acquired a dubious hallmark of other collectibles. They are being counterfeited. Of course, whether it's a "reproduction" or a scam depends on what the seller says about it after it's been altered. On quite a few occasions, though, Les Paul gold-tops have been doctored to resemble much more valuable sunbursts—sometimes with replaced tops, modified bindings, altered headstocks, inked-on serial numbers instead of stamped-in numbers, and other drastic changes that require plenty of lutherie skill.

Several people have cut down the headstocks of late-model Fenders, replaced the decals with fakes, switched neckplates (where serial numbers are usually stamped), and replaced the 3-color sunburst (or other color) with a '50s-style 2-color. (There have even been several reports of phony Gibson "patent-applied-for" decals.) While not rampant, such activities further complicate the market and increase the risks encountered by dabblers, since only a trained eye can detect a well-doctored fake.

The manufacturers; reissue guitars.

The companies responsible for making the now-vintage guitars in the first place are, for the most part, ironically removed from the contemporary vintage-instrument scene. Collectors and other buffs adopted a jargon of their own, and it is now used nationwide, having been settled upon after years of informal usage and exchanges of information. Everyday terms not found in catalogs include: P-Bass, Tele, Strat, sunburst (as a model name, as opposed to merely a finish), SG/Les Paul, dot-neck, gold-top, patent-number and patent-applied-for, cream coils, flame maple and tiger stripe, 2-color and 3-color, belly and pyramid (Martin bridges), 3-bolt and 4-bolt (types of Fender neck attachments), stack-knob (concentric tone and volume pots on the earliest Fender Jazz Basses), tweed (cloth covering on early Fender amps), reverse and non-reverse (Firebird body shapes), and pre-CBS.

In terms of public awareness, so-called reissue guitars have further darkened muddy waters. For example, Gibson's Les Paul 55, or 55/78, is described in the May '78 price list as "a reintro-

duction of the 55 model Les Paul." It is nothing of the sort. The "Les Paul," or "Les Paul Model" was a gold-finish carved-top solidbody. The "reissue" more closely resembles a flat-body Les Paul *Special* of that era, though there are also substantial variations in construction and features between the Special and the reissue.

The '79 price list is a little more accurate, calling the reissue "a new version of the 55 model Les Paul guitar," but again the obvious "Special" qualification is omitted. The same brochure describes another guitar, the Les Paul Special Double Cutaway, which includes a body shape and features never before combined on any Gibson guitar, as "a popular reintroduction of a vintage Les Paul model." Gibson Firebird reissues also had mixed features from various models, and the reissue Flying V's weren't even close.

Gibson's Director of Research and Development, Bruce Bolen, was involved with all of the company's reissue guitars. He explains: "It's really not that simple, this distinguishing between old ones and new ones. Take our first Flying V reissue, for example. The idea was to reproduce the shape; it was never our intention to make the thing exactly like the original . . . sometimes an original material might not be available anymore . . . and some of the changes we made were improvements."

Second, Gibson should be commended for again making available functional, reasonably priced instruments such as the flatbody Specials. Third, Gibson is hardly the only company with occasionally inaccurate catalogs, and fourth, the reason that collectors are quick to point out the discrepancies is simply that they care so much for those wonderful old Gibsons in the first place. Still, when all is said and done, describing new and unique models as reissues of old ones further bewilders an already confused buying public.

Dave Wintz of Rockin' Robin says, "Take the reissue Firebird—to me it's just a guitar. On all of the reissues Gibson has done so far they use a lot of the new manufacturing techniques, and the headstock inlays are different, and on the [single cutaway] Les Pauls the binding in the cutaway is different. All that stuff makes a difference. They'd have to do an exact—*exact*—reproduction, and they haven't done one yet."

Manufacturers' marketing and administrative practices cause additional obstacles to the buyer, collector, or researcher attempting to make sense

This 1937 D'Angelico Excel arch-top acoustic was handmade by the master guitar builder, John D'Angelico.

Gibson SG/Les Paul Standard, circa 1960: Note fold-away vibrato tailpiece.

out of American guitar evolution. Aside from inaccurate catalogs there are problems of inconsistent serial numbers and incomplete records of manufacture. Companies routinely change a guitar's features with no corresponding change in model designation, and sometimes a new name is even introduced for a model that doesn't change at all.

Good and bad books have been written that deal in whole or in part with guitar history. Some (though not necessarily all) of the helpful volumes are: *Martin Guitars: A History*, Mike Longworth [The CF Martin Organisation, Box 329, Nazareth, PA 18064]: *The Fender Guitar*, Ken Archerd [Musical New Services, Ltd., 20 Denmark Street, London, England WC2H 8NE]; *The Guitar Book*, revised edition, Tom Wheeler [Harper & Row]; *Guitars From The Renaissance To Rock*, Tom & Mary Anne Evans [Paddington]; *Roy Acuff's Musical Collection*, Doug Green and George Gruhn [WSM, Inc.]; and *Gibson Electrics, Volume 1*, Andre Duchossoir [Mediapresse, Chatillon, France].

Old guitars versus new guitars. You can walk into any music store and get into an argument about whether old guitars are better than new ones. Right away all sorts of qualifications must attach to any such discussion in order for it to have any merit whatsoever. Which companies are we talking about, and which models, and which periods of manufacture? And given all the subjective considerations, who's to say what "better" means? Besides, even after details such as these are agreed upon, we are left with the indisputable fact that two guitars identical in brand, model, and date of manufacture will probably sound, feel, and look a little different—maybe completely different. Ed Seelig, of Silver Strings Music in St. Louis, recalls, "Every time I've been able to compare old sunbursts side by side, they all sound different. One time I traded one that I had, which was really in ragged shape, to Mick Ralphs [of Bad Company] because mine sounded exactly like the one that Eric Clapton used with the Blues Breakers. The one that he gave me was in much nicer shape, but mine had the sound he was looking for. And the variation in PAF pickups is just incredible."

Having enumerated various qualifications, one generalization may be made, and it is at the core of the vintage market: Old guitars are at least *perceived* by many people to be better than their modern descendants. For each of several important models, most

collectors can readily rattle off a list of ways in which they feel vintage editions are demonstrably superior to new ones.

The problems of the old-is-better assertion are similar to those of most generalizations; for example, there are fine *new* guitars and vintage gobblers, and buying a good instrument will always depend on intuition, knowledge, and experience, and not merely a general awareness that certain pieces are valuable (it is not unreasonable to assume that once in a while a seriously inflated price is paid for a clunker, and both buyer and seller think that a prized antique has changed hands).

On the subject of old versus new as it relates to Martins, Charley Wirz, of Charley's Guitar Shop in Dallas, says, "Martin just went from a lifetime to a one-year warranty, and that's got to make those old Martins worth even more."

Several dealers, some of whom sell new instruments as well, cite the guitar boom itself as an indirect cause of a claimed inferiority of new products. The boom gave rise to new retail structures, and Charley Wirz says, "There are these volume dealers—wholesalers and discounters and mail-order houses—and anybody who wants to sell something at cost plus ten [percent] can sell a thousand of them. So the factory is going to have to sell *two* thousand just to stay ahead. Therefore, they have to cut corners."

Dave Wintz points out, "New instruments are sometimes a little stiffer, but for the most part there's a lot of new stuff that I really like. A lot of the popularity of vintage guitars involves fads and psychological things, though there's the fact that new guitars depreciate, while old ones stay at the same level or go up."

Texan Tony Dukes is one of American guitar's most colorful characters. He takes instruments to clients (including dozens of rock stars) rather than operating out of a store. He has bought and sold over 50 sunbursts and wears a gold replica of one around his neck. Concerning old guitars, there is no doubt where his sentiments lie: "You take an old 'burst' with them old butterfly Kluson tuners, the nickel parts, the quality control they had, the lacquers, the neck angle—all that chemistry, that magic, is magnified through time. Plus there's the sunburst's being the geometrical wonder that it is, with aspects of a jazz arch-top and the best of the solidbodies thrown in. It has its own character. Each has its own temperament, and its charisma can inspire the player, pick him up

when he's down.

"They are getting so scarce, but a hundred years from now they'll still be turning up for $200 under some little old folks' bed or something—we got a saying, 'Even a blind hog can find an acorn now and then'—but they're harder and harder to find, and I think the sunburst's price is just going to keep clicking right on down the road."

Guitars and stars. Whether it is Elvis Presley with a steelstring on *Ed Sullivan*, Jimi Hendrix with a white Strat in *Woodstock*, or Lee Ritenour with a red dot-neck on the cover of *Guitar Player*, anytime a famous person with a certain instrument is seen by a few million people, the market is affected to some degree.

It's an understandable but odd phenomenon, really. Eric Clapton goes through a hundred guitars and picks one that suits his touch and his fingers—one that feels good to *him*, sounds good to *him*. The guitar shows up on the back of *Layla*, and suddenly thousands of people want one for what in a sense is the opposite reason—because someone else chose it for himself.

Guitar/star associations make for strong medicine, and it is common for a buyer, particularly a novice, to believe consciously or subconsciously that by selecting *this* Stratocaster he can somehow, through some unfathomable cosmic Stratocaster oneness, tap Eric's magic. Ask practically any buyer, and he or she will affirm that what *really* counts is talent and practice; but mystique alone accounts for many a dollar to change pockets nonetheless, and most of the currently popular items owe much of their success to the fact they they showed up onstage or on album covers with various stars.

Thus, buyers are both fad oriented and quality oriented. Guitars come in and out of style, and models of questionable merit have sometimes enjoyed periods of popularity, but quality and practicality are still essential factors in a guitar's worth over the long run.

Aside from the famous person's formal or implied endorsement of a certain guitar, there is also the question of the price he or she can pay for it. Musicians famous enough to be exceptionally influential are usually wealthy enough to pay much higher prices; they can write off the costs as well. Many famous guitarists like to bargain over an extra five-spot as much as anyone, but the fact remains that their budgets are bigger than the average rock and roller on the street, and a few high-dollar

Left: 1924 Gibson L-5 arch-top steel-string acoustic. Opposite: 1958 Flying V, one of Gibson's radical, futuristic solidbodies designed in the '50s.

sales can influence the model's market value.

Diminishing sources. Did you hear about the D'Angelico with a missing tuning key that sat on a pawnshop wall for six years and finally sold to a twitching collector for $40? Or the mint sunburst with unwrinkled tags still on it that was under a grandmother's bed since 1959 and was never played even once because the kid she bought it for got hit by a train so she gave it away? As Tom Wittrock notes, there seem to be more stories than guitars. Every collector has a trunkful, and many of the tales concern prized instruments that sold for pittances to luck-struck buffs.

But the days of inexpensive Super 400s on pawnshop walls and of attics yielding up dusty Herringbones are drawing to a close. "The last two years things have really dried up," says Larry Henrikson, "although the occasional things that do turn up seem to be nicer than ever. The first and most common source of guitars are the things people see on bandstands—they get picked up first. The second group is, 'Hey, my uncle has such and such.' The next level is word-of-mouth, where you hear about it just in passing. Then the fourth is simply—wherever you can find it."

Tom Wittrock says, "Pawnshops have changed so much in the past few years that they've practically turned into little antique stores. Prices have jumped to almost market levels; they won't bargain like they used to, and they're not anxious to sell. I once bought a Martin at a pawnshop for twelve bucks, but that's the only deal like that I've ever found, and I've been going to these places regularly for four years straight."

Danny Thorpe adds: "Pawnshops used to be nice places, but now everybody goes there looking for old instruments, and because of that the pawnshop guy's even got a big head. You can walk in there and find a Fender Mustang for $250. A Fender Mustang's not *worth* $250, but they think it is because the guy sold a '59 Strat two years ago for $350. So now he says, 'Somebody said that the Strat I sold for $350 is worth a thousand bucks.' So now Mustangs start becoming worth $250 in the pawnshop. Someone knowledgeable tells somebody who's not knowledgeable that he goofed, but the guy doesn't have any conception of what he really did or what the stuff was really worth, other than the name Fender on it, or Gibson, or whatever."

Many dealers actively seek out guitars through want ads, pawnshops, and

other local sources, sometimes employing buyers to scour the newspapers and music store bulletin boards. Other dealers, particularly larger, established shops, rely heavily on the buy-back policies extended to returning customers.

Collector/dealer Ed Seelig voices a concern common among vintage guitar buffs: "You run into people who aren't playing or barely play but have 50 or 75 guitars. And there are apparently guys out there—and a lot more than we thought—who have 100, 200, or 300 guitars put away.

"The effect of it depends on how rare the guitar is. If it's a mid-'60s 335 it's not going to make any difference because there are so many. But if it's a Flying V, that's a different story. At one point I tried making up a list of every original V I could account for. There were under 100 made, as I recall. Now, I would figure that probably at least ten of them have been destroyed—I don't think that would be unreasonable to assume—so they are long gone. So we've got something in the upper 80s left—that doesn't leave a whole lot that aren't spoken for.

And when you end up with a situation where the majority of a specific instrument is in the hands of someone who knows its current market price, there's no limit to how high that price can conceivably go. The Explorer is another prime example—there's no way that that's a $4,000 guitar, but that's what they've gone for, and the reason is their rarity. It's just gone out of sight; it's just crazy how high some prices are."

Danny Thorpe, of Heart Of Texas Music, adds, "I'm kind of caught in the middle. I like collecting what I play and I like lots of different instruments, although I think it's a bad thing for Joe Blow who has 35 mapleneck Strats or ten sunburst Les Pauls. It makes it that much harder for a good player to get a good instrument at a very affordable price. It's bad for a lot of people who just hoard guitars and pay outrageous prices to get something, because they can totally upset the whole market. To each his own—everybody is entitled to buy what they want to buy, let's face it, and you can't do anything about that. But I think that it's a drag when a guy buys ten Martin pre-War D-45s, or outbids some Japanese industrialist and pays ten grand for one. That can upset the entire market, and it does happen, especially on a guitar that there's only 91 of, like pre-War D-45s. Let's face it—if a guy's got ten of them, he's definitely got the stronghold on what's available.

"At the same time, some of these guys that have a whole bunch of sunbursts—if they decided one day to, say, dump 40 of them on the market for sale at a reasonable price, that would completely blow the minds of everyone that has $3,500 invested in one to resell to make a profit."

Modifications and refinishing. A guitar is often refinished, and that can substantially reduce its collector's value even if it's a skilled job that changes the finish from looking like a dinged-up '59 to a mint '55. When asked to compare a nicely refinished '56 Strat to an otherwise "identical" model, all the collectors surveyed agreed that the original would be worth hundreds of dollars more. But as Ed Seelig points out, "This is a very personal matter. It would normally make a difference of hundreds of dollars in the value, but some buyers don't care that much if it's refinished. The ones who are looking for an instrument to work with and play—if they can't afford, say, $1,250 for a '55 original Strat, and then they find a refinished one for $700, I say buy the refinished one. It looks as good, sounds as good, and plays as good."

Dave DeForrest of Guitar Trader in Red Bank, New Jersey, has over 600 vintage guitars in stock. He comments: "I see an insane persnicketiness on the part of ignorant buyers who want only perfect, unmodified instruments. A sunburst with Grovers is *not* a worthless guitar, but most of the people I deal with have standards of perfection that are counterproductive—they're bad both for the market in general and for the particular buyers. A lot of times I am in the unfortunate position of turning down a valid piece—valid both in practical terms and as a collector's guitar—because it has Grovers, or because the person has replaced the original Bigsby with a stop tailpiece or something. I do this because I know that when I go to resell it, buyers won't like the modification.

"It didn't used to be this way. It used to be that you were damned happy to get your hands on a '59 Les Paul in any kind of playable condition. The older, mature dealers don't have this attitude of—throw this acoustic away, it's got a tiny crack in the top. They cherish the things and recognize them for what they are. People have very bizarre criteria for what they will accept. Modifications reduce the saleability, not necessarily the value—if you see the distinction."

Whether or not it is a good idea to refinish your recent-issue guitar to look like an old one depends more on personal taste than investment potential. Danny Thorpe advises, "Sometimes you end up having as much in it as if you went out and bought an original. I've seen some guys pay $700 to refinish a '68 Les Paul and to make it look like a '59 sunburst. Well, by the time you do that, you've got $1,500 in a guitar that's not worth $1,500. Likewise, if you're going to pay $500 for a Strat, and then pay some guy $500 to restore it, it's hardly worth it."

The substitution of new tuning machines is a common modification, probably the least odious alteration that you can make to a vintage instrument from a dealer's point of view. "New hardware is not really a problem," says Larry Henrikson, "as long as you can find original parts to put back on the guitar. It is the permanent modifications that lower the value to what the thing is worth simply as a musical instrument. But if a guitar is really rare, like an old Explorer, then it will be worth something even if it's got a hole for an extra pickup routed out in the body, simply because there are so few of them around."

The sellers. Guitar traders deal not only in merchandise, but also in information. If you sold a Les Paul Custom for $1,000 to a fellow dealer, you would naturally be interested in learning that he had already found a buyer willing to pay $1,350 for it, or that one just like it recently sold for $1,500. If you had a good source for Epiphone hollowbodies but no longer cared very much about those models, you might be willing to trade phone numbers with someone who's got a line on a good source for P-Basses.

Guitar dealers are sometimes as cash oriented and tight lipped as Hasidic diamond merchants on the streets of New York City, while others freely extend credit and share information. A social gathering of four or five experienced collectors from various parts of the country can result in many tales, tall and true. The dealers may be able to trace one specific instrument's travels through the hands of various collectors, dealers, musicians, and investors.

One price can affect another, and if you're plugged into the right channels, information travels fast. An event at the Dallas Guitar Show provided a microcosm of what can happen on the general market. Dave Wintz recalls, "Everybody had rosewood Strats [with rosewood fingerboards as opposed to the earlier, more valuable maple-neck models]. When we got to the show

1955 Fender Precision Bass.

there were no prices on any of them. But as soon as one person—I don't remember who it was—started pricing the average, clean, rosewood pre-CBS Strat at $740, they went to that price all around. No one is afraid to sell, but no one wants to be bought out of everything just because he's uninformed as to what he can get."

Dave DeForrest comments: "I know of one dealer who requires customers to be sworn to secrecy as to the price, which is ridiculous and meaningless, of course. He feels that if he can keep the price a secret, he can continue to buy cheaply. A lot of dealers are so secretive and paranoid it's unbelievable. Try calling up a guitar shop, probably including my own, and tell them you're another dealer and that you want a certain piece strictly for your own personal use. Most of them won't admit to you what they're getting. Sometimes when I want to buy an instrument for my own personal use from another dealer, I have to send a representative to go and get it for me because sometimes a dealer won't sell to me if he thinks that I'm *really* trying to snoop around and figure out his profit structure."

Tony Dukes sees fundamental changes in the nature of the guitar market: "Ten years ago the market was a lot more player involved, with people like Robb Lawrence out in California and Robert Johnson down in Memphis. But it's being taken over by people who are from outside the music thing, businessmen. It's more money oriented and less music oriented. The traders, a lot of them, used to play in public themselves. The people who bought sunbursts used to be the Duane Allmans, the Billy Gibbons'. People used to feel responsibility when handling these guitars. Now you've got kids who blow in with trust funds or their daddies own a couple banks, and they buy a sunburst and play Kiss music on it. Speaking of prices, I sell 'bursts in the low threes all the time to players who can appreciate them, but some of these high-dollar dealers out there—it don't make shit from Shinola to some of them. They're just looking for prestige and profits."

Sellers of vintage guitars vary as to their personal attachments to the instruments. The typical dealer has been a musician for years and still likes to play, and he keeps a few prized items all to himself—his personal stash that isn't for sale. Some may well refuse to sell a guitar—even at an inflated price—to someone, perhaps a rock star, who has acquired a reputation for abusing instruments or for not fully appre-

ciating their subtleties. Old guitars are a finite national treasure, and every collector, every dealer, is aware of it.

The buyers. Most purchasers of vintage guitars are young to middle-aged musicians. Many are professionals, though the pros do not necessarily correlate with those who buy the highest priced items, or those who build collections. First of all, musicians generally aren't wealthy (though dealers report that if someone, whether amateur or pro, really wants a certain instrument, he or she will make surprising economic sacrifices to get it). Aside from rock stars with big bankrolls, many of the people who buy vintage instruments—especially those who buy several—are weekend musicians with non-music jobs.

Dave Wintz guesses that half of his many customers are amateurs. "There are a lot of people who work a daytime straight job," he says. "They just really like to play music. They read *Guitar Player*, go to rock concerts, and shell out a lot of money for old guitars. Then there are those that don't play too much or too well, but happen to have a lot of money. There are fewer of those people."

On the subject of general buyer profiles, Charley Wirz adds: "One of the most overlooked markets is the bluegrassers. Those people probably pay more for nonelectric instruments than anyone. It's not just rock and roll and electric guitars. There are desirable Martins, Gibson mandolins—even upright bass fiddles. Where can you go to find a decent upright bass? If you find a good one it's going to be $3,000. So there are buyers for all types of good instruments. Take carved-tops—how many good Gibson L-5's can you find these days? A decent instrument is going to bring good money in any section of the market."

Due to the proliferation of books and magazines (and in certain cases in spite of it) buyers are generally more informed than in past years, though comparatively speaking they still have a long way to go. Tom Wittrock says, "The average buyer in my part of the country [Missouri] knows the terms 'pre-CBS' and 'CBS' and that the pre-CBS is worth more, but that's about it."

Other shoppers are quite sophisticated. Ed Seelig comments: "Most of my buyers have specific musical requirements. They've been around, experimenting for many years, and they've tried things and know what they need. Some of these collectors have 40 or 50 guitars around and they're saying,

'Okay, I'm covered on everything, but I just would really like to have another '57 Strat with a nice V-neck,' so they buy one more guitar."

Irony abounds, or so it seems. Japanese musicians are among the world's most rabid guitar buffs, and they have worshipped vintage American instruments for years. Some time ago a Broadcaster would raise a lot more eyebrows in Tokyo than Tucson. Now the foreign buffs aren't just ogling those guitars; they're buying them, lots of them. "When you ship a guitar overseas," says Larry Henrikson, "You'll never see it again, not in this country. If I wanted to sell out my stock, I'd be a fool not to take it overseas. They've got more money to offer." Indeed, you can imagine that a buyer who flies from Tokyo to Chicago to shop for guitars isn't too pressed for cash in the first place.

Naturally, there's been much concern over the prospect of irreplaceable American instruments going overseas, probably forever (while at the same time—speaking of irony—Japanese guitars are making strong incursions into the new instrument market). Danny Thorpe says: "Those guitars are a big part of our heritage, and I'd like to keep them here in America. There are too few good instruments available to players as it is, and if all the good ones end up going overseas, then that's where they'll be, and they'll never be back here. All they can do in turn is import more stuff and make funkier stuff here to supply our market. It's just a never-ending deal.

Trends and speculation. What's the Next Big Thing? Will your maligned and dusty Jazzmaster someday make you rich? On the questions of future trends, some of the savvy collectors understandably play their cards close to their vests, offering few tantalizing tips. One thing they have in common, though, is a search for quality guitars yet "undiscovered" by the mass market. Larry Henrikson explains: "I've been buying Firebirds and haven't sold any recently, so from some people's standpoint that's a mistake. But I personally feel that the Firebird is one of the finest solidbodies ever made.

"You know, there are a lot of valid—and by that I mean quality—instruments out there that are only worth two or three hundred dollars today. There are 1960s Gibson-made Epiphone solidbodies, Epiphone thin-lines, Guilds—solidbodies and hollowbodies, electrics and acoustics—that just haven't really been discovered. Certain SG Specials

Gibson's first Les Paul, the 1952 gold-top.

Highly figured tiger-striping highlights this 1958-'60-style Gibson Les Paul Standard.

are just now taking off, at least for me. Old Juniors have always sold well, because they've been cheap. Jazzmasters—some of them are excellent, especially from about '58 to '62 or '63.

"I won't offer any advice about this guitar or that guitar, but I will say this

much to someone who is buying: Don't be pressured into buying a guitar on a particular day, because if it's a good deal today, it'll be a good deal tomorrow. Take your time, learn about guitars, and look at a lot of them, so that rather than having someone tell you what to get you can make your own choice."

Ed Seelig adds, "Be sure that the guitar is authentic, and deal with reputable people. A lot of the people I deal

with won't buy anywhere else, and there are customers that have other stores where that same situation exists. They know that the people are going to be straight with them, that they're not going to burn them, that if they say it's got patent-applied-fors, then they don't need to remove the strings and take out the pickups to look."

One law professor, when discussing the maze of interlocking rules that comprises the Internal Revenue Code, likens the effect of changing a single regulation to a big water bed: "If you push it in over here, it's got to pop up over there." A similar situation exists in the vintage guitar market. Larry Henrikson says, "The overwhelming popularity of Strats in the last couple of years has made a lot of other guitars soft—they haven't been selling well. You can take a pan of water and tilt it up, and then set it back down. The surface doesn't just go flat again right away. The water sloshes up one side, then the other, back and forth. It's the same with guitars, and probably every other business, too. These fads and trends, these waves, roll around the business for a while. Because of the Strat's popularity the Teles were real soft. Now we're noticing a little more Tele action here in the Chicago area. Other models are definitely happening, so it changes.

"I'm starting to call this high-price thing the 'Paul syndrome.' Les Pauls went up. Strats just went through the Paul syndrome. As old guitars have become recognized as being fine instruments, then those categories go through the syndrome, too. I think *Guitar Player* magazine was as responsible as anything else for Strats taking off because of so many covers that had Strats on them. Customers are becoming more educated—most of them are more aware than most store owners— but the market is still very fad-oriented. I think that a lot of instruments are going to become recognized, and this will spread out the market among several categories."

Concerning the stunning increases in the dot-neck's value, Charley Wirz remarks: "The days of three-chord rock and roll have been over for a while, and players are getting more musically educated. I think they are discovering that they can get several sounds out of just one type of guitar. I think dot-necks will continue to go up." When asked what mint dot-necks are selling for in Dallas these days, Charley responds with a laugh and a challenge: "Find one."

Tom Wittrock comments. "I feel that

jazz guitars—arch-tops—are extremely undervalued. It's a limited market compared to Martins and Strats and so on, but I think arch-tops are a good buy because of the amount of work that went into them. I remember one of George Gruhn's columns in *Guitar Player* that said one way to look at it is to ask what it would cost to duplicate one of these things, making it pretty much by hand the way it was done originally. Compare what it would cost to make an exact copy of a handmade arch-top like a D'Angelico or even something more common and cheap, like an Epiphone Broadway or a Gibson L-7. I don't think the present market value of those old arch-tops is anywhere near the exact cost of duplicating them. That's one way to look at it. There is plenty of talk about Jazzmasters, and there's certainly more interest in them, but I can't see them getting anywhere near Telecasters and Strats."

Dave Wintz agrees: "Maybe Jazzmasters will become really popular, and we've had some demand, but the average ones are still going for $300 or so, which isn't much. [Charlie Wirz reported $350 to $400, tops]. I really couldn't say. I certainly wouldn't sock them away in anticipation of it happening."

Dave DeForrest adds: "Outside of the very few popular models, there are many *fine* guitars that can be bought at ridiculously low prices. Gibson-made Epiphones are good, and the Epiphone Riviera is fully as good as a 335, though with a different pickup configuration. I'm not a big fan of 1960s Gibson acoustic flat-tops, but if I were I certainly would not bypass Epiphones of similar styles. But many people do, even though they were made in a Gibson factory by Gibson employees. Jazz guitars are basically cheap. You can buy a 1950s ES-175 for about the same price of a new one, maybe less. There are fabulous guitars out there, both solid- and hollowbody, to be had for well under $500. And there's not a lot of stuff that you can buy for that price.

"Not all good Strats are pre-CBS, either. The early CBS 4-bolt models are certainly nicer than the later ones with the 3-bolt array and the tilt-neck adjustment. You don't need to get a pre-CBS instrument to get an excellent Fender; in fact, CBS made a lot of fine instruments—rosewood Telecasters, for example.

"And not all prices are going up; I don't think a Les Paul is worth any more than it was a year ago. And I think the same could be said for the brown amps

and the tweed amps made by Fender, and there are others, too."

Concerning the future of the market from a businessperson's point of view, most of the collectors and vintage retailers surveyed for this article agreed on two points: The market will provide investment career potential for people who are both skilled in business and guitar experts: and the failures of some dealers to stay afloat may be due in part to market trends, but they are also inevitable consequences of the survival-of-the-fittest aspects of any business.

Danny Thorpe explains that keen commercial talents are more critical than ever: "As far as I can see, it's getting really hard to sell stuff. It's also getting harder to pick up stuff, because everyone is aware—or sort of aware—of what's going on. See, there are people who are really into the market and watch it and see what happens with it, but there are also people who just kind of know the market at one time, and they realize that their instrument is worth some money, but they don't know how much. A lot of times they want more than it's worth, or they ask less than it's worth. It's really becoming a lot harder to consistently pick up instruments to resell for a worthwhile profit.

"I think the vintage market as a whole is peaking. I can see sunbursts possibly going to five grand or over, but I can also see that peaking. Things that haven't peaked yet include Strats; you know, I can see a mapleneck Strat going to $2,500. I can see a rosewood neck Strat becoming worth $1,500. And 335s are definitely on the way up, especially dot-boards, but I think they will get to a point where they will also peak. I think the Dallas Guitar Show in a lot of ways was sort of the writing on the wall. People are finding that it's harder to get top dollar out of a piece than it used to be because people just don't have the money. And when you're dealing with vintage instruments there are a lot of rock and roll stars that have the money to buy them, but they already have them. And so the guy who really wants a sunburst Les Paul is not usually the star, but rather a guy who plays in a local band, He buys a $4,500 guitar, right? So he's sitting there with a $4,500 guitar—what's he going to do with it? He's scared to play it. I've got a sunburst myself and I won't take it out to a bar—you know—it will get ripped off, it'll break. I can't replace it, so I take my Ibanez.

"Collecting guitars differs from, say, collecting stamps or coins. Stamps and coins have their value because they're

rare, because they're no longer in production, or whatever. Guitars have that thing, but also a vintage guitar is not a good piece unless it is usable. Vintage guitars or guitars in general are utility tools that a musician must use to make his living, and that does not always warrant going out and spending $4,500 when you can go down and buy an Ibanez or a new Les Paul or a new Strat or something else that you can beat up or replace. So I think that one trend is that a lot of people are facing the reality of—I spent four grand for this, but now what will I do with it?

"Some collectors are branching into other things, and in my opinion that's also a trend. You know how a lot of rock and rollers are these days. They plug in three flangers and 13 distortion units and all that, so they really can't distinguish the difference between a '59 Strat and a Japanese copy of a new Strat or anything else. And that doesn't help the value of the old ones. A lot of people want to get out of the market while the getting is good.

"Finally, there's the economy. Let's face it, if you have to pay $3,000 for a guitar to resell for $4,000, okay, great, you can make $1,000—but *try and find a guy with $4,000.* That's hard, and you've got to make a living. A lot of guys that I know are dealing more new or used stuff, or just guitars in general, including some of the new lines that would be acceptable to someone who has been into vintage guitars for years, like some of the handmade types."

Conclusion. Some vintage guitar buyers truly appreciate their instrument's subtleties, and others have no idea what's going on, so the validity of spending thousands of dollars for a guitar simply comes down to a matter of "different strokes." But one common opinion, here expressed by Dave Wintz, is that "a lot of people are overly involved with the old instruments. I would sort of like to see people getting more involved with the music, as opposed to just the guitars. You can still make great music on a new instrument; you don't have to have an old one. A lot of people believe that an old guitar is going to make them a better player, yet only a few of them *really* know the difference. For those few people, yes, it really does matter whether it's an old sunburst or some reissue. I do have old instruments myself, and people will continue to look for vintage guitars because they have a certain kind of worn-in, soulful feel. There's just something about them."

Tom Wheeler

4.
GUITAR
CARE
AND REPAIR

INTRODUCTION

Taking care of your own guitar can bring you a great deal of satisfaction while saving you money, but you must know what you're doing. Repairman/luthier Dan Erlewine tells in the first section how to get started on a general maintenance program for your axe and how to assess your abilities to tackle some of the tricky jobs. The subsequent sections cover specific repairs and adjustments. Intonation, the basic "in-tuneness" of the guitar, receives three sections' treatment. The hows and whys are covered first, leading into a discussion of electronic tuning devices for adjusting a guitar's intonation. The final third of the trilogy is a detailed look at how the truss rod works, how it affects intonation, and how it can be properly adjusted. The next pair of sections covers bridge adjustments for acoustics and electrics, respectively. Proper bridge placement and set-up are as critical as correct truss rod adjustment for keeping your instrument in perfect playing order, and here the tools, measuring techniques, and principles of saddle-height adjustments are explored. Action Height At The Nut, the next section, covers techniques for measuring and cutting notches for optimum string height and intonation. The following two sections delve into string length adjustments for acoustics and electrics, outlining yet another indispensable process in the quest for proper intonation. Closing the chapter is a section on the care and feeding of your guitar's finish, addressing the various types of finishes, cleaning techniques, and tips for keeping your guitar gleaming.

GUITAR MAINTENANCE

June, 1983. "Damn! If I only hadn't tried to fix that myself!" A commonly heard complaint, as the repairman's fingers fly across the calculator. The old adage "When in doubt, don't mess with it" certainly governs guitar repair. But there's another side to it. As Dan Erlewine reports below, there are more than a few maintenance and repair procedures that amateurs can—and should—do themselves. Besides helping you gain a better understanding of your instrument, this knowledge can reduce repair bills and bring you closer to having the perfect guitar.

An expert repairman and custom luthier, Erlewine, 38, took up folk guitar at 14 and began fixing instruments a year later. Following high school, he worked for Herb David Guitar Studio in Ann Arbor, Michigan. Dan started Erlewine Instruments in the mid '60s with the assistance of his cousin Mark Erlewine, who later developed the Chiquita Travel Guitar. Seven shops later, Dan founded his current company, Dan Erlewine's Guitar Hospital [319 S. Michigan Ave., Big Rapids, MI 49307].

During his 23 years in the business, Erlewine has repaired guitars for countless rockers, including Ted Nugent, Mike Bloomfield, Clarence White, Bob Seger, and members of Alice Cooper, Blackfoot, and the MC5, as well as bluesmen Mighty Joe Young, Johnny Shines, and Luther Allison. Although the majority of his business today is repairs, he also builds fine custom instruments: Jerry Garcia owns one of his Strat-style electrics, and Albert King has a Dan Erlewine Flying V. Erlewine is proud of the fact that he has trained seven apprentices over the years, all whom earn livings fixing guitars. A performer since high school days, Dan plays everything from rock and blues to country guitar.

Why are many players afraid to work on a guitar?

Because they think that it's something really sacred. They've spent a lot of money for it, and it does seem sort of complicated if you don't know much about it. But there are a lot of little repairs that a person could do to their guitar that wouldn't hurt. You shouldn't be afraid of your instrument. Any serious player has to spend hours working on his guitars. Go to a repairman the first time around for simple stuff, and maybe he can help show you how to take care of it in the future.

How can someone avoid wasting money on repairs?

If people learned more about guitars before they even bought one, they could save a lot of money. People should spend more time buying guitars. Instead of spending $1,500 for six different guitars before you finally get your first good one, learn more about it and buy something good to start with. When people go out to buy an acoustic guitar, for example, they ought to have a mirror so they can look inside and find out what the guitar is built like. Look at how well the braces are glued. If you are dealing with a quality instrument like a Martin, Guild, or some Gibsons, you should get a good glue job. But a lot of people buy cheaper imports and have a lot of problems with them. If they checked out what they were buying before they got it, it would probably eliminate a lot of the junk that we get.

Is it the same way with electrics?

Sure. You're pretty safe with a brand name, but people should read every article they can get their hands on. It would be really smart to buy some of the exisiting guitar repair books before you ever bought a guitar, because you can find everything in there. I'm thinking in particular of both volumes of Don Teeter's *The Acoustic Guitar* [University of Oklahoma Press, 1005 Asp Ave., Norman, OK 73109] and Hideo Kamimoto's *Complete Guitar Repair* [Oak Pub., 24 East 22nd St., New York, NY 10023]. These three books are incredible. For about a $60 investment, you would know what you could and couldn't mess with, as well as what to look for when you buy a guitar. You should understand how a guitar is built so that you know what such things as warped necks look like. How many people do you know who bought a guitar and wish they hadn't? They can't even sell it. You can even get all kinds of famous brand-name guitars that don't have good wood in them. The

necks warp; they don't play well.

Let's start at the headstock and work down. Should a player adjust the neck himself?

Sure. If a guy can take a wheel off a car and change a flat, he should be able to handle a neck rod just by using a little common sense. Take a Gibson, for example. Anybody can come up with a nut driver that will adjust the truss rod. It doesn't have to be an official Gibson one, right? If you tighten the nut, the neck will straighten out. If you go the other way, it will loosen up and go with the strings. That's pretty obvious. You shouldn't be afraid of doing this. I don't believe that a neck should be perfectly straight, anyway. You want some relief on the fingerboard. If you were to sight down the neck from the nut towards the body, you'd want a little dip in there. If you put a straight edge on there, it wouldn't be perfectly straight. People expect the neck to be perfectly straight, but it can't be. Then the strings will buzz. It should have a little bit of curve. With a truss rod, you can control this.

What about installing new tuners?

People shouldn't try to put new tuners on themselves. I get a lot of cracked pegheads where people have taken a hand drill and tried to drill out the hole. The best way to do it is to clamp down and use a drill press or use a hand reamer and/or round file. And don't put oil on your tuning pegs. It goes down through the screw holes that hold the peg on and seeps into the back of the peghead. Most tuners shouldn't be oiled, anyway.

Can you put strings on in such a way that there's less slippage?

At least on my thin strings. I like to wrap the string around itself. I go through the hole, bring it back around underneath itself, and wrap the string against the shaft. Otis Rush used to put the string through the shaft hole twice. He could play all night long, bend strings like crazy, and never seem to go out of tune that much. It also helps to get a few windings around the shaft.

Do string winders present any problems by changing the tension too fast?

Not for me. I love them. But I always have my neck clamped in a vise on my bench when I use them. I can't see any problems. They're quick when you're in a hurry.

Can most people carve their own nut?

I think a nut and the fret job are the two most important things on an electric guitar as far as making it play well. Most people probably couldn't do a good job making their own nut, unless they were good with their hands. It's hard to make a good nut, and it takes a long time. People go out and spend a thousand bucks on a guitar that doesn't play right, and then they wail and cry when they have to spend 35 or 40 bucks to get a really nice nut made. A string should come up gradually over the nut and have its contact point right at the front of the nut. That's where the string length starts, right? With most factory nuts and nuts from a drawer at a music store, you can't even tell where the string is contacting because it's down too deep in the groove. It's very important to keep all the bone, ivory, or whatever you're using pretty much away from the strings.

How do you angle the grooves?

Towards the proper keys, so that the string will go where it naturally wants to lie. I like to back the sides of my nut grooves away from the string, so they are not pinching and muting it. You need a lot of different size files to make nuts. And a really nice nut won't last forever. If you hone it down carefully, so it's nice and comfortable to play in the first position and yet doesn't buzz, it will wear out in time, regardless of the material it's made of. You'll have to shim it up or have another nut made. It also helps to lubricate the nut with a little pencil lead.

Do you recommend using any spray or stick products designed for fingerboards?

I don't use them, never have. I tried one of them, and it seemed ridiculous— too slippery. I think they gum things up. I like just to keep the fingerboard and strings clean. A person can clean a fingerboard periodically, put some lemon oil on it. We used to use linseed oil years ago; it never hurt anything, but you don't use it all the time. Lemon oil is good for any wood. You wouldn't want to put anything on maple fretboards, of course, because they're lacquered.

How can caked-up fretboard grime be removed?

Very fine steel wool—0000—and warm soap and water. Soap and water can clean anything on a guitar if you're careful, especially on an electric guitar. If the frets are well seated, there's no reason you can't use a damp rag and soap to loosen that stuff.

If you remove all the strings to clean the fingerboard, should you make any compensations when stringing back to pitch?

It does upset the tension balance. You would probably be more concerned with that on acoustic guitars than electrics. If I were working on my nice old Martin, I would detune the strings really slow. I would tune down to D and play it for a little while, and then tune down to C and play it. It depends on how delicate the instrument is. Some instruments are tougher than hell, like a new Les Paul—you're not going to hurt that. They're all solid, and it takes them years to settle in. You should change strings one at a time on a nice instrument or else be willing to wait a few days for it to settle back in to play right again. Obviously, if you take all the tension off a neck and a body for any period of time, it's going to take a while to come back to what it was before. This is why it's good to get a guitar done *days* before the customer comes to pick it up. If it's a nice job, I like to get it strung up a week before they come to get it. Otherwise, it won't sound as good as when they brought it in.

Can an amateur change his own frets?

Refretting the guitar and dressing frets is the most important job that a repairman can do. That is something you shouldn't try yourself. And before you have your frets dressed or redone, spend some time trying different string gauges to find out what you really like. Then be sure the repairman knows what brand of strings you use. That's critical. If you get your frets done sensitively and then drastically change the gauges, it's not going to play the same.

Should tension be applied to the neck during refretting?

Yes. When I fret guitars, I use a jig that puts tension on the neck and holds it at concert pitch when the strings are removed. The body is also held, so there is no spring back. When I take strings off a Les Paul, for example, the neck will bow up a little bit because of the truss-rod tension. When I loosen the rod up, it sets right back down on the tension jig's neck supports. That is right about where the neck will be when you play it. Then I take the frets out and get rid of any humps or bumps. I put relief in the fingerboard and neck to make the action easier, and get rid of the hump up in the area around the 12th to 15th frets. The fingerboard should fall away a tiny bit when you get up around what people call the "box strings"—up on the body joint, the tongue. You should have a little fall away from maybe the 15th fret on up. If you were to put a straightedge on it, those frets should start to gradually fall away from the edge as they are going up to the last fret. This eliminates buzzing. A good fret job is one place a person should be willing to put a good deal of money.

Can you possibly mess up a guitar by adjusting the polepieces?

Like on a Gibson humbucking? You shouldn't be able to. That's something you should do yourself: Adjust your pickups up and down—as well as the polepieces within the pickups—to get the balanced tone you're looking for. As far as acoustic guitars, people shouldn't try to permanently install anything like a Barcus-Berry pickup themselves. That's a critical job.

Should players attempt their own bridge adjustments?

Absolutely. If you own an electric, you should be able to tune your own bridge and get it properly intonated. It's your own ear you're tuning to, right? My ear is different than yours, I can make a guitar play really in tune. When I go out and play a job, it sounds great to me. That doesn't mean that you'd like it. Our ears are different. You should also be able to clean your own bridge on an electric guitar. Take it apart and clean the pieces with naphtha or lighter fluid. If you get all the grease off the parts and put them back together, it'll work good again. Lightly lubricate it with oil. As far as substituting one type of bridge for another, though, you should avoid pulling bridge studs and moving bridge parts around, like trying to put a tune-o-matic on a guitar that doesn't have one. You should be very careful when putting a stop tailpiece on an ES-335 that has a trapeze on it; you might install it crooked. Take that to a pro.

Are there any difficulties involved with resetting the string placement at the bridge?

Most bridge inserts have pretty rough castings; they're not machined perfectly. They are filed quickly at the factory. Most people have to take their brand-new guitar out and have the bridge pieces replaced because the string spacings aren't right. The strings are too close to the edge of the fingerboard, they don't go over the polepieces properly, or they break easily. All you need is a little set of needle files and some 400- or 600-grade sandpaper. You should be able to go to the store, buy a new set of pieces, take your bridge apart, put the pieces on, and set the spacings the way you want them. I've got hundreds of customers, and they all like it a little bit different. Ted Nugent likes his strings really low, but he doesn't like them to buzz. I managed to do that for him, but I spent a week refretting one of his guitars.

Other than lubricating the nut, are there ways to help keep a guitar with a tremolo bar in tune?

It also helps to have a properly made nut that doesn't pinch. But other than a Floyd Rose system, there is nothing that will solve a tremolo problem on a Strat. I've installed a few of the Floyd Roses, and they work. It's amazing. You can also loosen the lower spring in the back of the Strat so it doesn't have very much tension. That will help keep it in tune. Try different spring combinations until you find what suits you. The older the Strats, for some reason, the better they play. I've found that old ones from the late '50s don't have as much difficulty staying in tune as newer, stiffer ones. The biggest problems people have with Stratocasters are pickups. If you are willing to lower the pickups as far away from the string as possible, you'll get a lot more accurate noting. The magnets are so powerful that when you fret in the upper areas, they pull the strings out of tune. Stratocasters are just weird birds. It's very hard to get the low E in tune on them. The Stratocaster is one of my favorite electric guitars.

How soon should cracks be repaired?
You should fix cracks on guitars quickly. Don't wait. This includes body cracks on acoustics and peghead cracks. I put pegheads back on guitars all the time—50 or 100 a year, mostly Les Pauls. People lean their guitars against the amp or trip over the cord. You should keep guitars in cases. You shouldn't polish the guitar with anything with silicone in it. It's hard to spray over guitars that have a silicone-type polish on them. If you crack your peghead, get it fixed right away. Don't be polishing your guitar and waiting three months because you don't have the money. Then it's loaded up with sweat and dirt and grease, and it doesn't ever want to glue up well. By the way, you shouldn't attempt any gluing unless you know what you are doing. And no epoxies or Super Glue, right? These are great, but you've got to know what to do with them.

How can checking—small cracks in the finish—be avoided?
That's more weather care than anything else. I've never seen a good guitar that I really loved that wasn't checked. Most of them are Gibson and Fender electrics. You'll very seldom see a guitar from the '40s on up that doesn't have some form of checking. You can avoid it by not taking a hot guitar out into the cold, and vice versa.

What's the latest on compensation for moisture or dryness?
You usually have more problems with guitars being too dry instead of too

moist; it all depends on where you live. If you have wood heat, be sure that you keep bowls or a kettle of water around to add humidity to the air. I try to keep around 40% humidity in my shop. I don't like those Dampits too well for acoustic guitars; I do like a soap box with holes drilled in it and a sponge inside. That works well if you put it in the string box. It's pretty hard to over-humidify a guitar in Michigan. It's dry out here. If you use a Dampit, be careful not to oversaturate it, or else the water may run onto the guitar. Goya makes a nice little humidifier with a stone in it.

Any advice for steel-string owners?
Check your guitar: Get an inspection mirror with a telescoping shaft from a hardware store or auto parts shop and look inside of it. If you have a 12-string, watch the bridge. I don't think there's a 12-string made that should be tuned over D, although some of the companies claim that theirs can hold it. Most 12-strings cannot hold concert pitch, and people are constantly doing that. Once in a while take an empty string package and see if you can slide the flap under any part of the bridge. If you can get it under there, you better get it checked out. I get an awful lot of bridges that should have been fixed when they first started coming loose. If people would catch these things right away, they'd get their money's worth out of their guitars.

Do classical guitars present special problems?
Classical guitar players are pretty much on their own. There is not a lot of good literature about classical guitars. It's hard to find a repairman who knows classical guitars very well. If you have a really nice classical, do a lot of looking around before you trust someone to fix it. The average repairman who works on electrics and steel-strings don't know anything about classical guitars—doesn't even know how to tie the strings on right, much less work on them. I find a lot of good classicals that are set up like steel-strings.

Should guitars be stored at concert pitch?
A lot of people have different opinions about that. I usually don't tune them down, or if I do, I might tune them down a whole-step. People are always asking: "If I'm going on vacation, should I take my strings off my guitar?" No, you shouldn't, unless you are putting it away for a long time. Even then, you always want to leave a little tension on it. But when you ship a guitar, you want to tune the strings down completely—no tension.

In general, should customers shop around for repairs?
Definitely. If it's a serious job, you should get two or three different estimates. This never offends me; in fact, I recommend it and even give the names of other repairmen. Get two or three opinions. See if they have a sample of their work around. You'd be surprised what you'll find out. People have different ways of fixing things. I sure wouldn't give a guitar to be repaired without knowing what the guy was planning to do. But that happens a lot, and people like me end up having to redo jobs. The bill is really high, they are sore about it, and it's too late. You can't get the money back, and half the time you can't even find the person who did the job. No repair person should be insulted by you getting other estimates. No one is the only person around.

Is there anything repairmen commonly overlook?
If he's going to set up a guitar for a serious customer, a good repairman should sit down and watch how that customer plays. Usually repairmen try to talk people into liking what they like; it makes it a lot easier to work on their instruments. But there are a lot of particular people out there. You don't just take a guitar in and do whatever you want to it. You want to see how heavy their attack with a pick is, how they note solo lines and bar chords. Do they squeeze hard? Do they play heavy? Instead of having a situation where the customer comes back and says, "Well, this buzzes," and the repaiman says, "Well, look how heavy you're playing," you should talk about it before-hand. That's something I've learned purely from experience. And you can't have the lowest action in the world, light strings, and no buzz. It doesn't exist.

Is there anything you wish customers would do more often?
Yes. Bear with the repairman. He's trying to do his best. The biggest problem I have is that people want a great job, and they want it yesterday. Serious work on guitars is not like putting soles on a pair of shoes. Usually people wait too long before they get it fixed anyway, and all of a sudden they get in a panic and have to have it fixed right away. I take the job on, but it's not done for two months and they call me all the time. If you want good work, you should be willing to wait for it.

Is there anything else owners could do to keep their guitars in good repair?
When you own a guitar, you should keep a maintenance log. Write down who fixed it, the date, and what was

done. Ask the repairman to list the materials, glue, and finish he used. Years later that information can be really helpful to someone like me. If I have a doubt about something, I could even trace previous repairmen. If it was a good guitar, he'll remember it. I wouldn't be surprised if I could remember every customer I've ever had, going back 15 years. I fix a lot of nice guitars, and it's hard to forget good guitars. Keep track of who worked on what, because before you know it, 15 years have gone by. It would sure make a repairman happy to have this information.

Jas Obrecht

INTONATION

January, February 1977. A good deal of repair information is based on traditional approaches or players' misconceptions, and many people (including some repairmen) will work on a guitar without having a good understanding of the instrument. For example, when something is wrong, they may make random adjustments, often overcompensating and thereby creating further problems. It is important to understand that every guitar has general requirements in terms of its own specific mechanical, physical, and acoustical properties. Also, different makes and models have their own peculiarities. Repairs, adjustments, and modifications should be based on a knowledge of these aspects of the instrument, while tailoring them to the needs and demands of the player. The principles and techniques which will be presented here are based on years of experimenting, studying, and working on guitars of all types.

Should you attempt repairs yourself? Although I will show ways to identify the problems and techniques for making the needed changes and adjustments, there is no substitute for skill or experience. Some repairs and adjustments require special tools or tooling techniques, while others are relatively simple. Most require a certain amount of skill or ability to be done properly. I do not recommend that the inexperienced attempt the more complex or unusual repairs, adjustments, or modifications (these often require expensive or unusual tools that you would be unlikely to have anyway). But if you do have some general ability or experience with tools, or just a lot of perseverance and patience, you can do many of the simpler repairs. Use your own judgment in deciding what to try. Even if you decide to take the problem to a repairman, by understanding the principles and techniques you can be sure that he has accurately identified the problem and done the work properly.

What is proper intonation? Attaining proper intonation of the instrument is the most common repair problem faced by all guitar players. Defined simplistically, it is the concept that the instrument should be in tune with itself throughout its various playing ranges, so that from key to key, chord to chord in various positions, and scale to scale all tones interrelate harmoniously. For example, your own instrument may be out of tune with itself in the sense that you have to make slight tuning adjustments when you change keys. Likewise, when you move from a basic E major chord to a D major chord the two may sound out of tune with each other, or when you play up and down the neck certain chords or notes may sound out of tune with others. Another test is whether the note pressed at the 12th fret of each string is sharp or flat in relation to the harmonic played over

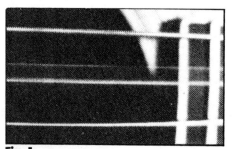
Fig. 1

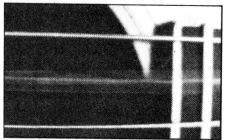
Fig. 2

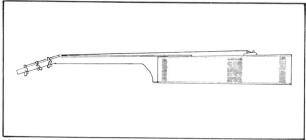
Fig. 3

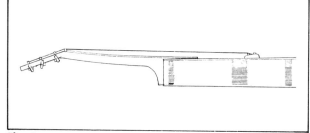
Fig. 4

the same fret on that string. The more demanding the player, the more critical these problems are. The subject of intonation deals with methods of adjusting or modifying the guitar to overcome these problems.

What factors affect intonation? The identification of intonation problems will be discussed in detail in the next section, but briefly here are some of the factors that affect it: action height at bridge and nut; string length (the distance between the point where a string leaves the nut and where it meets the saddle or bridge); string gauge; false or damaged strings; truss-rod adjustments. Of these factors, string length and action height are the most important. The methods (and difficulty) of adjusting, modifying, or regulating these factors vary with the types of guitar because of design variations among electrics, basses, acoustics, and classicals. They also each have different requirements in terms of precision of adjustment, but on all of them there are adjustments which can be made so that the guitar plays as in tune with itself as possible. There is no perfection, but it is possible to get close enough so that discrepancies are not noticeable.

On electric guitars and basses the adjustment screws located on the bridge make adjustments of string length relatively simple. On acoustics and classicals the bridge and saddle are usually fixed in place so that adjusting string length is much more difficult. The distance is correctly set to a general standard at the factory, and a good quality guitar will sound basically in tune with itself—but the various factors which are discussed here do affect precision of intonation, and even the fixed bridge on a Martin or Gibson may require certain adjustments. These are far more difficult than electric guitar and bass adjustments for string length, but both will be discussed in detail. The principles are always the same. The differences in guitar design lead to different remedies.

The frets on a guitar are spaced according to a scientific formula derived from the method of equal tempered tuning (the same spacing of intervals used in tuning keyboard instruments). Incorrect location of frets would create intonation problems by establishing intervals which do not conform to the equal tempered scale, but this is a remote possibility because most fingerboards are very accurately slotted by machine. However, if a guitar is handmade, errors of measurement or

cutting would create intonation problems.

Why new guitars should be intonated. Since guitars are made to appeal to a general public, the new guitar usually has the action higher than most players want, the strings are probably of a different gauge than the buyer will choose, and no fine intonation adjustments as to string length have been made. Even if makers could afford to make fine intonation adjustments, there is no way they could know the specific requirements of the person who is going to buy the instrument—particularly action height and strings. Therefore, a new guitar will usually need its action lowered for your playing needs, and it should be intonated with your choice of strings after the action is set. As noted above, these adjustments are much easier on electrics and basses. Whether or not a classical or acoustic needs string length adjustments after the action is set depends on how closely in tune it is in relation to the player's needs and demands.

Why guitars must be intonated periodically. Your choice of string type (gauge and alloy) and action height, in combination with string length, are the most critical factors of intonation. If the guitar is properly intonated and then any of these factors are later changed, it will probably have to be intonated again. Even if you keep these constant, the instrument will probably require re-intonating at some point, because all parts, both wood and metal, are subject to stress, settling, and stretching, all of which affect intonation. Obviously, the changes caused by these factors are slight, but it takes very little to affect intonation. Therefore, you cannot presume that the guitar will stay properly intonated for a given period of time. Each one is different. Some instruments (assuming string type, action, and string length are left the same) will stay in tune with themselves for long periods of time, while others will go out of tune (i.e., intonation) quickly. The various factors affect different guitars in different ways, and may cause the guitar to go in and out of proper intonation, requiring periodic adjustments to correct this. Even if you cannot hear the difference, you should keep your guitar at its optimum action and string length.

No two guitars are alike. Every guitar of a given make and model is unique, with its own sound and its own special set of intonation problems. Even two

instruments of the same make, model, and year are always different. Numerous factors cause this: human error (not all manufacturing processes can be done by machine); tooling wear (tolerances are thrown off); quality control variances (errors of differences in personal standards among inspectors); material variances (density of wood and its grain structure vary, affecting the guitar in many ways—action, intonation, buzzes, etc.); differing stress factors (one neck may tend to warp more than another, or one top pull more than another). Wood is not uniform; it is flexible and varies greatly, and any number of its numerous variables can affect sound and intonation.

Having discussed the problems of guitar intonation in general terms (i.e., setting or adjusting the instrument so that it plays in tune with itself throughout its various playing ranges), I will now look at the most common factors affecting intonation and explain how to identify them. Subsequently I will show step-by-step procedures for solving the problems on various types and makes of guitars. It is important at every stage to accurately diagnose the problem so that the proper solution can be implemented. (I am assuming that you already know how to tune the guitar and that you have put it into accurate standard tuning by harmonic or other methods before undertaking the type of analysis recommended here.)

False or damaged strings. The first thing you should check is the condition of your strings. A bend or kink in a string, manufacturing defects, corrosion, accumulated dirt, grooves caused by fret wear and aging, or any combination of these factors will usually cause the string to be "untrue" or "false." This means that it is not sufficiently consistent in diameter and density over its length to allow it to play in tune at each and every fret. Instead, it pulsates unevenly so that it creates more than one tone when played in certain positions, and this causes erratic intonation. This is the most obvious source of intonation problems, and should be corrected before attempting to identify the more subtle factors. Most people tend to leave strings on the guitar longer than they should, so the false string is a common cause of bad intonation.

How to identify false strings. Falseness can be heard, of course, since the dissonant or pulsating effect of the untrue string will prevent you from tuning the guitar properly or from playing in tune. But false strings can also be spotted visually. A "true" string played open vibrates evenly from a large pattern down to a progressively smaller (but still even) vibration. A "false" string played open vibrates unevenly and pulsates, rather than having one set motion, and in effect oscillates between one frequency (or tone) and others at a very rapid rate. You can see the falseness or trueness of a string by playing it open and observing the vibration pattern. (Note: the patterns of the three bass strings are more easily discernable than the treble string patterns.)

Remember that the vibrating open A or fifth string appears to be slightly false when viewed under fluorescent lights due to the nature of its frequency (a strobe effect), even when it is brand new. So this string should be examined under natural or incandescent light.

Strings can be found to be almost perfect, but they, too, will begin to get false with time. As a practical matter, a small amount of falseness may be acceptable for playing but when it is causing problems the string should be replaced. Whether or not a string is too false to be used for playing is a matter of personal judgment, but it is important to have the truest strings possible if you want accurate intonation.

A word of caution: Newness does not guarantee trueness. New strings are sometimes false (due to manufacturing errors or because of damage caused during packaging) and should be replaced. Be alert to spot kinks and other uneven spots in both new and old strings. These defects cause problems.

Excessive warp in fingerboard. Contrary to popular belief, the neck or fingerboard of a guitar is supposed to have a very slight amount of warp or curvature between the nut and the spot where the neck joins the body. This allows a pressed string to vibrate without striking the adjacent frets (since the strings travel in semicircular orbits, the bridge elevation alone is not sufficient to insure free movement of the string at positions below the spot where the neck joins the body). Excessive warp has a sharping effect because the string must travel extra distance to reach the fingerboard.

To test the amount of warp, press down a string simultaneously at the first fret and at the fret where the neck joins the body, and observe the space between the string and the frets at the halfway point. A proper amount of warp would be reflected by a distance of about .010" for guitar or .015"-.020"

for bass. If there is no space, there is a counterwarp, and warp must be added. If the guitar has an adjustable truss rod you can usually make warp adjustments easily, but if the truss rod is not adjustable (or if there is no truss rod at all) it is a challenging repair problem. These types of adjustments will be explained later.

The pulled neck. This should not be confused with excessive warp. A pulled neck may have the proper amount of warp, but it joins the body at the wrong angle. This is illustrated in the following diagrams: Fig. 1 shows the proper angle for the neck, while Fig. 2 demonstrates the pulled neck. Pulling is caused by stress, weak joining of the neck to the body, or a mistake in setting the angle of the neck during construction or repair. If this is the problem, sharpness of intonation results from the added distance the string travels to the fingerboard. A pull may not be as radically visible as in Fig. 2, but any pull is identifiable by the following procedure: First, test and observe the warp as indicated in the previous paragraph; then, do the same test, but instead press on the first fret and very topmost fret. If the distance between the string and the frets is substantially greater in the second measurement, the neck is pulled. If the distance remains fairly consistent with the initial measurement, there is no pulling problem. If the guitar has a pulled neck, even an adjustable truss rod will not solve it. The neck must be reset, or at least the frets removed, the fingerboard planed and refretted, and the action reset. Both of these solutions are major repairs.

Action height and string length. Scale length (the theoretical distance between the point where a string should leave the nut and where it should meet the saddle) is derived from a mathematical formula calculated to produce an accurate scale in conjunction with the fret spacing. But the theory of scale length does not take into account the fact that the strings are suspended above the frets and that this added distance of movement when you press down the string will have a sharping effect on the fretted tones. For example, if the string length (the actual distance between the point where a string leaves the nut and where it meets the saddle) were set to its theoretical distance (scale length), the 12th fret harmonic of a string could be tuned to exact pitch, but the corresponding fretted note at the 12th fret would be sharp in relation to the har-

monic. This is because pressing down the string increases its tension slightly, and this has a sharping effect, just as tightening the tuning peg increases tension and thereby has a sharping effect. The increase in tension occurs when a string is pressed at any fret, becoming greater as you move up the neck because the string is further from the fingerboard in the higher positions. (This is why an incorrectly adjusted guitar often sounds increasingly out of tune as you play up the neck.) To compensate for this, manufacturers set the string length a bit longer than the theoretical scale length by placing the saddle slightly further back from the position indicated by the formula.

However, the problem is not that simple. Since the height of the nut and bridge affect how far the strings must move to reach the fingerboard, these settings are interrelated with saddle placement. Obviously a high action requires the string to stretch further and therefore demands more compensation from the bridge, while a lower action requires less. Manufacturers produce instruments for a general market, with action usually set a little high and saddle placement to general compensation standards. Thus, subsequent alterations of the action will affect intonation and may require alterations in saddle placement ("saddle adjustment"). Raising or lowering the action of any guitar, new or used, will probably require these adjustments.

It should be noted that saddle placement is sometimes too far back, so that instead of causing a sharping at the 12th fret, a flatting effect occurs. Here the saddle must be adjusted forward to compensate for flatness. Obviously, the adjustments are much easier on electric guitars and basses than on acoustic guitars, since the latter rarely have adjustable saddles. But all types can be adjusted or altered to varying degrees, and I will discuss all of them as we go along.

String gauge and tension. The gauge and alloy (or material) of a string affect its tension, and tension has effects on saddle placement or adjustment, because a higher tension string requires more compensation at the saddle than does a lower tension string. For example, if you replace a given string with one that is the same except that it has a larger core diameter, the new string will have more tension due to its higher gauge, and this added tension will increase the sharping effect. This is because the higher tension causes the string to change pitch more radically when fretted than would a lower gauge string moving the same distance to the fret. (This is easy to understand when you consider how much turning of the peg it takes to change the tone of a very loose string as compared with one that is already up to pitch.) Therefore, choice of string gauge and tension (along with action height) must be considered in locating or adjusting the saddle.

As a practical matter, you should put on your choice of strings (gauge and alloy), set the action to the desired height, and then make whatever saddle adjustments are necessary. These matters will be dealt with in detail later. As I pointed out earlier, manufacturers cannot know ahead of time what strings and action you will choose, so some saddle adjustments are almost inevitable in conforming the guitar to your playing needs (this is true of used guitars, too). Also, both new and used guitars flex and change over time and therefore need periodic adjustments.

Checking intonation at the 12th fret. The most commonly used method for determining the correctness of string length or saddle placement is to compare the fretted note at the 12th fret with its harmonic. If the fretted note is higher than the harmonic for that string, the saddle must be moved back to compensate for this sharping effect (the added length from the 12th fret to the saddle will compensate the sharping effect). Conversely, if the fretted note is lower than its corresponding harmonic, this is a flatting effect which must be compensated by adjusting the saddle slightly forward in regard to that string. Both these phenomena occur commonly. Solutions include adjusting the mechanical bridge inserts (for electrics and basses), angling the saddle forward or back (acoustics), or even relocating the saddle in the case of acoustics.

The 12th fret is used as the testing point because it is approximately at the center of the scale length, and it provides an octave point for making the comparison between the harmonic and the fretted note. This comparison at the "halfway point" gives an average measure of the overall intonation. (The comparison can be made between the open string and its 12th fret octave, but the harmonic is clearer than the open tone and is the same pitch as the 12th fret tone, making it easier to detect sharpness or flatness. This is especially true if you are using an electronic tuning device, since the open string creates too many overtones, and makes reading the dial difficult.)

John Carruthers

TUNING DEVICES AND INTONATION

March 1977. Electronic tuning devices. There are several types of electronic measuring devices which can be used for checking intonation. They employ various methods including stroboscopic, meter, cathode tube, and light pulsation. But all operate on the basic concept of translating the incoming signal (i.e., musical note) into a visual image that accurately indicates whether the notes are on pitch, sharp, or flat. Figures 1 and 2 illustrate two of the most popular types of tuning devices.

Operating the device. Most machines which test intonation work in the same manner. When the note being played is on pitch, the indicator holds on center. Movement to the left indicates flatness, while movement to the right indicates sharpness. (On stroboscopic tuners the speed of movement to the right or the left indicates the degree of sharpness or flatness.) For example, play the open A string harmonic at the 12th fret and adjust the guitar tuning peg until the tone holds the indicator at center. Then play the fretted note at the 12th fret of that same string. If the indicator moves to the left, intonation is flat, and you must shorten the string length. Conversely, if movement is to the right, you must lengthen the string. (The principles underlying these adjustments were explained earlier.) When both the harmonic and the fretted note create a centered reading, the string is properly intonated. Due to the device's extreme sensitivity to even the slightest irregularities in the string, there may be small oscillations around the center point of the indicator. When the string is in tune these movements are equidistant from the center.

Why use an electronic tuning device? It is not absolutely necessary to use such a device, but they are far more accurate than the human ear because they: (1) detect much smaller frequency changes; (2) register only the actual pitch of the note, while the ear often has difficulty, because pitch is obscured by tone quality; and (3) are consistent indexes of absolute and relative pitch, while the ear is subject to fatigue. The stroboscopic devices are usually accurate to within one "cent" (pronounced "sont"), which is 1/100th of a semitone (a semitone being a normal chromatic half-step, say, C to C#). Even some of the simpler and less expensive devices are accurate to within five "cents." If you frequently do your own intonation adjustments a tuning device can be a worthwhile investment.

Tips for using tuning devices.
1. Before using the machine, be sure it is properly calibrated in accordance with its instruction manual.
2. Pre-tune the guitar to concert pitch (a pitch pipe is adequate, but a tuning fork is preferable). This is important for two reasons. First, it is necessary to have full tension on the neck when making adjustments, since tension affects action and therefore intonation. Second, a string which is not tuned to correct pitch may produce a false reading on a strobe, because these devices pick up and register harmonic overtones. For example, if the machine is set to *E*, a string tuned accidentally to *A* could produce a stable pattern on the indicator because *E* is the 5th harmonic (or overtone) of *A*. By pretuning the guitar, you insure that the indicator is registering the fundamental tone for which you have set the machine.
3. Hold the guitar in normal playing position when testing intonation. Holding the guitar adds slight stresses to the neck and body, and these stresses affect intonation. Testing in this way insures adjustments

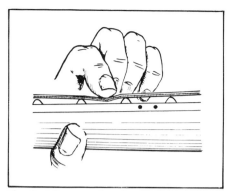
Fig. 1: Adequate fretting pressure.

Fig. 2: Excessive pressure.

that compensate for playing conditions.

4. For electric guitars and basses use a standard patch cord to plug directly into the tuning device. Then set the volume and tone controls at full to insure an optimum signal, and tune a given string to the device (using the 12th fret harmonic). Then continue to play the harmonic while you experiment with the pickup selector switch to determine which pickup gives the clearest reading. Usually it is the rhythm pickup. Also experiment with levels of volume adjustment, because

these can either improve or distort the image.

5. For acoustic guitars you can use the microphone supplied with the unit, or you can use a contact pickup to plug directly into the tuning device. Contact pickups are useful, because they eliminate the outside sounds that cause interference on a normal microphone. (Note, however, that some contact pickups do not have a strong enough signal to register on the tuning device.)

6. Always use the 12th fret harmonic instead of the open string when tun-

ing to the device. The harmonic creates more vibrations per second, causing a more continuous signal and therefore a clearer image.

7. On stroboscopic machines you must be aware of the fact that the different bands on the strobe dial are for different octaves, and that one of the bands will be most appropriate for the note you are testing. This is usually easy to determine, because the spokes in the correct band will be substantially clearer than those in the other bands. Non-strobe machines often have an octave selector switch; experiment with these settings to find the clearest image.

Finger pressure. Guitar players often press too hard, stretching the string excessively and producing a sharping effect, or pull the string off center with the same result. Fig. 1 shows the proper pressure, just enough so that the string touches the fret firmly. Fig. 2 shows the added stretching that occurs when excessive pressure is used. Avoid these errors when playing or when testing intonation.

John Carruthers

INTONATION AND TRUSS RODS

April 1977. Intonation adjustments must be carried out in proper sequence: (1) truss rod, (2) action height, and (3) string length (saddle adjustments). While the first two do not relate solely to intonation, they affect it by raising or lowering the distance of the string from the fingerboard, thus causing a sharping or flatting effect. Therefore, these first two procedures must be done before the final length is established.

Truss rod and warp. Contrary to popular belief, the neck must have a certain amount of warp for the guitar to play properly. If there is no warp, the vibrating string will tend to buzz against the fret immediately above the one on which you are pressing the string. This is because the string vibrates in a slow curve, and a slight warp in the fingerboard is needed to accommodate this motion. Too much warp has a sharping

effect, since it increases the distance the string must stretch to reach the fret. It makes playing more difficult for the same reason. A reverse warp, or "counterwarp," usually causes the buzzing effect described above. In extreme cases the counterwarp may cause buzzing even on open strings, making the guitar unplayable other than in the higher registers.

Warp is normally created by the tension of the strings, and its amount is regulated by the truss rod, a metal rod running inside the length of the neck. Classical guitars rarely have truss rods, since string tension is so low that the neck can normally handle the load without additional support. Most steel-string acoustics, electrics, and basses require additional reinforcement in the neck to support the higher tension of

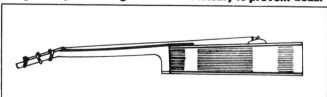
A slight warp in the fingerboard is necessary to prevent buzz.

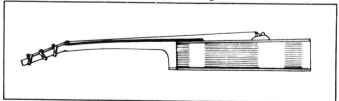
Counterwarp can cause even open strings to buzz.

steel strings and prevent excessive warp. A few makes of steel-string acoustics, most notably Martins, have non-adjustable truss rods, but most commercial brands have adjustable ones. (Those found on the vast majority of electric guitars and basses are adjustable.) If your guitar has no truss rod, or has a nonadjustable type, changes in neck warp cannot be made without difficult modifications. With the adjustable type, regulating the warp is relatively easy, although skill and a great deal of care are necessary to do it properly.

How the truss rod works. The non-adjustable truss rod works by reinforcement, strengthening the neck and preventing the string tension from causing too much bend. The adjustable variety works by creating stress on the neck. Although there are design variations, basically the pre-curved adjustable rod is fixed at one end and has a hex-nut or screw at the other end so that tension can be added or released, thereby changing the degree of warp. On most guitars the adjustment is just above the nut, under a removable plastic plate, though some guitars have it at the heel of the neck.

With most truss rods, warp is reduced by turning the hex-nut clockwise, which strengthens the neck. Counterclockwise movement causes a relaxation in the neck, increasing the natural warp created by string tension.

You should always *face* the screw and turn it in a clockwise or counterclockwise direction (depending on the desired adjustment) regardless of whether the hex-nut appears at the head or the heel of the guitar. Obviously, you must have full string tension on the neck when measuring the amount of curvature and making these adjustments, since the tension of the strings is the primary factor creating warp. Therefore you should retune after each adjustment in order to maintain actual playing tension.

Testing for the proper amount of warp. To test the amount of warp, press down a string simultaneously at the 1st fret and at the fret where the neck joins the body. The amount of warp is the space between that string and the top of the fret lying halfway between the points you are pressing. (Since you will need a free hand to measure this gap, you can have a friend hold down the string at the 1st fret or you can use a capo. Set the capo just tight enough to touch the strings to the fret. Too much pressure can cause an arch in the string, resulting in a false reading.) Important: To get accurate measurements (1) you must string the guitar with the make and gauge of strings you will be using; (2) all strings must be on the guitar; and (3) the instrument must be tuned to playing pitch. These factors all affect the amount of warp.

It is not a good idea to check warp merely by sighting down the neck, because your eye can be deceived by the binding or optical illusions created by irregularities in the frets and/or fingerboard. Also, the sighting method does not provide a means of measuring the exact amount of warp.

The procedure for measuring the amount of warp is the same for electric, bass, and acoustic guitars, though height specifications will vary. The amount of warp necessary depends on the type and particular characteristics of the instrument balanced against the needs and demands of the player. However, the following guidelines provide a basic adjustment that will usually suffice.

Having pressed the two points on the string as indicated above, find the midway spot and measure between the string and the top of the fret (the sixth string is usually the most convenient for this). Most repairmen use a mechanic's "feeler gauge," the kind used for adjusting points and valves on cars is an effective tool for this measurement. I have found the following basic standards to be the most useful for the widest variety of guitars and playing styles: for acoustics and electrics, .010", for basses, .015"-.020". If slight variations from these specifications are necessary, they can be determined by further experimentation.

Caution: All adjustments should be carried out in small increments and very cautiously. In fact, this is one area where you may wish merely to understand the process and leave the actual adjustment to a skilled repairman. The amount of adjustment on the truss rod is very critical, and too much movement can either break the rod or cause a counter-warp. Usually it takes very little adjustment to achieve the correct amount of warp. Also, allow a certain amount of time between each adjustment (approximately five to ten minutes) to allow the wood to settle to its new point of equilibrium under the pull of the strings (retuning the strings immediately to playing pitch will expedite this).

John Carruthers

Truss rod adjustment nut accessed at headstock.

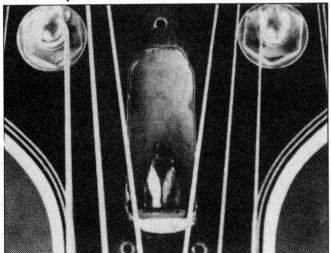

Screw-type adjuster located at the body end of the neck.

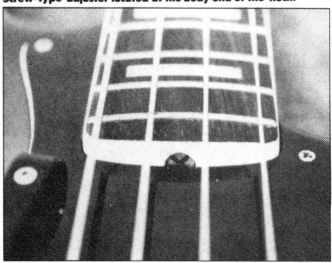

BRIDGE ADJUSTMENTS FOR ACOUSTICS

May 1977. After the truss rod is adjusted action height must be set before final intonation adjustments are made. First we will cover adjustments at the bridge on acoustic steel-string and classical guitars, and next we will treat the same subject in regard to electric guitars and basses. Subsequently we'll discuss action height at the nut and final intonation.

Important reminder. All action height measurements, like truss-rod measurements, must be taken with a full set of strings on the guitar—the gauge and type you will be using, tuned to playing pitch. This is important because the degree of tension and specific playing properties of the strings affect action height by stressing the neck.

Fig. 1 illustrates files, pliers, and nippers. Fig. 2 shows how to carefully remove frets with the nippers. Fig. 3 illustrates the proper contour for steel-string and classical bridge saddles.

Useful tools (see Fig. 1). To measure action height at the upper end of the fingerboard use a small steel rule measured off in 64ths of an inch. This is inexpensive and can be purchased at hardware and auto supply stores. Most saddles on acoustic guitars are wedge fit. This may require the use of end nippers to facilitate removal of the saddle from the bridge. (Pliers could be used as a substitute, but there is a risk of crushing or damaging the saddle, because they do not distribute the pressure over a large area, and they lack the end nippers' cutting edge, which firmly grasps the saddle.) The concave cutting surface of a fret file makes contouring and curving the saddle much easier, but this tool is rather expensive and must be ordered from a dealer. Careful use of a mill file (followed by fine sanding) will accomplish similar results. A mill file and medium grade sandpaper are effective for removing

material from the bottom of the saddle.

Saddle contour and curvature. The saddle's profile should conform to the curvature of the fingerboard. Both are slightly curved on most acoustic steel-string guitars, while both are flat on most classical guitars. Before proceeding with measurements and saddle height adjustments, sight along the neck from the bridge and be sure that the saddle conforms to the curvature or flatness of the fingerboard. If it does not, loosen the strings and remove them from the bridge. Then remove the saddle from the bridge by carefully gripping it with a pair of end nippers, as illustrated in Fig. 2. Don't use too much pressure and don't try to force the saddle out of its slot. Work the nippers from one end of the saddle to the other, rocking it slightly if necessary. If it won't yield to moderate pressure, take it to a repairman. It may have been mistakenly glued into the saddle groove, in which case normal removal procedure may cause damage to the saddle or bridge.

After removing the saddle, shape its curvature to conform to that of the fingerboard. Work slowly and carefully with either a fret file or mill file. At the same time you are doing this you should be either maintaining or modifying the contour of the saddle. Saddle contour is illustrated in Fig. 3. The rounded saddle is the most commonly used on acoustic steel-string guitars. The *beveled* saddle is recommended for classical guitars

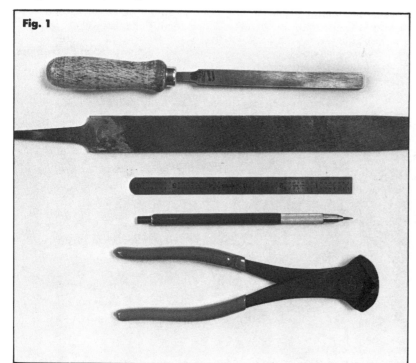

Fig. 1

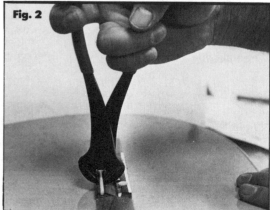

Fig. 2

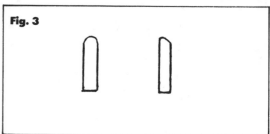

Fig. 3

because the string windings tend to vibrate against the rounded saddle, causing extraneous buzzing. For a rounded saddle, the curved cutting surface of a fret file automatically creates the necessary contour, but a mill file and sandpaper can be used instead. For a beveled saddle, a mill file and sandpaper give the best results. Be sure to round the leading edge slightly (with a fret file or sandpaper) to prevent string breakage and excessive saddle wear. There are some marginal intonation aspects of saddle contour in regard to string length. I will discuss these later.

After correcting the saddle curvature, reinsert the saddle (being careful that the bass and treble ends are in their respective positions). Then tap it lightly with a mallet to insure that it seats properly.

Measuring action height and specifications for measurements. Measuring action height at the upper end of the fingerboard is done with a steel rule at the fret where the neck joins the body. Follow the procedure illustrated in Fig. 4, sighting across the fingerboard to measure the gap between the top of the indicated fret and the bottom of the string you are checking. It is best to make this measurement while holding the guitar in playing position. When resting on a bench the weight of the guitar may affect the neck position, making the reading inaccurate.

It is impractical and unnecessary to adjust each string to its required height at the bridge. The other strings will automatically arrive at appropriate heights when the first and sixth are set (assuming that the saddle curvature correctly follows the curvature of the fingerboard, as previously described). An ideal height for acoustic steel-string guitars is with the sixth string at 3/32" and the first string at 5/64"; classical guitars play well with the sixth at 5/32" and the first at 2/16" (normal setting), or sixth at 2/16" and first at 3/32" (low setting). Action is set higher on the bass side, because these strings travel in a wider arc than the treble strings. Some players require lower or higher adjustments for their playing styles, but the above settings usually provide easy playability while avoiding intonation and buzzing problems.

The doubling factor. As a rule of thumb, if you need to lower a string by a given amount you must remove approximately twice that amount from the saddle. This principle applies to both removable and nonremovable

saddles, but the adjustment procedures differ (as explained below).

Removable saddles. Having measured and determined the correct amount to be taken off, remove the saddle from the bridge with a pair of end nippers (as explained above). Then measure off and mark the needed amount from the bottom of the saddle on each end (for the sixth and first strings) and draw a line between these points. By grinding down the saddle to that line (with a mill file or sandpaper) and reinserting it into the bridge, you will find in most cases that the height is then correct at the sixth and first strings, while the other strings average out at correspondingly appropriate heights. (Caution: when reinserting the saddle be sure that the bass and treble ends are positioned properly; then tap the saddle lightly before reinserting and tightening the strings. If the saddle is not properly seated, all measurements and adjustments are thrown off. Also, remember to retune prior to each measurement.) If this method (doubling the needed distance) does not suffice, remove an additional amount, but work slowly and cautiously—it is easy to remove material and difficult to replace it.

Nonremovable saddles. On bridges where the saddle slot extends into the bridge feet (e.g., some older style Martins) the saddle is usually glued in. This type should be left intact and material removed from the top surface, since attempts to extract it may result in damage to the saddle or bridge. Even if the saddle is loose and can be safely extracted, material should only be removed from the top. These saddles are usually tapered on both ends to conform to the shape of the bridge feet, and removing material from the bottom would shorten the saddle's length. The shortened saddle would then not fill the entire length of the saddle slot.

To remove material from the top, use the same procedure described above in regard to curvature and contour, maintaining these factors while lowering the saddle the required amount. (You must be careful not to damage the bridge surface or the face of the guitar. Avoid this by protecting these areas with masking tape and cardboard. Caution: tape should be pulled off very slowly and carefully to avoid damage to the finish.) This procedure is much more difficult than the previous one and is best left to an experienced repairman.

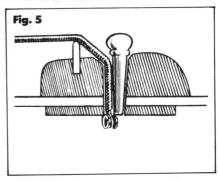

Fig. 4 shows how to measure action height. Fig. 5 illustrates the proper amount of angle for a string passing over a bridge.

Shaving the bridge. Lowering the saddle flattens the downward angle of the string between the saddle and the bridge pins, and this reduces the tension between these two points. This rarely creates problems, but in extreme cases the reduced tension against the saddle and the closer proximity of the strings to the bridge may cause them to buzz against these surfaces. Shaving the bridge and reangling its string channels usually remedies this problem by restoring a sufficient amount of angle and tension. Fig. 5 illustrates an optimum amount of angle. If shaving the bridge is necessary, it should be handled by a competent repairman. It is an involved process which I will discuss later.

Raising the saddle height. If you cut off too much (or if the saddle is already too low) you will either have to shim up the saddle or make a new one. Making a new one is difficult, requiring considerable skill and experience. If you do not have to raise it more than a small amount, one or two shims made of a business or index card will do, but too many shims will not work, since the saddle will begin to lose stability. At least half of the saddle height should be below the top surface of the bridge (see Fig. 5).

John Carruthers

BRIDGE ADJUSTMENTS FOR ELECTRICS

June 1977. *Important reminder:* All action-height measurements, like truss-rod measurements, must be taken with a full set of strings on the guitar—the gauge and type you will be using, tuned to playing pitch. The degree of tension and specific playing properties of the strings affect action height by stressing the neck.

Necessary tools. The only tools ordinarily required for these adjustments on electric guitars and basses are small screwdrivers and/or Allen wrenches of appropriate sizes for the given bridge-adjustment screws, studs, or set screws (either Allen or slotted type). These are available at your music dealer or at hardware stores. (The Allen wrenches are frequently supplied with the guitar.)

Recommended Action Height Settings

Bridge Type	6	5	4	3	2	1
A	3/32"	X	X	X	X	5/64"
B	3/32"	Follow Fingerboard Contour				5/64"
C	X	X	5/32"	9/64"	9/64"	2/16"
D	X	X	2/16"	7/64"	7/64"	3/32"

Legend
A —Thumbwheel and stud-type bridges (precurved)
B —Bridges with individually adjustable string heights
C —Bass guitars: lower setting
D —Bass guitars: higher setting

Principles of saddle-height adjustments. Theoretically, the doubling factor explained previously would also apply to electrics and basses, but since the adjustment is done mechanically on these latter types of guitars it is unnecessary to consider raising or lowering the saddle twice the amount of necessary height adjustment. Here you simply take the initial measurement and either raise or lower the saddle-height adjustment screws until the measurement meets the specifications. This procedure is explained below in regard to different types of bridges. Specifications for electric guitars and basses differ from acoustic steel-string and classical guitars. The table below gives recommended action-height settings (at the fret where the neck joins the body) for electric guitars and basses.

Measuring action height at the upper end of the fingerboard. Measuring action height on electric guitars and basses is done the same way as for acoustic guitars described previously. The measurement is taken at the fret where the neck joins the body, by placing the end of the rule on top of that fret and sighting across the fingerboard to measure the gap between the top of the fret and the bottom of the string you are checking (see Table). Remember that it is best to make this measurement while holding the guitar in playing position. When resting on a bench the weight of the guitar may affect the neck position, making the reading inaccurate.

Making the adjustments. Electric guitar and bass bridges are of two basic types. The simplest type has adjustment wheels or adjustment studs on each end, and relies on a preset curvature that is supposed to conform to the curvature of the fingerboard. With these, as with a properly curved acoustic saddle, it is impractical and unnecessary to adjust each string to its required height at the bridge. The other strings automatically arrive at appropriate heights when the

first and sixth are set. (This assumes that the bridge is properly curved. If it has lost its curvature, it should be replaced.)

Having determined the appropriate height measurements for the first and sixth strings (at the fret where the neck joins the body), adjust them accordingly at the bridge: Clockwise rotation of the stud or thumbwheel normally lowers the bridge and counterclockwise movement raises it. The other basic type of bridge has individually adjustable saddle heights for each string. On these you must adjust each one, so that the string settings follow the fingerboard curvature. (Note: With this type, clockwise rotation usually raises the string and counterclockwise movement lowers it.)

Recommended height specifications for both these types of bridges are given in the table above. With regard to the individually adjustable saddles you should combine use of the specifications with your visual judgment, sighting along the neck from the bridge to determine proper conformity between bridge and fingerboard curvatures. Adjustments for electric basses are done in the same way as for electric guitars but with different height specifications, as indicated in the table.

Needless to say, some players require lower or higher adjustments for their playing styles, but the recommended settings usually provide easy playability while avoiding intonation and buzzing problems. If necessary, you can vary these standards to conform to the characteristics of your instrument and meet your playing requirements.

Caution: Many stud-type bridges have set screws (located behind the studs) that regulate string length. On this type, to avoid bending these screws, you should loosen string tension before making height adjustments. Also, on some Gibson basses there are locking set screws that must be loosened to allow upward or downward adjustments.

Note regarding bridge curvature. In some instances, the curvature on the preset bridge may be inadequate for your guitar. This is usually the result of curvature modification of the fingerboard during refretting. Also, a bridge may collapse from excessive string pressure over a long period of time. Insufficient curvature usually causes buzzing on the middle strings and makes clean bends difficult, if not impossible. The best way to remedy this situation is to replace the bridge.

John Carruthers

ACTION HEIGHT AT THE NUT

July 1977. Remember that all action height adjustments must be taken with a full set of strings on the guitar, the gauge and type you will be using, tuned to playing pitch. Variances in the tension and playing properties of the strings change the stress on the neck and thereby affect measurements.

Necessary tools. To measure action height at the nut you should have an auto mechanic's feeler gauge which measures widths of at least between .018"-.022." These are available at auto supply or hardware stores and cost no more than a couple of dollars. For cutting the nut slots deeper you can use an X-ACTO saw for the treble strings and a nut-file for the bass strings (or a fine-tooth hacksaw blade can be used in place of the nut-file). For classical guitars the X-ACTO saw is unnecessary since the strings are all of wider diameter. (Nut-files come in varying widths that correspond to string diameters and can be ordered from your music dealer. However, they are somewhat expensive and the fine-tooth hacksaw blade achieves similar results.) End nippers are useful for removing Fender-type nuts. The picture below illustrates all of the above-mentioned tools.

Measuring action height at the first fret. Measurements at the first fret (to determine proper action height at the nut) are done with a feeler gauge: You must hold the gauge parallel to the string surface to get an accurate measurement; avoid the common error of tilting the blade. For steel-string acoustic guitars, .020" between the first fret and the bottom of each string is usually an ideal height—low enough to be comfortable, but high enough to avoid buzzing when the string is played open. For classical guitars, .022" to .026" works well, depending on the player and the instrument. For electric guitars, I recommend .018," and for basses .020." Lower or higher settings than these may be used, depending on the guitar's resonance factor, structural strength, type of strings used, etc., but these recommended heights will work well for most players.

Reslotting the nut to specifications. If the string is too high, you must carefully slot the nut deeper and remeasure until the gauge touches both fret and string—yet does not push the string upward. The fit should be exact. Cutting the slot deeper can be done with an X-ACTO saw for the treble strings and a nut-file (or fine-tooth hacksaw blade) for the bass strings. On electric basses a small rat-tail file of proper diameter is a good substitute for the fret file; if using a nut file or saw, rock it laterally to widen the cut as you work. *Caution:* It takes very little cutting to lower the string, though this varies with the hardness of the nut material, the sharpness of the tool, and the amount of pressure exerted. Proceed cautiously, cutting a small amount and then remeasuring. Repeat the process until the adjustment is correct. Remember to restore full tension to the string each time you remeasure. And remember that it's easier to remove material than it is to replace it.

Techniques for cutting the slots deeper: (1) When cutting the slot, the cutting tool should be held parallel to the angle of the headstock: (see Fig. 1) *not* parallel to the fingerboard. Otherwise, the string may buzz against the slot groove due to inadequate string tension at the point where the string reaches the nut. Tension is increased when the string angles downward from the nut as shown in the drawing (see Fig. 2). Some guitars have headstocks that run parallel to the fingerboard. With these you must angle the nut slot as though the headstock was

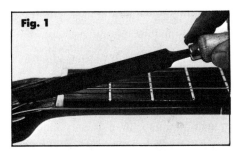

Fig. 1

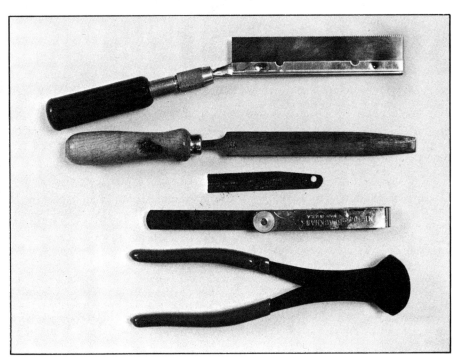

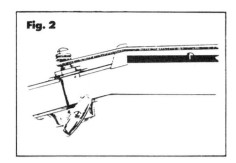

Fig. 2

angled normally. This ensures that the breaking point of the string is at the surface of the nut which faces the fingerboard, thereby increasing tension and preventing buzzing. (2) When deepening the slot be sure to use a wide enough saw or file to accommodate the full width of the string. If the string fits too tightly in the slot, it may sit at the proper height initially but later settle into the groove and begin to buzz. On the other hand, if the slot is too wide, the string may oscillate in the slot, causing extraneous sounds.

What if the slot is too deep? Buzzes caused by the nut slot being cut too low

occur when the string is played open; once you press a string at a given fret, the string vibrates between that fret and the bridge. (However, a string fretted in the higher registers may buzz sympathetically against a lower fret if the nut is too low. This occurs rarely, and may also be caused by inadequate neck warp or by fingerboard irregularities.) If you have cut too low and the string begins buzzing (or if this condition already exists), the nut may have to be shimmed or replaced. I do not recommend putting glue in the slots to shim up the string. This makeshift approach is short-run and unreliable. It may be possible to shim the entire nut by placing a strip of business card or index card under it and regluing it in position (using sparing amounts of white glue on the nut channel, shim, and bottom surface of the nut).

Note: After regluing the nut, return the strings to their respective slots and restore normal tension; this serves as a vice to ensure that the nut is securely seated. Wipe off excess glue with a damp cloth. If the nut requires more than one or two shims, it should prob-

ably be replaced. This requires a high degree of technical skill, since each nut must be fashioned to fit the particular guitar. Removing the nut for shimming should also be done by an expert; attempts by the inexperienced often cause damage to the nut channel or to the finish surrounding it. For those with some experience, the procedure is as follows: loosen all the strings and remove them from their slots; carefully score the finish around the edges of the nut with a sharp X-ACTO knife then place a small block of wood against the nut surface adjoining the fingerboard and tap the block gently with a mallet to dislodge the nut, as it is usually glued in. One light tap with the mallet will usually suffice. Proceed cautiously, taking note of the design of the nut slot, finish, and headstock veneer. *Caution:* Guitars with the Fender-type nut design are very likely to suffer splitting of the headstock surface during the above procedure and must be handled differently. Coax the nut out slowly with end nippers. This procedure should also be followed on guitars with a deep nut channel and thick headstock veneer.

John Carruthers

STRING LENGTH ADJUSTMENTS ON ACOUSTICS

August 1977. Now we will discuss string length adjustments on acoustic steel-string and classical guitars by means of reangling or sloping the saddle, and the same method in regard to f-hole guitars with nonmechanical bridges.

A word of caution: Be sure that you understand the principles of string length adjustment, as explained in the chapter on intonation, before proceeding. Also, be alert to problems of false or damaged strings and the pulled neck, as these phenomena may create intonation problems no matter how carefully you follow all the procedures and specifications. Remember that your strings should be the kind you will be using regularly; this is especially

important for final string-length settings, since changing the make or gauge of strings can affect intonation (just as changing action height affects it).

Necessary tools (See Fig. 1). Only a few tools are necessary for reangling the saddle to correct intonation: end nippers to remove the saddle, a mill file for reangling large sections of the saddle, a needle file for angling individual sections of the saddle, and 220 grade sandpaper for rounding and smoothing the edge of the saddle. Needle files and point files are available at hardware and auto supply stores. I find the point file (designed for filing automobile distributor points) particularly useful for reangling portions of the saddle.

Reangling the saddle. As explained previously, if a given string is going sharp at the 12th fret, the saddle (or the string's breaking point on the saddle) must be moved back, providing added string length to compensate for this sharpness. If the string goes flat at the 12th fret, this must be compensated by moving the saddle (or breaking point) slightly forward, overcoming the flatness by shortening the distance (or string length) from the 12th fret to the breaking point. By reangling the saddle, as illustrated in Fig. 2, the breaking point can be moved forward or back to alleviate flatness or sharpness respectively. (The black markings in Fig. 2 were rendered in for the purposes of this article to delineate the different settings.)

Limitations of this method. Sloping or reangling the saddle will suffice to correct intonation only when the necessary changes in string length are minimal, since the range of adjustment is limited by the width of the saddle. A further restriction is that you must not angle the saddle to such a sharp point that it becomes a string cutter, i.e. you must leave a certain amount of surface for the string to break across. It should also be noted that when the bevel is re-

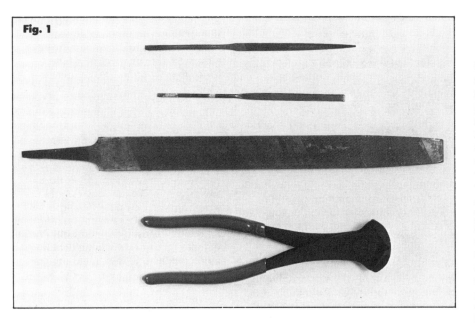

Fig. 1

versed for intonation purposes (with the apex of the saddle adjacent to the bridge pins or the point where the strings tie into the bridge), the tendency is for the strings to cut into the saddle, resulting in inadvertent lowering of the action and consequent buzzes. The danger of this effect is reduced by providing a somewhat wider and rounded breaking surface.

Procedure. Make a chart listing all six strings in order and write down sharp or flat (in "cents") for each string as you test it at the 12th fret (it is best to use an electronic tuning device, but if none is available the testing can be done by ear). Also indicate the make and gauge of strings you are using, action height (at nut and bridge), and truss-rod adjustment height. If you have future intonation problems, this information will enable you to determine whether or not settings have remained stable since the time you set the string length. Thus, the chart helps you make the adjustments initially and also forms a useful reference point for solving problems in the future.

After completing the chart, mark with a pencil the portion of saddle to be reangled for each string. Then remove the saddle from the bridge with end nippers. Angle a small amount at a time with an appropriate file, rechecking intonation as you go along; keep doing this until you reach the optimum result attainable with the given amount of saddle. *CAUTION:* When reangling the saddle, be careful not to reduce its height, as this will lower your action. It is easier if you hold the saddle in a vise

while filing. After angling, smooth the edge with sandpaper to provide enough breaking surface, so the string will not cut into the saddle and vice versa. When putting the saddle back into the bridge, be sure that it is seated properly. Remember to have full tension on all the strings when testing intonation for any given string, as the pull on the neck affects overall string length.

Changing the gauge of strings. If reangling the saddle does not suffice, changing the gauge of a given string can achieve marginal intonation effects. For example, if a string is still slightly flat after you have angled the saddle forward as much as possible, use of a larger diameter string will have an additional sharping effect that may alleviate the problem. Conversely, a smaller gauge string will have a flatting effect. If these solutions do not produce enough change, or if the larger or smaller diameter string is unacceptable in terms of tone or playability, then it is necessary to relocate the saddle. This is

a radical procedure and should be approached only by experienced repairmen.

Classical guitars. When there is a string length problem, you angle the saddle as needed, using a mill file. The procedure is the same as described above for steel-string guitars, but do not make snap decisions or carry out adjustments after trying just one set of classical strings, since individual strings tend to vary widely in regard to intonation properties. Keep a record for several months, comparing several sets of your choice of strings, before concluding which strings are sharp or flat. Test after the strings have been on for several days to allow for stretching. Classical strings have more overtones than steel, making intonation adjustments more difficult; also, the strings are made of substances that tend to stretch, thereby changing the diameter and affecting intonation. Thus, improvements are best made by averaging your tests over the long run and making adjustments accordingly.

F-hole guitars. Some f-hole guitars have nonmechanical bridges; the bridge is held on by string pressure, and intonation is altered by moving the bridge for string length adjustments. The best method is to locate the proper intonation positions for outside (E) strings and let the other strings fall at the average between these two. This may not get all the strings into proper intonation, but it is a good basic procedure. Most f-hole guitar bridges with compensated saddles were designed for much heavier strings and different relative diameters than are now in common usage: They may, therefore, be inadequate for your choice of strings. It is possible to make an unnotched saddle blank and compensate for each string, but this is highly skilled work. Another solution is changing string diameters; the problem with this, as indicated above, is that you sacrifice your string preferences.

John Carruthers

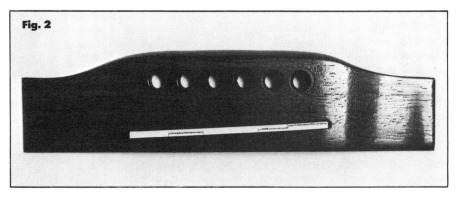

Fig. 2

STRING LENGTH ADJUSTMENTS ON ELECTRICS

October 1977. This article treats string-length adjustments for electric guitars and basses. Be sure you have carried out all preliminary measurements and adjustments (truss rod, action height, etc.) in proper sequence before doing final string-length settings. Also, make certain you understand the principles of string-length adjustments and use of electronic tuning devices.

Be alert for false or damaged strings, since these will create intonation problems no matter how carefully you follow all the procedures and specifications. You should always adjust string length with a new set of strings on the guitar, but remember that even new strings are often false due to manufacturing defects. If you find a string to be persistently difficult to intonate, it is probably false. Replace it and try again. However, on electric basses it should be understood that due to the large string gauge, created by numerous windings, it is more difficult to find a "perfect" string or to achieve "perfect intonation." Normally, the overtone structure will mask any imperfections, assuming they are not extreme and the bass has been intonated as accurately as possible.

Fig. 1 illustrates the basic procedure for adjusting the intonation on tune-o-matic bridges. Fig. 2 shows a bass bridge that only allows for intonating the strings in pairs.

When making intonation adjustments, also remember to employ the choice of strings you will be using regularly. Changing the make or gauge of strings later on will probably affect your intonation and require that the string lengths be reset. Also, the strings should be left at full tension on the guitar for a few hours before setting string length. This allows the pull on the neck to reach its stable level and the strings to stretch completely.

Basic procedure on electric guitars and basses. Nearly all electric guitars and basses work on the same principle in regard to adjusting string length. Slotted-, phillips-, or allen-headed screws at the bridge enable you to adjust each string's saddle forward or backward to alter string length. On some guitars the screw heads face the neck end of the instrument while on others they face the other direction (on Tune-O-Matic type bridges you can face them either way). An appropriate screwdriver with an extended shank provides easy access to adjustment without scratching or damaging the top of the instrument (see Fig. 1). Turning the screw one direction will move the saddle forward toward the neck to compensate for flatness. Turning it the opposite direction will move the saddle

back away from the neck to compensate for sharpness. The appropriate direction is easy to determine by experimenting. Using an electronic tuning device to test harmonics and their corresponding notes at the 12th fret, it is possible to set string length accurately on electric guitars and basses.

Fender two-foot and three-foot bridges. The old style Telecasters have only three bridge feet, so that there are two strings per bridge foot, or saddle. Similarly, some Fender basses have only two bridge feet, as shown in Fig. 2. With these types of bridges it is often difficult or impossible to get both strings perfectly intonated since the direction and/or amount of adjustment required for each is rarely the same. Thus, you must find a median point between the two optimum adjustments. Keep going back and forth, testing how many "cents" (1/100ths of a semitone) sharp or flat each is, until you achieve an average between the two. This is not really satisfactory, so Fender came out with a replacement for these units, which provides a six-foot bridge for basses. Also, the Telecaster Deluxe comes with a six-foot bridge, which is similar to the Stratocaster bridge.

Extra margins for adjustment on Fender-type bridges. Sometimes the adjustment range of the bridge is inadequate for the proper setting of a given string. For example, on Fender-type bridges the saddle may be back as far as it will go and the string will still be sharp at the 12th fret. This can be compensated by removing the spring behind the saddle (see Fig. 2). If only a small amount is needed, cut a portion off the spring and put it back on (this holds the saddle in position). If all of the available distance is needed, just leave the spring

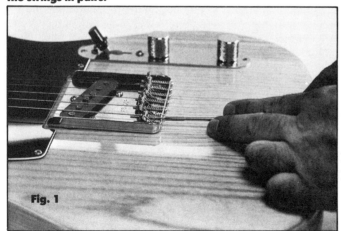

Fig. 1

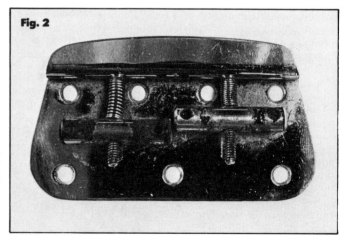

Fig. 2

off. On Strats, sometimes the saddle may be moved forward to the point where it hits the mounting screw, and the string will still be flat. In this case, you can gain the added distance by removing the corresponding screw. It is safe to remove one or two of these screws, since there are a total of six holding the bridge assembly on the guitar.

Extra margins for adjustment on Tune-O-Matic type bridges. When you have reached the outside limits of adjustment on the Gibson Tune-O-Matic (or bridges of the same basic design), the individual saddles, which I call bridge "inserts," can be reversed to achieve further intonation adjustment. For example, if the insert is all the way back, and you still need added string length, this can be achieved by removing the insert and reversing the direction it faces (assuming it was in correctly to start with). Fig. 3 shows the insert in normal position for the fifth string and reversed for the fourth (the adjustment screws are facing the neck). The breaking point of the fourth string will now be about 1/8" farther back (away from the fingerboard) than it was, adding to the string length. If an already reversed insert has gone as far forward as it can, and you need to shorten the string length further, returning the insert to its normal position would achieve the desired results. Fig. 3 shows the second string with a reversed insert and the third string with the advantage gained by returning a reversed insert to normal position when further shortening of string length is needed.

The procedure for removing the inserts is slightly different for old and new Tune-O-Matic bridges. On the old model the inserts are held in place by a fine steel spring that reaches across the six insert screws, as in Fig. 3. After taking off the spring, remove the appropriate insert, being careful not to spill out the other inserts (the spring holds them in when the strings are off). Then replace the insert, facing it in the other direction. When this is done, replace the retainer spring. On the new style Tune-O-Matics the inserts are held in with individual cir-clips (semicircular retainer clips). Remove the appropriate clip by prying it with a compass point or other sharp instrument, then reverse the insert and replace the clip. A pair of surgeon's hemostats, or surgical clamps, are useful for replacing both the cir-clips and the old-style retainer spring. They can be purchased at medical supply or electronic shops and some hobby stores.

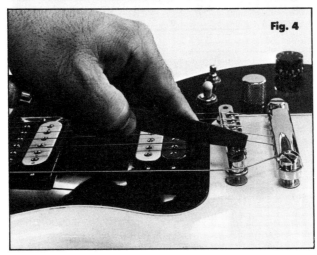

Fig. 3

Fig. 4

Fig. 3 shows the insert in normal position for the fifth string and reversed for the fourth on a tune-o-matic. Fig. 4 illustrates proper technique for renotching a bridge.

Renotching the bridge insert. After the insert has been reversed, it should be renotched so that the angle in which the string travels across the insert is down toward the point where the strings attach to the bridge or body of the guitar. This prevents buzzing. It can be done with a tri-corner file or nut file, as shown in Fig. 4. The cut should be just deep enough so that if you bend the string it will not jump out of the saddle. Normally the string should break across the point furthest forward on the saddle (facing the neck), but this can be varied if additional minute adjustments to string length are necessary and can be achieved by no other means. If the slot has worn too deep, or someone has miscut it, the reversed insert may not be able to properly accommodate the string, causing it to buzz. Replace the insert, remembering to renotch the new one properly.

Using compounds to hold Tune-O-Matic settings in place. After you have the string length set properly on a Tune-O-Matic type bridge, there is a tendency for vibrations of the guitar to change the settings slightly, throwing intonation off. A good solution to this problem is to apply a caulking-type compound to the screws holding the inserts. (It should be a substance that is pliable and does not dry out.) This holds the settings in place but allows for future adjustments. I find that the best material for this is the mastic that is used to attach Barcus-Berry pickups to acoustic instruments. Remove the insert screws, coat the threads with the mastic, and reinsert. Do this before making the adjustments. Once they are made, the mastic will hold the settings, but also allow for future adjustments that may become necessary because of changes in string guage, weather, etc. This is the great advantage of such compounds over using clear nail polish or lacquer, which hold the settings but must be reapplied when there are future adjustments. After setting string length, apply a dab on the thread where the screw and insert meet. When you make adjustments later, a reapplication may be necessary.

Relocating the bridge. If all the above approaches have been taken and there is still a problem of intonation that requires further string-length adjustments, you can try different gauges of strings to achieve marginal effects. The problem with this approach is that it is very limited in effect, and it requires you to sacrifice your string preferences. The only remaining solution is to relocate the entire bridge assembly.

John Carruthers

FINISH MAINTENANCE

October, November 1978. Caring for the guitar's finish is a relatively simple procedure but one which must be carried out with the proper materials and an understanding of their use. Periodic maintenance of the finish enhances the beauty of the instrument and also helps to prevent permanent surface damage that may result from the cumulative effects of wear, acids from the hands, etc. The two basic areas covered by such maintenance are: (1) the finished surfaces of the neck and body; and (2) the usually unfinished surface of the fingerboard. This column will explain both the cleaning of these surfaces and the application of appropriate waxes and polishes for protection and preservation. Read everything before applying any previously untried substances to your guitar.

Types of finish. Before cleaning and polishing finished surfaces, first determine the type of finish so that the appropriate cleaning solvent and polish can be chosen. Incorrect solvents or polishes may irreparably damage the finish. Guitars and other fretted instruments are finished with a variety of protective substances, the most common of which are nitrocellulose lacquer and synthetic finishes such as polyurethanes and polyesters. Acrylic lacquer is also used, though less often. Instruments occasionally have composite finishes in which a synthetic is used as a sealer, followed by a final lacquer coating. Older guitars and some custom-made instruments may have varnish or shellac finishes. Also, some fine classical guitars are finished with French polish, which is a hand-rubbed shellac application.

Most of these finishes are subject to oxidation and fading; all are subject to abrasion and the accumulation of residues on the surface (grime, perspiration, wax, smoke films, etc.). If these effects are not regularly dealt with, they may lead to unnecessary and permanent damage to the guitar's surface. Using the following guidelines, you should be able to determine the type of finish. This in turn will enable you to proceed with choosing the appropriate cleaning solvent and polish. Obviously,

if the guitar is new and free of the above-named problems, cleaning will not be necessary, and you can start polishing.

Identyfying the type of finish. Most guitars made prior to about 1930 were varnished or French polished—those methods being the most practical. Thereafter with the development of more sophisticated spray equipment, nitrocellulose lacquer was used on most makes. In recent years, synthetic finishes such as polyurethane and polyester have become increasingly popular with some manufacturers, because they dry quickly and evenly (qualities which are advantageous to mass production) and are highly transparent. The age of a guitar will not necessarily pinpoint the type of finish, but depending on the make and kind of guitar, it may give you an indication when combined with the following standards for visual judgment.

quer, and synthetic finishes such as polyurethane usually have a deep, high-gloss appearance, except when they are applied or rubbed-out so as to create a satin finish. Varnishes tend to have a shallower depth, less gloss, and a somewhat hand-rubbed and satin effect. However, varnish may be either high- or low-gloss, depending on its quality, the degree to which it has been polished, etc. Thus, high-gloss varnish may look like lacquer in some cases, but few contemporary guitars (other than some which are custom-made) have varnish finishes. Shellac, normally applied by the French polish method, has an extremely shallow depth; it seals the wood so minimally that you can usually see the actual texture of the wood grain, and it ordinarily has a hand-rubbed, slightly satin patina. Even when French polish has a higher gloss, there is a soft glow and delicacy that distinguishes it from other finishes.

Choosing the correct cleaning solvent and polish. Use of a solvent or polish that is chemically incompatible with a given finish may cause irreparable damage. (Some guitar and furniture polishes contain cleaning solvents

as well as polishing and waxing agents; it may be unsafe to assume that a polish will not react with the finish.) Such incompatibility is most likely to occur with shellac (French polish) because of its extreme sensitivity to chemical solvents—even the appropriate ones. For this reason, exercise the utmost care when cleaning and polishing this type of finish, as indicated later. Also, exercise caution with the more durable finishes such as lacquers, synthetics, and varnishes. Furthermore, you must keep in mind the age and condition of the finish. The amount of necessary care is related to all of these factors.

Even when you are certain as to the type of finish, make a preliminary test (as explained below) before cleaning and polishing. Probably 95% of contemporary guitars are finished either in nitrocellulose lacquer or synthetics and lend themselves to the basic methods described here for cleaning and polishing. Varnished guitars may likewise be treated in the same manner, although the method specified for shellacked (French polished) surfaces may also be used, particularly in the case of varnishes having the same base—alcohol—as French polish. **Caution:** Under *no* circumstances should you employ the solvents, cleaners, or polishes recommended for lacquers or synthetics when dealing with French polish, as this will certainly cause serious damage to the finish. Furthermore, regardless of the surface or methods used, always proceed with caution. By testing first you can avoid noticeable damage to the instrument from a reaction between the finish and the substance applied to it.

Polishing cloths. All cleaning and polishing should be done with flannelette, a soft cotton flannel available at yard goods stores. Do not use pre-treated flannelette cloths, since they may harm the finish due to chemical elements. Also, avoid using ordinary rag material or paper towels, as they may have an undesirable abrasiveness. Fold the cloth into a small pad for applying the solvent, cleaner, or polish. Always do one section at a time, wiping it immediately with a clean, dry piece of flannelette. Turn and/or replace both cloths as necessary for clean applications of solvents and polish. (Flannelette can be washed and re-used, although washing lessens its softness.) Make sure that the cloths are free of debris (e.g., wood or metal particles) that might scratch the guitar's surface. Cloths used for one cleaning or polishing operation should not be used for another (e.g., a cloth

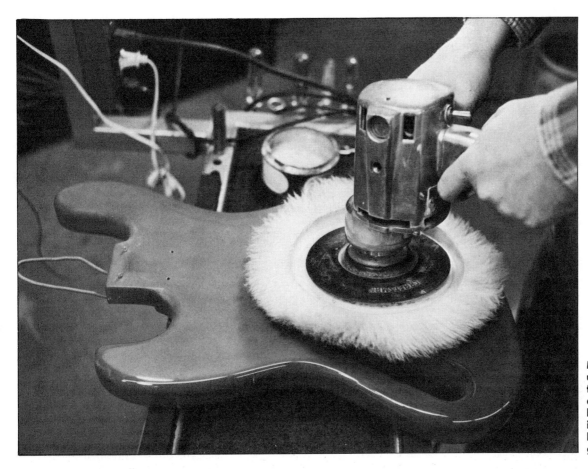

Manufacturers use various buffing compounds and waxes to bring their finishes up to a bright, reflective gloss.

used with cleaning compounds will contain abrasives that will interfere with subsequent polishing and waxing).

Testing solvents, cleaners, and polishes. Whatever the substance (water, chemical solvent, cleaning compound, wax, or polish), test it on a small section of the guitar before working over the entire surface. For example, you can choose a small spot adjacent to the heel of the neck to test whether there will be a reaction between the substance and the finish. With the vast majority of guitars it is highly unlikely that there will be any problem, but in the rare case where there is a reaction, using this approach will assure that the damage will be slight, particularly if you wipe off the substance immediately after application and confine your test to a very small area. Even if there is a reaction in the test spot, you may be able to disguise it to some extent by application of a wax or polish. The chances of a reaction are extremely remote, but it is easier to be cautious in the first place than to correct substantial damage in the rare instance when it does occur. It is particularly important to use this method of testing when you are treating French

polish, even when the correct solution is being used; more on this later.

Preliminary cleaning with damp and dry cloths. In most cases, some of the accumulated substances on the finished surface are water soluble, while others require a chemical solvent or cleaning compound. As a matter of procedure, it is best to clean carefully the surface with water first before using chemical solvents or compounds. One method: Slightly dampen a flannelette pad and clean the finish a small section at a time, wiping immediately with a dry cloth after each application. **Caution:** Do not use this method on French polish, since shellac reacts badly to water.

Cleaning lacquer and synthetic finishes with chemical solvents. After completing the steps just explained, repeat the procedure using an appropriate chemical solvent to dampen the flannelette pad. Work a small section at a time and clean it with a fresh, dry cloth as previously described. Be sure to remove all residues before moving on to the next section. For lacquer and synthetic finishes, "mineral spirits" paint thinner, available at hardware and

paint stores, is effective and safe. Another good solvent is xylene, which can be purchased from chemical suppliers and some pharmacies. This solvent is not as readily available as mineral spirits paint thinner, and it is highly toxic, even when absorbed through the skin. Nevertheless, it is an excellent solution for cleaning guitar finishes. (If you use xylene, avoid breathing the fumes or bringing the liquid into direct contact with your skin; wear rubber gloves and/or moisten only a small portion of the thick cloth pad.) **Caution:** Always use solvents sparingly and carefully. They may be applied to varnished surfaces, but extra care is advisable. Never use solvents on French polish.

Occasionally the application of a chemical solvent will result in a thin, hazy film on the surface of the guitar. This is usually due to oxidation or a wax residue that is resistant to the solvent. In such a case, the haze can be removed by application of cleaning compounds in accordance with the instructions in the following paragraph.

Removing oxides and abrasions from lacquered and synthetic finishes. In many cases, cleaning with

rubbing marks created by abrasives in the first application. The compound will always leave minute marks, but these should fill in when the polish or wax is applied. Nevertheless, use the compound sparingly and carefully, remembering that it removes a very thin layer of finish in order to expose fresh gloss. **Caution:** Once again, this method does not apply to French polish but may be used on varnish. Make sure all residues are removed before polishing and waxing. The use of a cleaning compound should be necessary no more than once every one or two years, depending on the guitar and its use. Exercise some restraint in deciding when to apply it. For example, only one section of the guitar may need this treatment; refrain from using the compound on all the surfaces merely as a matter of routine, and apply it only when necessary.

Waxing and polishing. Once the finish has been cleaned, gloss can be further restored and heightened with a high quality guitar or furniture polish. If possible, choose one containing carnauba (one of the hardest natural waxes); this will leave a strong shine that both enhances and protects the finish. Spray waxes and polishes are easy to apply, since you can spray a small amount directly onto the surface and polish with a flannelette cloth, but other liquid waxes and polishes are equally effective. Apply the polish sparingly, covering a small area at a time. Use fresh cloths for polishing and to remove all residues.

Recommended cleaning and polishing solution for shellac (French polish) finishes. The previously outlined methods for cleaning and polishing apply to modern lacquer and synthetic finishes; varnish may also be treated by the same means. (A good approach for handling a varnished surface might be first to try the solution for treating French polish; if that proves inadequate, then the lacquer/synthetics method can be employed.) The cleaning/polishing solution for French polish is inappropriate for use on lacquer or synthetics; its effect is to leave an oily residue even after you have dry-polished it with a clean cloth.

Caution: Even the correct solution can harm French polish if application is not properly carried out. Never apply the solution directly to the guitar (i.e., by pouring it onto the finish), and make certain that you shake the solution well immediately before each application to

water and chemical solvents will be sufficient to prepare the surface for final polishing or waxing. However, sometimes oxidation of the finish has dulled it to such an extent that wax or polish alone will not restore it to a high luster, or there may be minor abrasions that mar its appearance. After cleaning the entire finished surface of the instrument with water and solvent, you can determine the state of the finish. Oxidation or minor abrasions can be handled with a cleaning compound. (Note: Deep marks, dents, abrasions, or scratches cannot be removed in this manner. Such problems require expert attention—refinishing in most cases—and will not be covered here.) An excellent agent for

removing minor abrasions or oxides and restoring depth and luster is mild "car cleaner," a compound that contains both mild abrasives and polishing agents. Reputable brands are available at auto supply or hardware stores.

Place just a bit of compound on a flannelette pad and work it over the finish, covering a small area at a time and wiping immediately with a clean, dry flannelette cloth. Use small circular motions on solid colors; work with the grain where it is visible. The amount of pressure should be light to moderate, depending on the severity of the problem to be corrected. A second application of the compound, using a lighter pressure, has the effect of reducing the

Rubbing and polishing compounds and wax come in various consistencies.

the flannelette pad. This is critical, because the alcohol will harm the finish if applied in excessive concentration; by keeping the alcohol mixed thoroughly with the water and mineral oil, it is buffered; by applying the solution only with the cloth pad, the amount on the surface is kept to a minimum. Do a small area at a time, and dry-polish with a clean cloth immediately after initial application, removing all residues. With French polish, always follow the method previously described for testing solvents and polishes on a small section of the guitar. If there is excessive disturbance of the finish, reduce the amount of alcohol in the solution. Proceed with extreme care.

French polish is very thin and may wear through with time, requiring that the surface be repolished with the methods originally used. This should be done only by a qualified person, as it takes a great deal of practical experience and skill to do it correctly. In regard to maintaining the finish, use the cleaner/polish only when necessary. You can reduce the need for revitalizing the finish by keeping the guitar in its case, wiping it down with a clean flannelette cloth after playing, and avoiding exposure of the instrument to the elements. (These practices should be followed with all guitars, regardless of finish, but are particularly important with respect to French polish.)

Cleaning and polishing the unfinished fingerboard. Fingerboards with lacquer, varnish, or synthetic finishes should be cleaned and polished with the same methods described above for those categories. Unfinished fingerboards should *not* be cleaned and polished by those means, since raw wood requires special treatment and the avoidance of certain substances contained in polishes and cleaners.

Most unfinished fingerboards are made of rosewood or ebony. To clean the fingerboard (and to shine the frets simultaneously) use 0000-grade steel wool. This is the finest grade available; do not under any circumstances use a coarser grade such as 000. Work the steel wool across the fingerboard and frets, scrubbing perpendicularly to the length of the neck. Be careful that the steel wool touches only the surface of the fingerboard and not the headstock, the finished portion of the neck, or the body of the instrument.

On electric guitars, put masking tape across the tops of the pickups so that the iron particles from the steel wool will not attach to the magnetic polepieces (the particles may affect the functioning of the pickups). Once the fingerboard is cleaned, the natural oils from the hands will lightly polish it in the course of playing. In most cases this is all that is needed. However, if extra smoothness is desired, carnauba paste wax can be used on the fingerboard. Apply it in accordance with the directions provided with the product.

A caution against oils and silicone. Oils and silicone-containing polishes should never be applied to the fingerboard, because they may cause deterioration of the glue that laminates the fingerboard to the neck; furthermore, if oils or silicone seep under the adjoining finished surfaces, it may be impossible to refinish those areas in the future. Also, some organic oils will turn rancid, creating an unpleasant smell. In general, avoid putting oils or materials containing silicone on *any* part of your guitar, as they may work their way into the wood through breaks or cracks in the finished surfaces, making future refinishing difficult or impossible. When refinishing guitars, it is also advisable to avoid a hand-rubbed oil finish, since it does not adequately protect the wood and may reduce resonant quality. Always bear in mind that wood (even when it has a protective finish) is extremely sensitive and must be treated with the utmost care.

John Carruthers

5.
BUILDING
AND
CUSTOMIZING
YOUR OWN
GUITAR

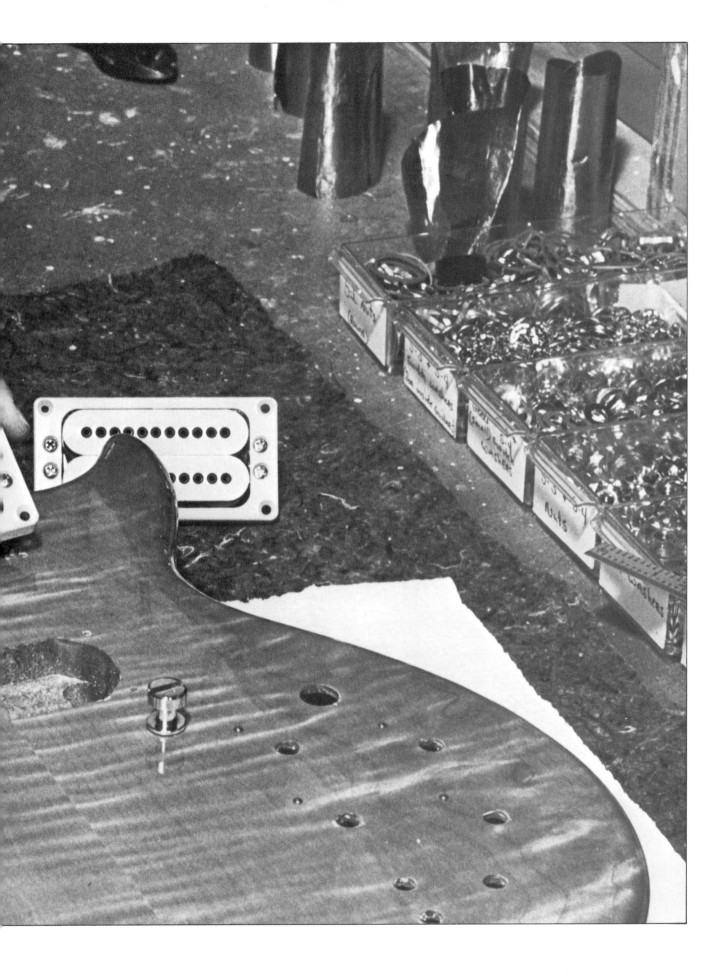

INTRODUCTION

Not everyone is content with a stock guitar, so the first section of this chapter gives an overview of do-it-yourself kits for the player who wants a custom job from the ground up. It covers everything from the selection of necks and bodies, to the pickups, bridges, and nuts—the components that bring the instrument to life. It also contains detailed discussions of weight, feel, cosmetic appearance, and sonic characteristics. Specific tips on installation of parts, sealing and finishing of the wood, and final tweaking are included. The next two portions of the chapter provide a cross section of the marketplace for hotrodding accessories of all types, and include tips from Eddie Van Halen and Pat Thrall, as well as repairmen who customize for a living. For the electronics-minded, the final two sections of the chapter, Understanding On-Board Preamps and Building An On-Board Pre-amp/EQ, explain how preamps are constructed and how they work. A do-it-yourself project shows how you can give your instrument a distinctive, powerful edge and open up a whole new range of tones.

BUILDING A KIT GUITAR

August-November 1982. Deep within the heart of many a player there lies a desire to create his or her own instrument. Sometimes this desire is for cosmetic reasons, while other times it is for functional aspects, or a combination of the two. Everyone has seen guitars that have been rewired, reshaped, carved or refinished either by the player or at his behest.

Enterprising individuals noticed this trend and decided to start manufacturing a large variety of guitar parts and subassemblies. This created a whole new market, while allowing the player easy access to the necessary supplies to fulfill his or her desires. These parts range from lookalikes and workalikes to the wild and bizarre, and everything in between. Some assemblies are interchangeable without modification to the instrument, while others require extensive modification.

Making a guitar and its associated components from scratch requires a great deal of knowledge, skill, and equipment. The aim of the kit guitar is to eliminate as many of these restrictions as possible while still allowing a suitable outcome. There are many kit manufacturers, and it is not an easy task to select which one or mixture of manufacturers will give you what you want. Still, there are certain guidelines to follow in the selection of the various components, regardless of manufacturer.

Basic considerations. Before we get into fine detail about the proper selection of components there are some overriding considerations we must first make. Is the cost of the kit guitar cheaper than buying one that is already assembled? You can save money by building a kit guitar, but in many cases players end up spending just as much as they would on a manufactured instrument, or more, because they don't consider all the cost factors in planning the project (such as outside assistance in completing the guitar, or correcting mistakes they have made during construction).

Is the cost of the kit guitar competitive with other kit guitars? It pays to shop around, but there are usually trade-offs between price and quality, and it is necessary to check carefully before investing in components. You can sometimes investigate them at a local music dealer, or perhaps you have friends who have used some of these kit parts. Many are available from guitar manufacturers or their dealer network as replacement parts.

You should take the time to closely examine the alternatives, and make an effort to determine which are the most functional for the cost. Are you planning to build a complete guitar or only to modify an existing one? Even if you only want to partially modify your guitar, kit supplies and the techniques described in this series can be invaluable. Even though the articles are directed toward building kit guitars, the subject matter applies to modifications and repairs of existing instruments. It is also very important to remember that parts on guitars have interrelated dimensions and functions, and you must consider this when making substitutions. Finally, does the manufacturer offer any warranties on its products?

Criteria for selection. There are certain fundamental issues that you should consider when planning a kit guitar or the selection of a replacement part or accessory. The following are some examples:

Type of wood. The type of wood you select affects weight, balance, resonance, sustain, resistance to climatic and temperature changes, and appearance. Although some hardwoods are very attractive, they may be too heavy for easy handling or lack the proper resonance for the sound you wish to achieve. Also, some woods are more difficult to tool than others, and this is significant, particularly if you do not have access to sophisticated wood- or metal-working equipment. It may be advisable for people who lack experience in this field to take extension courses in industrial arts to gain skills and also access to shop tools and guidance at minimal cost. You may want to also consult with a local repairman for additional guidance.

Interfacing various components. Even when you buy the components from a single manufacturer, quite often the tolerances of the various parts do not correspond well enough to allow assembly without modification. Under these circumstances, you can imagine the problems one might encounter when buying parts from multiple suppliers. When placing an order for components, determine whether or not they will be compatible with other parts. However, should you encounter tolerance problems, we will endeavor to explain how to solve these or work around them in the course of assembling your kit.

Functional aspect of hardware. It is also very important to ascertain whether or not the mechanical and electrical components measure up to your expectations. Not all tuning machines, bridges, pickups, and other such components are created equal. Once again, to the extent possible, try to get some hands-on evaluation experience with a particular line of components before you send away for parts. In regard to pickups, it is particularly important to make certain you will get the type of sound you want, without undesirable side effects, although you must remember that the sound involves the interplay of wood and electronics, not just the amplification of the strings.

These are just a few examples of the considerations involved in determining whether you should get involved in building a kit guitar, or modifying your guitar with kit parts, and—if so—making sure the kit or modifications come out as anticipated. The following are some of the issues that we'll cover: determining neck and body materials; body contours and routing for pickup assemblies, neck mounting, and controls; neck shape and width, fretting and fret dressing, headstock angle, tuning machine configuration, and truss-rod functionality; finishes and finishing procedures; electronics (switching controls, pickups, active and passive shielding) and layout; pickguards; criteria for evaluating tuning machines, bridges, and other hardware; techniques for proper assembly, including layout and modifications of kit parts to ensure optimum results; proper sequence of procedures; and some secrets for making these tasks both easier and more effective.

There are several important factors worth considering when selecting a guitar neck: strength, resonant characteristics, feel, weight, toolability, finishability, cosmetics, replication of vintage

models no longer available, etc. Obviously, you have to balance these factors, and how much weight you apply to any or all of them will depend largely on your own particular needs or values.

Strength. The neck has to withstand constant stress from both string tension and various applied forces during use or handling. There are a couple of considerations. If the neck has a truss rod, this may allow more flexibility in regard to selection, since the rod makes up for certain deficiences in woods. However, the rod rarely, if ever, extends into the headstock, and the most common break point on a neck is at the junction of the nut and headstock. Therefore, the wisest choice is a wood that is resistant to breakage or splitting. On the other hand, you must bear in mind that all the criteria are interrelated. For example, you may choose the strongest wood at the sacrifice of certain sound characteristics, since the neck has some effect on the overall sound.

Types of wood. The two most commonly used woods for guitar necks are maple and mahogany. Different varieties of maple and mahogany display different characteristics. The strongest maple is eastern rock maple. The climate in the Northeast produces a slow growth, resulting in a hard, dense wood. This variety is not always as cosmetically attractive as some others, but it can be relied on for its strength factors. (Though some varieties of maple may have more figure than others, they may not exhibit the characteristics that make for a strong neck.)

The mahogany family is comprised of an immense variety of types. In recent times the most popular for use on musical instruments has been Honduras mahogany. It has been favored for its fine, even grain and workability. However, the availability of quality Honduras has diminished, largely because of increasing expense and decreasing quality. This has resulted in increased usage of African and other mahoganies.

As a rule, rock maple is considerably stronger than most types of mahogany, and most kit guitars provide maple necks. Some kit makers offer necks made of exotic woods such as rosewood, which tend to be more cosmetically oriented rather than chosen for sound or functional reasons. In terms of strength, cost efficiency, and reasonable cosmetics and sound quality, maple is a good buy.

Grain structure. The type of wood is not, however, the only issue. Grain structure must also be considered. Basically, with a maple neck, the two most common selections for grain arrangement are either slab or quarter-sawn (see Fig. 1). Both of these cuts are strong, and are quite unlikely to twist or warp over the years. The most reliable way to determine the type of cut is to view the end of the cut (in the case of a neck, either the heel or the top of the headstock). Remember that the type of cut can change from one end of the piece to the other due to a twist or change in the grain structure, called run-out; the best pieces are those with minimal run-out.

Resonance. Resonant characteristics of neck materials are not nearly as important as those of body materials, but they do have a contributing effect to the overall sound. Necks with higher resonant factors are usually made of softer hardwoods, such as mahogany. The flexibility of softer woods tends to cause certain frequency ranges to be emphasized and others diminished. Harder woods tend to be more uniform in their response, because they don't contribute as much resonant quality to any one frequency. This, however, produces a somewhat thinner sound in terms of overall overtone reinforcement. Whether you desire a thinner or a resonant sound is a subjective matter. However, in most cases it is advisable to consider strength over resonant properties, since most of the instrument's resonant properties originate from the body.

Weight and feel. The denser a hardwood, the heavier it will be, and one must keep in mind the balance relationship between the body and the neck. Also, when you combine the neck with the body, the overall weight can contribute either to player fatigue or comfort. Also, hardwoods have grain structures that vary in fineness or coarseness. This will be most noticeable in regard to fingerboard texture. Assuming the back of the neck is properly finished, the only significant difference in feel among neck woods would be evident in the fingerboard texture. Fingerboard woods such as ebony exhibit a very fine texture, while coarser-grained woods like rosewood have the opposite characteristic. Again, how important these differences are is a matter of personal conjecture.

Toolability. Some woods have characteristics that allow them to be machined more easily than other types. While necks supplied with kits are already pre-shaped, the more adventuresome, and skilled, builder may wish to further modify the neck. If so, there are several factors to be considered: the denseness of the material, its soil or wax content, and its figure. Some unusual woods, such as lignum vitae, are so dense that they cannot be machined with ordinary woodworking tools. Conversely, mahogany and unfigured maple, the most commonly used neck woods, are very easily tooled. Most figured woods, although attractive, tend to be very difficult to work, and may require special techniques and tooling. Teak and some types of rosewoods, to give just two examples, have such a high oil and wax content that they are difficult to shape and smooth, as they load up the sandpaper or other abrasive mediums. They also tend to create finishing problems because the finishing material often does not adhere effectively to the oily or waxy surface.

Cosmetics and replication. There are many hardwoods that, because of their attractiveness alone, are offered by kit manufacturers. Some of these, however, pose problems in regard to finishing. Extremely coarse-grained structures present major obstacles to achieving a smooth, gloss finish. Also, in certain cases where a player has decided to duplicate a vintage instrument that no longer is available, the wood selection may be based on the woods used in the original instrument. Most of these early instruments used fairly conventional woods that should not be too difficult to acquire.

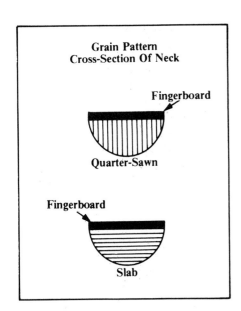

**Grain Pattern
Cross-Section Of Neck**

Fingerboard

Quarter-Sawn

Fingerboard

Slab

Always check tuners for backlash and sloppy movement; also make sure they fit the headstock of your guitar.

January 1983. After discussing sizing up and choosing neck materials, let's forge ahead now into body materials—we'll discover many similar issues involved. As with necks, *you* have to be the ultimate judge of the "best" materials, letting your goals determine which qualities are of foremost importance.

Remember that these discussions on materials are not yet concerned with procedures for crafting, dimensions, interfacing, or finishing. We'll deal with these critical areas later. This cautionary note: Wait until you understand your materials before buying so much as a bridge saddle, and save yourself many an aspirin dose tomorrow. Going ahead without a grasp of the glitches latent in kit guitars can be disastrous! But with reasonable care and attention, the project can prove most rewarding. Now, the factors you should consider.

Strength. As a rule, nearly all woods commonly used for solidbody kit guitars are equal to the task. The requirements for neck strength are considerably more important than those for the body.

Type of wood. Probably the two most common woods used for kits are ash and alder. These woods, each of which varies in weight, grain, and resonance, are used primarily for their moderate cost, long acceptance by well-respected manufacturers, and relative ease of tooling. Many other woods are suitable, including such exotics as zebrawood, rosewood, and teak, or the more conventional hardwoods such as maple or mahogany.

While manufacturers do offer the alternative woods, you should consider some of the problems you may encounter, such as difficult tooling, oily or waxy characteristics that can interfere with certain types of finishing, and excessive weight. But over the years players have consistently shown an overwhelming preference for alder or southern ash. When questioned as to why they favor these materials, they generally cite the weight and resonant quality of these woods. This latter characteristic is of particular importance in duplicating the sounds of certain vintage instruments without enduring the financial hardships that result from buying an original.

Whenever acquiring a kit guitar body, you should make sure that the wood was at least kiln-dried, if not naturally seasoned over a long period of time. You are essentially forced to take your supplier's word in this matter, so deal with a reputable company.

Laminations. Many of these woods do not grow large enough to provide a single-piece body, thus bodies are frequently laminated. Ideally, some care has been exercised in the selection of the pieces to be joined, with an eye toward an aesthetically pleasing result. But many people have complained of mismatched or poorly proportioned bodies—for example, a three-piece body whose thirds are not equal. This may be of no concern if you are going to paint the guitar with an opaque finish. However, some makers will laminate several kinds of wood in the same body, and this may cause finishing problems (due to uneven coefficients of expansion and contraction and/or different finish absorption qualities).

Resonant quality. Body material will make a significant difference in how the guitar sounds. Lighter, more resonant woods make for a fuller, richer sound, while heavier woods tend to produce a thinner sound with fewer overtones. Sustain may vary with wood weight, too, but not as much as resonant quality. Sustain is a difficult matter to generalize about because there are so many characteristics that contribute to it. Therefore, your chief concern should be with finding the kind of resonant quality you prefer.

Weight and Feel. Weight and feel of the guitar may either enhance or detract from your enjoyment in playing, and balance is a related matter that must also be given close attention. Excessive weight or a lopsided distribution can result in fatigue, discomfort, or other limitations on playing. When determining the highly important balance between neck and body, allow for the addition of hardware and electronics. Generally speaking, a lighter body will be more comfortable—not only in terms of total weight, but also because the body, hardware, and electronics will add up to counterbalance the neck and tuning machines.

Many hardwoods are offered by kit manufacturers especially for their attractiveness. A few were mentioned above. Unfortunately, some pose finishing problems because their coarse-grain structures present major obstacles to achieving a smooth, high-gloss finish. Others, as we mentioned, have excess natural oils or waxes that may interfere with the adhesion of finishing materials. More conventional woods will avoid these problems and at the same time achieve excellent replications of vintage instruments either too costly for the average budget, or simply no longer available. Even if you are not trying to duplicate a particular vintage instrument, the conventional woods have significant advantages in price, weight, balance, finishing, and resonance.

Toolability. As with neck woods, different body woods may either enhance or complicate tooling. In general, ash and alder are fairly easy to work, while some of the more exotic woods may, in some cases, create special problems, again, because of such characteristics as high density, oils and waxes, or complex grain. Since the kit body normally comes precut, including pickup cavities and so forth, this may present no obstacle. Still, complications could arise if you are planning to sand the body or perform modifications such as relocating the pickup cavities. Of course, this will also depend on how experienced you are and what kind of equipment you have available.

November 1982. Tuning machines come in various shapes and sizes, but perhaps the most obvious and immediate consideration is whether you want a tuner plated with gold or chrome. The decision may involve the bridge and the jack plate as well, since many players desire matching cosmetics among all components. Although a matter of personal taste, remember that chrome outwears gold by at least a factor of ten to one.

More important than cosmetics is the tuning machines' gear ratio. Machines vary in ratio from 9:1 to 25:1; the higher the ratio, the more sensitive the response. Also, for easier, more sensitive tuning, it is important to get a machine that is relatively free of *backlash*.

It is a simple matter to test either of these factors. In order to test gear ratio, draw a line on a piece of masking tape and stick it on top of the machine capstan; then count the number of times you must turn the knob to rotate the capstan 360 degrees. If you have to turn the knob 15 times to rotate the capstan once around, then the gear ratio is 15:1, and so on.

The backlash test must be done with the machine on the guitar and under load from the string; backlash is the amount of free play when you tighten or loosen the machine—in other words, the "transition" between the tightening and the loosening. Backlash is undesirable because it interferes with accurate tuning.

Another consideration is knob size and mounting. On certain headstocks with space limitations, such as six-on-a-

side (in-line) designs, the use of smaller knobs is of great benefit. On three-on-a-side designs, space limitation is rarely a problem. It is not advisable to use machines designed for three-on-a-side headstocks on six-on-a-side guitars since they tend to overlap and get in the way.

Bridge hardware. Bridges come in a variety of designs, and with several combinations of features. Considera-

Top: Strap buttons and string tree components. Middle: Strat and Tele bridges and studs, stop tailpiece, tune-o-matic, and mounts. Bottom: Various types of jack holders.

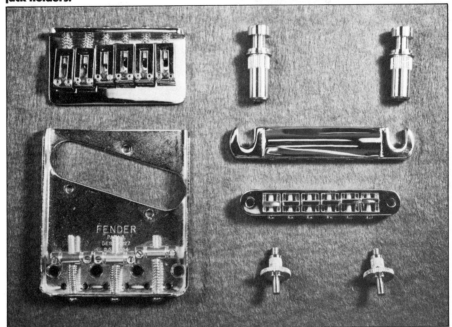

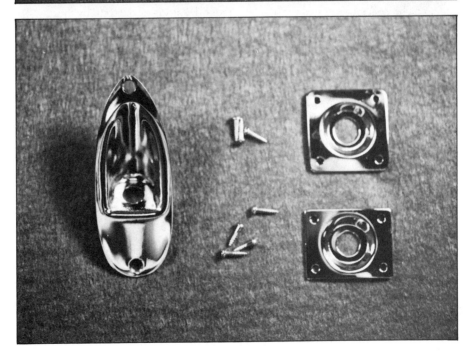

String trees (retainers). On guitars with shallow headstock angles, it is usually necessary to use headstock-mounted string trees to achieve sufficient downward string tension across the nut slots; this provides clearly defined tone when strings are played open. String trees will be covered later, since their choice can only be properly determined during final assembly stages. For example, some guitars with steep headstock angles (seven or eight degrees) do not require retainers, while others with shallow angles (one or two degrees) may need all six strings pinioned. Protruding capstans can also reduce the downward angle of strings. It's advisable to wait before ordering these items; but if you are determined to order ahead it's possible to approximate by comparing your kit to its commercially available counterpart. tions include: combination bridge/tailpiece vs. separate bridge and tailpiece; string height and/or string length adjustments for all six strings vs. individual adjustments for each string; tremolo vs. nontremolo; and front string loading vs. rear loading.

Probably the most functional design has six string saddles, independently adjustable both vertically and horizontally. This allows complete control for conforming the bridge to the fingerboard curvature, while also providing for individual intonation of strings.

Strap buttons. Recently there has been a proliferation of strap buttons and strap button locking release devices. Several factors should be considered in making a choice. Conventional strap buttons are the least expensive. For convenience, reliability, or quick changes of instruments, these newer locking/release devices have distinct advantages over their old counterparts. However, be sure that the brand you choose has a reputation for reliability among other players. Earlier versions have been known to break free unexpectedly during playing, causing damage to guitars.

January 1983. Since the number and size of the various pickups, controls, and switches will determine the cutouts in both the body and pickguard, it's very important to preselect all electronic parts and related components. Many manufacturers offer stock configurations based on well-known commercial design, but you may have a different arrangement in mind. If so, options are often available, and some companies will even do a custom body or pick-

guard design, perhaps at additional cost.

Suppose you build a Strat-type guitar, but instead of the standard three single-coil pickups you'd rather have two humbucking pickups. If you require a separate volume and tone control for each pickup, a careful layout of controls will avoid complicating the electronics. Occasionally, when your concept is very unusual or radical, you may have to make the body modifications and custom build the pickguard yourself. When purchasing electronic components, many people have learned the hard way that lack of careful forethought can result in unanticipated headaches. Paying attention to the following details can save you a lot of grief and additional expense.

Excess magnetism. Choosing pickups with excess magnetism is one of the most common errors with kit guitars and pickup replacements in general. In the quest for more power, some manufacturers have greatly increased the amount of magnetism in their pickups. But this approach involves a tradeoff: beyond a certain threshold, increased magnetism has negative side effects, including reduced sustain, buzzing, and intonation problems. These adverse effects are aggravated by the degree of excess magnetism, number of pickups, and their placement.

Sustain. An excessively powerful magnetic field will tend to draw the string to rest, rather than allowing it to vibrate freely. You may get a loud attack, but that advantage is undercut by the limited sustain.

Fret buzzing. A more obvious effect of excessive magnetism is abnormal fret buzzing, which may even occur on a guitar with a properly aligned neck. This buzzing can occur over the entire playing range, becoming worse as you play higher on the neck, since this brings the string nearer to the pickup. An easy way to diagnose this problem is to raise and lower the pickups, comparing the degree of buzzing at the high and low settings. In some cases the pickup(s) will have to be replaced because the magnets are so powerful that even the lowest setting won't provide enough compensation.

Intonation. Another ill effect of excess magnetic pull on the string is a wavering of pitch that makes it extremely difficult to play in tune. Sometimes, when the pickup is located very close to the bridge, this effect may be rather insignificant.

Polepiece alignment. Make sure that the polepiece spacing on your pickups corresponds directly to the string spacing. Because strings diverge as you move toward the bridge, the alignment of polepieces and strings will vary, depending on where you locate the pickup. Some slight misalignment is all right, but too much will noticeably decrease the gain in the affected strings. The first and sixth strings are the most frequent trouble spots since there are fewer neighboring polepieces to help pick up the signal that might otherwise be lost.

Phase alignment problems can occur when two or more pickups are used simultaneously. Basically, two factors are involved: magnetic polarity (north or south), and the direction of coil windings. When the polarities of pickups in simultaneous use are mismatched, certain frequencies are cancelled with significant loss of volume. The resulting sound is commonly called ''thin.'' In some cases an out-of-phase tonal effect is desirable, but this is usually controlled by a polarity reversal switch so that the player may return to the normal, in-phase mode at will.

Buying pickups that allow you to change the phase (either by reversing output leads or, with some pickups, by reversing the magnet position) may prove convenient, since there is no standard phasing of pickups. In general, units made by the same manufacturer have the same phase relationships. If you encounter a recalcitrant phase problem, don't go into the pickup yourself, since this may cause irreparable damage. A qualified repairman will usually be able to change the phasing for you.

Switching functions. Many different tonal combinations are possible with two or more pickups. Your switching should allow you to use each pickup individually or to combine them in various ways in order to obtain the maximum range in tonal color. You may have to use more than one switch. For example, in a Strat-type configuration a single five-way switch allows you to use each pickup individually, mix the lead and middle pickup, or mix the rhythm and middle pickup. But what if you also wish to combine rhythm and lead, or put all three pickups on simultaneously? Access to all these combinations is most easily accomplished by using three miniature toggle switches. There are, of course, other possibilities. For example, if someone were to use three *three-*posi-

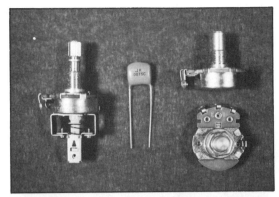
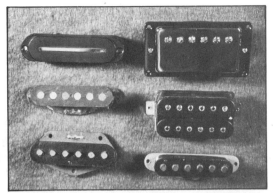

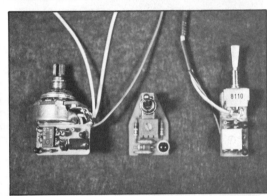
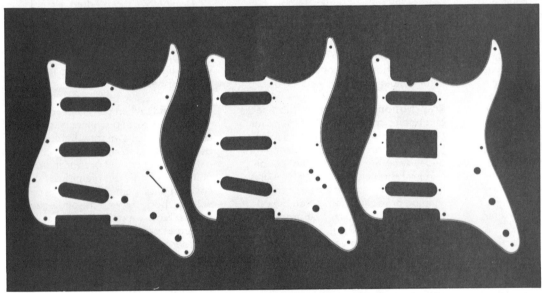

Clockwise from top left: Pots for volume and tone controls (the capacitor in the middle is a vital component in the tone circuit); single-coil pickups (left, bottom right) are bright and clear, while humbuckers offer better midrange; three onboard preamps; pickup selector switches. Three versions of Strat-style pickguards cut for (left) a blade switch, (center) miniature toggle switches, and (right) a humbucking pickup.

tion (on-off-on) switches with center-off (double-pole, triple-throw, or DPTT) for a Strat setup, this would provide in-phase and out-of-phase, as well as off—the maximum number of combinations for a Strat-type configuration. Note that these switching decisions affect the choice of a pickguard. (In our Strat example you would need three 1/4″ switch-mounting holes instead of a knife-switch slot.)

Location of components. Controls and pickups sometimes interfere with play-ability, depending on the individual's style. For example, an inadvertent bump into the volume control or certain switches when playing might well cause some undesired changes. Obviously, there are fewer options when locating pickups because of the limited available space and the need to achieve optimum tonal range. But switches and pots (potentiometers) lend themselves more easily to relocation. Standard pick-guards allow some range of choice as to control location, and the number and type of pickups.

Onboard electronics. Onboard electronics (preamps, equalizers, compressors, etc.) are very popular, and some electronically oriented players even design and build their own. Since many units are commercially available, certain criteria should be kept in mind when choosing—functionality (is the effect significant?), signal-to-noise ratio, size, power requirements/battery life, and access for battery replacement. Also remember that such accessories usually require additional controls and more space in the guitar body.

February 1983. Using the guidelines given in previous articles, we've selected all the components for our kit guitar—wood pieces, electronic and mechanical parts—and now we're ready to begin putting it all together. The first step is to prepare the body and neck for joining. For demonstration purposes we'll be using an alderwood body with a stock pickup configuration, and a Strat-style neck with a rosewood fingerboard already fretted by the manufacturer. The body and neck are both unfinished, so we can provide pointers on every phase of the operation.

Preliminary checkup. Avoid problems and wasting time later on by checking all fits and alignments between the neck, the body, and the other components *before* doing any finishing work. The alignment between the neck and body is a primary concern. First, make sure that the neck will fit into the body—in many cases the heel of the neck turns out to be wider or narrower than the neck pocket. If the neck is too wide, the pocket must be enlarged. This is a critical adjustment since it will eventually affect the way the strings align with the pickups and the fingerboard.

To handle this particular problem, simply establish the centerline separately on the body and the neck, then align them both with a straightedge before joining. The body's centerline connects the center of the neck pocket and the center of the bridge location. Carefully measure the neck pocket to find its centerline; the bridge location on most Strat-style bodies is predrilled and this usually provides an accurate reference point. In other cases, it may be necessary to use a line bisecting the lead pickup cavity as your other reference point.

Once you've established the centerline of the body, do the same for the neck by drawing a line from the center of the nut to the center of the heel. (On finished fingerboards, place masking tape over the heel section of the board and draw the line on the tape.)

Aligning the neck. Now set the neck in its slot, and use a straightedge to guide you as you link the centerlines of the body and neck. (It may be helpful to enlist the aid of another person to ensure stability.) Once the point of perfect alignment has been found, trace the

Unfinished guitar neck with rosewood fingerboard (frets installed by the manufacturer).

outside edges of the neck heel with a sharp pencil in order to determine what part of the neck pocket must be removed.

Shaping the neck pocket can be done with a chisel, router, or milling machine. Regardless of the method, exercise the utmost care to ensure that you remove no more material than the exact amount required. It pays to check as you go along, taking out just a little at a time. Remember, it's much easier to remove wood than it is to replace it!

Oversized neck pocket. If the pocket is slightly larger than the heel, finishing coats applied to the neck, body, or both may take up the slack. But if it is obvious that finishing will not close the gap, you can bond a wood strip to either or both sides of the pocket, using the same type of wood used for the body. Centering considerations outlined earlier apply as you decide how much wood to use and whether to put it on both sides. If the body is already finished, or you lack the proper tools and skills for adding these strips, unfixed side shims may also be used at the time of final assembly. (This technique will be treated in more detail in a future article.) Whatever the method, the essential thing is to have a tight fit between the neck and the heel pocket so that tuning and string alignment remain stable.

Preparations for finishing. Most necks and bodies come from the kit supplier either unfinished or with just a sealer on them. Many are inadequately sanded, and leaving the surface in that condition invites an unsatisfactory final finish. If the wood is relatively free of deep sanding or tooling marks, you may start working it with a fairly fine grade sandpaper, such as 220 grit. But if marks are visible, start with a coarse sandpaper, such as 120, then work down to a finer grade.

Sanding techniques. There are certain rules you should follow in sanding:

When doing large, flat surfaces, use a block and always sand *with* the grain. This helps avoid creating high and low

areas that may interfere with finishing and mar the instrument's appearance. Wood grain consists of hard ridges with pulpy soft material in between, and sanding without a block tends to remove a disproportionate amount of material from the soft areas, especially with the coarser-grained woods.

There are various types of power sanders available, but the most useful are the medium-sized, high-speed orbital sanders. A very small orbital pattern is best for avoiding sander marks, and some of the newer models leave virtually no trace at all.

When sanding over areas where there are cutouts or cavities, use scrap wood inserts to prevent the sander from rounding off the surrounding edges. Just make sure that the top surface of the filler insert is flush with the rim of the cavity.

When sanding around the area where the neck joins the body, be careful not to undercut the body beyond the width of the neck heel. (Insert the neck into the heel pocket periodically, and draw guidelines to monitor your progress.)

Don't leave sharp edges, except along the edge of the neck pocket. Sharp edges do not take finish well, and will cause rub-throughs during final finishing procedures. To soften an edge, sand it lightly—just enough to relieve the sharpness.

April 1983. When you build your own guitar you are, in a manner of speaking, captain of your own fate. But fate can be tricky—and so can finishing chemicals. Without careful preparation, your guitar may come out blemished. We've covered alignment and fit of the neck with the body, as well as sanding techniques. Now we go into some further steps and precautions you should take in order to ensure that the final coats of finish will be smooth and durable.

Sealing the screw and mounting holes. Do this with a small amount of wood filler after sanding is completed. Sealing the holes will prevent the absorption of water or solvents by the end grain, which could eventually cause

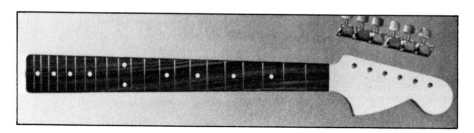

the neighboring finish to lift or crack. (The filler can easily be removed following application of the finish.)

Grain fillers. There will be some shrinkage of the finishing coats as volatiles evaporate during drying and aging. This shrinkage can leave unsightly grain patterns. The antidote: grain fillers, which provide a smooth, flat surface for finishing and inhibit absorption of the finish into the wood grain. (Grain fillers are usually unnecessary for very close-grained woods—maple or alder, for example—but they are a good idea on coarser-grained woods such as ash, rosewood, and mahogany.)

Grain fillers are usually made up of solids—such as pigmented cellulose—suspended in a volatile solvent. With a variety of colors and tints to choose from, you will want to select the one that best suits the type of wood and finish you are using. As a rule of thumb, either closely matching or darker fillers are best: If you want to highlight the grain, the filler should be darker than the wood. Where to buy? Grain fillers are used primarily by professional wood and furniture finishers, and are generally available from companies that cater to these industries.

Filler application. Since fillers tend to settle out while sitting on the shelf, they should be thoroughly mixed before using. Occasionally, more solvent will have to be added to the mixture in order to provide the correct consistency. (Follow instructions on the container—in most cases the filler should have a paste-like consistency.) Be sure to blow out all sanding residues with a compressed air jet before applying the filler. Application is usually accomplished with a cloth, wiping across the grain in circular strokes. This forces the filler into the open pores. The residue should be taken off with a fresh cloth.

Always follow the manufacturer's drying instructions, as applying the final finish too soon may cause problems—solvents may be incompatible, or shrinkage of the filler may draw the finish into the grain. Even if your final finish is opaque, it is still advisable to use a filler, since grain marks will show through opaque as well as transparent finishes. After the filler has been applied and allowed to dry, you may wish to lightly resand the guitar with 220-grade sandpaper to further highlight the grain. Filler is usually applied before any stain.

Stains. There are basically two methods of applying stain to the wood: rubbing and spraying. Oil-based stains can be rubbed directly on the wood with a soft cloth—a method with both advantages and disadvantages. On the plus side, it doesn't require expensive spray equipment, yet it gives an even result, free of lap marks (areas where multiple strokes have resulted in a buildup of color). Oil-based stain goes on evenly because it is *absorbed* into the wood, rather than *adhering* to it in a film (the principle behind spray lacquers). The wood can only absorb so much—the rest is wiped away, resulting in a uniform coat, though it will be darker on end grain. On the negative side, oil-based stains have a longer drying time, their darkness is difficult to adjust (due to their dependence on the wood's absorptive powers), and they are slightly more opaque than the alternatives.

Spray-on stains are usually made by mixing some stain or staining pigment with a finishing material, such as lacquer. (Not all stains and finishes are compatible, so be sure to follow the manufacturer's recommendations and instructions.) This method has certain advantages: no disproportionate absorption on the end grain, plus possibilities for subtle shading and highlights through overcoating and concentrating the lacquer. Also, by means of subtle tinting, it is possible to simulate aging effects. All this presumes a good spray technique, with quality spray equipment a necessity. In order to avoid runs or beading, always allow the coats to dry thoroughly between applications.

Sealers. After the body has been properly sanded and filled, the next step is applying the sealer. Sealers provide a smooth, flat surface for the final top coats and fall into two basic categories: lacquer base and synthetic resins. Lacquer-based sealers have a higher volume of solids and should be thoroughly mixed prior to each usage. Extra solids cause the coats to build faster due to reduced absorption, and they allow easier block sanding.

Synthetic sealers (polyurethane, epoxy, or polyester are the most common types) usually come in the form of resin and catalyst, which are mixed together just prior to application. The resin sets and cures as a result of chemical reaction, rather than the evaporation of volatiles. Advantages: builds finish thickness very quickly, and dries and reaches maximum hardness in a minimal amount of time with little shrinkage. Disadvantages: tends to reduce reso-

ant quality of the instrument (especially important with acoustic or semi-acoustic instruments); more difficult to sand flat; not as transparent as lacquer finishes; extremely hazardous to one's health, with special precautions to minimize inhalation required.

Sealer application. It is advisable to follow the manufacturer's label instructions. Most sealers are applied using spray equipment, following normal spray procedures. Since the sealer will be sanded out before final coats are applied, a flawless application is not crucial.

May 1983. We've looked at filling, staining, and sealing your kit guitar's body and neck, and now we'll discuss the fine art of wielding a spray gun—it's not as simple as it looks.

Spray equipment is necessary for applying both the sealer and the top coat. The results should be excellent as long as you keep an eye on the four major variables: viscosity, air pressure, volume, and fan.

Viscosity essentially means thickness, or resistance to flow. Most spray equipment is designed to spray liquids of a certain viscosity, so be sure that your finishing product and your equipment are compatible.

In order to function properly, most spray guns require a certain amount of *air pressure*, typically specified in cubic feet per minute, or *cfm*. The cfm rating is usually given as a maximum, although your operating pressure may be lower, depending on the interrelationship of *volume* (the rate at which atomized fluid is blown from the gun), *fan* (the width of the spray jet), and viscosity. You can find the optimum pressure through experimentation.

Spray gun adjustments. On most spray guns there are two settings—one for volume, one for fan width. When set properly, the volume allows a smooth, even coat, free of runs. If runs appear, just turn down the volume. The fan control is set according to the size of the object being sprayed. For example, a narrow target requires a narrow fan. Wasteful overspray results when the fan is too wide (overspray is a term for atomized material that misses the target).

General precautions. Spray equipment must not be contaminated with oil or water. In order to prevent this, a device called a *trap* is usually installed between the compressor and the spray gun. Traps typically employ centrifugal force or a dessicant (drying agent) such as silica gel to catch or vent off contaminants.

It is also very important to spray at temperatures above 70° Farenheit and in conditions of low relative humidity. Too much humidity in the air causes a problem known as *blushing,* in which a normally transparent finish becomes clouded with a whitish hue. This results from condensation of moisture due to the cooling effect of rapidly evaporating solvents. Some manufacturers offer finish additives that slow down the rate of evaporation, thereby eliminating the blushing effect.

Excess temperatures are also to be avoided. Too much heat may speed up evaporation and cause blushing. Heat may also dry the finish before it has a chance to flow out, resulting in an ''orange peel'' effect. Again, additives are available to modify the drying time, thus eliminating flow-out and blushing problems.

Filtering. The finishing material and solvents should be poured through a filter before useage in order to remove any particles that may pass through the spray gun and lodge in the coat, mar-ring the overall results. Filters are usually available from finishing materials suppliers.

Spray techniques. It is very important to maintain a set distance from the object you are spraying. Depending on your fan and volume adjustments, you should establish a spraying distance of between 8" and 14". Initiate each stroke at either the right or left of the subject by pulling the trigger. Then, while maintaining your distance, direct the gun evenly across the target area. After you've passed the outer edge of the subject, release the trigger to end the stroke. For the next stroke, repeat the process in the opposite direction. As you move down, slightly overlap each sweep so that no area is missed.

Corners and edges, as a rule, tend not to take finish as well as flat surfaces. For example, the sides of a solidbody guitar—particularly on the lower bouts—never seem to get as much finish as the surfaces of the front and back. This is partly due to the higher absorbency of the end grain, and also partly because of the wide spray pattern normally used to cover the top and back surfaces. A wide spray pattern simply deposits the finishing materials in smaller concentrations. The best remedy consists of prolonging the stroke over these areas and adding extra coats. Extra coats should be done immediately after the initial one so that the finish merges properly with adjoining areas.

Practice spraying. Spraying appears to be fairly easy, but proficiency requires a great deal of practice. If you are new at the craft, you may want to practice on a piece of scrap wood (or even cardboard) similar in size to the item you plan to finish. Look closely at the practice subject to see whether you are getting runs, orange peel, the proper amount of overlap, etc.

Spray bombs. Most spray bombs (cans of spray paint) have an excess amount of plasticizers to make their application easier. This results in a finish whose hardness never comes up to that of a conventionally formulated mixture applied with professional equipment. Spray bomb finishes are also difficult to overcoat. The subsequent coats often react with the previous ones, producing a variety of problems such as an ''alligator skin'' or ''parched earth'' effect, lifting of the finish, crackling, or permanent softness. In general, very few spray bombs are suitable for finishing

Binks Model 69 spray gun, ideal for application of sealer and finish.

guitars. The best ones are those made for touch-up jobs by companies that produce finishing materials for professional spray work. You may choose to use spray bombs if—for economic or practical reasons—you can't gain access to professional spray equipment. But if you intend to go this route, be aware of the problems.

Tacking. Suppliers of finishing materials usually carry *tack rags* for the removal of dust and other contaminants from the surface of the wood to be sprayed. Use the rag (usually cheesecloth or a similar material impregnated with a sticky substance) to wipe the surface of the target immediately before you apply the finishing material. It is also advisable to do this between coats *after* the finish has fully dried.

July 1983. Spray-gunners (and others): Many of you have been following our epic saga of kit guitar construction for a long time—most recently through a discussion of methods of surface preparation and basic spray technique. Those of you whose trigger fingers are getting itchy will be pleased to learn that this episode concerns the applied practice of finishing: putting on the layers of sealer and topcoat, and what to do in between.

Left: The kit builder must be careful to avoid overzealous use of the block sander; rub-throughs are difficult to correct. Below: Always use spray equipment in a well-ventilated area.

Application of sealer coats. Sealers are basically a colloidal suspension; that is, they consist of a large amount of microscopic solid material dispersed in a liquid medium. The solids fill the grain, but you must agitate the spray canister periodically to keep them in suspension. Because of the high concentration of solids in sealers, it is generally easy to sand between coats. The number of coats will vary according to the porosity of the wood, but from five to eight will usually suffice to form a suitable foundation for the topcoats.

Sanding techniques. Use a block sander to avoid creating low spots or other irregularities on the large, flat surfaces of the guitar body. Between sealer coats, 400-grit wet-or-dry sandpaper is usually best. For final coats, 600-grit is preferable because it leaves finer sanding marks, which makes buffing and polishing easier. Coarser paper is used on sealer coats because they are not buffed out. You can save sanding time by using a coarser grade, and the sanding marks left by the 400-grit will not interfere with the appearance of the topcoats. Regularly immerse the sandpaper in sanding solvents such as water (mixed with soap) or mineral spirits. This will prevent the paper from loading up, speed up the sanding process, and prolong the life of the sandpaper.

To promote surface leveling, move the block in diagonal or circular motions across the grain. Don't use the block on curved surfaces; fold the sandpaper in half to provide a natural gripping surface for your fingers. If there are any hints of coloration under the sealer, be extremely careful not to sand through to them; the resulting damage would be difficult to undo. When there is any question of this happening, be sure to wipe off the sanding solvent periodically and check your work. Sanding solvent may mask the presence of a rub-through.

Rub-throughs. The precaution of wiping off the sanding solvent and checking your work periodically applies not only to sealer coats, but also to final coats. An accidental rub-through to the sealer, the coloration, or to the wood itself are all possible. Any of these mishaps are extremely difficult to touch up without noticeable and undesirable scars and blemishes. For example, if you rub through to the sealer, that section will not attain the same gloss as the topcoat on final buffing. Rub-throughs of color or down to the wood itself not only cause lustre problems; they create discolorations. The least critical rub-through is from topcoat to sealer, since no color variance results, and the finish can be restored with additional topcoats.

Topcoats. After you have completely sealed and sanded out the body, the final topcoats may be applied. The full treatment normally requires eight to ten coats. Although you should always apply finishes sparingly to avoid runs, it is *particularly* important to do this on topcoats. Volatiles do not evaporate as quickly in areas where the finish is thicker—a run is a case in point. This results in hardness variations that interfere with uniform leveling by the block sander. Follow the spray instructions from the last article and remember: Never stay in one spot for too long, as this invariably results in runs. Again, use 600-grit instead of 400 for sanding. Also, it's a good idea to tack rag any dust or residues from the surface between coats and after sanding.

John Carruthers

GUITAR KITS AND REPLACEMENT PARTS

March 1980. Five years ago players had little indication that one day they would be able to pick up a phone, make a call or two, and order the electric guitar of their dreams—whether it be a near-exact copy of a vintage Fender Strat, or a cocobolo neck and a custom zebra-wood body decked out with gold-plated tuners, a brass/bone nut, jumbo frets, a mirror pickguard, Les Paul, Telecaster, and Charlie Christian pickups with matching mounting rings, an assortment of switches and speed knobs, a vibrato tailpiece, an anodized aluminum jackplate, and a Straplock button. Recent ads hint that a do-it-yourself electric guitar kits and replacement parts industry was beginning to spring to life: Charvel's Electronics announced an unbreakable jack holder for $2.50, and the Rowe-DeArmond company offered a humbucking pickup for thin-

body, f-hole, and solidbody guitars. Those were still the days when the most common cliches around repair shops were, "Gee, I could fix your guitar if I could just find the part," and "Yeah, we can do that, but it's custom—I gotta make it by hand."

Today the choices in over-the-counter replacement parts and do-it-yourself kits are staggering, as more than 30 companies compete to cater to your instrumental needs. Manufacturers advertise not only exotic necks to stroke, clear pickguards, black chrome hardware, bridges of steel and brass, pickups that will "blast your rocks off," and potentiometers with built-in boosters that are guaranteed to "blast you into the '80s with low-impedance output and revitalized highs," but also such intricacies as tapped pickup assemblies (available in several custom colors, with

drop-in installation) that offer you 21 different tonal combinations. For those who'd rather do it themselves, two companies feature kits, one of which will give you everything you need to build your own Strat-style guitar for $169.00 suggested retail—no wood-working or electronic skills required.

What does all this mean? Basically, anything that you can unscrew, unbolt, or yank off an electric guitar or bass can be replaced with a custom part, and the time for cloning your favorite instrument—or anyone else's—is at hand. Although major guitar manufacturers such as Fender, Gibson, Guild, and Ibanez offer parts and accessories, we'll examine the independent manufacturers who have made replacement parts and kits available to the general public. First we'll consider some of the pros and cons of doing it yourself and take a look at the companies offering guitar kits or nearly complete lines of bodies, necks, pickups, hardware, and accessories—the one-stop shops of the replacement parts world—as well as a couple of body and neck carvers. An upcoming second installment will deal with the specialists—companies offering pickups, bridges, pickguards, machines, pots and electronics, or brass parts.

The motivation behind the desire to build or customize an instrument are many, but perhaps more than anything

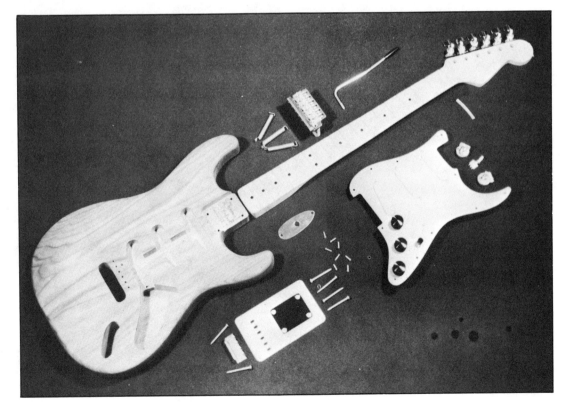

EMG (dist. by Over-lend) Strat pickup assembly, Mighty Mite hardware, Boogie Bodies bird's-eye maple neck, Kharma walnut body, Schecter pickguard and back-plate. Schaller Mini-L tuners, DiMarzio brass bridge, Torres brass nut, Alco knobs and switch, DiMarzio pots.

else, the kits and parts industry is built on fantasy—the player's desire to combine the best qualities of Gibson, Fender, Rickenbacker, or other favorite guitars with his or her own ideas of sound, aesthetics, and playability. Like the hot rod kits of the late '50s, it's an industry where cosmetics play a major role.

The major advantage of doing-it-yourself is that you can get what *you* want, and in the process gain a better understanding of your instrument and a feeling of accomplishment. Some products, if installed correctly, can help cut down onstage hassles and may give you an extra edge over other musicians. You can tailor an instrument to suit your needs. If, for instance, you like a certain neck shape that is unavailable in off-the-rack models, you can buy a new neck and shave it to your specifications. If you prefer the old 4-bolt pattern that Fender offered in their Strats before going to a 3-bolt pattern several years ago, no problem—you can order one without having to dissect a vintage Strat. Kit guitars and custom-made instruments also allow you a wide choice in wood types and finishes.

When Edward Van Halen began his search for a trademark instrument several years ago, he turned to a replacement parts company for his wood and his own imagination for the rest of the guitar. Today, he plays some of the best-known homemade guitars in rock and roll: "The reason I started experimenting was I wanted a Gibson-type sound, but with a Strat vibrato. I stuck a humbucking pickup in the Strat and it worked okay, but it didn't get a good enough tone. Then I found out about a company that sold necks and bodies, and I went to them for my wood. The guitar I made looks like a Strat, but it only has one pickup in it which I made from an old Gibson PAF that I rewound, and one volume knob—no tone, no fancy garbage. It's painted the way I like them. I made a guitar that you could not at the time buy on the market. The main reason I did it was to have something that no one else had. I wanted it to be *my* guitar—an extension of myself." Van Halen has since put together several other instruments, learning by trial and error as he went along. He estimates that he has the actual time of assembly down to about an hour and a half. On an average, the wood for each guitar cost him $150, and this includes having the neck made to his specifications—wide across the fingerboard, almost like a classical guitar, but fairly shallow in depth.

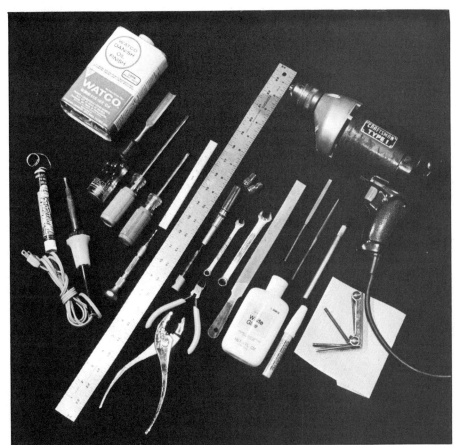

Pat Thrall, formerly with the Pat Travers Band, also plays an instrument that is made to his specifications. He built a Stratocaster-style guitar to accommodate a Floyd Rose setup. He duplicated his favorite neck—a '60 Strat—and put three pickups and a mid-range roll-off control in the body. Pat found that with this setup he could approximate both the sounds of a Gibson Les Paul and a Fender Strat. The instrument is now an integral part of his onstage act.

While the acquisition of a guitar custom designed to fit your needs is bound to appeal to every guitarist, there are several factors to consider before plunging into a store with a fistful of money and visions of the ultimate axe. First, be forewarned: You should not attempt to build any of the more expensive kits or perform any modifications if you are unsure of how they are done. It's a well-known fact that many players wreck their instruments while trying to build or modify something they know little about. If you have any doubts, take it to a repairman. Although product literature doesn't always state this, most manufacturers agree that modifications and kit building should be left to the pros. Because of the newness of the

industry, there is little written information on building kits and installing replacement hardware. To properly assemble an electric guitar or bass, the craftsman should have at least a basic understanding of woodworking, metalworking, plastics, and electronics.

A slight controversy exists as to whether or not it is less expensive to assemble a guitar from a kit or a gathering of various replacement parts as opposed to buying an off-the-rack instrument and having it customized to your specifications. The majority of kit manufacturers agree that while their products are, in the long run, more expensive than store-bought guitars, having an individualized instrument can compensate for the added cost if the materials and workmanship are of high quality. One manufacturer points out that in areas of the country where the discounting of off-the-rack guitars is less prevalent, kit guitars can, in fact, be cheaper. According to repairman John Carruthers, "Probably somewhere between 75% and 85% of those kit projects turn out to cost more than what the person expected, and they usually end up costing more than if the person had bought an already-made guitar. There are only a few times when it's of some value, and that's if you understand up front that it's going to cost you more money. By building a kit guitar or modifying a stock instrument, you can get some specific requirements that you can't get on, say, a factory Fender Strat—like if you want two humbucking pickups in there instead of three Stratocaster pickups. Then, in that case, you couldn't buy a stock Strat that would fit your needs, and it might be advisable to put a kit thing together. But in most cases they end up costing you more money, and they create a lot of headaches, especially when people attempt to do things they don't understand completely."

A major portion of Dan and Dawne Torres' business at Torres Guitars [14467 Big Basin Way, Saratoga, CA 95070] for the last five years has centered around installing replacement parts and working on kits. One of the main problems they find with kit guitars is that after you get them assembled, you have to know how to adjust the action. "Often the neck and bridge won't line up, and then you're in trouble; you don't have anything to start with," Dan explains. "When you buy a guitar off the rack, you have some action to start with—a reference point. You can lower it, you can adjust it, you can have it worked on. On a kit project you may not be sure you have the neck straight and tilted correctly. Sometimes even from the same manufacturer you'll get things like where the neck and the body won't meet properly, or you'll get them on and the bridge will be off-center, so it has to be filled and relocated. The neck-bridge problem will take about $40 to $50 to repair because usually people mess it up so badly that it's more work to fix than if we had done it, and we only charge about $15 to do it in the first place.

"Do-it-yourself kits are a job, a nice hobby project. It's more rewarding when you deal with the higher-quality stuff—the Boogie Bodies, the DiMarzios, the Schecters, the Kharmas, the Mighty Mites, and products like these. You end up with a better guitar than you can buy—*if* you're good enough to put it

together. You can't build your own guitar cheaper than you can buy one stock: It's not the way for a kid looking for an inexpensive guitar to go. There isn't one single thing that doesn't take some effort and work. There is very little that you can just purchase and, with no knowledge, install."

The Torreses and Carruthers agree that a clean job of assembling or customizing a guitar will often require highly specialized and expensive tools, such as reamers or Dremel tools for installing machines, precision files for bridge notching, and small electronic soldering irons for pickup work. "It's hard for someone who doesn't have the tools to get the same results." Carruthers adds, "Plus, there's nothing like experience. If you've done a job a thousand times, chances are you're going to do it a lot better than someone who's just doing it for the first time."

The type of finish you choose and the time it will take to apply it is an important factor to consider when figuring the cost of a kit. Torres contends that a good job of finishing takes about 10 to 14 hours for someone who knows how to do it. Carruthers figures it even higher. "If you went to Sears and bought a compressor and then you got a spray gun and bought all the stuff, you could spend $400 just to get ready to spray. It's possible to do a marginal job with spray cans, but the problem is

that most of the paints and lacquers in spray cans have too many solvents in them. They don't harden up properly when they're applied to something. It could be months or years before the coat hardens up to where you could polish it or buff it out.

"If you're doing a lacquer job, the lacquer itself won't even harden up until two or three weeks after it's been on. So you have to figure you've got the time of preparing the wood and putting the filler and stuff in it, and then you've got to build up several coats of sealer and go through several coats of lacquer. Just the spraying alone can take a day or two, and then there's a waiting period where you've got to let the stuff harden up. After maybe two or three weeks of waiting, you have to buff the stuff out, sand it, buff it, and then assemble the guitar. I've made a lot of guitars myself, and I've remade a lot of guitars, and one of the hardest things to do properly is finish them."

Edward Van Halen, on the other hand, finishes his guitars quickly and inexpensively. Although his methods may cause lovers of finely finished guitars to cringe, they do help him achieve a unique and easily identifiable trademark instrument: "I use Schwinn acrylic lacquer bicycle paint—it's good stuff," he says. "I use tape to make the stripes. For me painting is the most involved part of making a guitar. If you want it to

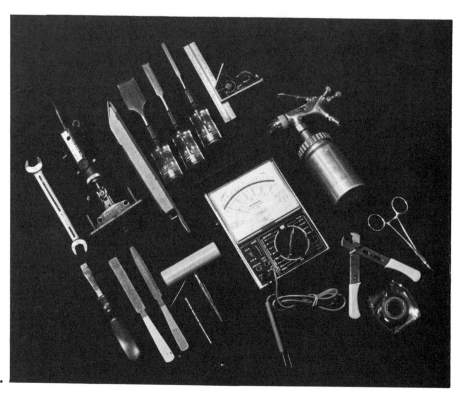

Basics for kit-builders, including wrenches, small power drill/router, sanding block, chisels, ruler, screwdrivers, files, reaming tool, voltmeter, spray gun, wire cutters, and electrical tape.

come out good, you have to spray it and let it dry overnight. Then wet sand it and spray it again—do that about six times. The more coats you put on and wet sand, the more glossy it will look. I've painted bodies in two hours. I leave the neck unsprayed; I hate lacquer. I leave it bare because I like the feel of the wood—I don't like to slip and slide on the neck."

With replacement parts and kits alike, other important things to look into are the types of warranties and instruction material included with the product. When shopping around, it is advisable to keep in mind the ancient maxim, "Let the buyer beware," for reasons Dan Torres explains: "Many companies carry the same things, but prices vary. You'll find the same part with different prices over a very wide range. One company will sell us a 5-way position switch for the same price that another company retails it—one will retail it for $4.95 and another will retail it for $10, and they are identical parts. You almost think that they are buying it from each other and remarketing it. A lot of the stuff is not made by the company that's selling it. It's totally random and the guy on the street has no way of knowing that he's buying exactly the same thing at different prices. And there's no list of retail prices unless you are lucky enough to wander into a store that's giving them out. They don't advertise retail prices very often, so it's really difficult to compare." If your store doesn't have price lists available, write to the manufacturers and request them (a list of addresses concludes this article).

When your kit guitar is finally assembled the way you want it, what will it be worth? Obviously an imitation '59 Strat won't have the same price tag as an original, but it still may have a good resale value. Compared to Gibson, Fender, and other major guitar manufacturers, the kits industry is still in its infancy. The way things look now, the value of the kit guitar will be directly proportional to the skill with which it was assembled and the quality and popularity of the components used. Vintage instrument dealer George Gruhn addresses the question: "Right now there is no going market rate—it's a matter of supply, demand, and precedent. The resale value is going to depend on who put the thing together. If it looks prime and plays great, it will be worth more. Obviously some of the kits are better than others. A kit that was made in Japan, costing $100, is not as good a kit to start with as, say, a

Schecter. Some of these cheaper kits have poorly seasoned and pooly fretted wood, and they are not capable of as much. A Schecter kit assembled by the right person is capable of giving you a very good guitar. But if you take a Schecter kit and give it to a butcher to assemble, you'll have a piece of crap. The finished product is the reflection of not so much the Schecter kit, but the Schecter kit assembled by *whom*."

One final advantage to do-it-yourself kits and replacement parts is the boom in business it has brought to guitar sales centers and repairmen. Neil Henderson of Mighty Mite points out that retailers can save themselves time and money by selling kits: "A lot of times when a dealer gets a factory guitar, it's not going to be set up properly—it'll be factory set up, which means it might need a little bit of fretwork here and there and adjustments and intonation. All a dealer has to do with kits is stock parts."

Since the kits and parts industry began to flourish five years ago, several companies have come and gone, and new ones enter the field every month. Currently the companies offering the largest selection of products are Carvin, DiMarzio, Mighty Mite, Schecter Guitar Research, and Stars Guitars. Founded in 1946, the **Carvin** company of Escondido, California, was one of the first manufacturers of replacement parts; as early as 1952 they were selling replacement pickups. Among the guitar and bass products Carvin offers today are tailpieces, jackplates, brass nuts, necks, pickup wiring kits, switches, and pots. Their replacement humbucking pickups are warranteed for 10 years against malfunction of any kind; this is voided only if the pickup is subjected to misuse. The rest of their guitar-related components are warranted to be free from any failure or malfunction for five years. Carvin also retails sound systems, mixers, amps, basses, and single- and double-neck guitars. They sell directly to consumers via their catalog, and allow a 10-day trial period during which customers can return products for a full refund.

Except for pickguards and a few small parts, you can buy nearly every component for an electric guitar from the **DiMarzio** company in Staten Island, New York. Although they still carry the line of pickups for which they are best known, in the last year the company has begun offering a wide array of hardware for Fender- and Gibson-style guitars and basses (including brass and chrome products), replacement electri-

cal parts, miniature amps, and bass strings. They also feature custom bodies in the styles of Strats, Telecasters, Precision basses, Jazz basses, and Explorers, all available with a choice of routing patterns. The Strat-style bodies are made of ash, mahogany, padauk, maple, and striped woods; the Tele-style comes in ash or mahogany body with a maple top and binding. Recently they have introduced a line of guitar and bass necks. Company spokesman Steve Blucher urges that until they complete their product-information literature, any installation of DiMarzio parts should be done by someone with experience. DiMarzio products come with a five-year warranty; they are sold over the counter in stores across the U.S. and are available abroad in 50 countries.

Started in 1974, the **Mighty Mite** company of Camarillo, California, sells replacement pickups, a large selection of brass bridges, pickguards, hardware, and other parts. Their guitar kits come complete, including strings. The bodies are styles like Strats, Teles, Les Pauls, Explorers, Flying V's, Firebirds, and B.C. Rich Mockingbirds, Biches, and Eagles. In addition to ash, these come in a variety of exotic woods, including mahogany, shedua, teak, walnut, koa, rosewood, and figured maple. Their maple necks are available with optional ebony or maple fingerboards. The assembly of a Mighty Mite kit guitar may require some drilling, filing, and reaming, and company spokesman Neil Henderson advises that necks be set up by a professional repairman. Optional lacquer or oil body finishes are available for an added cost. Pickups carry a lifetime guarantee, as long as the magnet remains intact. Other products exhibiting manufacturing defects will be replaced. Mighty Mite products are sold in guitar stores and are also available in Europe.

Schecter Guitar Research, located in North Hollywood, California, manufactures and stocks over 400 different items for building or customizing guitars and basses. They have replacement parts for instruments in the styles of Strats, Teles, Gibsons, and Rickenbacker guitars, as well as Rickenbacker basses and Fender Precision and Jazz basses. Schecter also carries pickups, pots and switches, screws, springs, and pickguards. In custom bodies they offer a choice of 17 woods, ranging from ash, maple, and walnut to such exotic species as macacuba, koa, shedua, zebrawood, and imbuya. Necks come in almost as many types of wood, including cocobola, wenge, pau ferro, purple heart, Macassar ebony, and Hong Kong rosewood. Kits are available, and spokesman Hershel Blankenship figures that buyers should add an additional cost for assembly if they have it done by a repairman. Schecter's warranty extends for one year from the date of purchase, as long as the buyer retains the receipt. Their products are sold in stores or by mail order, and can be found in Europe, Japan, and Australia.

San Francisco's **Stars Guitars** manufactures hardware for other companies; in addition, they offer their own line of brass and chrome-plated brass hardware for guitars and basses. Although they don't carry pickups, they do have a line of electronic parts. Stars also makes bodies for Strat-style, Precision-bass style, or custom-order instruments; these come in rosewood, walnut, and irroko. A Stars spokesman reports that their products are warranted for the life of the purchaser. They are sold over the counter at the company, in music stores, and through mail order.

Saga Musical Instruments in San Francisco offers two do-it-yourself kits for Strat-style guitars: the ST-10 and the ST-20. The ST-10 features a birch-mahogany laminate body; the ST-20 has a solid ash body. Since the necks come with truss rods and frets installed and the instruments' three single-coil pickups are pre-mounted in a pickguard assembly, Saga owner Richard Keldsen figures the time of assembly for the kit to be about an hour and a half. No electronic

or woodworking skills are required, he adds—all you need is a Phillips screwdriver. Instruments are shipped with a coat of sealer on the wood. Keldsen says that Saga's warranty is "vague, although anything that has ever been sent back to us has been replaced free of charge."

Two companies that manufacture and sell necks and bodies are **Kharma Bodies** in West Hempstead, New York, and **Boogie Bodies** in Puyallup, Washington. Working alone, 28-year-old Marc Carlin produces Kharma's products: bodies in the styles of Strats, Teles, Explorers, and Flying V's, as well as necks carved of bird's-eye maple with optional ebony, rosewood, or maple fingerboards. He uses ash, walnut, maple, red oak, mahogany, zebrawood, teak, rosewood, and figured maple for his bodies, and recently added the Rhama series of bodies, which have walnut wings and a striped center made of a maple and walnut insert. He also handles brass bridges, pickup mounting rings, tailpieces, strap buttons, nuts, and knobs. His wood products are shipped with a coat of oil, and they are warranted against any defects in workmanship.

Boogie Bodies originally supplied wood components to other replacement parts companies. Today they sell directly to stores and customers. Ken Warmoth, now 28, fronts the two-man operation, turning out bodies of flame and burl maple, mahogany, walnut, koa, and other exotic woods in the styles of

Strats, Teles, Les Pauls, and Flying V's, as well as Precision, Jazz, and Les Paul basses. His Les Paul and Flying V guitar and Les Paul bass bodies accept only Fender-style hardware and bolt-on necks. Boogie Bodies manufactures many types of custom plastic pickguards, and a pickguard made of a wood laminate mounted on aluminum. The company also builds made-to-order instruments. Ken reports that necks are available in different sizes and in all stages of completion, and can be bought either finished or unfinished. Boogie Bodies warrants everything except the finish on their products.

For more information on kits and parts manufacturers and their wares, feel free to write the companies for their catalogs and price lists.

Jas Obrecht

Company Addresses

Boogie Bodies, Box 1244, Puyallup, WA 98371

DiMarzio, 1388 Richmond Terrace, Staten Island, NY 10310

Kharma Bodies, Box 82, West Hempstead, NY 11552

Mighty Mite, 4809 Calle Alto, Camarillo, CA 93010

Saga Musical Instruments, Box 2841, South San Francisco, CA 94080

Schecter Guitar Research, Box 9783, North Hollywood, CA 91609

Stars Guitars, 818 Folsom St., San Francisco, CA 94107.

ELECTRIC GUITAR REPLACEMENT PARTS: TIPS FOR THE BUYER

May 1980. *Guitar Player*'s investigation into the pros and cons of building and modifying your own electric guitar began with "Guitar Kits And Replacement Parts." In that series we examined the motivations behind wanting to build a customized instrument and considered

the cost, time, and skill factors involved. We also looked at companies offering complete do-it-yourself kits or extensive lines of necks, bodies, pickups, hardware, and accessories—the one-stop shops of the parts world. These included Carvin, DiMarzio, Mighty Mite, Schecter

Guitar Research, Stars Guitars, Saga Musical Instruments, Kharma Bodies, and Boogie Bodies. Here we'll consider some of the specialists—companies offering one or more types of replacement parts for electric guitars. It's important to note that this is not a catalog or buyer's guide, but simply an overview of what's available and what's involved with installing it.

The replacement parts industry began its boom in the mid-'70s. Today, with enough cash in hand, players can literally trade anything on their guitar for a custom counterpart: bridges of steel and nuts of bone for brass pieces; stock pots for better-tapered custom units; cranky old tuning machines for smooth-turning aluminum wonders; dull pickguards for acrylic mirror flash; or worn-out pickups for cleaner, dirtier, or hotter models. The industry has grown to the extent where you can now even replace something as simple and inexpensive as a stock strap button with a device that, the ads lead you to surmise, will never leave you standing in horror as your guitar crashes to the floor. Due to the vast extent of replacement, special effect, and customizing products, however, this article will only cover those that are designed to function generally the same as stock parts. A listing of manufacturer's addresses concludes this article; feel free to write them for catalogs and further product information.

The reasons for replacing parts are legion, changing old for new or adding something to help you get an onstage edge over other guitarists being among the most common. Perhaps more than anything else, though, the replacement parts industry caters to players' fantasies, their desire to have the sharpest looking, best playing, and hottest sounding axe in town. Many are inspired to replace parts in order to approximate the sound or appearances of a favorite player's instrument, like Eddie Van Halen's one-pickup Strat-style guitar, Billy Gibbons's "Pearly Gates" (a vintage Gibson Les Paul), or Roy Buchanan's Fender Telecaster. But before you rush out to get whatever you think will bring you that special sound, remember: Pickups (and to a lesser extent bridges, nuts, and other parts) are only links in the signal chain that begins with your fingers or picks on the strings, goes through the pickup, guitar body, and cord or wireless transmitter to your effects if you have any, and then the amp, speakers, and maybe a PA or recording equipment. Even the type of wood your guitar is made of and the position of your pickup will affect the sound. A general rule to keep in mind when purchasing replacement parts is that until you have them installed in your guitar and hear them through your complete system, you won't be sure of how they will affect your overall sound.

Pickups. All too often guitarists find that shopping for pickups can ultimately lead to a real "let the buyer beware" situation. Many players are unaware of the complexity of some of today's products, and often factual shortcomings exist in advertising as intelligent discussions of products are bypassed for mountains of hype. According to Dan Torres, who acts as a consultant to many major pickup manufacturers, "The most common problem people run into is not understanding what they are getting. The ultimate problem is with distortion pickups—they expect it to be a fuzztone. You put a distortion pickup in their guitar, and they flip it on and it sounds louder. None of the distortion pickups are fuzztones; they just have a higher output. I had another troublesome problem when someone came in and said he wanted his guitar to sound real clean. So I rewound the pickup so he sounded clean. But what he meant by sounding clean was sounding like Carlos Santana! Terminology is not standardized across the industry, and so far there's no way to objectively measure pickup performance.

"The next most common problem is not understanding how the pickups are going to change the sound of the instrument. There are compromises made: When you go to a higher output, you may lose highs. When you go to a cleaner output, you might lose middle or bass—again, misunderstanding. And often pickup manufacturers, like most businessmen, won't give you a comparison: 'My pickup sounds like so-and-so's, but this is what's different about it.' No advertiser says that their product is mediocre or lacking in anything; they all say their product has everything. Often music store salesmen—and they sell the largest amounts of pickups—don't know very much. There are complete misunderstandings because there are so many brands; the average music store doesn't carry all of them, definitely. They've got what they've got, and say whatever they have is the best. Nobody would say, 'I've got the worst one here.' So they sell them, and often these are the incorrect pickups for what the person wanted. So players end up trading, changing quite a bit."

Probably the best place to start on your road to finding the right pickup is with self-education. First of all, take your guitar with you. When you go to a store, you have to be able to articulate the sound you want. Compare it to a sound on a record or cassette, or with what you have now. Explain what you would like to add or subtract. Shop around and find out different store policies on returns in case the pickup doesn't work in your system the way you would have intended. Ask if you can have a pickup installed for a trial demonstration (this may prove well worth any extra labor charge). Be sure you understand the product's warranty

Left: Parts are often available pre-packaged, including necessary installation hardware. Right: Pickups, clockwise from top: Mighty Mite Strat, Gibson single-coil, Fender Precision Bass, Fender Strat, Lawrence L-220, Fender Precision with DiMarzio cover, Fender Precision.

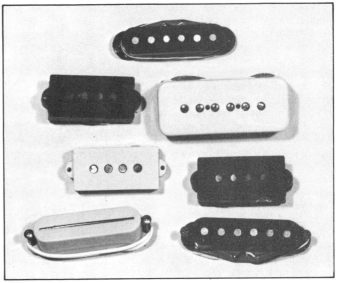

terms. Learning about the technical aspects of pickup design can also help you achieve your sound. Unfortunately, due to the newness of the pickup industry, there is little written information on the subject.

The wide choice in replacement pickups also demands that repair and salespeople know more about products so they can better advise their customers. Sometimes products are shipped with little information explaining their design and function. Torres reports that he and other repairmen have found it useful to sacrifice one of these pickups to the knife so that the pickup's resistance, metal content, type of magnet, and other facets can be better examined, thus allowing a better understanding of the device.

Most of the replacement pickups sold today are modeled after the basic single-coil and humbucking (double-coil) units. Used on Fender Strats since their introduction, most Telecasters, and many other guitars, single-coil models are the oldest. The most important and imitated humbucking is the pickup designed by Gibson's Seth Lover in the '50s. "Today innovation is not the going thing among pickup manufacturers." Torres contends. "The going pattern is variations on a theme. There are only so many variations you can make, but you can juggle them endlessly so that you can come up with 50 different pickups. There is no proper way to make one—it's the way that sounds best. You can put more wire on the coils; that will make it hotter, louder. You can put less wire on the coils; that will make it cleaner. You can change the magnet or add helper magnets to the outside of the coils. When you get that much structure, you can get a real hot pickup with a lot of highs, but you also get so much magnetism the pickup can't be very close to the strings or it will attract them and cause a damping problem, making the guitar play out of tune. One of the innovations has been to build a preamp into the pickup. These are low-impedance units; they have very little wire in the coil. You get a very clean pickup with a good volume." Another innovation manufacturers have come up with is a single blade instead of polepieces in order to compensate for the absence of intense magnetic energy between the polepieces—the area a string travels during a bend.

Ultimately the beauty of any pickup will rest in the ears of the listener. Once you have found the pickup of your choice, if you have any doubts about how to install it, take it to a professional repairman. Pickup installation requires skills in soldering, electronics, and oftentimes woodwork.

Currently Fender, Gibson, Guild, Ibanez, and other major guitar manufacturers sell replacement pickups. Some of the larger parts companies profiled in an earlier article—Carvin, DiMarzio, Mighty Mite, Schecter, and Stars Guitars—also feature lines of pickups. Bill Bartolini, an independent pickup manufacturer, heads **Bartolini Guitars** in Livermore, California. His company sells over 40 models of pickups, including exact replacements for Fender Precision, Fender Jazz, and Rickenbacker basses, Strats, and older Gibson Johnny Smith guitars; and they have three mini humbuckers and five large humbuckers (two of these come with an active preamp). He also carries hexaphonic and quadraphonic pickups for Strats, and Precision, Jazz, and Rickenbacker basses, as well as hexaphonic and quadraphonic humbuckers. He warranties his material and workmanship for one year, as long as the pickup is not subject to misuse.

Rowe-DeArmond in Toledo, Ohio, sells two models of humbuckers, the 2300, which comes with a chrome cover and is standardized to a Les Paul size, and the 2400 super-humbucker, which is an extra-high-output pickup. The company also carries toggle switches and volume pots. Their two-year warranty covers defects in workmanship and materials, provided the warranty card is mailed in on time.

Seymour Duncan owns **Seymour Duncan Research Laboratory** in Santa Barbara, California. He rewinds pickups, duplicates them, or manufactures them to specifications. He now carries over 90 models, including 15 for Strats, 12 for Telecasters, 18 for Jazz Basses, and replacements for Precision basses, Fender Jazzmasters, and Fender Jaguars. He also handles humbuckers, seven-pole stereo pickups, and quadraphonic bass models. He keeps a record of the specifications of every pickup he has wound, and also has the specifications of pickups used by many well-known performers. Seymour guarantees that if you're not happy with your Duncan pickup and call within ten days, he'll redo it, replace it with a different model, or send a full refund.

EMG of Santa Rosa, California, lists ten different pickup models in four basic designs. They use both ceramic and Alnico magnets, and their products come complete with pots. The pickups are available in sizes designed to fit in the place of Les Paul humbuckers, Les Paul Deluxe mini humbuckers, Strat single-coils, and Precision bass pickups. They are warranted for two years. Nashville's **Bill Lawrence** manufactures 12 different pickup models, all humbuckers. These are designed to fit Les Pauls, Les Paul Deluxes, Telecasters, and Strats. He uses a special magnetic alloy that, he says, operates at a high output with a low magnetic flux. Lawrence products come with a five-year written warranty. "If it's our fault," Bill adds, "we'll replace it." Although they're best known for their acoustic guitar pickups and transducers, **Shadow** in New York City carries three electric guitar humbuckers and an eight-pole Jazz Bass pickup.

Brass. The use of brass parts for guitars has increased substantially over the last few years as manufacturers have maintained that bridges and nuts made of the metal may tend to enhance the instrument's sustaining qualities and aid in holding the intonation. Cosmetic appeal also plays a major role in the business, and because of this you can now buy dozens of brass replacement parts to match the bridge and nut. Brass

Finished Strat-style guitar with Schaller tuners, Torres brass nut, Schecter shedua neck, Boogie Bodies zebrawood body, Schecter pickup assembly and jack plate, and Mighty Mite bridge.

is finding favor among repairmen because it can be used for making kit guitars or for replacing parts that may be hard to get from manufacturers. Working with the metal, though, calls for experience and skill, for reasons Dan Torres explains: "To replace a bass bridge, for example, which is one of the easiest installations there is, you need special files to cut the notches in the proper position, and then you have to reset the action and intonation. With some bridge installations you have to pull the old studs and replace them. Even the amateur with some experience in fixing guitars is usually going to mess up a brass nut or get no benefit from it. When you buy one of these, all you get is a piece of brass. It isn't notched because every guitar is different. Notching them is more difficult than doing a bone nut, and you need the right files to do it. Most repair shops carry a file for each string diameter." If you have any doubts about installing your brass hardware, especially bridges and nuts, you'd probably be best off taking it to a qualified repairman.

Most of the major guitar manufacturers offer brass hardware, including the Fender company, which recently announced a whole line of these parts. Stars Guitars, Mighty Mite, Schecter, and DiMarzio carry lines of brass parts, too. **Guitar Man** in Santee, California, has a vast assortment of products for Les Pauls, Telecasters, Precision basses, and Strats, including tailpieces and bridges, buttons, plates, pickguards, speed knobs, toggle plates, tailpiece studs, pickup mounting rings, string inserts, nuts, and string tension guides. The **Phil-Lu** company in Ocean, New Jersey, offers solid brass bass and guitar

bridges, and **Rex Bogue** in San Gabriel, California, carries a brass guitar bridge. **Lado,** a guitar company in Ontario, Canada, sells brass accessories such as guitar and bass bridges, control knobs, pickup rings, and plates. **Leo Quan** in Oakland, California, manufactures Badass Bridges, which fit into existing mounting bolts of many models of Les Pauls, SGs, Firebirds, and other Gibson guitars, as well as a couple of Epiphones.

Machines, pots, and pickguards. John Carruthers discussed the installation of tuning machines in his series of articles. Since replacing tuners is a delicate operation, it should be attempted only by those who know what they are doing. **Grover Musical Products, Schaller, Gotoh,** and **Sperzel** all manufacture and sell tuning machines. Pots are available from nearly every major guitar manufacturer, as well as DiMarzio, Mighty Mite, Schecter, Stars guitars, Bill Lawrence, and other parts manufacturers. **International Sales Associates** (ISA) and **Power Pots,** both located in southern California, also sell replacement pots. Pickguards are also widely available. A transparent Plexiglas pickguard is sold by **Axis Guitar Works,** and **Zon's Guitars** handles Les Paul-style Mirror-Guard pickguards.

The listing of companies and products in this article is by no means complete; rather, it should serve as an overview of the wide variety of what's available. Countless other small companies and independent craftsmen are involved with the production of replacement parts, and new products are announced all the time. What's most important is that buyers understand the

extent of the options. If no one in your area has *exactly* what you are looking for, chances are somebody else will— only shopping around will tell.

Jas Obrecht

Company Addresses

Axis Guitar Works, 508 No. 5th St., Jeanette, PA 15644

Bartolini Guitars, Box 934, Livermore, CA 94550

Seymour Duncan Research Laboratory, Box 4746, Santa Barbara, CA 93103

Overlend-EMG, Box 4394, Santa Rosa, CA 95402

Gotoh, c/o Coast Wholesale, 200 Industrial Way, San Carlos, CA 94070

Grover Musical Products, 1278 W. 9th St., Cleveland, OH 44113

Guitar Man, Box 278, Santee, CA 92071

International Sales Associates, Box 9783, N. Hollywood, CA 91609

Lado, RR1, Uxbridge, Ontario LOC 1KO, Canada

Bill Lawrence, 1003 Saunders Ave., Madison, TN 37115

Leo Quan, 5359½ College Ave., Oakland. CA 94618

Phil-Lu, 1206 Herbert Ave., Ocean, NJ 07712

Power Pots, Box 896, West Covina, CA 91793

Rex Bogue, Box 751, San Gabriel, CA 91778

Rowe-DeArmond, 1702 Airport Highway, Toledo, OH 43609

Shadow, 22-42 Jackson Ave., New York, NY 11101

Sperzel, 7807 Lake Ave., Cleveland, OH 44102

Zon's Guitars, 129 Military Rd., Buffalo, NY 14207.

UNDERSTANDING ONBOARD PREAMPS

May, June 1980. Internally installed (onboard) preamp units for guitars and basses have become very popular lately, with many different types making their way into the marketplace. Since

the installation of preamps is fast becoming a common guitar modification, players frequently ask me to explain what they are, how they function, how to interpret their specifica-

tions, and how to choose the right preamp for their playing needs.

Understanding how a particular preamp operates will give you a good idea of its compatibility with your instrument and how the two can be integrated. If you have some understanding of electronics, you should have little difficulty with the terms used here; if you do not know some of the terminology, you may find it helpful to procure a basic electronics dictionary from an electronics store (such as Radio Shack) or a bookstore.

Types of preamps. Preamps are now available with a variety of functions, ranging from the single-stage buffer preamp to more involved units offering active tone controls or equalization. All of these units use transistors, FETs (field effect transistors), or IC (integrated circuit) op-amps (operational amplifiers) and depend on a battery or batteries for their operation. (A breakdown of the type of voltages necessary to operate these devices will be explained later.)

The most common type of preamp used in guitars and basses is the single-stage buffer or driver, which serves a variety of functions. It is usually placed directly at the output of the instrument, after the controls, converting the output of the guitar to low impedance. The high-frequency response of the signal is thereby increased (providing the pickup can produce the higher frequency range) because the pickup becomes isolated from the guitar cable and its associated filtering effect (which normally causes high-frequency loss when output is at high impedance; this effect occurs on most conventional guitar pickups, which are "passive"—i.e., use no external power source). This isolation also minimizes the line loss normally occurring when longer cords are used between the guitar or bass and the amplifier. Another advantage of a low-impedance output is that it permits direct input to a mixing board (either in the studio or live performance) without going through a "direct box."

Most single-stage preamps offer variable gain, thus allowing you to boost the output of the instrument with a simple adjustment. However, any noise produced by the pickup (such as hum or buzz) or by the controls on your instrument will also be amplified by the preamp proportionately with the increase in signal. Therefore, if you have problems with this type of voice you should consider this when choosing a preamp. Single-stage units can usually operate on a single 9-volt battery and ordinarily do not require a large amount of space for a clean installation.

Active tone control or EQ units. These are preamps offering active tone control or equalization (EQ) that has been specifically designed for use with guitar or bass, the units, tone circuits being optimized for the different frequency ranges of these two basic types of instruments. Some EQ units also contain a buffered input stage identical to the single-stage preamp described earlier. However, instead of sending the signal directly out of the instrument after the buffer amp, it is sent through additional stages of circuitry required for altering tone. The variety of tone options varies from unit to unit, with some offering ± 20dB boost or cut, variable frequency controls, rolloff contours, and/or EQ controls. Active EQ units usually have from one to six stages of preamp circuitry. Some will require only a single 9-volt battery, while others may require two, either in series or in parallel. This is an important consideration, not only in regard to the space required for mounting two batteries inside the instrument, but also because the supply-voltage requirements for other types of active gear you may want to use may be incompatible with the requirements for the EQ unit. Also, preamps with active tone controls usually require more space in the guitar than buffer preamps, and thus may require some body modifications.

Interpreting the specs. Whether you choose the single-stage preamp or a unit with other capabilities, give close consideration to its specifications. There are a variety of specifications associated with preamps, but the main concerns are the following: input impedance (specified in ohms), input level (specified as volts, peak to peak), noise (stated in dBs), and current requirement (microamps or milliamps). The following paragraphs discuss these factors.

Input impedance. A general rule in the electronics industry states that the input impedance of a preamp should be at least ten times greater than the device you are putting into it. The resistive value of a guitar's volume and tone controls, typically 250K or 500K, provide a direct correlation with how high the input impedance of the preamp should be. Both single- and dual-coil pickups usually require an input impedance of 250K to 500K. The reason for a high-input impedance in a preamp is to avoid any loading (gain loss) and to prevent a loss in high-frequency response. *Caution:* Manufacturers may

L-R: Onboard preamp fits into the control cavity of a guitar; external preamp that plugs into the instrument and requires no rewiring; external preamp attached to guitar strap.

lower the input impedance of a preamp in order to gain better signal-to-noise ratio specifications. Therefore, pay close attention to the input impedance specs to make certain they are compatible with your pickups. Pickups for acoustic guitars, usually piezoelectric types, require a very high input impedance from a preamp, generally above 1 Meg (million) ohms. If you are in doubt about the output impedance of your pickups, consult the manufacturer, and electronic technician, or a knowledgeable guitar repairman; they should be able to answer your questions.

Noise specifications. The noise specification of a preamp depends mainly on two separate sources. One is thermal noise (hiss), produced by all electronic components, not only from the electrons passing through them, but also from materials used in their construction. Resistors are notorious noise makers, especially those that combine high resistive values with carbon-type construction. The other source is junction noise, which also manifests itself as hiss, adding to the thermal noise of the circuit components. This type of noise is confined to semiconductors (transistors, FETs, ICs etc.) and is directly dependent on how the input stage of a preamp is designed or determined by circumstance. Since the pickups normally used in guitars are high impedance, the preamp must exhibit a like or higher input impedance; this presents problems since it is very difficult to get low-noise performance in high-impedance circuits. The ultimate solution is to use pickups that involve active circuitry that provides conversion from high to low impedance at the source (i.e., at the pickups themselves instead of at the controls). The closer the conversion is to the source, the better the signal-to-noise ratio.

Preamps designed with high-impedance inputs usually have a noise figure in the –65dB to –80dB range, whereas preamps designed with low-impedance inputs will have noise figures that typically exceed –85dB. A figure of –65dB is in all probability the limit for acceptable noise from a preamp. EQ units with more than one preamp stage may not suffer from a poor noise figure, but if the gain of high-frequency response is increased too much, it may produce an audible amount of noise.

Input level. This specification (stated in volts, peak to peak) is the maximum input voltage that can be put into the preamp from a pickup. Pickups are

capable of producing very large voltage transients, depending on the construction of the unit (single or dual coil) and on the way you play your instrument. The output of your pickups can be accurately determined by the use of an oscilloscope, or roughly determined by classifying it in one of the following groups.

Low-level devices. This group includes piezoelectric contact pickups (used primarily on acoustic guitars), single-coil pickups, and some dual-coil (or humbucking) types. These all usually exhibit transient voltages of less than 2 volts, peak to peak. Piezoelectric pickups are considered low-level devices because the transients (attack voltages, from the time you hit the notes until they peak out and return to their lowest levels) from the strings are picked up from the instrument's body, not from directly under the strings. Placement of contact pickups on the guitar body is very critical and may dictate using a preamp to achieve the desired tone and output, regardless of whether the manufacturer claims his pickup does not require a preamp.

Single-coil and some humbucking pickups using Alnico magnets in their construction generally have transients of less than two volts, peak to peak. However, with certain pickups in this category, this may not be the case; so it is wise to measure the output signal from these models. Alnico magnets generally do not generate a lot of power when used in pickups (unless the magnetic mass is very large), but are desirable due to their addition to midrange frequency response. Integrating a preamp into an instrument equipped with low-level pickups is relatively easy, usually requiring a single 9-volt battery for up to a maximum of 18dB of signal boost, either straight gain (gain uniform in all frequency ranges) or frequency equalization gain (gain allocated differentially among various specific frequency ranges). You should make certain that the preamp you purchase can handle at least a 2-volt transient; otherwise, input distortion from the preamp may also become a part of your output signal.

High-level devices. Pickups capable of putting out large voltage transients, sometimes called "hot" units, usually are made with ceramic magnets, which aid in producing voltages from less than two to peaks of from four to six. Preamps designed for use with these pickup inputs should be capable of handling input signals of 3 volts, peak

to peak. Preamps used on hot pickup signals are most useful for lowering the output impedance of the instrument and for allowing the advantages slated previously (buffering effect, reducing line loss, and eliminating the need for "direct boxes").

Input-level overview. The attack transients or maximum peak-to-peak voltage produced by the pickup will dictate the input level that the preamp must be capable of handling. If you plan to use a preamp to get distortion (overdrive) from your instrument, it is not necessary to overdrive the preamp with the pickup signal. In fact, this can often result in an unnatural distortion or clipping of the waveform for the period of time the pickup signal exceeds the preamp's input capabilities. If you overdrive the preamp, there is a good chance it could be destroyed, and if the device is encapsulated in plastic (unserviceable) or does not contain input protection, it will be rendered useless. The input capability of a preamp can be raised by simply increasing the battery supply voltage from, say, +9 to +18. If your installation dictates these circumstances, you may want to provide extra room for an additional battery. However, you should first check with the manufacturer to make sure the preamp can operate with a higher supply voltage before attempting a voltage increase.

Current requirement. Most preamps not only require a DC supply to operate, but also need a regular amount of current from the battery or batteries. Manufacturers state their products' current requirements in microamps or milliamps. Microamps represent a very low amount of current consumption, and 1 milliamp equals 1,000 microamps. Preamps can require anywhere from 10 microamps to 2 milliamps at their stated operating voltage (i.e., 1 milliamp drain at 9 volts). Alkaline batteries are usually preferred for most electronic installations due to their longer lifetimes and current capabilities. The typical alkaline battery is rated at 500 milliamp hours (MAH), meaning it will supply a 1 milliamp drain for a period of 500 hours. Depending on how often you will be playing your guitar, you can determine how many months a battery will last. The MAH rating will apply only to a fresh battery. To ensure that you are getting fresh ones, you should purchase them at a shop or retail store where you can test them or can be sure their stock is frequently renewed.

Batteries. Often a player will purchase a battery for a new installation or as a replacement only to discover that the preamp either performs poorly or does not operate at all. Current drain of a preamp under 1 milliamp is considered "shelf life" (i.e., the device requires no more current than the battery loses while sitting on the retailer's shelf). The shelf life of a battery can vary from six months to a period of years. Naturally, preamps that require larger amounts of current from the battery will necessitate battery replacement more often. If you are planning to use a pickup with a large output signal, it may be necessary to increase the supply voltage to the preamp. Most, if not all, electronic devices such as preamps contain resistive components in their bias networks. For example, if a preamp requires 1 milliamp of current at 9 volts, it may require 2 milliamps when supplied with 18 volts. Battery life will not be extended by raising the supply voltage. If you determine that your installation will require batteries more often than you are willing to replace them, you may want to consider using an external AC power supply for your system.

John Carruthers

BUILDING AN ONBOARD PREAMP/EQ

July 1983. Three pickups on a guitar can offer tremendous versatility, and the sounds produced by such a configuration can be quite distinctive. However, because the unusual number of pickups creates a potential for an overabundance of knobs on the guitar's surface, manufacturers often pare down the number of controls in favor of more understated cosmetics, simplicity of operation, and a lower price. After all, with just one volume and one tone knob per pickup, the clutter of six knobs can detract from even the most beautiful of sunbursts or make it difficult for the player to quickly readjust tone and/or volume settings.

Perhaps the best known of the 3-pickup electrics is the venerable Fender Stratocaster; countless variations (and direct copies) have been based on its design. It has a *very* distinctive timbre, and offers a good deal of control over the tone of two of its pickups, while leaving the lead (bridge) pickup without a tone control. This is fine for many guitarists: It provides a bright lead sound, plenty of control over most tonal parameters, and keeps the knob count down to an easy-to-use three. Nonetheless, some guitarists feel that control over the shape of the lead pickup's tone would be useful.

For those players, here's an inexpensive (usually less than $20.00) modification that yields a different approach to control over any 3-pickup instrument's sonic spectrum, and includes the boosting capabilities of a preamp. And in most cases, no extra knobs need be added. It's an onboard active preamp/equalizer. The circuit actually consists of two separate sections: tone and preamp. The construction of this project is pretty straightforward, although before attempting it, you should have at least a rudimentary knowledge of electronics (be able to tell a resistor from a capacitor, know how to solder, etc.). If you aren't versed in the ways of electronics, you may want to forgo this project. Additionally, you may be able to prepare yourself by reading Craig Anderton's *Electronic Projects For Musicians*, or get help from a skilled friend.

The key to this preamp/EQ project is making it compact. The electronics cavity on a Stratocaster, for instance, only allows for a circuit board that measures about 2" x 2" or 3½" x 1⅛". Before you rush to build the circuit, measure the control cavity of your guitar—it may be smaller than the dimensions mentioned here. If it turns out to be larger, then you may not have to condense the circuit to such a small package, thereby making it easier to construct.

Difficult as it may seem, building the preamp/EQ that small can be accomplished. A single integrated circuit can be used instead of three separate ones shown in the accompanying schematic diagram (quad op-amps such as the TL084 or the RC4136 offer low noise and low distortion, easy connection, and low price). If you have enough room, you may use three high-grade op-amps such as the LM318, LF351, or TLO81. Most parts are readily available through Radio Shack or other retail electronics outlets (check ads in electronics magazines, too; there are often bargains from mail-order firms, provided you are willing to wait for the order to arrive).

This preamp/equalizer also calls for two 9-volt batteries for proper operation; these can be fitted into the tremolo spring cavity in the instrument's back *if* you have a tremolo and *if* you are willing to use only two springs. Don't rely solely on a ruler to measure the available space—place a couple of batteries in there. Once replaced, the cover plate can usually hold them in place; otherwise, a thin piece of foam rubber may be necessary.

If routing of the cavity is required, examine your needs for the preamp/equalizer carefully. There are many fine commercially available preamps and EQ circuits that don't have to be fitted into the guitar. Quite simply, any routing or other modification most likely will have an adverse effect on the resale value of a guitar—particularly a vintage one. So be careful. If you're at all hesitant, build the circuit and install it in a separate metal floor box. (Connect point A of the circuit to the "hot" lead of the box's input jack, and substitute a 250K or 500K pot for R14. Wire the input and output jack's grounds together.) Use a short cord between the guitar and preamp/EQ. In this way you can get many of the benefits of the unit without modifying a thing on your guitar.

The prototype of this circuit was installed in a Stratocaster that has a 3-way pickup selector and three single-coil pickups. It will work with a 3-pickup guitar with a 5-way selector, as well as with a 2-pickup instrument. It was originally designed as a tone circuit exclusively for the bridge pickup, but it offers a treble boost/bass cut (or vice versa)

Top: Preamp controls can replace the original ones without pickguard or body modifications. Bottom: Measure your guitar's control cavity carefully before building the Preamp/EQ.

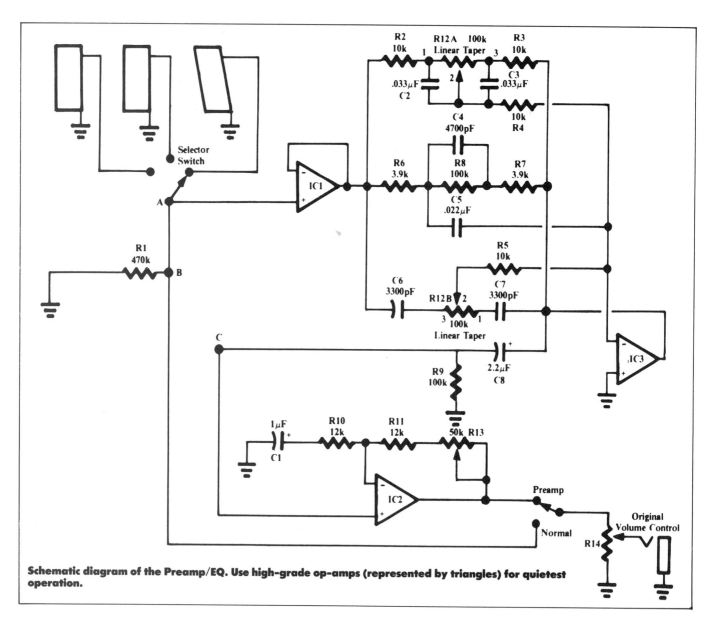

Schematic diagram of the Preamp/EQ. Use high-grade op-amps (represented by triangles) for quietest operation.

and a level boost that works well with all three pickups.

The tone control circuit incorporates a dual-ganged pot (two 100K potentiometers connected back to back, and operated by a single shaft). These are cross wired (see schematic) to give a simultaneous bass boost and treble cut when turned fully in one direction, and a treble boost and bass cut when turned the opposite way. By using a ganged pot, only one knob is needed for controlling the tone.

The guitar's existing volume control is used to govern the overall loudness produced by the guitar, whether the preamp is engaged or not. The 50K preamp gain control can be a pot, operated by one of the guitar's knobs, or it can be a trimmer (small variable resistor) placed inside the guitar. The

former approach affords more control, while making it necessary to drill an extra hole in your pickguard to accommodate the preamp/normal switch. Using an internal trimmer allows you to place the switch in one of the existing holes. Note: The circuit shown here is designed so that the preamp/normal switch bypasses *all* of the circuitry, including the tone section, whenever the "normal" mode is selected. To alter it so that the tone section can be activated independently from the preamp, disconnect the wire between point "A" and point "B," and solder a jumper wire between points "B" and "C." This makes it impossible for you to bypass the circuitry should the batteries go dead or the circuit fail. If you want to be able to bypass all of the electronics, as well as independently activate the

tone control or the preamp, follow the original wiring scheme, but use a 3-way switch, and connect the third pole to point "C." This will permit a selection of "tone circuitry without preamp," "preamp and tone circuitry," and "system bypass."

Obviously, there must be a means of controlling the battery's flow of power to the unit, and this requires an on/off switch. You can use a double-pole/single-throw switch, but that would necessitate drilling yet another hole in your pickguard. There is a simple solution: a jack with built-in switches that activates the power when you plug in your guitar. An easy-to-find jack of this sort is Radio Shack's 3-conductor double closed-circuit stereo jack (number 274-277). It contains two switches that are toggled whenever a plug is inserted.

To install it, connect the "+" power pin of your op-amp to pin 1 of the jack, and attach the "+" wire from one battery to pin 2 of the jack. The "−" lead from that battery should be connected to ground. For the second battery, connect the "−" pin from the op-amp to the jack's pin 5, and connect the jack's pin 6 to the "−" lead of the second battery. Finally, attach the "+" lead from that battery to ground. The "hot" output of the original volume control (R14) connects to pin 4 of the jack; the ground point from the circuit board connects to the jack's pin 9.

Before building this circuit, lay it out on paper first (graph paper with ten squares per inch is ideal, since perfboard—which should be used for this project—has its holes spaced at similar intervals). Bear in mind that R13, the preamp gain control, can be either a trimpot or a standard control; if you decide to use it as a trimpot, leave room on the circuit board. Also remember that the two 100K pots, R12A and R12B, are the ganged tone control pots.

Make sure the polarity of C1 and C8 is correct, and use a socket for the IC. Because excessive heat (such as that generated by a soldering iron) can damage ICs, solder in the socket and

the rest of the components, and just before giving it a trial run, insert the IC. Beware of static electricity—it, too, can harm the chip.

Once the circuit board is assembled, examine it carefully for bad solder joints, miswired components, and correct polarities. Next, place it in the guitar's cavity (or a metal box). Without the batteries activated, insert the IC. Make sure that none of the circuit's connections touch the jacks, pots, or any shielding that may be present. A piece of construction paper can serve as a good insulator between the board and other parts if necessary.

Reassemble your guitar, plug in the cord, and turn on your amp (make sure that the volume is way down—malfunctions or a high-gain setting of the preamp may result in a loud roar). If the unit fails to work, unplug everything, disconnect the batteries, and re-check the circuit's construction.

The Preamp/EQ outlined here should give you a great deal of control over the tonal parameters of your guitar. And even if you're satisfied with your current sound, you may find that the new expanse of tones and the volume boost can add a new dimension to your sonic capabilities.

Colin Drew

Preamp/EQ Parts List

Resistors (all 1/4-watt, 10%)

R1	470k ohms
R2-R5	10k
R6, R7	3.9k
R8, R9	100k
R10, R11	12k

Capacitors (all rated at 16 volts)

C1	1uF electrolytic
C2, C3	.033uF
C4	4,700pF
C5	.022uF
C6, C7	3300pF
C8	2.2uF electrolytic

Pots

R12A, B	100k linear taper, ganged pot
R13	50k linear taper
R14	guitar's volume pot

Miscellaneous parts

DPST switch, SPDT switch, battery connectors, knobs, wire, solder, perfboard, output jack.

6.
ELECTRONIC EFFECTS AND ACCESSORIES

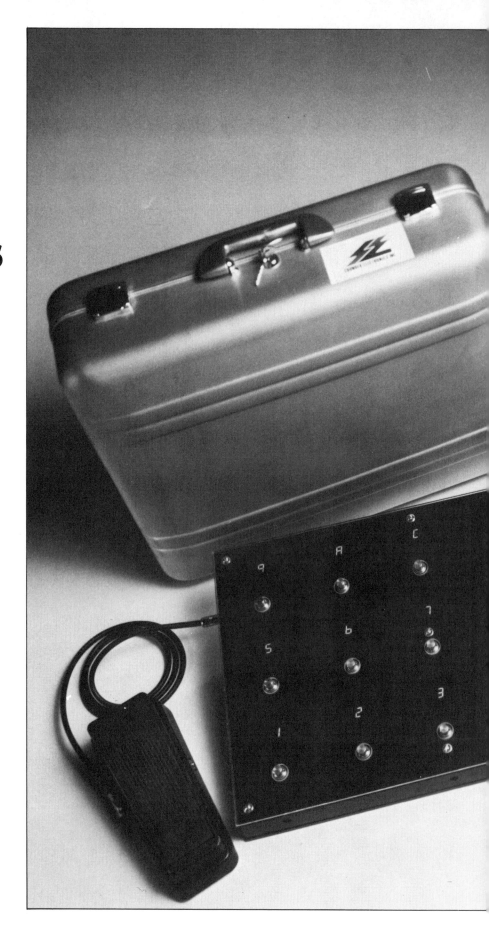

INTRODUCTION

Thomas Edison rejoiced over his invention of the light bulb, but he never dreamed that electricity would be used to power fuzztones, equalizers, choruses, and the dozens of other sound processors so vital to today's guitarist. The sixth chapter starts with a section on the vital link between all amplified gear, the cord. Often the last piece of equipment given consideration when guitarists buy instruments, amps, and effects, it can either be the key to a good sound or an Achilles heel. Choosing, repairing, and building your own cords are covered within. The next six sections of the chapter cover effects devices and their management. First, there's a look at how several common devices work, followed by detailed examinations revealing how chorusing and other time-delay devices work and a comparison of graphic and parametric equalizers. After the discussions of "what they are" and "how they work," you're ready for the section by electronics wizard Craig Anderton explaining how to connect those little boxes for your guitar's best sound. The final two sections cover how to build a pedalboard (the next logical step in making your bundle of effects and wires portable), and how to streamline your setup by including multi-effects devices and computerized programmers.

THE GUITAR CORD

October 1979. Without your guitar you couldn't strum a single note. If you're an electric guitarist you also must have a means of getting the guitar's sound to the amp; otherwise, nothing that you strum will be heard. Unless you can afford a wireless transmitter to link the guitar with the amp, you will have to do what most electric pickers do—plug in a cord.

If you have been playing electric for any amount of time, you know how important a cord can be to your sound. If you've ever forgotten to bring one to a jam session, practice, or gig, you can remember how your wellspring of tricks, technical wizardry, and hot licks had to go untapped (unless another player happened to have a spare cord to lend). It's hard to believe that a simple length of wire with a plug at each end

could be so important, so *needed*. But it's a fact of life that electric guitarists must face if they want to convey their music to an audience. The guitarist, the guitar, the strings, pickups, cord, and amp all comprise a system. If any part of that system is missing, nonfunctional, or otherwise put out of commission, the end product of all your practicing will be nothing.

Almost every guitarist who has played an electric has uttered on at least one occasion, "I'd give anything for a good cord," as their failing cords caused their amps to crackle, whistle, and pour forth sighs of weird hisses. Everyone has their own set of priorities, and for guitarists one that sits at the top is obtaining dependable equipment. No one can get up onstage and just hope that their gear is going to work. A musi-

cian must *know* that everything will function correctly. Of course there has to be a certain margin that allows for the unavoidable frustrations—strings that break, PAs that howl from feedback—but only so much patience can be expected from an audience. It's part of your job to keep your guitar, amp, and peripheral equipment in good working order. When things break down, your listeners are generally only aware of the end result—flawed music. If things keep going wrong in a performance it makes *you* look bad, too.

In a guitarist's setup, one of the most common items to self-destruct is a cord. It's no real wonder, either, when you consider that in a given performance a cord will be yanked upon, twisted, stepped on by any number of people, and in general exposed to more potential hazards than you could ever foresee. Such wear and tear on a day-to-day basis takes its toll: Almost every

Left: (Top) Raw cord showing conductor, insulation, braided shield, and jacket; (bottom) see-through coil cord. Right: Various kinds of cables and their components.

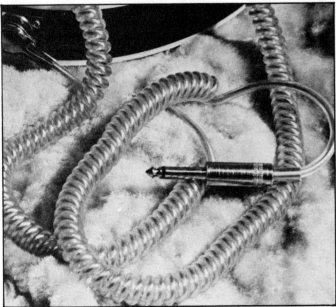

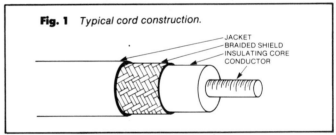

Fig. 1 *Typical cord construction.*

JACKET
BRAIDED SHIELD
INSULATING CORE
CONDUCTOR

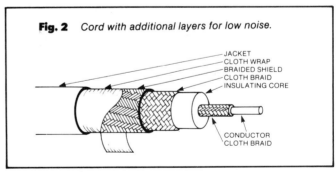

Fig. 2 *Cord with additional layers for low noise.*

JACKET
CLOTH WRAP
BRAIDED SHIELD
CLOTH BRAID
INSULATING CORE

CONDUCTOR
CLOTH BRAID

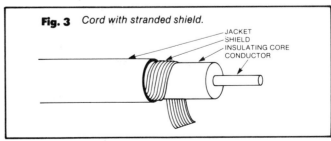

Fig. 3 *Cord with stranded shield.*

JACKET
SHIELD
INSULATING CORE
CONDUCTOR

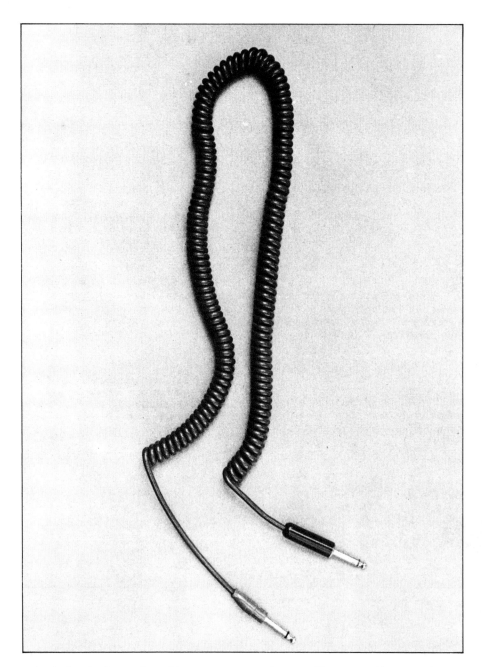

from the guitar to the amp, either the volume or the tone will be impaired.

In order to understand the possible problems, you must first be familiar with a cord's construction. Don't be put off, though. Cords are far simpler than you may at first think. In general it is nothing more than an insulated wire surrounded with a stranded or braided shield of aluminum or copper and then covered with an insulating jacket. The central wire carries the signal to the amp and is generally called the conductor, or "hot" wire. It is most often composed of several strands of wire in a bundle, rather than one solid wire. This makes the cable flexible so that the cord will not be stiff, and therefore will lay flat on the floor. This inner wire can be found in a variety of gauges (depending on the manufacturer's specifications). The wires will range from 25 AWG (American Wire Gauge) to 16 AWG (the smaller the AWG number, the thicker the wire). Naturally, some will be larger or smaller, but for the most part conductors will be constructed within this range. Ideally, every bit of the signal of the cord should be present when the cord terminates at the amp. But if the material used for the cord is of high resistance (thereby restricting the flow of electricity), the signal will be attenuated, resulting in a loss of volume from the guitar. Too much resistance can be present if the wire is too thin, although such wire is almost never used in the construction of cords. Resistance and a similar property called *reactance* combine to make up what is known as a cord's *impedance*. Impedance is simply an overall opposition to electrical flow; it is measured in ohms. The higher the impedance, the larger the corresponding ohm value. Although every cord can be expected to have a few ohms' worth of impedance, you should try to find one with as little impedance as possible.

Another property of wires is *capacitance*, or the ability of an insulator—such as the one between the conductor and the shield—to hold an electrical charge. The capacitance of a cord is generally expressed in units of picofarads per foot (pF/ft). Excessive capacitance causes the cord to behave as a lowpass filter; that is, it allows lower frequencies to travel freely, but removes high-frequency content from the sound. Since the "edge" of a guitar's tone is

guitarist has had a cord crackle, act as a radio antenna, or do absolutely nothing. They'll curse the cord, or curse themselves for not having a spare, even though they're rough on their gear. Even if you do little playing outside of a few slow shuffles at home once a month, chances are your cord will eventually give you some trouble.

Two things are important in assuring a long cord life and the proper transfer of the guitar's signal to the amp. First, you need a good cord at the outset, and second, you must properly treat it and maintain it. To get a good cord, you must know what you're looking for. Basically, you will want something that can clearly transmit your guitar's signal

to the amp. That seems like a simple request, right? But surprisingly, there are many cords that, even when brand new, will not give you a true sound. Why a cord will or won't give an accurate sound is due to a number of factors related to the construction of the cord and the properties of electricity.

The signal put out by a guitar's pickups is an electrical representation of the sound being produced by your strings. This electricity is in the form of low-level alternating current (usually less than one volt) with a frequency corresponding to that of any note played on the guitar. Your amp boosts this signal and converts it back into sound. If anything should happen to the signal on the way attributed mainly to its higher harmonics, it is therefore desirable to have a cord with low capacitance.

The amount and type of shielding is also an important component of a cord. Strands of copper or aluminum are often wrapped in a spiraling (helical) form around the insulation of the center conductor. This shielding usually functions as the ground, or return, wire of a cord; it also helps to block out spurious noises from radios, motors, fluorescent lights, etc. An alternative to using strands of wire as a shield is to use a braided wire tube that fits around the conductor. It works in basically the same way as a stranded shield, but is woven in a crosshatch pattern, making it more able to withstand stretching.

A third type of shielding is a foil of aluminum or a combination of aluminum and polyester. Because it has no gaps between wire strands, its effectiveness can be 100% in guarding against spurious noises entering the conductor. For the most part, though, good braided or stranded shields offer adequate coverage that range anywhere from 70 to 90%—enough to shield the conductor from most radio interference and buzzes from fluorescent lights and motors.

Good shielding is vital, and bad shielding can leave your system open to some unpredictable effects. One minute, the sweet sound of your guitar may be coming through the amp itself, and the next minute you will find yourself being accompanied by someone saying, ''Ten-four, good buddy,'' or (stranger yet) by a totally different song coming from a powerful radio station. If you're like most musicians, you'll find these uninvited, disembodied guests an annoyance that you can live without; if you have cords with good, effective shielding, then you will be able to live without such interference.

Now that you know basically what to look for—and what to avoid—in a cord, how should you go about checking out various cords? There are certainly a lot of them on the market. Go to just about any music store and they are sure to have a variety of them. Try several without changing the control settings on either the guitar or the amp, and compare the sound. If any of the cords make your guitar sound muddy or lackluster, steer clear of them. If any of them cut down your volume, again, avoid them. Shake and flex the cords. Do you hear any crackles or rubbing noises? If you do, you are experiencing what are called *microphonics*. They are noises caused by *triboelectricity*—small

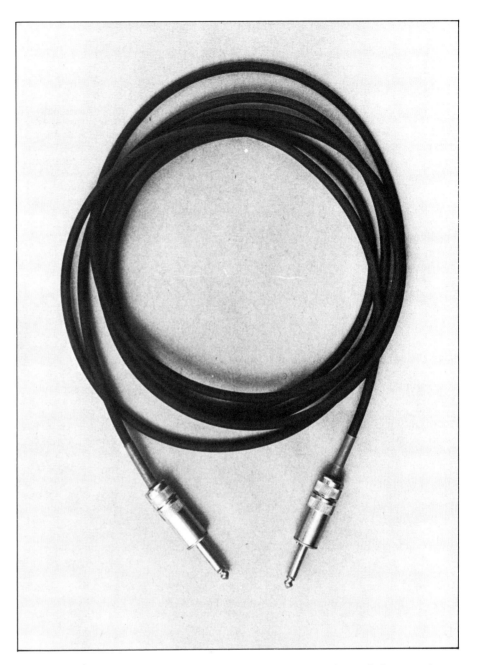

trickles of electricity generated by friction between the cord's components. Some manufacturers add windings of cotton, rayon, polyester, or other fabrics between the various layers of insulation, shield, and conductors to lessen the effect. If one cord exhibits more microphonics than others you have tested, forget it. Chances are, you will move around onstage, and you don't need ''popcorn'' noises coming from your amp.

Try out a cord that is the length that you need. Cords over 20 feet long, no matter how good they are, can start to have a degrading effect on your sound. A bad cord will start to change your guitar's tone at much shorter distances.

If you don't need a really long cord, don't buy one. In fact, don't even bother trying one, because you want a cord that sounds best for what you are actually going to be doing. Also, if you are looking for cords to patch between effects such as fuzztones, phasers, etc., try to use the shortest possible. If, say, your fuzztone is only 10 inches away from your phaser, you don't need a 12-foot cord. The longer the cord, the greater your chances are of introducing unwanted signals into the system.

Look carefully at the cords you are trying out. Molded plugs are a common feature on store-bought production model cords, as well as those given with a new guitar or effect. These can be a source of annoyance if you are the least bit rough on a cord. Because the plug is molded directly onto the cord, it is impossible (without the benefit of an X-ray) to tell how good the connection is between the cord and the plug itself. Some cords with molded ends are excellent; others are doomed from the start. As with buying any other type of cord, a buyer should beware. Try one out in the store; you may find that is suits your needs.

Beware of coil cords. Like straight cords, some are good and some aren't. Many guitarists are attracted to them because they look snazzy, and they're often very convenient in situations where you don't want to be tripping over miles of cords, but some have hidden pitfalls. Because of the coiling of the cord, many do not have adequate shielding, or contain abnormally thin wire (a tradeoff to make coiling easier). This isn't to say that *all* coil cords are bad; it's just that some manufacturers take production shortcuts that result in a less durable, harder-to-repair product than a straight cord. To be sure that you don't get a flawed cord, try a good straight cord between your guitar and amp. Then try the coil cord. If you really want a coil cord, and if it sounds as good as a straight cord, and looks like it can handle whatever amount of punishment you normally dish out, then buy it. Treat the purchase of a cord as if it were an amp or guitar: Don't buy solely on the product's looks. Also, just because a cord has the words "military specification" on it does not guarantee that it is any better than a cord designed to the specification of private industry. Test this sort of cord as carefully as any other.

A good guitar cord isn't always cheap. Some can cost as much as $20.00—or even more. But since you paid hundreds of dollars for a guitar *with the right sound*, and a few hundred more for an amp *with the right sound*, are you going to spoil it all with a junky cord just to save five or ten dollars? Get a good cord; they tend to last, and even if something should happen to go wrong with it (due to accidents, wear and tear, or careless handling), it can almost certainly be repaired.

If you're careful with your cords, they can last for several years. A few precautions will help in assuring a long life for them. First, don't try to roll them up into a small ball and then tie them with their loose ends. This puts excessive strain on the connections of the wire and the plug, and can crimp the shield and conductor in the cord. Many cords have a natural tendency to coil themselves neatly into about an eight-inch circle. Use this feature to your advantage—if the cord wants to wind itself that way, let it. Use string or wire twist ties (such as those for closing garbage or sandwich bags) to tie the cord at two or three places. Clean your cords occasionally. Hold a rag in one hand and pull the cord through it with the other. Excessive dirt that accumulates on the cord acts as a slight abrasive that accelerates wear on the insulating jacket. Also, a clean cord looks better.

Never jerk a cord's plug out of the amp or effects! Hold the plug and pull *that* out. When you tug on the cord, the tension is transferred through the soldered connections of the plug, placing an excessive amount of pull on them. Even if your plugs have strain reliefs (springs that wrap around the cord near the plug), some of the stress is still going to be transferred. Be kind to your cords. The better you treat them, the longer they will last, and the less money you will have to spend fixing or replacing them.

Despite how well you may treat your cords, inevitable tragedies may occur. You must be prepared to deal with bad situations of all kinds. For instance, what would you do if you were to trip over one of the many cords strewn about the stage and yank on it sufficiently hard to dislodge it from its plug? Well, life must go on, and so must your performance. The best thing to do is to have a spare cord in a readily accessible place—on top of the amp, in your guitar case, in a tool box, or anywhere close by. For the time being, you can simply plug in the spare and go on playing. If you're quick enough, you can change a cord in a couple of seconds, and in such a short amount of time you can be back wailing away as if nothing happened.

After the gig, though, you may want to repair the cord that bit the dust. It's not too difficult to do, and no doubt you're aware of what a new cord can cost—motivation enough, particularly if you break cords with any amount of regularity. If you have basic soldering skills, or if you know someone who can guide you through soldering procedures, fixing a cord can be an easy job.

There are two basic plug-to-cord connections found on most cords: (1) The cord is simply soldered to the proper conductors inside the plug, and (2) the cord and plug are integrally molded together with their soldered connections encased in hard plastic. The molded type of cord will often break down near the plug, but you won't be able to actually see symptoms of fatigue. The cord will simply fail to work, or at best work intermittently when you jiggle it. With a plug that is not an integrated part of the cord, you can usually remove the shielding cover, or shell, and examine the connection or connections that have become dislocated. If your cord has a molded plug, you will have to cut the cord about one-half of an inch from the plug itself. After this the procedure for repairing both types of cords is the same. You will need a phone plug—one with a metal shell is advisable, since plastic shells tend to break if you step on them.

Remove the shell and the sheath (the plastic or cardboard insulating collar inside the shell). Place these on the cord in the proper order, so that you don't forget them. It's very common for a person to get all done soldering the cord to the plug and then find that they've forgotten the shell. It can be terribly exasperating to have to undo your work and then redo it. Always plan ahead!

To repair a cord, you will need a few tools—some of them are probably sitting in your tool box already. These are: a small screwdriver, a pair of pliers, a soldering iron, a pair of safety glasses, and a sharp knife or single-edged razor blade. You will of course need solder, and you may want to consider a soldering station (a stand that holds the hot soldering iron), a vise, and perhaps a piece of plywood or particle board to work on.

Always use rosin-core solder for this and any other type of electronic work. It contains an alloy of lead and tin that is designed for a good balance of electrical conductivity and fast melting. *Never* use acid-core solder; it is designed for plumbing and some other nonelectronic applications and it can ruin anything you work on. If you have any questions as to which is which, tell the salesperson at the hardware or electronics supply store what you're using it for. They'll set you on the right path.

With a very sharp knife, razor, or craft blade, cut a half-inch-long slit in the outer insulation of the cord. Peel back the insulation until a total of about three-quarters of an inch of shielding is exposed. Trim off the insulation that you have pulled back. Now unravel some of the shielding—about half an inch should be sufficient—and twist this into a conductor. Don't worry if some of the shield's strands fall off; they were probably damaged when you slit the shield. They are of little consequence, as there are plenty more left to work with. Next, cut away a quarter inch of insulation

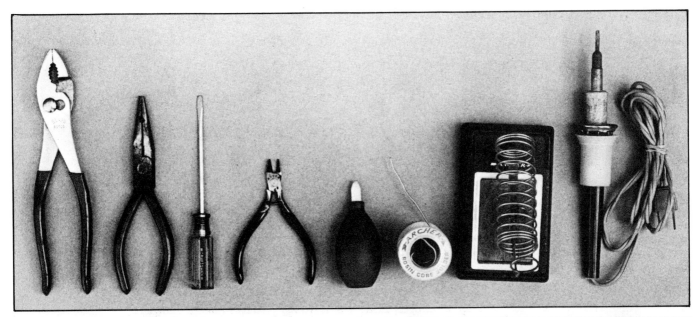

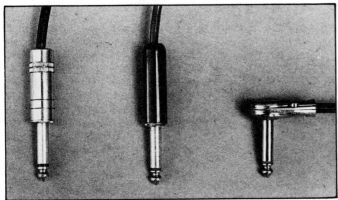

surrounding the center conductor; be careful not to cut any of the wire strands of the conductor. Remove that insulation and twist the strands together.

The following steps involve soldering. There are a few precautions you should take: (1) Don't solder on a "good" surface. A table top can be permanently marred if hot solder should drip on its finish. Formica, veneers, and any similar materials can be ruined in the blink of an eye. Use a piece of plywood for a work surface, or better yet do your repairs on a workbench in the garage or basement. (2) Wear eye protection. A pair of safety glasses usually cost less than a set of strings—a hell of a cheap price to pay when you consider that your eyes can't be replaced at *any* cost. Soldering in itself is not dangerous, but solder sometimes splatters small drops of rosin (the brown material in the center of the solder that enables the solder to flow smoothly onto connections). Also, whenever you snip excess bits of wire, they can inadvertently be

sent flying. Such occurrences may or may not come to pass, but there's no reason to tempt fate, and being prepared puts you in control. (3) Use a vise, pliers, or a clothespin to hold a plug while you are soldering. That metal gets hot enough to blister your fingers, and if you just leave it on your work surface chances are good that it will roll. It can then land on your legs, in your lap, or on your foot. This brings up another precaution—don't wear short pants or go barefoot when soldering. You never know when or if something hot will land on your legs or feet. Play it safe. Pants—particularly jeans or corduroys—afford acceptable buffering from the heat. Any shoes will do.

Now that you're going to solder, lay your tools out, put on your safety glasses, and plug in the soldering iron. The heating element will take a few minutes to reach operating temperature. The first soldering you will want to perform is a process called *tinning*. You should tin the center conductor and the twisted shield. To do this, hold the sol-

dering iron to the wire, wait a few seconds for it to heat up, and touch the solder to the *wire*. The solder should melt and flow onto the wire. Remove the solder, then the iron. Only put a light coat of solder on each wire. Tinning helps insure a better connection to the jack, and improves conductivity. After tinning both wires, trim the lead made from the extra shield so that it is about a quarter of an inch long.

If there are any screws in the plug, remove them. Screwing the cord to the plug does not afford the best connection; the screws can come loose, and with them any attached wires. There are two connecting points on the plug: the tip (hot) connection and the sleeve con-

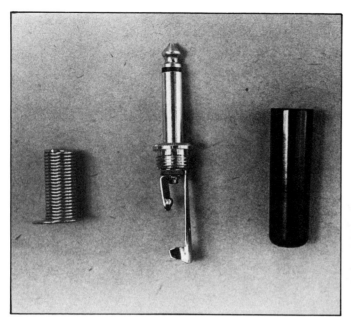

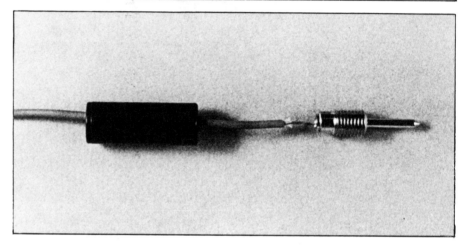

Clockwise from top left: Disassembled plug (shell, plug, and coil-spring strain relief), switched plug, and pin-style plug with single conductor.

nection. The tip connection most often sticks straight out of the middle of the plug, and is short. The sleeve connection attaches to the main part of the plug and is about twice as long as the other.

To solder the shield lead to the sleeve connection, hold the lead against the connection and heat both with the soldering iron and touch the solder to both connecting surfaces. Remove the solder and allow the junction to cool. The solder should have a shiny, silvery appearance when cool. If it looks very dull, the connection should be redone.

To attach the hot lead, pass it through the hole in the tip connection from the inside out. Heat the wire and the connecting point with the soldering iron. Touch the solder to it. Remove the solder, then the iron. Allow it to cool. Snip off any excess wire and bend the tip connection in slightly. This will help prevent any sharp edges (burrs) of the snipped wires from cutting through the insulating collar and shorting out against the shell.

If there is a cable clamp (two flaps protruding from the end of the sleeve connection), bend these around the cord with pliers. This clamp helps take any excess strain off the conductors. Don't make it too tight with the pliers, since too much pressure will cause the clamp to cut through the insulation. Slide the insulating collar over the connections, then slide the shell, too, and screw it onto the plug.

It may take practice to be able to repair a cord quickly and in a way that looks acceptable, but in the end you can save a bundle. In fact, you can make your own cords if you're so inclined. Most electronic supply houses sell cord designed for microphones and guitars. Buy the best quality cord available. If you go through the trouble to make a cord, make a good one. Variations on the standard phone plug are also available. Angle plugs, solid brass plugs, plugs with switches to eliminate thumping when they're unplugged from the guitar, so-called military plugs, some with diamond-shaped tips, and even some with gold plating are offered. While each has its good points, all function in basically the same way. Talk to guitarists who have tried the various kinds and then try them yourself. To avoid disappointment, don't buy anything without first investigating.

Cords are a necessity for every electric guitarist, and once you have heard what a bad one can do to your sound, you'll always want the best. A final caution: Never use a guitar cord to link an amplifier with a speaker cabinet. However good the cord may be, there is always some resistance—perhaps two or four ohms, and possibly more—this can cause undue loading of the amp's output circuitry and possibly damage the unit. It will detract from the amount of power reaching the speaker, too. Also, most guitar cords can't take the higher voltage that an amp can crank out (20 volts and up), and will seriously attenuate your volume and perhaps even burn out. Use a speaker cord for this application. It is usually made of zipcord (standard lamp cord) and can handle up to about 10 times the power an amp can deliver. Because zip cord isn't shielded, never use a speaker cord for a guitar-to-amp transmission, or else you'll be back to accompanying a broadcast from a local radio station.

Tom Mulhern

EFFECTS DEVICES

May 1976. Today's guitarist, by using some of the growing number of electronic modifiers available, can make dramatic changes to the basic tonal color of an electric guitar. Whether these changes are meaningful musically, or whether they are just effects for the sake of effect, depends strongly on the musical sense of the performer and the viewpoint of the audience. However, the more you know about an effects box, the better your chances of extracting musically satisfying sounds from it. Below are some of the explanations of how electronic modifiers actually work.

Wah-wah pedals. A wah-wah is the name in guitar circles for what synthesizer players call a *filter*. Filters are similar to amplifiers in that they provide gain, but they do so in a premeditatedly lopsided way. For example, a *lowpass* filter amplifies lower frequencies while rejecting higher frequencies: conversely, a *highpass* filter amplifies higher frequencies while rejecting lower ones. This principle of controlled amplification lies behind the bass and treble controls you find on hi-fi and guitar amplifiers. Wah-wah pedals are a third class of filter, called a bandpass filter. This type of filter puts a large amount of gain at a specific frequency only. By making the filter tunable (that is, having the ability to put that gain peak anywhere within the audio frequency range), and varying the tuning with a pedal, you obtain the wah-wah effect. Depending on the filter design, you can sweep over a one octave range, or up to six or more octaves. A wider sweep range is not necessarily an advantage, as pedal action becomes more critical.

The name wah-wah derives from the fact that a bandpass filter is similar to the filter inside your own mouth that allows you to make 'wah' sounds. One of the first people to use a commercially available wah-wah was Eric Clapton, on "Tales of Brave Ulysses" from the album *Disraeli Gears* [Atco, 33-232]. Jimi Hendrix also used a wah-wah, as evidenced on virtually all his albums. Some players rock the pedal in a rhythmic fashion to accent the tempo, as in the theme from "Shaft," whereas others use it more as a tone control, rocking the pedal slowly to accent certain guitar notes.

Fuzzboxes. A fuzzbox is another variation on the amplifier theme, but it's an amplifier whose gain is set at an abnormally high level. This means that even the slightest sounds are going to be amplified so much that they overload the fuzzboxes' internal amplifier, causing distortion. The greater the overload, the greater the fuzz effect. This massive gain not only adds distortion and sustain, but increases the chance of both controlled and uncontrolled feedback since it amplifies every little vibration the guitar produces. You don't necessarily need a fuzzbox to achieve the fuzz sound; for example, by turning up your amplifier volume to an outrageously high level, you can force your electronics and speaker to overload, again giving distortion. In fact, one of the advantages of a fuzzbox is that you can obtain the sound of a high volume setup at low levels, like in the studio or small clubs.

A variation on the normal fuzz is the triggered type. Since fuzztones are so sensitive, they tend to pick up hum, noise, and other extraneous sounds. A triggered fuzz shuts itself off if you are not plucking the strings, or if the guitar note is at the very end of a decay. Although it doesn't sustain in as predictable a manner as a conventional fuzz, the lack of noise more than offsets this effect for certain styles of playing.

Many bass players have noted that a guitar fuzzbox doesn't sound all that good with bass, giving a thin sound. This is because a fuzzbox generates many high-frequency harmonics, these high frequency sounds tend to dominate over the original bass bottom, giving that tinny effect.

Compressors (sustainers). I prefer the term compressor over sustainer, because there are ways to sustain a sound other than compression. Compressors are yet another special-purpose amplifier circuit.

With a conventional amplifier (or preamplifier), the more signal put into it, the more signal you get out of it (up to the point of distortion, that is). A compressor does just the opposite: the more you put in, the less it gives out. Therefore, when you first pluck a guitar string, the compressor tends to reduce the output, and as the string decays, the compressor amplifies more and more to maintain a constant output. This is how it creates sustain. The mark of a good compressor is smooth compression; in other words, it doesn't sound choppy as it adjusts to the changing signal input. Also, a compressor should have low noise. Because of the large amounts of gain available, a compressor will sometimes think its own noise is a low-level signal and try to amplify it.

Compression is so widely used in recording to limit dynamic range (otherwise, tape machines and disc cutters would not be able to handle the average live performance caused by distortion from the peaks and valleys) that it would be hard to name a record that doesn't use it. Also, compression gives the illusion of louder volume, since the constant dynamic range gives a much higher average signal level. For this reason, it's used on TV commercials to make the ads stand out, and many Top-40-type stations compress their overall signal to get the extra talk power.

One of the most obvious examples of compression is the acoustic guitar sound in "White Summer," by Jimmy Page from the Yardbirds' album *Little Games* [Epic, BN 26313]. Notice how every little nuance, finger slide, and string noise comes through; and when a sharply hit chord appears, it seems no louder than the single note lines. Drums are also favorite candidates for compression—listen to "Hole in My Shoe" from Traffic's *Dear Mr. Fantasy* album [English import only—Island, ILPS 5906], as well as the middle-period *Beatles Magical Mystery Tour* [Capitol, 2835].

Compression is a valuable effect; it doesn't color the guitar sound like a fuzztone or wah-wah, but gives a smooth, sustaining sound that is pleasing to the ear and actually makes the guitar somewhat easier to play, since you don't have to hit the strings as hard to get a good output level. Singers also like compression: Whether you yell or whisper, the sound level is more or less constant.

Octave splitters. These are also called octave dividers. They've never really caught on that well with guitarists, mostly because guitars don't mate well from an electronic standpoint with octave-dividing circuitry. Saxophones

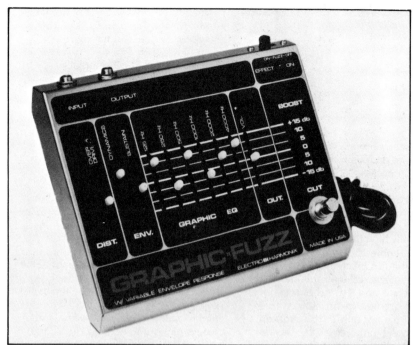
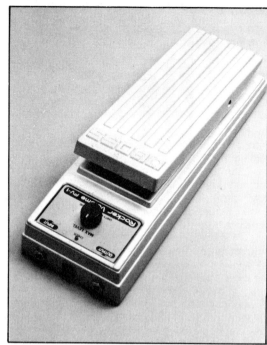

L-R: Electro-Harmonix Graphic Fuzz (combination fuzztone and graphic equalizer), Boss PV-1 volume pedal, Morley Stereo Chorus/Vibrato, Ibanez Compressor, Mu-tron Octave divider.

give out a much more compatible signal, and most recorded examples of octave division feature the saxophone. The long sax solo on Frank Zappa's "King Kong" from the *Uncle Meat* album [Bizarre, 2024] is a good illustration. Eddie Harris also uses an octave box extensively in his recorded work. The only guitarist I know of who uses an octave box extensively in his playing is Tal Farlow.

The sound of an octave box is generally a raspy duplicate of the guitar pitch, but an octave (sometimes two) lower. The raspiness is due to the fact that an octave box can't divide a guitar down directly, but must fuzz it first, and then divide it down. The divided output, in turn, sounds fuzzed. Filtering can help improve the tone, but it adds cost. Another problem is that octave boxes like consistent input signals. A guitar is anything but consistent, a string gives out more harmonics when first plucked, fretted strings give less output than open ones, and so on. As a result, many early octave dividers worked sporadically or only over a certain portion of the guitar's neck. By judicious use of different pickups and tone control settings it's possible to tame these things, but it requires practice. If you are willing to work with them, however, the effect can

be most dramatic—like a bass doubling along with your guitar run exactly.

Octave multipliers. This is the opposite of an octave splitter; rather than giving a tone an octave lower, it gives one an octave higher. Since all but the most expensive custom types work on the same principles as the octave splitter, the same kind of problems occur, and the same kind of cautions hold. The only commercial octave multiplier I've ever seen was used by Jimi Hendrix in the studio, although I'm not sure he used it 'live.' If memory serves, it was built by Roger Mayer in England (it also looked homemade—not the product of an assembly line) and was called "Octavia." Since the octave higher sound can occur in other ways (hitting harmonics through a fuzz, certain wah-wah techniques, etc.), it's difficult to single out any one of Hendrix's cuts as the definitive octave multiplier sound; however, it sounds to me like he used it extensively on the first *Are You Experienced* album [Reprise, 2621].

Tremolo and vibrato. Tremolo was one of the first available electronics modifiers; in fact, Bo Diddley couldn't have gotten his sound without one. A tremolo simply causes a cycling volume change, as if you were turning your guitar's volume control up and down really fast and evenly. Usually, the speed of this change is variable, from slow (1 or less Hz) to about 15 cycles per second.

Vibrato sounds similar, but is much

more complex to generate from an electronic standpoint. Instead of giving a periodic volume change, it gives a periodic pitch change. There are, to my knowledge, no commercial vibrato boxes on the market, although phase-shifting devices may be modified to produce a vibrato effect. Most vibrato you hear on record comes from an old series of Magnatone amps, which had built-in vibrato (to be different from the many amps at the time that had tremolo, I presume). Vibrato can also be introduced with the guitar's vibrato tailpiece; however, this method can give a much wider pitch change than the electronic types.

Volume Pedals. There are two distinctly different types of volume pedals around, so we'll touch on each one. The passive type simply places a volume control (technical name: potentiometer or pot), like the kind on your guitar, in a footpedal configuration. The chief disadvantages are when the pot gets scratchy, so does your guitar sound; there may also be some loss of signal. The photocell type is somewhat more complex. It uses a light-sensitive volume control called a photoresistor (or pair of photoresistors in some models), and the ultimate volume level depends upon how much light shines on the photoresistor. A small light bulb inside the pedal provides the light, a pot then controls its brightness.

Although this may sound like a roundabout way to accomplish the

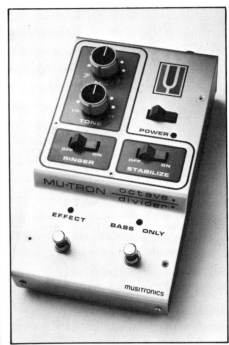

same task, there is one big advantage. Since the pedal volume depends upon the resistance of the photoresistor, and photoresistors don't get scratchy like pots, you can achieve a much smoother and pop-free sound. Even if the pot controlling the light bulb should get dirty and scratchy, the overall sound still remains clean because the light bulb, photocell combination is not fast enough to respond to the little ticks and pops of a dirty pot.

I like using a volume pedal for live playing. For one thing, it can help control fuzzes and compressors. When they feel like they might feedback uncontrollably, simply pulling back on the volume usually straightens things out. Volume pedals also allow you to make volume changes without having to take your hands away from the guitar—very useful. Finally, they can give an effect; by plucking your guitar string with the pedal off and then pushing the guitar pedal in, you get a bowed-like sound, sort of like a subtle cat's meow. Steve Howe of Yes uses this technique (catch the intro to "Roundabout" on *Yessongs* [Atlantic, 3-100], as does Larry Carlton for example, "Put It Where You Want It" from the *Crusader 1* album [Chisa, BTS 6001.

Other types of pedals and filters may also be tuned by photoresistor instead of pots, and the same general comments about passive vs. photoelectric types apply there, too. Although companies use the terms photocell and photoresistor interchangeably, there is a

difference. A photocell generates a voltage when illuminated; a photoresistor changes resistance.

Preamps. Preamps simply take a guitar signal and make it stronger. They are necessary for driving amplifiers with low sensitivity; for example, many hi-fi amplifiers are designed to give out their maximum-rated power with a half-volt of input signal, yet a guitar only gives out about one-fifth of that on the average. A preamp can also overdrive an amplifier with high sensitivity, giving a fuzz-type sound. Robin Trower and John McLaughlin derive much of their guitar sound by using a preamp to overdrive their normal amplifier. In essence, this is electrically equivalent to using a fuzz, although the actual sound may be slightly different.

Preamps are fairly simple circuits, and as a result they can easily mount inside a guitar. Many of the new guitars with built-in electronics simply contain a preamp to give a level boost, and some kind of electronic filter instead of the guitar's standard tone controls.

Echo units. The echo unit is basically a miniature tape recorder. In simpler models, your signal gets recorded on a tape loop at the record head, then travels to the playback head (travel time is the echo delay time) where the signal is fed to your amp so you can hear the delayed signal, and passed on at reduced volume through a volume control to the record head again, so

that next time the tape loop goes around you get another echo, but this time a little softer. Echo units also have blend controls to mix the original guitar signal with the echo signal.

Most of the echo you hear on recordings is not from an echo unit, but from using the echo capabilities of the studio's recorders. Studio recorders are far superior in terms of frequency response, lack of noise, and freedom from wow and flutter (or, cyclic pitch variations) than the average commercially available echo unit. Therefore, echo units are mostly a way to get studio effects in an onstage situation. One band that uses echo extensively 'live' is Pink Floyd, as do many of the more experimental jazz groups (Miles Davis, Billy Cobham, etc.).

Since most echo units are tape recorders, it's important to remember that it's necessary to demagnetize and clean the tape heads about once a month, or more frequently with heavy use. [*Ed. Note: Now solid-state delay lines based on digital technology have made the standard tape echo unit all but obsolete.*]

Reverberation. This gives a feeling of spaciousness, as if the instrument were being played in a large hall. Reverb is a natural for studio use; studios are designed to be acoustically dead, so adding reverb makes the sound a little more live. Many instrument amplifiers also have built-in reverb units.

The principle of operation is as fol-

Clockwise from top left: Boss TW-1 Touch Wah envelope-following filter, Roland rack-mountable guitar preamp with overdrive, tone, and level controls, Roland RE-100 Space Echo.

lows: Your instrument feeds into a speaker-like device that couples your signal into a set of reverb springs. Going through these springs introduces a delay that is then picked up by a microphone-like transducer at the other end. Also, the signal doesn't just go down the springs once, but bounces back and forth until it dies out (decays) completely. The amount of time it takes to decay determines the duration of the reverberation effect. Reverb units generally include the facility to mix part of your straight signal in with the reverberated signal.

Ring modulators. Producing a highly unusual sound, a ring modulator accepts two frequencies as inputs, and gives you the sum and difference of the two frequencies at the output. One of the two input frequencies is your instrument, the other is provided by an internal oscillator (or tone generator). For example, if the internal oscillator is putting out a 1000Hz tone, and your guitar is laying an A-440Hz, you will hear the sum (1000 + 440, or 1440Hz) and the difference (1000 - 440, or 560Hz). So at the output you have two tones, one at 560Hz and one at 1440Hz; additionally, you don't hear either of the original input signals due to the nature of ring modulator circuitry.

Although ring modulators aren't as popular as fuzzes and other modifiers, they've caught on with a lot of jazz people; for example, listen to Jan Hammer's solo on ''The Noonward Race'' from the Mahavishnu Orchestra album *Inner Mounting Flame* [Columbia, KC 31067]. One aspect of his playing is that he tends to vary the internal oscillator frequency manually, giving a unique kind of vibrato.

The sound of a ring modulator is difficult to describe, the overall effect is

sort of percussive and gong-like. The added overtones and sub-harmonics (which frequently aren't consonant with the guitar signal) also add a sort of mechanical timbre. In fact, since the straight ring modulator sound is kind of harsh, it's common practice to add a little natural instrument sound to the ring-modulated output. Most ring modulators have this capability, using a control called either mix or blend. Additionally, since changing the internal oscillator frequency drastically alters the final sound, the oscillator is usually variable and controlled by either an external potentiometer or pedal of some kind.

Phase shifters. Phasing began as a studio process in the '50s; it requires two tape recorders (one with variable speed operation) and a relatively hip engineer or producer. However, you can't phase in *real time*, in other words, you can't phase a track at the same time you lay it down, but usually have to wait until the mixdown process. Tape phasing itself consists of recording your instrument on two separate tape recorders, then listening to the outputs of both

recorders simultaneously and varying the speed of one of the recorders. This produces a small time delay or time lead, which creates all kinds of sonic phenomena—harmonic structures change, the phase of the signal changes, etc.

When phasing was first introduced, it was not an immediate success . . . people thought the unusual sound meant something was wrong with the record. In the '60s, however, many groups started to use phasing, creating sounds characterized by a swooshy, milky, spacey effect. Some of the most lavish examples of phasing are on Jimi Hendrix' album, *Axis: Bold As Love* [Reprise, 6281], particularly on the final section of the title cut; another example is the mid-part of the Doobie Brothers' ''Listen To The Music'' from their *Toulouse Street* album, [Warner Brothers, 2634]. However, while American recording engineers were ''phasing'' their records, English engineers called the process ''flanging,'' presumably because the engineers would put their thumb along the flange of the tape reel to create speed variations necessary to the phasing process, although Beatles producer George Martin claims that John Lennon coined the term duing one of their recording sessions.

Due to the complexity and expense of phasing in the studio, there was growing pressure from musicians to have a box that could simulate the sound of phasing "live." This led to the phase shifter. Like tape phasing, the phase shift sounds occur by taking a signal, giving it a variable time delay, and listening to it at the same time as the original signal. To produce the phase shifting effect, you don't have to put in much delay (nowhere near as much as an echo unit, for example), so most companies use a series of little amplifiers that can change phase in a continuously variable manner from 0 to 180 degrees, which produces an apparent time delay. By putting a whole bunch of these stages end to end, or *in series*, the phase changes add up; for example, with four stages you get 4 x 180 or 720 degrees of phase shift, which produces a delay sufficient to give a phasing effect.

By electrically varying the phase shift at a slow rate, such as 1 to 10 cycles per second, it is possible to simulate the swirling effect of rotating speakers. A low frequency *control oscillator*, which usually has either an adjustable speed control or buttons for slow, fast, or medium speeds, actuates the periodic phase change.

Although these phase shift boxes make neat sounds, they don't really have the sharp clarity that only tape phasing can give. This is because all those phase shift stages produce an apparent, rather then real, time delay.

Enter the '70s, with the technology to create actual time delays rather than simple phase changes. These *analog delay lines* take a signal and pass it down a series of stages (bucket brigade fashion), to create a delay. This sounds much closer to tape phasing—but manufacturing companies using analog delay lines couldn't call their new boxes phasing units, since they'd already used up that name on their phase shift type circuits. So, they call these newer, more realistic sounding boxes "flangers."

One of the best examples of the phase shifter box sound is Joe Walsh's "Turn To Stone" from his *So What* album, [Dunhill, 50171], although many albums and songs (sometimes too many, I'm afraid) also use this effect.

Digital delay lines. Digital delay lines have been in existence before the newer analog delay lines, and still offer sev-eral advantages. Analog delay lines (see above) pass a signal along down hundreds of little delay stages—but sadly, each stage contributes a little bit to degrading the signal. Therefore, you can't have too much delay without adding noise and distortion to the signal, so there is a limit to how much delay you can coax out of an analog delay line. The digital delay line, while using the same principles, makes one important distinction. A signal presented to it is first "coded" into *digital* form, which is the same kind of language that computers talk. This coded signal is then delayed through a number of stages; but because it is a code and not a real signal, there is no degrading action on the signal itself. After the delay, the signal is decoded back to its original form. NASA uses a procedure similar to this to clean up pictures from outer space by coding the pictures, sending the pictures as a code rather than as pictures, and then decoding again at the receiving end.

Digital delay lines (or DDLs) are also inherently more expensive than analog types, which has relegated their use pretty much to high-ticket recording studios and PA companies. DDLs are used mainly to create more accurate phasing effects than those possible with phase shifter boxes; they can also add enough delay to give a distinct but short echo, which makes an instrument sound like it's doubling with itself. Although analog delay lines can do many of the same things, in critical applications the DDL is the way to go. [*Ed. Note: In many cases, digital delays are actually less expensive than equivalent analog devices due to recent breakthroughs in computer technology.*]

Envelope-dependent devices. A fairly new class of device, as represented by the Mutron and Seamoon's Funk Machine, these two boxes basically allow you to get the effect of a wah-wah pedal, but without the pedal. The process is a mite complicated, so hang in while we go into the electronics.

Instead of being pedal controlled, the loudness of the signal input controls these filters. A strong signal kicks the filter open, as if you pushed a pedal down to its treble position. As the signal decays, the filter behaves as if you were pulling the pedal back to its initial position, but exactly synchronized to the volume of the input signal. This type of machine works best with instruments that are percussive (i.e., guitars, basses, electric pianos), because the percussiveness makes the filter go through a batch of changes due to the many volume level changes. Envelope-dependent units therefore have a sensitivity control, to adjust the filter's excursion sweep relative to the volume input. A slight filter excursion sounds like a burble; a wide excursion sounds like a wah-wah. Recorded examples of the Mutron can be found on Steve Howe's *Beginnings* album, [Atlantic, SD 18154]; Larry Graham uses the Funk Machine with his bass on the *Release Yourself* album, [Warner Brothers, BS 2814]. Like many other effects, these often sound better when combined with some straight signal; this is especially important with bass, so you don't lose the bottom.

Talking bags. Joe Walsh's solo on "Rocky Mountain Way" from the *Smoker You Drink* album, [Dunhill, DSX-50130], shows off the talking-bag effect; Link Wray use a homemade setup that was a cross between a wah-wah pedal and talking bag back in the '50s. In any event the principle of operation is as follows: Your guitar signal goes to a little amp-speaker combination, and the output from the speaker goes through a plastic tube whose end sits in the back of your mouth. By putting a PA microphone up to your mouth, you hear the guitar signal through the PA—but filtered through your mouth cavity, which incidentally makes a pretty good filter. One warning, though: A dentist friend of mine once had the opinion that these things could rattle your teeth around, leading to a premature loss of teeth if used extensively. I have little knowledge on the subject, and it seems a bit alarmist considering how little the average guitarist actually uses the effect; I pass the information along, anyway.

Equalizers. An equalizer is basically a fancy tone control. Rather than just boosting or cutting in the bass and treble range like most tone controls, an equalizer has several points (usually five or more) distributed throughout the audio range. You can boost or cut the gain by a fair amount at any of the points. Thus, if you had points for bass, lower midrange, midrange, upper midrange, and treble, you could boost the bass to make up for a deficient speaker cabinet, while cutting the treble a bit to deemphasize any noise, and beefing up the upper midrange a hair to give more bite or presence. The other points can be left in the flat position, which neither boosts nor cuts. Equalizers mainly allow you to shape frequency response in any way you want; this is how studios add more bite, bottom, or whatever tonal quality desired to a sound.

These are the basic modifiers, although as different technologies start to grow and mature, we will see even more devices made available to expand the guitar's sonic options. The guitar is such a supremely expressive instrument by itself that some people question the validity of effects, and some people look down on them. But it seems to me that good musicians, when and if they use effects, use them well; and if an effects device can help somebody express their musical dreams better, then I figure not only are they valid, but raise the quality of life of a musician. Unless, of course, they break down . . . but that's another story.

Craig Anderton

CHORUS LINES

February 1982. Pure tones are boring. Turn on your TV at 4 AM and listen to the test tone that accompanies the color bars. Very boring. The ear, working in conjunction with the brain, actually *craves* dynamics in sounds—changes in timbre, pitch, loudness, rhythm. When confronted with a simple or steady sound, the listener is easily fatigued, and the tendency is to let the mind wander. Harmonically complex sounds, such as those produced by a plucked guitar string, stir the mind and delight the ear. Even something so seemingly simple as a major scale produces an avalanche of stimuli.

For years, electric guitarists have been accustomed to new electronic effects that alter the basic timbre of their instruments in one way or another. However, not all guitarists want to change their sound—they just want it *fatter*. To such an end, the chorus device provides an electronic means of enriching the texture of an instrument without drastically altering its basic timbre.

The *choral* effect, produced in nature by multiple voicing, has been a part of music and instrumentation for many centuries: from the many-stringed lute and piano to the modern 12-string guitar and mandolin. In much the same way, a group of people singing in unison produces a rich, thick blend, which bathes the listener's ears in interesting, dynamic sounds. Just by adding voices to sing the same part creates incredibly complex overtone structures that add size and shape to even the most one dimensional of musical pieces.

Historically, instruments have had doubled or tripled strings; until a few hundred years ago, this was often to increase their volume (single strings of gut, soft iron, brass, or bronze didn't vibrate strongly enough to create a tremendous amount of sound). However, more than greater volume was achieved through doubling. A more complex, well-rounded sound was produced as a result of the chorusing between strings.

What is it about the chorus effect that makes it so apparent? How can you tell two strings plucked in unison from a single one? Two factors play the greatest role in determining this: the time between the sounding of the voices (such as two strings) and the relative pitches of the voices.

Let's use the 12-string guitar as our reference to examine the effects of time delay and relative pitch on our perception of the chorus effect. When the two strings are tuned perfectly in unison, and are picked, they sound almost as one. As the pick passes over one and then the other, there is a natural time delay—however slight—between when you hear the first string and when you hear the second string. Such a short delay—only a few milliseconds (thousandths of a second)—is much shorter than the 20 millisecond gap necessary for the ear to detect a discrete delay. If the two strings are tuned closely enough, and picked rapidly with the same amount of force, many people can't tell that there are actually two strings involved.

By slightly detuning one of the unison strings, it is possible for almost anyone to discern two distinct voices. This pitch disparity doesn't need to be very great; our ears are quite keen, and can detect pitch differences of only a few *cents* (hundredths of a semi-tone, or half-step).

Musicians and composers have long been aware of the thickness produced by instrumental doubling. A solo violin, for example, can be pleasing to the ear, but several violins performing in unison create a rich, warm effect. This richness is due to phase differences between sounds created at multiple sources. Minute differences in the time when sound waves from different sources begin, coupled with differences in pitch (rarely, if ever will two instruments be *exactly* in tune), produce complex harmonic interaction.

Cancellation and reinforcement of certain frequencies, caused by the meeting of sounds from multiple sound sources (including reflected sound) create a spatial image, giving the sound a three-dimensional feel, and thereby creating an illusion of size.

Of course, not every guitarist wants to play a 12-string or a lute. The doubling strings generally make it harder to finger notes or to vibrato, plus they make fast cross-string picking a nightmare. Today, through the wonders of electronic wizardry, a guitarist can plug his instrument into any of dozens of electronic chorus devices and get a fatter sound—without *having* to play a 12-string (or using a second guitarist). And 12-string players can get even more shimmer and size out of their instruments as well. In fact, any electronic signal can be fattened up through the use of a chorus effect.

Electronic production of the chorus effect relies on the same two fundamentals as natural chorusing: pitch difference and time delay. The delay itself does little to thicken the texture of the overall sound. A short delay added to a sound can create an illusion of two separate sounds. However, they are identical—their nuances and timbre are exact duplicates, and the gap of time separating them is constant. In essence, the two sounds are mirror images of each other.

This is not to say that time-delay effects such as echo, reverb, or automatic double-tracking are flawed. They lack nothing when taken for their face value, and can be quite beneficial as musical tools. However, their effects tend to be too perfect, and they add more ambience than richness. To fatten up the sound's harmonic structure, one has to alter the pitch of the double as well as the time lag between the original and the clone. Luckily, changing a sound's pitch electronically is easy: It's simply a matter of changing (modulating) the delay time.

This process can be demonstrated with practically any echo unit—analog or digital delay, or tape echo with variable-speed operation. Set a delay time and leave the echo regeneration control up fairly high. Now play a note through the unit. Shorten the delay time while the sound is echoing, and the pitch will rise; lengthen the delay time, and the pitch will fall. Naturally, a pitch change produced in this way is quite drastic and difficult to control, and therefore it's not very useful in most musical contexts.

Suppose that you could electronically shift the pitch *slightly*—in fact almost imperceptibly—in a controlled manner. This is usually performed by controlling the delay time with a modulation LFO (low-frequency oscillator):

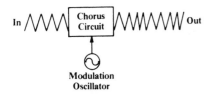

The result would be frequency modulation, or vibrato—a bending of the pitch similar in effect to using a hand vibrato tailpiece or moving a finger slightly while fretting a string. If you were to use only the vibrato output from an electronic circuit, you would get only vibrato. As with echo, reverb, etc., it's a nice effect in some contexts, but it's not chorusing.

Simply mixing the vibrato with the straight signal creates some interesting harmonic interaction, but still the result is merely the original sound flavored with a bit of pitch bending. To achieve chorusing, it is necessary to delay the original signal, add vibrato, and then mix it with the straight signal.

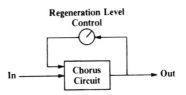

The composite result is a sound whose shape is determined by cancellations and reinforcements of certain frequencies that are delayed, frequency modu-

lated, and mixed. In fact, for an even more pronounced effect, *regenerating* (recirculating, or feeding back) the output from the effect back into the input creates a delay and vibrato of the already delayed and vibratoed signal. This adds even more richness to the final sound.

How are chorus units related to other time-delay signal processors? The key is in how their delay circuitry is employed. Delay times lasting from about 15 milliseconds to 80 milliseconds are used for automatic double-tracking, where an image of two identical sounds in unison is created. The delay employed is too short to be perceived as distinct echoes. The pitch of one of the voices may be modulated slightly. Discrete echoes lag behind a signal by about 80 milliseconds or more, and can be heard as distinct single events.

When delays of approximately 40 to 160 milliseconds in duration are regenerated (in nature, this would mean reflected and re-reflected), the result is reverberation. The actual echoes are so close together that the sound is smoothly ambient, without sharp attacks.

Extremely short delay times of about 10 to 30 milliseconds are characteristic of chorus units. Slight modulation of the sound's frequency passing through the unit and mixing with the original signal creates peaks and notches in the frequency spectrum. Flanging works in much the same way, although the requisite delay times are shorter—varying from .25 millisecond to roughly 20 milliseconds. Also, the amount of modulation used for flanging is greater than that of chorusing. The result is more

pronounced peaks and notches higher up in the frequency spectrum.

Whereas chorusing typically tends to be soft and unobtrusive, flanging is often drastic, and can produce a sound similar to that of a jet taking off. Depending on the number of controls and the intentions of the effect's designer, some of these tune-delay devices may be able to perform double duty. For example, by shortening the delay time and increasing the modulation amount on a chorus, one can obtain flanging.

Choosing a chorus box. There are many electronic devices capable of producing the chorus effect. These range from inexpensive (under $100) floor boxes designed specifically for chorusing, to multi-purpose units (such as delay lines) that not only give chorusing but other sounds as well (flanging, doubling, echo, etc.). First, we'll cover the basics of floor-box chorus units.

Floor-box chorus units. Virtually all well-known effects manufacturers (such as MXR, Electro-Harmonix, DOD, Boss, Ibanez, and literally dozens of others) make some kind of chorus box. However, many of these boxes feature significant design differences, so it is important to audition as many of them as possible before making your final decision. For example, one chorus unit might offer less overall delay than another unit—and while the box with the shorter delay will probably have a lower price tag, the final sound could resemble flanging more than chorusing. When shopping for a chorus box, check for the following characteristics:

Noiseless footswitching. When you switch from effect in ("active" mode) to effect out ("bypass" mode), there should be no "pops," dead spaces, or pauses.

Quiet operation. Your ears are the best guide for this. One good test is to play bass through the chorus, since low frequencies do not mask the high fre-

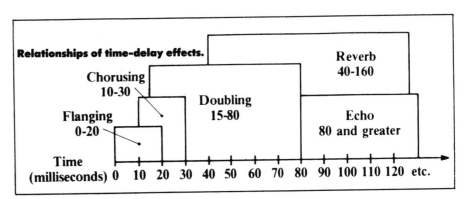

Relationships of time-delay effects.

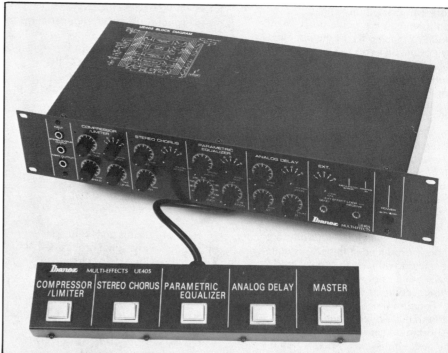

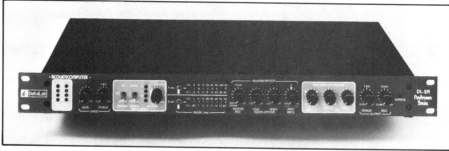

Clockwise from top left: Morley Chorus/Flanger, Ibanez Multi-Effects rack-mountable four-in-one effects system, DeltaLab DL-2 Acousticomputer reverb and image enhancer, MXR Stereo Chorus.

quencies where hiss is most obvious, thus making any noise more apparent. Note that noise is not always a constant—in fact, in some cases the noise level will be extremely low if you're not playing, but will increase in level as you play more loudly. Therefore, it's important to actually play through the chorus for at least a few minutes, under a variety of circumstances, in order to best gauge its overall noise level.

Wide dynamic range. A guitar is a highly percussive instrument, and since chorus units often have a limited dynamic range, the wide dynamic range of a guitar signal can create problems. Strike a highly percussive note or chord when playing through a chorus; there should be no popping or distortion. With more costly chorus devices there is usually some kind of input level indicator to show if you are overloading the unit, along with a level control to help you adjust the level of the input signal feeding the unit.

Low current consumption. Batteries

are expensive, so check how much current the chorus box draws. This figure is usually given on a spec sheet in "mA", which is short for milliamperes (a unit of current measurement—1 mA equals 1/100th of an ampere). The more mA a chorus box draws, the more often you will have to replace the batteries. Less than 5 mA is considered low current consumption, 5 to 10 mA is acceptable current consumption, and anything over that is going to cost you a fair amount in batteries. If the chorus unit does draw more than a few mA of current, make sure that it includes provisions for an AC adapter. That way, if battery costs start getting out of hand you can always switch over to AC power.

Pedalboard compatibility. Many manufacturers now make "pedalboards" which neatly group effects together and provide a common source of non-battery power to all effects. If you have such a pedal board, make sure any new chorus unit is electrically and mechanically compatible with pre-

viously existing effects.

Status LED. Since many guitarists use chorusing in a very subtle manner, it's important to know for sure whether the effect is in or out of your signal path. A status LED indicates this unambiguously.

Synthesized stereo outputs. Synthesized stereo outputs can produce dramatic stereo effects under some conditions, but there are some precautions to consider. The main problem is that while synthesized stereo sounds great "live" or through headphones, if this stereo sound is played back in mono rather than stereo (for example, over an AM radio), the chorusing effect will drop out entirely. As a result, most groups do not use synthesized stereo outputs when recording. If you want to create true stereo chorusing that doesn't cancel in mono, you will need two chorus units—feed your instrument into both devices simultaneously, route the outputs to different channels, and adjust the two sets of chorus controls for the best sound.

Musically useful controls. Some chorus units include several controls, some only one or two. While names of these controls vary from unit to unit, their functions are very similar. *Speed* controls the rate of pitch shifting, and therefore, the perceived rate of change of the chorus effect. At slow speeds, the effect is languid and lush; at higher speeds, the sound resembles that of a rotating speaker system set for high speed. *Width* controls the range of the pitch shifting. Large width settings can create an out-of-tune effect, since you are shifting pitch over a wide range; shifting pitch over a narrower range gives a more subtle, shimmering sound. *Depth* usually controls the mix of the delayed and straight sounds. When these are mixed equally, the chorusing effect is strongest; turning down the delayed sound makes the chorus effect less pronounced. Some units also include a *feedback* or *regeneration* control. Increasing this control gives a sharper, more metallic timbre.

Rack-mount chorus units. While there are few (if any) rack-mount devices dedicated exclusively to chorusing, there are many rack-mount digital (and occasionally analog) delay lines that are capable of producing the chorusing effect. Rack-mount devices typically include more controls than floor boxes. For example, while floor boxes seldom include feedback controls, rack-mount units will not only have feedback controls but also may let you select positively or negatively phased feedback, thus giving you a choice of two distinct timbres.

Delay lines may also include other features, such as programmable control settings, more sophisticated modulation (pitch-shifting) capabilities, integral AC power supply (no more batteries!), and other goodies. Of course, the tradeoff is that delay lines usually cost more; typical list prices range from around $200 to thousands of dollars. The more expensive devices may even include dual delay lines, long-delay options, the ability to match levels with anything from a guitar to a recording console, and so on. However, if music is a big part of your life, or your equipment doubles for studio use as well as on-stage use, it might well be worth spending the extra money for a good rack-mount delay line rather than going for a less sophisticated floor box. In fact, the more expensive unit may actually be a more cost-effective alternative in the long run.

To create chorus effects with a typical digital or analog delay line, select an initial delay in the 10 to 25 ms range (whichever ends up sounding best to you), and introduce a little bit of pitch shifting via the delay line's modulation depth control. For the most spacious sound, keep the speed control fairly slow. Generally you will want minimum feedback; however, for certain special effects a little positive feedback sounds absolutely great. Above all else, experiment with the various control settings—delay lines are capable of producing far more sounds than most people realize.

Select your chorus carefully, and you'll find that it is one box that can really make your axe come alive without sounding "gimmicky." And don't forget to try plugging bass into one of these boxes as well—if used subtley, chorusing can make a bass stand out and sound more "animated."

Craig Anderton

GRAPHIC VERSUS PARAMETRIC EQ

March 1979. If you want to know what's going to show up in the guitarist's bag of tricks next year, look at what the professional recording studios are into this year—a case in point involves equalizers. A few years ago, studios started installing graphic and parametric equalizers to replace their older units, and now these same devices are showing up as less expensive accessories for onstage and small-studio use. There is a certain amount of confusion over just which type of tone control is "best" for guitar. This installment will help clarify matters somewhat.

First of all, let's get some basics out of the way. The term equalization simply means tone control, and it is a holdover from the days when tone controls were used specifically to compensate for frequency response problems. For example, if the system's treble response to a particular signal were unequal to the bass response, then an equalizer might be used to compensate for the discrepancy, thus balancing, or *equalizing*, the response. However, today equalizers are used just as much to create "*unequal*" (custom-tailored) responses by boosting or cutting certain parts of the frequency spectrum, so the name equalizer seems possibly a little pretentious—if you want to call these things tone controls, I certainly won't object. Since "equalization" is a mouthful, engineers use the term EQ, as in, "Let's add some EQ and see if we can make this thing sound decent."

Alternatives to equalizers. Equalizers are wonderful and useful devices, but they also have some drawbacks. They add noise to a signal, they are relatively expensive, and the parametric types in particular are somewhat hard to adjust. But there are alternative ways to expand your tone-control options, such as guitar-rewiring projects. Using tapped humbucking pickups for single-coil or double-coil sounds from one pickup, as well as combining pickups in different ways (series, parallel, and out-of-phase options) can create quite a number of interesting and useful tone changes. Also, replacement pickups are now available from a variety of sources that can change the basic sound of your guitar to something that's "hotter" or has more "presence." So, before you get too involved with effects boxes, check out your guitar and see if there are some simple ways to improve its tonal quality. One example: If your pickups are not adjusted correctly and you experience a loss of treble as a result, you're probably better off trying to correct the pickup adjustment than adding treble with an equalizer.

The graphic equalizer. There are now quite a number of graphic equalizers available to the musician. A graphic takes your guitar signal and splits it into a number of different frequency bands, and the most important characteristic of the graphic is how many bands it offers.

Each band may be boosted (augmented) or cut (diminished) in intensity. Clearly, the more bands, the greater the degree of control. Some graphics will have only five bands, which can be considered as bass, lower midrange, midrange, upper midrange, and treble—not that great an improvement over the standard tone controls found on most amps. Having ten bands is much better; you can now control one-octave ranges throughout the audio spectrum (with one popular equalizer, for example, the centers of these bands—measured in Hertz, or Hz—fall at 31, 62, 125, 250, 500, 1K, 2K, 4K, 8K and 16K). There's no reason to stop there, though; some manufacturers offer 31-band equalizers that give you control over areas of the audio frequency spectrum only 1/3 of an octave apart—this is quite a degree of control.

One of the original applications for the graphic was in smoothing out loudspeaker response curves. The response of a loudspeaker is never "flat"; instead, there are little peaks and dips throughout. A multiband equalizer can add a dip where a speaker peaks, cancelling that problem; or, it can just as easily peak where the speaker dips. The graphic is also popular for equalizing *program material*—fairly complex sound sources, such as signals from several instruments and vocalists mixed together. In this application, its relatively gentle boosting and cutting action offers flexible control of tone without sounding too unnatural.

The parametric equalizer. The parametric trades off a large *number* of bands for increased *flexibility* in controlling each band's effect. A parametric

may have, say, only four bands. But whereas a graphic's band is fixed at a particular frequency, the parametric's bands will be able to cover any spot in the audio spectrum; not only can the parametric boost or cut, but the sharpness of the band will often be adjustable. In other words, you can boost/cut a very narrow or a very broad range of frequencies—your option. (For more information on these types of equalizers, see pages 53-59 of my *Home Recording For Musicians* [Music Sales, 24 East 22nd Street, NYC 10010.]

Which one is for you? Naturally, if you can afford it, it's nice to have both types of EQ and simply patch in whichever one is appropriate for a given situation. But how do you tell which type is appropriate? Here are some guidelines:

1. The parametric is more difficult and time consuming to adjust than the graphic. So, for onstage use where it is vital to totally change a sound in a matter of a few seconds, the graphic is my favorite choice. Also, most graphics use slide pots for the boost/cut controls, so the actual arrangement of these levers on the front panel provides a *graphic* depiction of the frequency response (which is why they're called graphics). And since we're on the subject, here's a note to manufacturers: How about incorporating some memory presets into your equalizers so that guitarists can store 16 or 32 favorite sounds for later recall? It would really be a big improvement over changing all those pot positions all the time.

2. When it comes to solving specific response problems in an instrument, the parametric is your best bet. Let's say you have some nasty 60Hz hum you want to *notch out*, or eliminate. With a graphic, one band had better be at exactly 60Hz if you want to solve the whole problem; with a parametric, you simply adjust one of the low-frequency band controls to a precise 60Hz. Another problem with the graphic is that the sharpness of the notch is fixed; with the parametric, you can set an extremely sharp notch that cuts out 60Hz and very little else. Or, say that you want to emphasize a certain note on the guitar. With a parametric it's easy; with a graphic, unless the band is located exactly where you want it, you are in trouble. All in all, if you simply want to expand the standard bass/treble/midrange amp controls, the graphic would be a good place to start. The parametric is for more specific applications.

3. The parametric not only has the ability to make some really good sounds, but it also has enough effect to make some really awful sounds. If you are heavy handed with the controls, you can come up with some really over-emphasized, overboomy, and over-cooked sounds—it's like letting someone with no taste buds decide how much spice to put in your dinner. With a graphic you can check over the sliders and see which ones are radically boosting or cutting, and get them back to ground zero if the sound has gotten out of

Sound-shaping gear: Ibanez parametric equalizer (L) in a small foot-pedal and (R) Moog graphic and parametric equalizer.

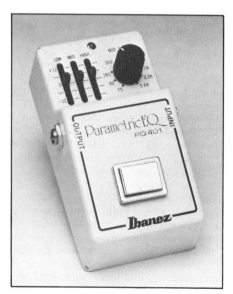

hand; with a parametric, settings are not quite as obvious. Another note to manufacturers: *All* equalizers should have an in/out switch so the user can compare the equalized and non-equalized sounds. This would allow people to compare the results of their knob twiddling with the original signal, and demonstrate exactly what changing certain controls will do to a sound.

I hope that the preceding has helped give you a little better handle on what type of equalization is best for your situation. Just remember that no one equalizer can solve all types of response problems, which is the reason why new designs are constantly being introduced and older designs are constantly being improved.

Craig Anderton

HANDBOOK OF MULTIPLE EFFECTS

November 1979 - January 1980. The purpose of the next few installments is to give you some insight into particularly useful combinations of effects—what increases sustain, how to minimize noise in a given setup, how to make a phaser appear more intense, and what effects should follow (or precede) other effects. You'll find that a switching system that allows you to combine multiple effects in various combinations is an ideal way to experiment with multiple effects; and *experiment* is definitely the operative word. Due to the non standardized nature of the present-day effects scene, some combinations might work well with one brand of effects, and not so well with a different brand. Then again, most musicians put their wah-wah pedal after the fuzz—but Jimi Hendrix did just fine by putting the wah-wah in *front* of the fuzz, which helped give him a special sound on certain songs. There is no "right" way to hook together multiple effects, only the way that is right for you. Don't be afraid to plug things into each other; you won't blow them up, and you might discover a sound that really makes it.

The first part in our handbook deals with *series* combinations of effects. With series combinations, your instrument plugs into one effect, whose output plugs into another effect, whose output plugs into yet another effect, and so on until you reach your amp. For the sake of convention, we'll call the *first* effect the one closest to your guitar and the *last* effect the one closest to the amplifier.

How to avoid noise in multiple-effect setups. There are three golden rules you must follow if you wish to minimize noise in multiple-effects systems.

They are:

1. Use the *fewest* number of stages possible. Every op-amp, every transistor, and every resistor contributes noise to the system—so avoid redundant stages. For example, if the first effect you're feeding includes a buffered input, there is no need to add an additional buffer board between the guitar and the first effect. This cuts out just one more stage of noise.
2. Feed the strongest signal level possible, short of distortion, into the input of an effect, and use the effect's output control to trim back to unity gain. An effects box has a fixed amount of noise; by increasing the signal level going through the device, you therefore increase the signal-to-noise ratio. This will sometimes mean an excessively large signal coming out of the effects box, but since most boxes have some kind of output control, you can trim it back to keep the signal level constant throughout a chain of effects.
3. Keep all interconnecting cords as short as possible. This is less important with well-designed effects, but it never hurts to use the shortest possible patch cords necessary to get from one effect to another.

The all-important first effect. The first effect in the signal chain is vitally important, since it sets the operating level and character of the system as a whole. Let's look at what happens when you choose a compressor as your first effect, and why it's an excellent candidate to be the first.

A compressor increases sustain by *increasing* its gain as the input signal *decreases* in level. Therefore, as a string decays, the compressor will amplify more to bring up the apparent level, thereby increasing the sustain. Many guitarists favor the use of compression today to the point where compressors are extremely popular effects.

However, we need to note something very important. If there is an electronic device before the compressor that contributes any noise at all, then the compressor will interpret that noise as being a low-level signal, and attempt to amplify it—producing the sound of Niagara Falls in your amplifier. For example, if you plug a guitar pickup directly into the input of a compressor, you will get the lowest possible noise figure; if you buffer the guitar signal first with a buffer board, then the compressor will bring up any residual noise contributed by the buffer board. This also points up one of the reasons I'm not in favor of onboard electronics: *Any* preamplification included in the guitar also contributes noise, which the compressor will try to amplify.

So, it makes a lot of sense to plug our "naked" guitar directly into the compressor. By leaving out a buffer board, or any onboard guitar electronics, we're following rule number one of minimizing noise. However, this means that for best fidelity and overall sound, you need to use a good compressor with built-in buffering so that the guitar is not loaded down. The way to test the quality of a compressor is pretty simple: Plug your guitar directly into an amp and note the tonal quality. If going through a compressor dulls the high frequencies, move on to the next model. After finding a couple of compressors that don't affect the frequency response of your axe, choose the one that gives the lowest average noise under a variety of operating conditions and that also has a good sound.

A compressor is a unique kind of device in that if not overused, it can be left in the signal chain at all times (unlike, say, a fuzz, which you tend to cut in and out as needed). However, be aware that almost all musicians have a tendency to overcompress when first exposed to compression. While over-compression does give drastic amounts of sustain, it can also add distortion and contribute to an unnatural sound. Compression is most effective when used judiciously—I can't emphasize that enough.

In some cases it's handy to have *two* compressors connected in series. The first compressor can act as a buffering/preamping type of device with a very light amount of compression, while the second one can be set for extreme amounts of compression for use during solos or to bring out the best in subsequent effects. When you really want to sustain, you can punch them both into the signal line (but expect a lot of noise!). Alternately, you can modify one compressor to include a couple of preset positions.

For those who dislike the effect or sound of compression, then I would recommend that you use a buffer board or buffering preamp as the first step in your series signal chain. This will isolate the guitar from subsequent loading caused by other effects, add a little volume boost (remember what we said about keeping signal levels up), and still preserve the entire dynamic range of the guitar.

You may find it helpful to think of a series effects chain as comprising three parts. The first section (Group 1) contains devices that alter dynamic range and/or synthesize frequencies; Group 2 comprises equalizing and filtering devices; and the final section, Group 3, includes time-altering devices (echo, analog delay, digital delay) and output devices.

Here are some thoughts about particular combinations of Group 1 effects:

Compressor before fuzz. This increases sustain and gives a more even fuzz timbre; however, it also creates a lot of noise while not playing. *Fuzz before compressor* gives the same sort of sound, but is usually noisier.

Fuzz before ring modulator. This allows you to ring modulate the fuzzed instrument sound. I feel the *ring modulator before fuzz* produces a more varied texture, since the multiple harmonics going to the fuzz produce thicker, dirtier sounds.

Octave divider before compressor. While I prefer to have a compressor first in the signal chain, many octave dividers only give satisfactory results when they are directly preceded by your guitar. Additionally, switching in the compressor allows you to compress the octave-lower note along with the original note.

Octave divider before fuzz. Al-

though fuzzes generally don't like to receive two notes at once, in the case of an octave divider the notes are spaced *exactly* one octave apart so everything works out all right. It also gives the fuzz more bottom.

Putting these effects in an order based on the information given above, we have Fig. 1, showing the connection of Group 1 effects.

Some of you would doubtless prefer the fuzz before the ring modulator; that's what patch cords are made for—experimentation.

In group 2, we have devices such as wah-wahs, filters, equalizers, and phase shifters (which more closely resemble filters than time-delay devices). These types of effects are not that critical about the order in which they connect; series filters basically just add their effects together, so it doesn't matter whether a wah-wah is added to a graphically equalized signal, or whether a graphically equalized sound is added to a wah-wah sound. However, there are some combinations that seem to work well:

Phase shifter before phase shifter. Running two phase shifters in series at different speeds creates some really beautiful effects. I highly recommend this configuration, especially for four-stage shifters (usually the less expensive models).

Graphic equalizer before phase shifter. This way, any noise contributed by the graphic becomes phased, and sounds more musically pleasing. On the other hand, if the phase shifter is particularly noisy, you might want to have the graphic *afterwards* so that you could trim down some of the treble (where noise is most noticeable).

Wah-wah (or envelope-followed filter) before equalizer. Not all that important, but wah-wahs and envelope-followed filters tend to have pretty high gain, so you don't want to have too many noise sources preceding them in the signal chain.

Taking the above into account, our Group 2 effects connect as shown in Fig. 2.

Unlike Group 2 devices, Group 3 effects sound very different when placed in different combinations. Here are some examples:

Flanger before noise gate. This allows you to cut out any residual noise of the flanger; *noise gate before flanger* serves no useful purpose.

Echo unit (or delay line) before noise gate. This combination has the advantage of cutting out noise contributed by the echo unit. However, the noise-gating action will also cut out some of the low-level echoes, which may not be desirable. In many cases I prefer *noise gate before echo unit,* as it gives a more

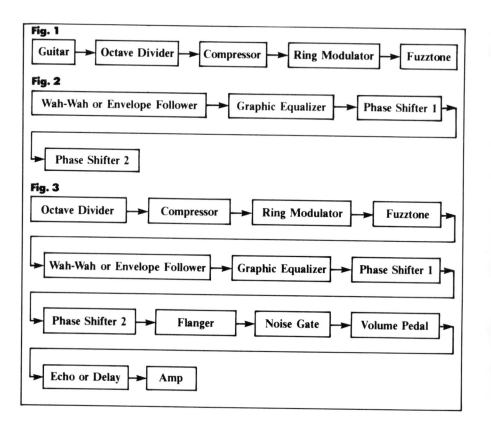

Fig. 1

Guitar → Octave Divider → Compressor → Ring Modulator → Fuzztone

Fig. 2

Wah-Wah or Envelope Follower → Graphic Equalizer → Phase Shifter 1

Phase Shifter 2

Fig. 3

Octave Divider → Compressor → Ring Modulator → Fuzztone

Wah-Wah or Envelope Follower → Graphic Equalizer → Phase Shifter 1

Phase Shifter 2 → Flanger → Noise Gate → Volume Pedal

Echo or Delay → Amp

natural sound.

Volume pedal before echo unit (or delay line). With this arrangement, when you pull back on the volume pedal the echoes will keep on going. Placing the volume pedal *after* the echo unit means that when you pull back on the pedal, you shut off all sounds. . .including the echoes. Don't overlook the switching circuit; it allows you to interchange the positions of the two series devices and comes in particularly handy in this instance.

Connecting the Group 3 effects after the Group 1 and Group 2 effects gives us the "ideal" series combination of multiple effects in Fig. 3.

With smaller effects systems, retain the same general order, but just ignore the spaces created by the effects you don't have.

Here are some other recommendations for this configuration:

1. Keep the volume level consistent through the chain so that cutting in several effects doesn't create a big volume boost. Use the footpedal to control the overall level.
2. The first stage (preferably a compressor) should bring the instrument up to the highest possible level that the system will take—short of distortion—for the best possible signal-to-noise ratio.
3. Do not precede an envelope-followed filter with any other effects unless the envelope-follower section has a separate input for the control signal.
4. When the graphic equalizer is not used so much as an effect but rather as a tone control unit that's left in the signal path at all times, place it last in the signal chain.
5. Noise gates based on filtering (i.e., those that alter frequency response to get rid of noise) are well suited to going towards the very end of the signal chain—say, right before the graphic equalizer in the situation described above.
6. Because Group 2 effects sometimes cause sharp changes in amplitude at different frequencies, it is often useful to insert a limiter between the Group 2 and Group 3 effects. In the "ideal" series combination given above, the limiter would go either between phase shifter 2 and the flanger, or between the flanger and noise gate. Limiting at this point also allows you to put more *average* signal level into the echo unit or delay line, thereby effectively increasing the headroom and

lowering noise.
7. Look for effects with relatively high input impedances (greater than 100K), relatively low output impedances (less than 10K), and true bypass switches that disconnect the input of the effect from the signal line when not in use. This gives you the best chances for compatibility and a good match between effects.
8. Experiment with different orders; the above pointers are suggestions and *not* rules. Here's a simple test to determine whether one effect sounds better before or after another effect: Patch them together both ways, and listen carefully; whichever combination sounds better to you is the right combination for you, and whatever sounds best to others is the best combination for them. There is no "perfect" way of combining effects boxes, because different combinations involve different trade-offs; but by looking over the above guidelines, you should have a good point of departure.

Why parallel? I don't necessarily like to have an effect that jumps out at me; I prefer sounds that add ambience to, or enhance the expressiveness of, that natural sound of an instrument. While series combinations give you the most dramatic effects, parallel connections allow you to achieve more subtle ones. These complex sounds can sustain the listener's interest much longer than, for example, the *whoosh-whoosh-whoosh* of a traditional phase shifter. Also, it is often difficult to add effects in parallel due to out-of-phase cancellation problems. Should you put two effects in parallel and the sound becomes weaker instead of stronger, adding a phase inverter (see Fig. 4) in series with *one* of the parallel effects will solve the problem.

Basics of parallel patches. One of the first principles of parallel effects is that generally the unprocessed signal makes up the majority of your final sound, with the effect mixed in at a lower level. For

example, think of a wah-wah pedal. Although punching in the wah-wah gives the desired effect, you also acquire a thinness to the sound because the pedal's filter is only passing a particular band of frequencies, while rejecting others. However, by mixing the wah-wah in parallel with the unprocessed signal, the effect is *added on top of* your unprocessed signal instead of replacing it. While the wah-wah may appear less dramatic, the overall sound is fuller and less gimmicky. Another example: Many players find that ring modulators are just too quirky sounding to use effectively. However, mixing the ring modulator sound in at a lower level than the unprocessed signal adds the bizarre harmonics that are the trademark of a ring-modulated sound (but they are put in a different perspective by being made subservient to the unprocessed sound).

Interestingly enough, studios are using devices like the Aphex Aural Exciter that have little to do with recreating reality, but rather enhance reality through electronic means that attempt to replicate the way we actually hear. With virtually all exciter and "animator" devices, signals are added at a low level in parallel with an unprocessed signal to create the desired effect. Thus, the principle of parallel mixed effects extends beyond guitar processing into realms that are, for all practical purposes, unexplored.

Here are some thoughts about particular parallel combinations:

Dual phase shifters in parallel with an unprocessed signal. Such a combination adds more diffusion to the sound, and creates a less gimmicky, more ethereal result.

Dual filters added in parallel with an unprocessed signal. This is particularly useful with devices such as the Super Tone Control (project #17) from my book *Electronic Projects For Musicians* (EPFM for short), [Music Sales, 24 East 22nd Street, NYC 10010], since you gain very subtle control over tone, and you can add just a tiny bit of high-frequency response to give some sparkle and a

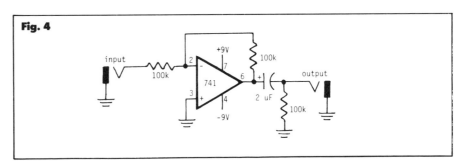

Fig. 4

subtle midrange peak to increase the intelligibility of a solo. While in theory you should be able to do the same thing with a graphic or parametric equalizer, for my purposes the parallel filter route gives less noise and more flexibility.

Using voltage-controlled filters also adds to the interest. While voltage-controlled devices are mostly the province of modular keyboard synthesizers, you can expect to see more and more guitarists taking advantage of synthesizer modules for guitar processing. Parallel filters that are either swept asynchronously or swept in opposite directions (i.e., as the resonant frequency of one filter goes up, the other filter's resonant frequency goes down) produce results that are fascinating and novel—you can even achieve human-like vocal sounds with some experimentation.

Paralleled time-delay effects. These are useful for the same reasons as the other parallel patches: more ethereal sound, more subtlety, and less noise (you only use as much effect as you want to).

As a final note, many effects (such as tape echo units) have blend controls to mix the effect sound in parallel with the straight signal. I think it would be a good idea if more effects offered blend controls, as long as both signal paths are noninverting with respect to phase.

Using effects in conjunction with the switching system. As you may recall, the switching system has a series line of five effect stations (A, B, and 1-3) in parallel with two parallel stations (4 and 5). These combine in a mixer, which is followed by one more effect station (6). Stations A and B can choose between two different effects, while six other effects can switch into any of the other six stations. Although it's great to be able to switch around, there are some "stable" combinations of effects which I tend to use as a point of departure. These are:

Station A: Chooses between compressor (EPFM project #8) or the Tube Sound Fuzz (EPFM project #24). This brings the guitar signal up to line level for the best signal-to-noise ratio throughout the system.

Station B: Chooses between Ultra-Fuzz (EPFM project #6) or Ring Modulator (EPFM project #9) to add harmonic enhancement when required.

Station 1: This and Station 2 usually hold phase shifters so that I can have two phase shifters in series.

Station 3: Usually holds a Super Tone Control, as does Station 4. By having these two parallel filters with separate high-pass, low-pass, and band-pass outputs, you can get very precise tonal control. If you don't build your own effects, then putting a pair of graphic or parametric equalizers in these stations will approximate the same effect.

Station 5: This usually holds either a Multiple Identity Filter or the delay-only output of a flanger or a delay line.

Station 6: The most frequent occupant of this station is an Electro-Harmonix Memory Man Deluxe for echo effects, although occasionally I'll switch a phaser or flanger into this station. Also, sometimes I take the echo output from this device and patch it into Station 4 or 5 for parallel echo effects, or process the echo sound and *then* patch it in parallel.

If you look over the above setup, you'll see that it gives a lot of options for creating an interesting, expressive guitar sound. Additional support devices for the switching system include a Goodrich output volume pedal, and a number of homemade control-voltage generators to drive the voltage-controlled devices. I should mention that these control-voltage generators have very little to do with the ones used in keyboard synthesizers. (I firmly believe that guitar and keyboard are entirely different instruments, and therefore require different modules. What makes a good synthesizer filter does not necessarily make a good guitar filter, and so on.)

Finally, I often insert special-purpose effects between the guitar and Station A. The ones I use most often are the ELectro-Harmonix MicroSynthesizer, modified; the Octave Doubling Fuzz; an A/DA Harmony Synthesizer; and a Mutron Octave Divider. Sometimes I'll patch a station into my PAIA modular synthesizer and use its modules in addition to my other modules . . . but that's a different story.

Craig Anderton

BUILDING A PEDALBOARD

November 1980. When the electric guitar boom hit in the '60s, playing the instrument required little knowledge of electronic gimmicks and doodads. All you had to do was plug your guitar into your amp, turn it on, and play. But during the second half of the decade, prominent guitarists began displaying some interesting possibilities for timbral enhancement on their records. Studio tricks such as flanging and phase shifting became legendary but were light years beyond the grasp of average axe

men—who wanted them all the more.

A wide variety of effects devices appeared, including wah-wahs, fuzztones, vibrato circuits, and tape echoes, although few guitarists included more than one in their setups. Not only were most of the units expensive, but often they were noisy, hard to control, unreliable, and seldom able to reproduce the sounds advanced on records. For many, a new guitar or amp seemed like a better investment.

In the '70s a revolution in the

microelectronics field produced virtually unlimited possibilities in sophisticated circuit design. As integrated circuits and other components became more complex, yet conversely smaller and less expensive, a cornucopia of effects became available. These included the long sought-after "studio-only" devices such as phasers, flangers, ring modulators, and filters. Evolution in the effects industry was hastened by fierce competition, until the number of products became almost mindboggling. Guitarists now have their choice of phasers, flangers, pitch shifters, octave doublers, chorus units, and even guitar synthesizers. And new approaches have been applied to old favorites: FET circuitry is used in some fuzztones; parametric filters are included in some wah-wahs; optoelectric and magnetic components are employed in some volume pedals; and voltage control has been added to

electronic vibratos.

As record and TV producers became increasingly aware of the electronic effects available to a few recording stars, they began placing increasingly greater demands on studio guitarists to produce "this sound" or "that sound." But because time is money on a session, guitar players couldn't just run out and try effects until they obtained the necessary timbre, or fiddle around with "toys" from their bag of tricks while other high-priced musicians sat idly by. Furthermore, the time spent connecting, disconnecting, and stowing several effects could be better used for extra sessions.

Necessity being the mother of invention, many professional guitarists—studio and stage performers alike—have started to rely on pedal boards and/or racks of equipment in order to expedite moves from studio to studio and city to city. They don't have time to pull apart all the cords and pedals and put them back together. It's much easier and quicker to place the pedalboard with its many effects in a flight case and move it all *en masse*; plus, it saves wear and tear on jacks, cords, plugs, and the effects.

Another point in favor of pedalboards is familiarity. With every device firmly planted in one place, you don't have to search to find, say, your wah-wah, which was on your left yesterday—or was it your right? By having all your effects at the same place day after day, you can almost rely on your reflexes to guide your foot to the right place.

Because of the increased availability in the last five or six years of low-cost, low-noise effects, no longer are studio guitarists the only ones stringing several modifiers together. Guitarists on all scales now have a basis for a variety of

tonal embellishments at the press of a button—or two, or three. . . . One thing leads to another: More effects means more cords for interconnection between the units (and more things to trip over). Then the guitarist is confronted with two basic problems: What order do the effects go in, and which cord goes where?

Naturally, you'll want to experiment with various orders for patching the effects together so that you can optimize their use. For instance, if you want to create a composite sound (fuzztone through phaser, flanger through wah-wah, etc.), you should patch them in an order that befits the intended purpose. Also, keep in mind the proximity of one effect to another. If two switches must be activated to produce a composite effect, place them close enough together to facilitate stepping on them quickly; don't place them three feet apart (doing the splits over a bunch of gadgets can be potentially hazardous).

Once you have determined a working order for your effects, you should match the length of each cord to the distance between each device. Why use a six-foot cord to patch between boxes that are only ten inches apart? Short cords in a variety of lengths of one, two, and three feet are common, and they help reduce noise.

How do you determine your needs? Is a pedalboard really necessary? It depends on your current effects, current needs, and projected needs. If you have two or more effects—or think that you will eventually have an armful—and find that moving to and from practice and gigs is forever a hassle, a pedalboard may be just what you need.

Once you have decided that a pedalboard is for you, be brutally honest and ask yourself: "Do I want to spend the time building one?" And just

as important: "Am I handy enough to tackle it?" Constructing a pedalboard from scratch can not only wear on your patience (often what looks good on paper isn't so hot in reality) but also tax all of your mechanical resources.

If you want a pedalboard but don't want to build it yourself, you can buy one. Several prefabricated models are commercially available (ask your music dealer). Don't expect them to be *too* inexpensive. While some cost little more than a few effects, others will have you thinking that your guitar and amp were cheap. Custom pedalboards on a scale with Lee Ritenour's, Larry Carlton's, or other studio aces can be tailored to your needs. Ask repairmen or dealers in your area whether they undertake such projects, or if they know anyone who does. It may require a lot of legwork, especially if you live in an area where the music scene is limited. Good luck.

Now for those who still want to arrange their own effects, let's start to work. Save materials, expense, and *work* by first putting your head to use. The more advance planning you do, the smoother the job ahead will be. At first you'll need graph paper (preferably with six or more squares to the inch), a pencil, and a ruler.

Measure the length, width, and height of each of your effects, including switch boxes for amplifier reverb or tremolo, any outlets you will need for AC power, etc. If you expect to expand in the future, measure the device you anticipate adding, or at least approximate its size. If you aren't sure of a device's size, or if you aren't sure whether you'll be expanding in the foreseeable future, leave room anyway; it's easier to live with a little extra space than to have to start over again on a larger board. List each effect and its dimensions on a piece of paper.

Lay out your effects in their proper order, and experiment with the configuration now, *before* you start construction. It will save redundant steps. If Effect A is going to be plugged into Effect B, place them close together. Remember, for every extra bit of cable—no matter how high the quality—the signal is degraded. Also, if you use, say, your left foot to manipulate a device that requires more than just stomping a switch (e.g., a volume pedal or a pedal flanger), don't place the unit on the right side.

Don't waste space by placing among your other effects any devices that will be left on at all times. If you plan to leave operational several components such as a preamp, buffer, shock isolator, or noise gate (regardless of what you do with the other units), place them in a second row so that you won't have to deal with them. This can save space for other effects that your foot *must* reach quickly. Always consider the easiest way of working everything, and use your layouts for a few days during practice sessions, playing as you normally do. Just sitting in your basement playing nothing in particular probably won't help you to decide whether a device is impractically placed.

Once you have determined an order for your devices, write down a flow-chart of your system; that is: Fuzztone to Phaser to Volume Pedal, etc. Determine a scale for a drawing of your pedal board and write it down. Generally, a convenient scale is one square (on the graph paper) to one inch. Draw each effect to scale on graph paper, using the length and width you recorded earlier. For instance, if the box measures 3" x 5", and your scale is one square to the inch, then your paper representation will be three squares by five squares.

Cut out the representations of your effects, and lay them out on a sheet of graph paper in the same order as you placed the actual devices. Mark on each "effect" the locations of input and output jacks, power cords or power supply connections (if any), footswitches, and side-mounted knobs or switches. Now the juggling begins.

Wherever a cord must be plugged into an input or output jack, you must leave about 3½" between that jack and any adjacent effects. This enables you to unplug just about any cord without removing the effect from the pedalboard. A space of 2½" between boxes

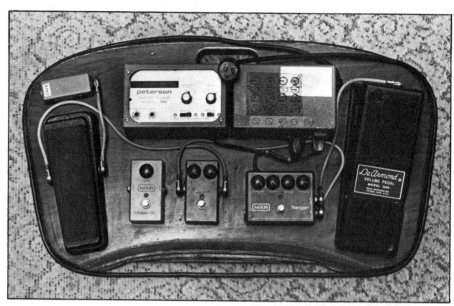

should be sufficient if your cords are equipped with angle plugs. Cords with two angle plugs or a combination of straight and angle plugs are ideal in some cases (they are sold in some music stores; if you can't find them, you or an electronically inclined friend can whip them up). Effects with knobs and/or power supply connections on their sides should be afforded the same amount of space as those connected with straight plugs: Even if you never change the settings, a little jostling in transit can alter your presets. Don't leave space for two plug lengths if a pair of adjacent boxes can simply be connected by a cord with straight plugs. Instead, move one device or the other about 1/2" forward or back on the pedalboard. Side-mounted knobs facing each other on juxtaposed effects need only about 1½" to 2" between them.

Now take your ruler and measure the width of your foot. If you place effects with top-mounted footswitches next to each other, you'll want at least one-half the width of your foot plus an inch between switches. Chances are the access spaces you allowed for jacks, switches, and so forth should afford sufficient spacing, but effects with inputs and outputs located at their ends, as opposed to their sides, will affect the measurements.

Once the spacing between effects is determined, check to see that the distance between the extreme left and right footswitches is no greater than about 30". This is usually enough space for six or seven effects and won't necessitate acrobatics on your part to get to all of them. A second row of effects, located behind the first and raised

Jefferson Starship guitarist Craig Chaquico's pedalboard: With everything fastened securely, there is less possibility for breakdown.

slightly, will be in store if you add more pedals. This, of course, will complicate construction, but the same procedures for a single-tier model can be used.

Measure the width of your layout from left to right. Add 2½" to 3" on each end (for handles), and you will have the overall width of your pedalboard. If you have AC-powered effects, or AC-to-DC battery eliminators, you will need a multiple outlet strip (a block of four, six, or eight electrical outlets) so that you can run one cord instead of several to a wall socket. Place outlet strips and power supplies at the rear of the pedalboard (transformers such as those found in battery eliminators sometimes throw off enough spurious fields to invade cords and effects, creating hum or crackle).

Now measure the length of your longest effect. That, added to the length of any second-row effects, plus the width of outlet strips or AC-DC converters (whichever is greatest), a 3" buffer zone between effects and power sources, and a 2" border on both the front and back of the board will yield the sum of your pedalboard's depth. Double-check your calculations, lay out the actual effects on the floor, and measure again (don't forget to leave space for projected additions). With your pedals arranged in the configuration you have mapped out, measure the length of each cord between effects, and obtain close fits. Don't make the cords too short, though: It's better to have them a few inches too long so that there is less strain on their plugs.

You're now ready to build the pedalboard. Obtain a piece of plywood that's at least 1/2" thick, or particle board that's at least 5/8" thick, and cut it to the width and depth that you determined on paper. Painting the wood with a nonglossy acrylic or epoxy paint will make it look good and help prevent chips and scratches.

Mounting the effects comes next. Screws and L-brackets aren't a good idea—they require drilling into the boxes, and make service and battery replacement difficult. Velcro fasteners glued with epoxy to the pedalboard and the effects may suffice if the boxes are fairly lightweight.

There's another approach for all devices, heavy or not. Many hardware and boating supply stores sell marine fasteners—small steel snaps used in conjunction with roundhead bolts designed for holding canvas covers on boats. They're fairly expensive (about $3.00 for six), but they're really versatile. And they can only be removed by pulling on the designated side of the fastener. When placed on both ends of a 1"-wide strip of no-roll polyester elastic, they provide an easy way to hold your boxes firmly in place. Two strips with fasteners should be sufficient for most effects; the size and weight of the devices will determine the final count. Rubber feet on pedals also help to further hold them in place.

Multiple outlet strips usually have provisions for screwing them directly to the pedalboard. Screw two handles onto each end of the board for easy moving by *two* people (if your board is wider than 30", it may be too heavy when completed to comfortably lift by yourself). Handy tip: Before turning screws into plywood or particle board, drill smaller pilot holes, and rub soap on the threads of each screw; use only wood or sheet-metal screws. The job will be considerably easier.

Once your pedals are fastened onto the board, plug your power cords into the outlet strip, and connect any AC adapters to their respective effects. Now install the patch cords between the pedals. Check to see that each output is connected to a subsequent input. Plug your guitar into the first effect, and a cord between the last effect and your amp. Plug the outlet strip into the wall, turn everything on, and try out your pedalboard.

If you connected everything correctly and have no bad cords, your guitar should come through loud and clear. If not, check each cord, make sure every battery is in good shape, make sure that every on/off switch is in the "on" position, and (once again) ascertain that all outputs are connected to inputs. Replace bad cords and/or batteries.

If you have more than one effect with a 3-conductor electrical plug, you may hear an overbearing hum, which is symptomatic of a ground loop (more than one path to ground). Try using 3-prong-to-2-prong adapter plugs on all but one plug, and leave their ground wires disconnected. If your amp also has a 3-prong plug, you may have to use the adapters on all of the effects' plugs. Also, some battery-powered effects are activated by plugging in a cord. Find out which of your effects function in this manner, and be sure to unplug them when your pedalboard isn't in use. In some cases, on/off switches can be installed to eliminate this hassle.

Once everything is working, you may want to fasten all cords to the pedalboard. Do not use staples or nails! Small plastic loops with a single hole, designed specifically for this purpose, are available from most electronics supply houses. The loop holds the cord, and the hole allows a screw to secure it to the pedalboard. One of these fasteners every 10" or 12" will keep your cords from jiggling, but still allow for quick removal. Excess lengths of AC cords from effects can be held close to the outlet strip using plastic cable ties (also available at most electronics supply houses).

Perhaps a case for protection of your pedalboard in transit would be a useful second project, or you might want to buy one ready-made. But with your pedalboard assembled, your gear is completely mobile and ready to travel anywhere at a moment's notice. Just pull out your two cords, unplug the outlet strip, and away you go.

Tom Mulhern

MULTI-EFFECTS AND PROGRAMMERS

June 1983. Hundreds or thousands of dollars can go into the average guitarist's pedal setup, simply through piecemeal accumulation. First a fuzztone, then maybe a wah-wah, followed by a chorus, an echo unit, a phaser, etc., etc. Each unit fits into the scheme of the player's music, and every addition to the setup increases the complexity of performing. If you're into effects, then in no time at all there can be several pedals, dozens of switches, and a tangle of patch cords staring up at you from the floor. Then it hits you: "Life is not simple." Serving to reinforce this revelation is the greatly increased time in packing everything for travel to practice and gigs, untangling the cords for setup (and hoping nothing goes wrong), and tearing it all down again.

In recent years, pedalboards have solved many of the organizational woes plaguing the guitarist or bassist so inclined to collect an unwieldy number of effects. However, a pedalboard has a finite size: It will only hold so many effects. This doesn't cause too many problems for the average guitarist with a handful of effects. However, for the fanatic with an ear for the difference between one kind of distortion and another, things can quickly get out of hand. For instance, when you get to your third fuzztone or more unusual effects such as vibratos, octave dividers, and pitch transposers, you may find that there just isn't enough space for them all.

Around the time that you start having anxiety attacks over where to put the next effect, you may have found that greater timbral complexity can be had by varying the order of your effects or activating several at once. You only have two feet, so at this point you'd better be a regular Baryshnikov in order to

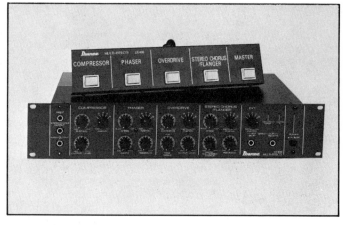

Left: MXR's Omni contains five effects in a rack-mountable unit. Right: The Ibanez UE400 has four effects and lets the user determine their order in the signal path.

make several simultaneous changes—for instance: switching from a combination that includes a fuzztone patched into a phaser and an echo unit, to an octave divider plugged into an envelope-following filter, a chorus, and a graphic equalizer.

Get the picture? You could make your complicated changes between songs, but you've probably found a great number of split-second changes that are essential *within* songs. After nonstop switch hopping for an entire evening, you could be ready for the chiropractor. And if the gymnastics aren't enough, what do you suppose fishing for footswitches can do to your concentration? It's hard enough to play a set without rushing an entrance, missing that stratospheric C# during your most difficult song, or balancing your singing and picking. Trying to remember what effects go on and off at what points can make a shambles of your confidence (especially if your audience is hostile, your drummer is drunk, or your *B* string won't stay in tune no matter what you do).

Pedal manufacturers got you into this mess, right? Well, you didn't *have* to buy their effects. However, several companies have seen the need for quick, easy changes, and have created equipment to help musicians deal with a multitude of sonic enhancers. Included among their wares are multiple-effects devices (three or more units in a single enclosure), programmers that switch effects on and off or vary their order, and programmers capable of governing every parameter of your sound.

And for those of you with a fully loaded (and no doubt expensive) pedalboard, your setup is *not* obsolete. You won't have to start from scratch. In fact,

some of these devices can add a lot of muscle to your existing setup, and in some cases afford you extra room on your pedalboard for even *more* goodies (I can hear that fourth fuzztone now!).

Of course, just as every guitarist has his or her own idea of what makes the perfect pedalboard, manufacturers also have their own ideas on the subject. Whether or not you agree with the manufacturer's design decisions goes a long way towards deciding whether or not you will find a particular device useful or useless. Different musical styles also enter into the picture; a C & W flatpicker would probably want different sounds than a hardcore player. In any event, rather than describe individual units (which, given the rapid rate of change in the music industry, would make this book obsolete within weeks of its publication), we'll consider what features are found on most multiple-effects units, so you can decide which are most important to you. We'll close out by talking a bit about programmers, and how they can also help you organize groups of effects.

When it comes to multi-effects units, there's more than one way to put more than one effect in a box. In fact, there are actually two ways: Make a single unit that consolidates a few popular effects, or make a box (sometimes called a "mainframe" or "pedalboard") into which a number of modular effects can be added. These modular effects can be complete, individual-effects boxes that may also be used without the mainframe, or effects that are designed specifically for installation in a specific mainframe and cannot be used except in the context of that mainframe. These days, many companies that make a line of effects also make matching pedalboards designed to hold their effects.

Both the multi-effects and modular approaches have their appeal. The first

approach—prepackaged multiple effects—is great for the player with no effects or just a few effects. Often, the most popular modifiers (distortion, phasing, delay, etc.) are housed in a single structure. Multi-effects units can free up some space on your pedalboard, or keep the floor clear if they are remote controllable. Another important aspect is that since all these effects were designed to work with each other, you should not have to deal with the incompatibility problems you sometimes run into when combining effects from different manufacturers. At the very least, prepackaged multi-effects units are highly portable and generally cut down on the number (and length) of patch cords necessary for the interconnection of multiple sound enhancers. Most even have provisions for interfacing with your current devices via effects loops.

Modular effects systems, while generally more expensive, can be more versatile since it is much easier to change effects (with nonmodular multi-effects units, upgrading is difficult or impossible). Regardless of which approach strikes your fancy, though, here are some general characteristics to consider when purchasing any kind of multi-effects unit:

Ability to handle effects from other manufacturers. You might have some cherished fuzz or wah-wah that is a vital part of your sound—no substitutes accepted! If so, make sure the multi-effects unit has provisions for an *effects loop.* This lets you insert external effects into the multi-effects system. Note, however, that even if the system doesn't have a loop, you can still insert most effects between your guitar and the input of the system, or between the output of the system and your amplifier.

Modular effects units are more versatile in that you can usually select from a number of possible effects. However,

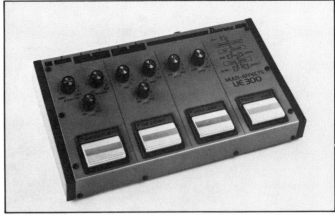

Left: Audio Envelope Systems' Axrac/FXrac contains modular effects devices. Right: Ibanez' UE300 floorbox multi-effects unit has three sound modifiers and a master bypass switch.

in many cases these alternative effects are provided by a single manufacturer, so your choices may still be limited. For this reason it's still a good idea to have a loop (or some other means of inserting additional effects) in your system, whether modular or not.

Loop location control. Some multi-effects units let you switch the loop into various points in the signal chain, since the location of an effect often influences its sound. For example, if you want to insert a wah-wah pedal into a multi-effects device that includes fuzz—phaser—flanger—echo, putting the loop between the fuzz and the phaser, or between the phaser and the flanger, will give significantly different effects.

Remote footswitch. While some multi-effects units are designed to sit on the floor, others are rack-mount units that are intended for installation in a rack frame. In the case of the former, a remote footswitch isn't important since the unit is on the floor anyway. With the latter, a remote footswitch is vital if you want to keep both hands free for playing. One hint is to pay particular attention to what kind of connecting cable links the footswitch and multi-effects unit together. If you're dealing with a complex multi-conductor cord, look out; better have some replacements around, just in case someone accidentally rolls a PA column over your cord. A better option is a unit that uses a standard guitar cord, since these are easily replaced in an emergency; the tradeoff is that using a single guitar cord to control multiple switches requires some electronic trickery that can add to the cost.

Master bypass switch. This is tremendously helpful if you want to switch a number of effects in or out simultaneously. The way to use a master bypass

switch is to start out with the master bypass bypassing all the effects. Next, you select individual effects with their individual footswitches. Finally, by simply hitting the master bypass switch, you can bring all the effects in at once. To return to the straight sound, hit the master bypass again. Using a master bypass switch is a lot more convenient than trying to punch multiple effects in and out at the same time.

Noiseless footswitching. As you switch effects in and out, or switch the master bypass in and out, there should be no "pops," dead spaces, or pauses.

Wonderful sounds from all effects. Don't be tempted to buy a multi-effects unit that has two sounds you like and two you don't; if you're only using two of the effects anyway, you're better off sticking to individual floor boxes. Also, check out the unit you intend to buy with the guitar you intend to play—I tested a multi-effects unit with one guitar and it worked fine, yet using a different guitar overloaded the phase-shifter section.

Status LEDs. With all these effects, it becomes very important to know which effects are in the signal path and which are not (especially if you use a master bypass switch). While most multi-effects units have status indicators, some of the rack-mount models include indicators both on the front panel and at the remote footswitch. This is very handy, since you'll probably spend more time looking at the footswitch status indicators than the panel status indicators. One multi-effects unit (the MXR Omni) even makes the status indicators do double duty by giving them two different brightnesses. If an effect's status LED is glowing at half brightness, the effect has been selected but not yet brought into the signal path; when brought into the signal path via the master bypass switch, the LED glows at full brightness. An unlit LED indicates that the effect is

bypassed completely.

Re-routing capabilities. Some multi-effects units let you alter the order in which effects occur. For example, preceding a fuzz with an equalizer produces a vastly different sound from following the fuzz with an equalizer; therefore, it's helpful if you can change the routing of these two effects at will, in order to obtain more than one sound. (In some cases, you may also be able to use the loop capabilities to tap different outputs from the multi-effects unit, or perform other patching tricks.)

Output level control. While not absolutely vital—you could always patch a volume pedal after the effects unit, or simply turn down the amp—an output level control lets you match the output of the multi-effects unit to a variety of signal inputs (guitar amps, recording consoles, PA systems, etc.).

Integral AC power. Most pre-packaged multi-effects units will include AC power. With units that are designed to accept existing effects, there will usually be an AC adapter that distributes power to the various effects. Either way, you save on battery hassles.

That pretty much concludes the section on multi-effects units. Effects programmers are another matter altogether; they generally control your existing effects (rack mount or floor box). Most include the ability to switch a number of effects—typically six to eight—in or out of the signal path. You may also assign each combination of effects a number, so that if one of your favorite sounds is fuzz followed by flanger followed by echo, simply punch up #12 (or whatever you call it)—and there's your sound. The number of possible "programs" varies; typical units let you program anywhere from about a dozen to over sixty possible combinations of effects.

Most programmers are pretty expen-

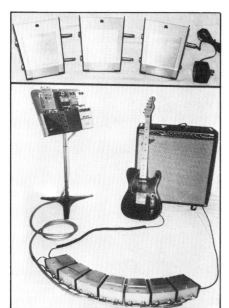

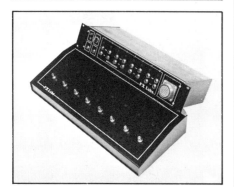

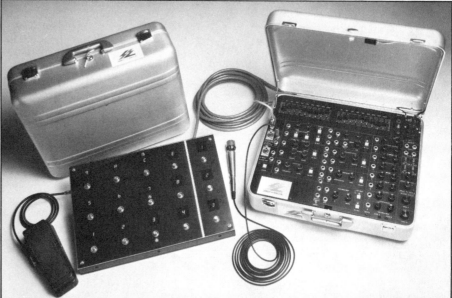

Left, top to bottom: Promark Sound Modular footswitch system for connection to other effects; FX Labs Switcheroo has a floorbox for selecting effects in a rack; Roland's SCC-700 Sound Control Center has a microprocessor for remembering chains of effects. Right, top to bottom: Shiino's Vesta Fire modular system; Sounder's Portable Effects System contains all effects in one flight case, the footswitch unit in another; Sequential Circuits' modular Pro-FX Model 500 features a memory bank for programming all parameters of each effect; the J.L. Cooper Effect Switcher allows the user to preset the order and combinations of 14 sound processors.

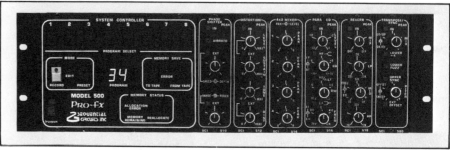

sive, and some boast deluxe features such as optional control-voltage outputs (suitable for use with many rack-mount devices), battery backup memory, switchable effects order, or cassette interface capabilities (this lets you permanently store the information in the programmer's memory on cassette for later use, and works in the same manner as cassette interfaces on programmable synthesizers, home computers, digital drum machines, and so on).

There's still more: At least one manufacturer (Sequential Circuits) has combined the concept of multiple effects *and* a programmer by making a programmable effects box. The difference between this programmer and the other programmers we discussed before is that the effects have been specifically designed to work with a programmer, unlike the normal situation where a programmer simply takes existing effects and switches them in or out of the signal path in a certain order. As a result, not only can you program combinations of effects to come in and out when desired, you can program actual control and switch settings on the effects themselves. Thus, when you come across a sound you like, simply assign it a "patch" number, press a button, and *all* the parameters of that sound will be "remembered" by the programmer. One example is that you could set up the unit's delay line for a great chorus sound, and give that one patch number; then, you could set up the same delay line for an echo effect, and give that a separate patch number. With one of the programmers mentioned earlier, you would probably need two delay lines—one set for chorusing and one for echo, with the programmer selecting whichever one was appropriate. Unfortunately, complete programmability is not cheap, but it is a tremendous time-saver (especially for live performances).

This look at multi-effects units and programmers is but a brief glimpse of the technology that is working its way into the lives of guitarists and bassists. No doubt, more devices of this nature will shortly be available, giving you a broader selection. Powerful tools such as these can truly expand your sound—and perhaps even clear up some of the clutter on your pedalboard.

Tom Mulhern and Craig Anderton

7.
AMP
SYSTEMS

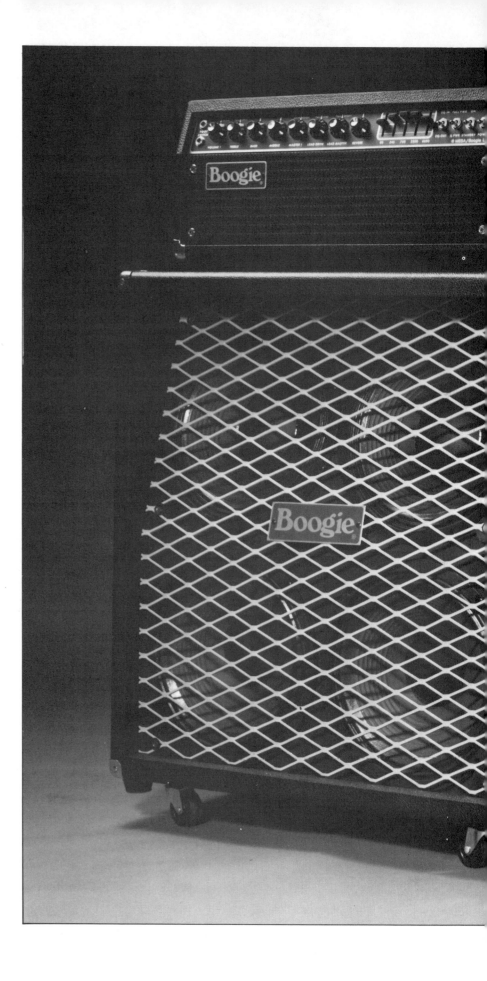

INTRODUCTION

You can put some of them in your pocket, you can stack others on a stage, but if you're an electric guitarist, you've got to have an amp. The opening section details how amps work, from input to output, explaining how all that circuitry pulls a great big sound out of a little guitar and how distortion, reverb, and tremolo function. Applications Of An Electric Guitar Amplifier, the second section, guides you toward obtaining the most from your amp, whether you're a bebopper or a headbanger. Potentially confusing subjects as correct speaker connection and matching, power ratings, and maintenance are clearly explained by repairman/amp designer Keith Reinegger. For those who've heard buzzwords such as "headroom," "FET," and "triamping" in discussions about amps but aren't sure what they mean, the next section, Amp Glossary, contains over 100 amp-related terms and concise definitions.In the next section by tube expert R. Aspen Pittman, the construction, function, care, and testing of tubes are spotlighted. A comparison of tubes and transistors in the creation of distortion and guidelines on when to replace tubes are also included. Rounding out this chapter on amps is a tour of the Mesa/Boogie factory, where you see how the chassis, components, cabinets, and speakers all come together.

ALL ABOUT AMPS

December 1973. What started out as a way to make musical instruments louder has become an industry that is responsible in part for the kind of music we hear today. The electric guitar is one of the mainstays of rock, country, fusion, and jazz. Without an amplifier there would be no electric guitar. This combination of guitar and amp has transcended the capabilities of acoustic instruments and has created ways to achieve new and exciting sounds. The screaming and powerful sound of rock, the crying and twanging notes of country, the sustain and blistering scales of fusion, and the staccato precise playing of jazz, all came about for the guitarist since the invention of the electric guitar amplifier.

Electronically, the guitar amplifier is a fairly simple, straightforward device. Any amplifier—guitar or hi-fi, tube or transistor, La Superba or El Cheepo—can be block-diagrammed as in Fig. 1. Guitar amps may have other goodies (reverb, tremolo, distortion, etc.) in addition to the basics, but always the preamp, power amp, power supply, and speaker will be there.

The initial signal processing is performed by the preamplifier. The preamp increases the signal level from the guitar, controls the output level via a volume control, and modifies the frequency response by the tone controls. The guitar's output varies with pick attack, guitar volume setting, type of pickups, pickup height, and strings. The average level for a single-coil pickup such as a Fender-Stratocaster is about 0.1 volts wide open with a strong pick attack. A Gibson Humbucking Pickup is about three times more powerful, and a high-output custom wound pickup can put out a volt. When the maximum level of clean power is attained, the signal level at the output of the preamp should be about 1 volt for solid-state circuits and 8 to 10 volts for a tube amp. This signal then goes to the power amp which drives it to full power before the point of clipping.

For a 100-watt amplifier with a 4-ohm speaker load the voltage level at the output is 20 volts. Using the 0.1-volt level of a Stratocaster as an example, the voltage amplification from guitar to solid-state preamp output (1 volt) is by a factor of 10 (1 divided by 0.1). The amplification of the power amp is 1 volt increased to 20 volts at the speaker. The amount of amplification of voltage is called gain. So, The gain of the preamp is 10 and of the power amp is 20. The overall gain required to drive the amp to full power is 200 times the input signal. Gain can also be expressed in dB. Amplification of voltage in the above example would be: 20 Log(200) = 46dB of gain. Guitar preamplifiers usually have much more gain available, initially, because pickups were a lot weaker.

Nowadays, an overdriven sound is often desirable. This requires more gain to drive the amplifier into distortion (beyond the point of clipping). This is why an amplifier may start distorting even though the volume is only a third of the way up. The voltage required to drive the amplifier to full power when the volume is cranked is called the sensitivity. Many of the newer amps have a very high gain with a sensitivity around 1 millivolt or 0.001 volts. Two volume (or gain) controls plus a master volume are employed to control a high-gain preamp. This overabundance of gain is designed to allow the guitar to overdrive the preamplifier stages to produce a controlled distortion and sustain at lower volumes. The power amp is distorted at high volumes as well.

The distortion occurs in the amplification devices used, such as a tube or transistor. These devices can only amplify to a certain voltage and then will clip or saturate when driven beyond their capabilities. The clipping point is determined mainly by the DC power supply. When the signal goes beyond the maximum available voltage level, it is chopped off at the threshold. This is called clipping. Sometimes diodes are employed to cause the same effect for a fuzzed signal. The sustaining of notes is another benefit of clipping. As the guitar signal decays, the volume of the clipped notes stays relatively constant until the signal has decayed enough to drop below the clipping level. If an amp has a 0.001-volt sensitivity and is driven by a guitar with an output of 1 volt, the sustain will seemingly last forever until the guitar signal has decayed less than 0.001 volts.

The other main feature of the preamp is the tone control. Many configurations are used, including bass, middle, treble, presence, or bright controls. Parametric middle controls (variable tone centers) and graphic equalizers are also used on some models. Tone

Fig. 1: Basic amplifier block diagram shows the flow from preamp to power amp. Fig. 2 illustrates the effects of tone controls.

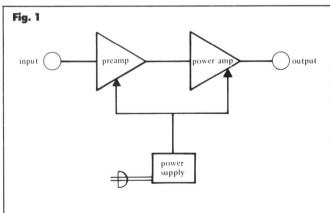

Fig. 1

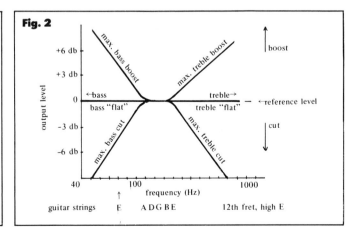

Fig. 2

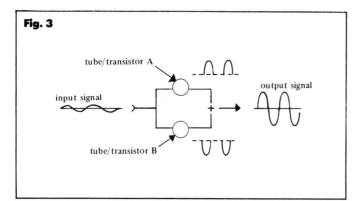

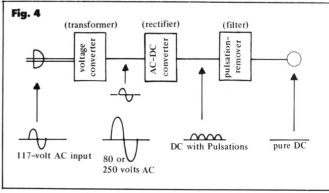

Fig. 3 illustrates the push-pull output concept. Fig. 4 shows how a power supply converts power for an amp.

controls are used simply to shape the guitar signal in relationship to frequency. Most tube amps utilize passive tone controls. Many solid-state amps imitate these same circuits, while others have active controls that are more precise and give better boost and cut capabilities. Passive circuits sometimes interact between the individual controls. The tone control increases or decreases the voltage amplitude at a specific range of frequencies. The bass control usually works below 200Hz, the middle control is from 200Hz to 1000Hz, and the treble is typically 800Hz and above. Presence controls or bright switches boost or cut the upper frequencies beyond 5000Hz. In general, the bass is affecting the low *E* and *A* strings on the guitar. Middle affects the reponse of the remaining open strings, and treble affects the notes on the high *E* string and the harmonics. Presence and bright can bring out the upper harmonics and string attack.

The preamp may be built with tubes or solid-state devices as the main element of amplification. Bipolar (ordinary) transistors, FETs (field effect transistors), or integrated circuits (a combination of transistors on a single silicon chip) are all solid-state devices that are used for amplification. From a performance standpoint, FETs and tubes have similar characteristics, except that tubes wear out much faster. Bipolar transistors perform differently, especially when overdriven to the point of clipping. When a transistor is clipped, the harmonic content has a harsher sound than a tube would have. Transistor distortion has a lot of third-order harmonics compared to the tube's strong second-order harmonic content. The pleasing, smoother sound of tube distortion can be simulated with some success by a properly designed FET circuit. Some transistor designs are susceptible to unwanted dis-

tortion from high-level input signals. The ability of an amplifier to handle these high-level inputs and transient peaks is called headroom. The lack of headroom is usually caused by too much gain and too low of a DC supply in the initial stages of the preamplifier. The signal is amplified to the clip point, causing distortion. Tube amps have a much higher supply voltage and can handle slightly higher input signals.

The power amp's main function is to provide the necessary energy to drive a speaker. The preamp signal is still a low-power signal and is only sufficient to drive line-level, high-impedance devices such as effects, mixing-board inputs or tape inputs. A speaker is a very low-impedance element (4, 8, or 16 ohms compared to a high-impedance input of 10,000 ohms or higher). In order for a speaker to be significantly loud, it requires more voltage and much more current than a preamp could ever deliver. An amplifier that is producing 100 watts into a 4-ohm speaker load will have an output voltage of 20 volts and an output current of 5 amps. The power amp can be divided into two sections. The input stages increase voltage, and the output stages provide the current drive to the speaker. The major components used in a power amp are either tubes or transistors. A combination of solid-state devices driving a tube output section is also used in some amps. Future amplifier designs may incorporate FET power transistors called MOSFETs or utilize digital power-amp technology.

The distortion characteristics of tubes and transistors in preamp designs hold true for power amps as well. When power amps are overdriven, they will distort too. There are many kinds of distortion in a power amp, such as nonlinearity (the input is not reproduced faithfully at the output), lack of frequency response (low or high notes are not reproduced accurately), and crossover distortion. Crossover distortion is

probably the most obnoxious distortion and is more prevalent in earlier transistor amp design. The ear can easily detect crossover distortion, and it is most noticeable at lower volumes when playing clean. The notes will have an underlying distortion that sounds like a fuzztone at low volume accompanying the main note.

Power output sections are usually designed so that one half of each cycle of the output signal is amplified by one tube or transistor, and the other half cycle is amplified by the other tube or transistor (see Figure 3). This arrangement is called push-pull, and it is analogous to a playground swing being pushed back and forth by two people. Each person does half the work.

When one output tube or transistor is working, the other is turned off or idling. At that instant when one of the devices is switching from off to on, the other is switching from on to off. Unless the design is exactly right, so that both devices switch at exactly the same time, the signal will be distorted at that instant. This is crossover distortion. In addition, transistors will produce a very brief click in the output signal at that instant, making the distortion more apparent. To keep the crossover switching from being noticed, current is sent through the output devices to keep them on or idling. If the bias is set properly, the crossover notch will disappear. However, if the bias current is excessive, the output devices will run too hot. Tubes under this condition of overbias will overheat and wear out rapidly, and transistors may consume too much power and fail.

So what is the difference between tube and transistor amps' sound? Part of it is the inherent distortion characteristics that were mentioned earlier. Another difference is the way a tube amp responds to speaker loads because of the output transformer that is necessary for a tube amp to match its output levels to the speaker. The output impedance (ratio of voltage to current) of a transistor push-pull stage is inherently low. In other words, transistors can handle large currents and can drive the speaker directly. Tubes are high-impedance devices. They operate at high voltages and low current. An output transformer is used to convert the high-impedance output to the low-impedance requirement of the speaker. Transformers are inherently nonlinear, distortion-producing devices. Through very careful design, the transformer can be improved to have acceptable distortion characteristics and frequency response. The transformer consists of wire wound around a steel core. As a rule, the size of the core determines the power and low-end frequency response.

The quality of the windings around the core affect the high frequency response. A good high-fidelity solid-state amp will have better high-frequency response. A good high-fidelity solid-state amp will have better high-frequency response than the average tube guitar amp. This isn't always desirable for the guitar player who prefers the softer warm sound of a tube amp. Pedal steel players like a precise high end, but for lead guitar, the sound becomes too crisp and brittle.

Tube power amps have other characteristics that differentiate them from solid-state amps. Transistor power amps are mostly referred to as constant voltage, highly damped amplifiers. Some manufacturers have designed their tran-

sistor power-amp circuits to behave like a tube power amp with constant current and a low damping factor. An amplifier that has a low damping factor will sound looser in the low end, and the speakers will have more excursion on bass notes. An amp, like a tube amp that is constant current, will respond differently to the speaker. A speaker's impedance will vary with frequency. A speaker's nominal impedance rating refers to the lowest impedance of the speaker at a specific frequency, usually between 100Hz and 400Hz. The constant-current amp will sound much livelier, especially in the high and low frequencies. This is due to the output's response to the varying changes in speaker impedance. The solid-state constant-voltage amplifier will tend to sound midrangier.

The part of the amp that supplies the juice to the preamp and power amp is the power supply. For tube amps, the power supply takes 117-volt alternating current from the wall outlet and turns it into 300- to 500-volt direct current plus 6.3- or 12.6-volt alternating current to heat the tubes. The tubes must be heated in order to function as an amplifier. AC is converted to DC voltage in the 20- to 80-volt range (depending on output power) for transistor amps. Contemporary solid-state amps use a plus and minus DC voltage for the supply. This allows the transistors to be directly coupled to the output without the use of a large DC coupling capacitor. The disadvantage of a direct-couple amp is if the power amp fails, it could also damage the speaker. Most ICs that are used operate on a plus and minus 15-volt supply.

The AC to DC conversion process requires three steps. The first step is the change from 117 volts AC to the voltage required by the amplifier. This is done by the power transformer, a big, heavy hunk of steel and copper wire. The output of this transformer is called the secondary AC voltage. The second step is to change (rectify) this AC voltage to DC. Rectification is done by diodes or a package of diodes called a bridge rectifier. Older tube amps that use a tube rectifier can be converted to diode rectifiers for more efficiency. Be careful. The DC voltage will be higher (giving more power) and may exceed some components' voltage ratings. The current at the output of the rectifier is still not pure DC. Some pulsation components are still present from the AC. Eliminating these pulsations is the last step of the power supply. This section consists of large supply capacitors

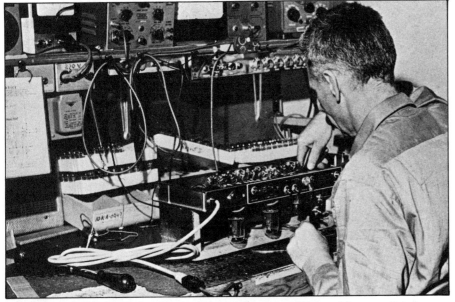

Top: Amp technician Bob Standen at his workbench in 1967 working on a Fender Princeton chassis. Bottom: Covering Marshall cabinets with Tolex.

and/or chokes to filter out these pulsations. If one of these capacitors or chokes is bad, a loud hum will be heard and possibly high oscillations as well. Some amps will have a fourth step incorporating voltage regulators to ensure the stability of the DC supply to the preamp.

In addition to the basic amplifier functions, many other special effects may be utilized to modify the sound. Older amps were often equipped with reverb and tremolo circuits. Some amps had two channels for running multiple instruments. Fuzz or distortion circuits were also popular until high-gain master volume circuits took their place. Most of the fuzz circuits utilize transistor or diode clipping, creating a hard-sounding distortion. Since natural amp distortion from tubes or FETs sounds much better, master volume circuits have replaced the fuzz circuits. Modern amps may contain the same effects that are available separately as effects boxes, such as phase shifters, chorus, graphic equalizers, vibrato, and compressors.

The reverb circuit is designed basically as shown in Figure 5. The reverb unit itself consists of long coil springs with transducers on each end. The

Fig. 5 schematically shows how a reverb circuit works. Fig. 6 shows the operation of a light-coupled isolator. Fig. 7 and Fig. 8 show the difference between a trigger-type fuzz circuit and a diode-type fuzz circuit, respectively.

transducers are coils wrapped around a metal core. The signal is sent to one of the transducers, exciting the spring. Then the signal proceeds down the length of the spring and is picked up by the other transducer. The reverb effect is produced by sound waves bouncing back and forth in the springs. The best reverb units contain six springs in three rows, giving different delay times. These units simulate the sound of an auditorium, with its large number of sound reflections. Usually the springs and transducers are shock mounted inside a steel sheet-metal enclosure. A complete reverb circuit also incorporates an amplifier drive circuit that excites the transducer and an amplifier to increase the signal from the output transducer. Most amps have a single volume control to set the amount of reverb signal that is blended with the original dry (unaffected) signal.

The tremolo circuit (sometimes erroneously called a vibrato circuit) provides a pulsating, rhythmic change in the intensity of the signal. True vibrato is like an opera singer's vibrato—it varies the pitch and intensity of the tone. When only the intensity varies, the effect is called tremolo. Tremolo is accomplished by a low-frequency oscillator driving a circuit that changes the volume of the signal. The modulation of the volume is performed by either a light-coupled isolator (or light-dependent resistor) or an FET. The

workings of the light-coupled isolator are diagrammed in Figure 6. Basically the photocell acts like a volume control whose resistance depends on the amount of light striking it. That light is provided by a small bulb or LED. The intensity knob controls the amount of volume amplitude change and the speed knob controls the rate of the low-frequency oscillator. The FET tremolo works similarly except its resistance varies directly with the pulsations from the oscillator.

When manufacturers realized that guitar players would rather select between two channels or sounds than share their amp with other players, the dual-channel amp became footswitch selectable. Usually, one channel is set up for cleaner tones and the other channel is the high-gain, master volume lead channel. On some amps the lead mode is done by adding in gain stages and volume controls in series to the original preamp. This is called cascading. Other designs incorporate two distinct preamps with separate volume and tone controls for each. One preamp is off when the other is on when this kind of circuit is in the channel-select mode. The input is fed to both preamps, and the switching is usually done in the final stages of the preamp circuitry. The player can select a channel by a footswitch or front-panel controls. Internally, the channel selection can be done by several methods. The simplest is a

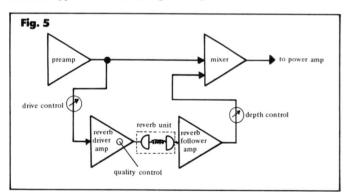

Fig. 5

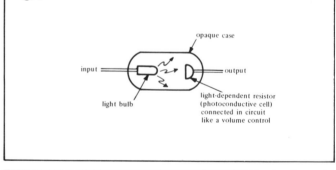

Fig. 6

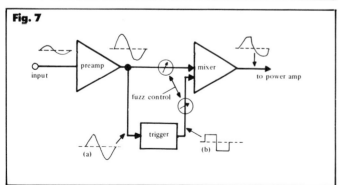

Fig. 7

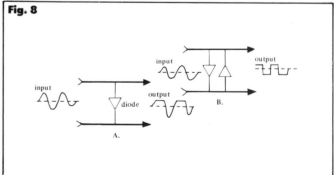

Fig. 8

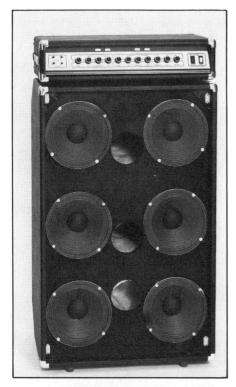  

dual footswitch that shorts one or the other channels, shutting it off. Relays, FETs, transistors, integrated circuits, and light-dependent resistors are used as a way to switch electronically. Switching circuits designed for solid-state amps may not work successfully with tube circuits. The high signal level in a tube preamp will exceed the voltage ratings of many solid-state switching devices.

With the popularity of outboard effects, effects loops are becoming increasingly important for a high-quality sound. Most loops are between the preamp and power-amp stages. Solid-state amps may have preamp-out and power-amp-in jacks that are essentially a line-level effects loop. Tube amps, again because of very high-level signals, require the output of the loop to be attenuated. Then, the output of the loop must be reamplified to the original level. The advantage of an effects loop is an improved signal-to-noise ratio. The noise generated by the effects used is not amplified by the preamp. The effects sound modification will not get washed out by a high-gain, distorted preamp if the effect is used after the preamp.

Guitar amplifiers incorporate all the basic aspects of amplifier design.

Because of the requirements of the guitarist, there are also many deviations from other amp designs to give a guitar a pleasing sound. In some respects, guitar amps are unsophisticated in comparison to a hi-fi amplifier. But the guitar amp is an extension of the guitar, since it is helping to create sounds rather than just reproducing them.
Richard Honeycutt and Keith Reinegger

APPLICATIONS OF AN ELECTRIC GUITAR AMPLIFIER

With so many kinds of music these days, there are a corresponding number of guitar styles. A guitar player's style is reflected not only in musical compositions and technique but in the equipment he uses to achieve the right sound. It is very difficult to find one amp that is suitable for all purposes and situations. An increasing number of amps are being manufactured with a lot of built-in flexibility through the use of multiple channels, built-in effects loops, and equalization controls. Small portable high-power amps have also become popular. Who wants to lug around 150 pounds of amplifier when a 60 pounder will do the job? Well, some players still prefer the power and low-end response of the big heavy stacks. Nothing else will do.

There is a direct correlation between the guitar player's amp and musical style. The two basic categories are clean sound and distorted. Usually, an amp that is used for clean, clear musical passages will have to be more powerful than a distorted amp at comparable volume levels. Distorted signals contain more harmonics and are easier to hear than the more fundamental notes of a cleaner signal. Also, an amp that is rated at 50 watts will put out more than that when it is overdriven and distorted. The power rating is measured at a low distortion specification, usually less then 5%. The input used during these measurements is a sine wave that is equivalent to a pure fundamental tone. A clean guitar note contains some harmonics, but the predominant signal is a fundamental. The distorted signal resembles a square wave, which contains almost all harmonics as well as fundamental. When a guitar signal is amplified beyond the maximum clean power output, the amplifier will clip or chop off the top and bottom of the signal, turning the waveform into a square wave. This distorted signal or square wave will have the same amplitude as the sine wave because of the power limitations of the amplifier (the power supply determines the available signal

voltage at the output). However, there is more power or energy in a square-wave signal than a sine wave of equal amplitude. If you were to compare a flute (which is a fundamental tone-producing instrument) with a sax (a lot of harmonics), and the voltage from peak to peak of the notes were the same, the sax would be significantly louder and easier to hear.

Good power and a faithful, accurate reproduction of sound are important in an amplifier intended for a clean style of playing. But this is not the only requirement. The tonality of an amp is also important to musical styles. Tone controls can do a lot to provide variation in sounds, but some amps' basic tonality, inherent in their designs, makes them particularly suitable for certain playing conditions. Some generalities can be made to correlate between playing styles and the amplification of the guitar. Of course, all players, all guitars, and all amps are different in some way, so there are no hard-and-fast rules concerning guitar and amp combinations.

The straight-ahead jazz player would want an amp that is percussive, giving a good attack and definition to fast passages. An even tone response is necessary so that all notes are equal volume. This means that from low *E* (80Hz) to the 17th fret high *A* (800Hz) the amp's output in combination with the guitar's output should be flat, especially in the 380 to 1000Hz range. Frequencies beyond 1000Hz are important for harmonic content and attack, but a dominant high-end tonal quality would detract from the warm, punchy jazz sound.

The amp requirements for an acoustic guitar with a pickup would be very different from any other electric guitar system. High-end and low-end emphasis, clarity, and equalization can help make an acoustic guitar sound like it is supposed to. This setup could be similar to a PA system, hi-fi like in quality. Upper frequencies need to be brought out to achieve good presence and bril-

liance, possibly with the aid of a tweeter. A good controlled bass response is also important. If the bass is excessive, muddiness and booming may result. As volumes get louder, the guitar resonances combined with peaks in the bass response of the amp will result in low-frequency feedback. The bass notes need to be there, but an over-resonant, low-end cabinet should be avoided. Equalization, such as parametric or graphic equalizers, can help solve tone and feedback problems with an acoustic guitar in a live situation. Midrange controls can help make an electric guitar sound more acoustic-like by cutting mids in the 200 to 500Hz region. Experimenting with high Q notches (mid cuts with a narrow range of frequency effect) can also produce some pleasing sounds.

A funky rhythm player or someone into twangy surf or country would want a sound in between the hi-fi acoustic sound and the flatter jazz sound. A Fender reverb amp and a single-coil guitar such as a Stratocaster or Telecaster are representative of this twangy style. In general, a bright and clear speaker adds to the twanginess, but too many highs or the use of tweeters can make the sound artificial, too steely. Anyone for a little reverb? This kind of tonality also works for bright, accented rhythm and chorusing. The doubling effect of chorus is brought out by a good clean high end.

Taking the jazz or twangier sound and adding a little edge of distortion gives you a raunchier, more aggressive style. This could lead to rock, blues, rhythm and blues, or fusion musical dimensions. Playing an amp at the edge of distortion, the guitar seems to respond easier, and the output becomes very lively. Tube amps really excel at this point because the distortion is soft and does not detract from the clarity and sweetness of the notes. However, older tube amps sometimes have parasitic oscillations or funny harmonic overtones. Solid-state amps, especially bipolar transistor types, can buzz at the distortion point, making an unpleasant transition from clean to dirty.

Shifting gears from lead to super lead opens up new dimensions to the electric guitar. It can either sound horrid or high-tech heavy. (Even the horrid sounds of a screaming guitar can be put to musical use as demonstrated by Jimi Hendrix.) Basically, high gain and overdrive cause the guitar to become self-playing. The notes become very distorted and take on the high harmonic content of the clipped signal. The amp is adding a lot of nuances and changing the tonality of the guitar sound completely. Playing the guitar requires a lot of technique as well. Hammer-ons, pull-offs, harmonics, and string muting create unique new sounds. Notes hold forever, and playing with the fingering hand alone—without the picking hand—is a snap. The player has to be on top of the volume control and be able to mute unplayed strings in order to control feedback. There are two major directions in these high-gain amplifiers to satisfy the differing musical tastes among rock players. The big stacks for that heavy English sound or the open back mini-amp with a sweeter, less nasty sound are very popular these days.

One thing remains the same: loudness and power help maintain the acoustic coupling between guitar and amp. To achieve the same kind of sustain and feedback at lower volumes, the amount of amp gain must be increased. Unfortunately, the clarity goes down as the gain and overdrive go up. Muddiness of a highly distorted amp can be corrected by reducing the low-end drive. If too many lows and mids are cut out, the fatness disappears and the amp will sound thin and screechy. Other weird sounds can emanate from high-gain amps when they are cranked. Overdriven too far, tubes or transistors can give a compressed sound. With multiple volume controls, many high-gain amps take a while to dial in the desired settings and achieve a balance between the amount of distortion and sustain. When the power amp is overdriven to the maximum, amps sometimes become atonal. The tonality changes of

the EQ controls get obliterated by the clipping and distortion occuring in the amplifier. With tone controls placed after the distortion stages, the equalization has more range, and their effect will be clearer.

A whole bushel of problems crop up when guitar amplifiers are modified or are high gain by original design. Many of these problems are magnified by the use of tubes and their nature. An amplifier that is very high gain is also sensitive. Extremely small signals at the input will be very loud at the output. This is great for amplifying the guitar signal, but included may also be hum, buzz, noise, squeals, oscillations, and radio stations. In other words, everything hanging out the front end of the amp turns into an antenna, picking up the slightest bit of unwanted noise.

The guitar pickups' high impedance makes the affinity for noise even worse. The buzz that occurs when the guitar is turned up (which gets worse when the player takes his hands off the strings) can be helped by such methods as extensive shielding, the use of a cordless system, or using low-impedance pickups. Most people prefer to keep their pickups unchanged and just put up with the high-impedance blues. Single-coil pickups are especially bad for picking up hum, thus the invention of the humbucking pickup. The choice of pickups is usually a matter of personal preference because of the distinct difference of sound between single- and dual-coil pickups. The use of a dummy coil can eliminate some of the hum picked up by the single-coil pickup. There are also single-coil-style humbucking pickups available. The hum is usually caused by

electromagnetic fields, such as lights, electric motors, and transformers. (Close proximity of a guitar to an amp will induce hum into the pickup.)

Pickup squealing is another annoying problem when the volume and gain are high. All pickups will squeal at some point as gain goes up. The pickups become microphones and a loop is created from guitar pickup to amp to speaker to guitar, etc. Potted pickups will perform better as will dense solid-body guitars. The squeal point will come at higher levels if sources of vibration in and around the pickup are damped.

Then there are the tube problems. High sensitivity causes preamp tubes to be microphonic, and they may start singing all by themselves. Tube selection is very important to eliminate the chances of microphonic oscillations. With everything turned up, the high-gain tube amp can reach the physical limits of the tubes. Usually, the first tube in the amplification chain will be the first to become microphonic. Solid-state devices have the edge over tubes in the high-gain situation in that they have a much higher threshold for microphonics. Solid-state circuits can also be designed to be lower impedance, which means a little less noise.

The original idea of high-gain amps probably stemmed from the addition of master volumes to amps to achieve a wide-open overdriven amp sound at lower volumes. Then gain boosting came along to create even more sustain. Old amps can be resurrected by such modifications. The best candidates are tube amps. Such hot-rodding techniques as gain boosting, master volume,

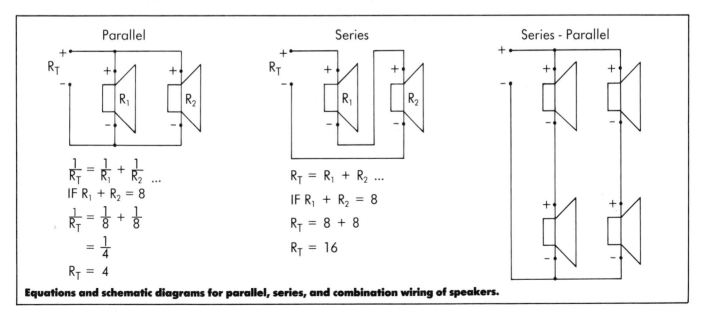

Parallel

$$\frac{1}{R_T} = \frac{1}{R_1} + \frac{1}{R_2} \text{ ...}$$

IF $R_1 + R_2 = 8$

$$\frac{1}{R_T} = \frac{1}{8} + \frac{1}{8}$$

$$= \frac{1}{4}$$

$$R_T = 4$$

Series

$$R_T = R_1 + R_2 \text{ ...}$$

IF $R_1 + R_2 = 8$

$$R_T = 8 + 8$$

$$R_T = 16$$

Series - Parallel

Equations and schematic diagrams for parallel, series, and combination wiring of speakers.

channel switching, tone boost, effects loops, power increases, and speaker changes have led manufacturers to adopt these modifications in their production amplifiers. Similarly, many of the innovations the manufacturers have created wind up as modifications in older amps.

Besides the preamp modifications, power increases to amplifiers can be performed. Again, a tube amp is easier to change than most solid-state designs. The difficulty in increasing power in solid-state amps is due to the extensive circuit redesign to ensure stability and current drive capability. A heavier duty output stage along with additional heatsinking and a beefed-up power supply would be a necessity for a power increase. The commonality of designs amongst tube amps allows power increases by changing transformers and changing or adding tubes. A 50-watt amp can be turned into a 100-watt amp, if space is available, by adding two tubes to the original pair and changing to 100-watt transformers.

Another way to increase power is by changing speakers or speaker systems. The power output of an amp is determined not only by watts but also by speaker efficiency. Output power can double by swapping a high-efficiency, high-quality, cast frame speaker for a stamped frame speaker that is standard equipment in many amplifiers. Some manufacturers will offer the good speaker as an option.

Quality of construction, materials, and tolerances have a great effect on speaker efficiency. The speaker transmits sound by converting electrical impulses into air motion. As the electrical energy or pulses enter the voice coil (many turns of wire wrapped around a cylindrical form), a magnetic field is generated by the coil. This field reacts to the magnetic field already present in the magnet assembly of the speaker. The direction of current flow (the electrical impulses are alternating current) determines the direction the voice coil will move in the voice-coil gap. The voice coil is situated in a magnetic field, a cylindrical slot in the speaker magnet assembly, called the voice-coil gap. Expensive, high-efficiency speakers have very close tolerances so that the space between the voice-coil gap is minimized. The smaller the gap can get without the coil rubbing, the more concentrated the magnetic field and the more energy transfer. Also affecting speaker efficiency is the ratio between the voice coil and the speaker's magnet size and material. Although alnico is a more efficient

magnet material, its lack of availability in recent years has led most manufacturers to use ceramic magnets. The bigger the magnet, the more concentrated the field in the voice-coil gap. However, when the voice-coil diameter is designed to be larger, the magnet must be increased in size to maintain efficiency.

The diameter of the voice coil can determine the power-handling capability of a speaker along with the materials selected for the voice-coil form. The ability of the voice coil to dissipate heat determines its survival under high-power conditions. A large-diameter aluminum voice-coil form is probably the best for heat transfer. Older designs used a paper-coil form, which sounded the most natural but could not stay cool and would burn up rather easily when attacked by flailing guitar notes. Composite or glass-impregnated voice-coil forms are also used as a compromise between the natural sound of paper and the heat-transfer ability of aluminum. Another trick to achieve better power handling and heat dissipation is by injecting a heat transfer material called Ferro-fluid into the voice-coil gap.

The voice coil transfers the electrical energy into motion. The actual sound waves are created by this motion through the speaker cone, which is attached to the coil. The speaker cone is suspended in two places. The outer edge of the cone (called the surround) is attached at the rim of the speaker frame (basket). The other attachment is the spider, which is affixed to the cone at the connection point to the cone and coil. The spider is connected to the basket where the magnet assembly is attached to the speaker frame. The amount of flexibility of the surround and spider determines how loosely the cone will move. The looser the suspension, the lower the frequency range of the speaker. The heavier the cone and voice-coil assembly, the lower the frequencies produced. Finally, the cone diameter affects frequency response as well. Large-diameter speakers will produce better low frequencies. It is difficult to design a speaker for a wide frequency response. Most speakers can only reproduce a limited spectrum of sounds. Speakers with a strong bass will sacrifice highs, and speakers that are bright will have a limited bass response. Metal domes are sometimes added to speakers to extend the high-end response, but this can lead to a metallic-sounding treble.

For guitar, the 12-inch speaker is the

most popular choice. It has good balance of lows and highs for the guitar frequencies. Tens are often chosen for a brighter sound and fifteens for more bass emphasis. However, when using multiple speakers in a cabinet, the combined speaker cone area will have the same kind of bass response as a larger speaker. That is why four 12-inch speaker cabinets have such a big, low-end response. Cabinet volume can determine bass response, but the more resonant the cabinet becomes in the lower frequencies, the muddier the speaker will be in the high end. Small cabinets will have poor bass. The resonant peaks of the small cabinet will move into the low notes of the guitar. This will cause some notes to become overpowering, and the low mids will tend to honk.

Small cabinets function better if they have an open back. Open-back cabinets are very convenient but provide very little loading of the speaker. This could lead to overdriving the speaker with strong bass notes since the speaker cone can move so freely. Reflections of sound from the back of the cabinet can give an impression of a full sound compared to the tight, controlled, and directional output of the closed cabinet. Again, personal preference determines the choice of cabinets, whether for sound quality or portability.

A speaker that is intended for heavy distortion should have a power rating in excess of the amp's power rating. This safety factor is necessary since speakers don't like distortion or clipped signals. Speaker power ratings don't take into account these nasty guitar signals. There is nothing wrong with putting a 200-watt speaker into a 100-watt amp. In open-back cabinets, the safety factor is even more important. Speakers typically fail from too much power or too much speaker-cone excursion. When a speaker starts distorting heavily, this can only lead to failure. It is always best to let the amp distort and the speaker to reproduce the amp's output. Never let the speaker do the distorting on its own.

Another important consideration for speaker selection is impedance. Impedance is the resistance to the current flow of an AC signal. The output of an amp is designed to operate at a specific output impedance. Some amps have selectable output impedance to allow them to have full power potential into different speaker combinations. This is achieved by way of an output transformer with multiple taps that varies the output voltage. No amp should have a speaker load less than the minimum load for the amplifier. Speaker impedances less than an amp's minimum impedance rating will draw excessive power from the amp. This could cause an overheating problem and direct failure of the output stages. Impedances greater than the amps rating will not harm the amp, in fact, the amplifier will cruise, since power output will be less. Transistor amps can run forever into a no-load situation but some will blow immediately when the output is shorted. Some transistor amps have protection circuits or such heavy-duty outputs that shorts are not a problem. Tube amps may fail when plugged into an open load because the output will go into severe oscillation and possibly cause the output transformer to fail. Most tube amps have speaker jacks that short to ground to prevent failure when the speaker is not plugged in. The tube amp can play for a limited time into a short.

When hooking up multiple speakers, it is important that they be phased properly. The speaker cones should all move in the same direction at the same time. If they don't, power will be lost because cancellation will occur. Loss of bass will be very evident when speakers are out of phase. There are three ways to hook up speakers: series, parallel, and series-parallel. Parallel is the most common. Speaker jacks on most amps are wired in parallel. The more speakers that are plugged into these parallel jacks, the lower the total impedance becomes. Two 8-ohm speakers in parallel become 4 ohms, and four 8-ohm speakers become 2 ohms. The number of speakers used, the type of wiring scheme, and the speaker's impedance must be carefully planned to achieve the desired impedance rating required by the amplifier. No matter what wiring configuration is used, the sum of the individual speaker's power rating will give the total power capability. When mixing different impedance speakers or cabinets, the power dissipated by each speaker is inversely proportional to the speaker's impedance. An 8-ohm speaker will use more power than a 16-ohm speaker when they are hooked together.

Interconnecting guitar amps can be done with a Y cord or a patch cord tying the inputs together, assuming there are two parallel jacks at the input. Other means of using two amps are becoming more popular since the proliferation of stereo effects. Some players are trading in their big amps for two little ones and using a stereo chorus or delay. This makes the sound incredibly full. Each side of the stereo output is sent to an input of each amp. An even better hookup utilizes an effects loop in the amplifier. The guitar signal is fed to one preamp, which eliminates duplicate controls of two preamps. The signal then proceeds from the effects loop output to the stereo effect. The signal is split into stereo by the effect, and one side returns to the amp's effects-loop input. The other output of the effects device is sent to a slave amp. This setup achieves a stereo sound with only one preamp and the effects are post-preamp, offering better noise and sonic performance. The only problem that can arise with effects loops is the incompatibility of signal levels with the effects. Some amps, especially tube amps, may have too hot of a level for the effects. In this case, the amp must be modified or outboard attenuators and amplifiers must be used. When using multiple amp setups or AC-powered effects, there can occur a nasty buzz (a ground loop due to duplications of ground paths) that requires lifting or isolating the ground on the AC cord of all but one of the amps.

When an amp breaks down on the gig, its a disaster. And it happens. No sound, crackling, distortion, loss of power, and embarrassment are the risks the electric guitarist faces when he takes to the stage. One sure cure for these potential dangers is to carry a spare. (Those many stacks of amps in concert aren't always there just for show.) This may be a bit out of reach for many players. The next best thing is to try to keep an amp well maintained and avoid rough handling. Allow a tube amp to cool down before moving it or exposing it to sudden temperature changes. Playing for four solid hours and then immediately wheeling the amp outside into the cold night air across the bumpy pavement and into the trunk of a car will do terrible things to those poor power tubes. Heat and vibration are the destructive forces an amp must try and survive. Proper ventilation of power amps is very important to prevent premature failure. Fan cooling of tubes or transistors will increase their life. Periodic checking of tube and jack connections is a good maintenance procedure. Bad cords should be repaired or destroyed, and always carry a spare. Input jacks usually make important circuit ground connections to the chassis. If the jacks are loose, they will cause crackling.

Power tubes should be replaced frequently if the amp is used hard and often. It is best to keep power tubes fairly well matched with the same brand and age. Of course, matched sets of power tubes are optimum. When tubes get tired from use and age, they can cause other component failures if the tubes were to short out. An amplifier that consistently blows fuses usually has a serious problem. Overfusing or by-passing the fuse is asking for trouble and expensive repair bills. Never use a fuse more than 1 amp higher in rating than the original fuse. Sometimes, noisy or scratchy pots can be corrected by vigorous turning. Otherwise, disassemble the amp and shoot volume-control cleaner or tuner cleaner into the controls. Never use anything else, like WD40. If the controls are still scratchy, they could be defective or possibly have a defective component causing DC voltage across the pot. Any other repair other than tube replacement should be referred to a qualified technician.

So much interest has developed in the electronic musical instrument field that amplification and systems are bound to change and improve. Digital technology is creeping into the music field, especially in recording, synthesizers, and delay effects. Amplifiers already incorporate logic circuits for switching, and other digital circuits are bound to be used in the future. In the future, programmability and memory for preset tone and volume controls may be incorporated into guitar amps. Solid-state amps will continue to be designed to imitate the tonal qualities of tube amps. One thing is certain, tubes will continue to become more expensive. Ultimately, the musicians will benefit from the technological improvements and the ever-widening range of sound an amplifier can produce.

Keith Reinegger

AMP GLOSSARY

October 1982. The following *Guitar Player* Amplifier Glossary features definitions of terms commonly associated with guitar amplifiers in an amp-related context rather than in cold technical terms as do most electronics dictionaries. Consequently, this glossary will go a long way in making often ambiguous electronic jargon found in manufacturers' brochures, operator's manuals, and magazine articles easier to understand.

Included are definitions of terms regarding such diverse areas as electrical phenomena, concepts, and amplifier hardware; note that many are conveniently cross-referenced for further explanation.

A

AC (alternating current). Electric current that reverses its direction (alternates) at regularly occurring intervals. Power from a standard wall socket is generally 110 to 120 volts AC, alternating at 60 cycles per second. Audio signals in amps, effects, wires, etc., are also AC. See DC.

AC outlet. Frequently referred to as a convenience or courtesy outlet (usually found on the back of an amp), this feature provides an extra socket for powering auxiliary equipment.

Active. Pertaining to electronic circuits (e.g., tone controls) that add to as well as subtract from a given signal. Such circuits often require power sources. See Passive.

Active tone controls. Tone controls that add to and attenuate, rather than just cut from, an audio signal.

Amplifier (amp). An electronic device that increases the level of an audio signal, usually for the purpose of driving one or more loudspeakers, or for maintaining proper levels in long signal chains (multiple effects, long cords, etc.).

Attenuate. To reduce the voltage, power, or frequency of a signal.

B

Balanced connector. A 3-conductor connector—commonly referred to as an XLR or Cannon connector—that terminates a cord carrying a signal over three wires. One wire acts as a ground, while the others carry the signal in the form of positive and negative voltages.

Bass control. A tone control that affects low audio frequencies (typically below 500Hz).

Biamping. The utilization of two amplifiers in a given sound system in order to separately amplify different frequency ranges and thereby reduce distortion. Usually, a full-range audio signal is divided by means of an electric crossover; one amp is designated for low frequencies, while the other is designated for highs.

Bright switch. A feature that emphasizes an amp's high-frequency range.

C

Cascading. Switching or wiring in extra preamplifier stages in series to achieve higher gain.

Channel. A complete sound avenue, usually consisting of a preamp, a voltage amp, a power output, and power-supply stages.

Channel switching. A feature that allows an audio signal to be routed from one channel to another, usually by means of a footswitch.

Chassis. The sheet-metal frame to which electronic components (capacitors, transistors, resistors, etc.) are mounted.

Circuit breaker. A device found on the backs of some amplifiers that automatically interrupts a circuit carrying potentially damaging current; often used instead of a fuse.

Compression. A feature of some amps and effects that reduces the signal's dynamic range by making loud sounds quieter and quiet sounds louder. See Limiter.

Crossover. A circuit that divides a signal into two or more bands of selected frequencies; often used in biamping or triamping.

Crossover distortion. Distortion caused by a slight delay in amplification at the crossing-over point between the top and bottom devices in a push-pull amplifier circuit.

D

dB (decibel). A unit of measurement for expressing the ratios of various quantities including sound level, power, and voltage.

DC (direct current). Electric current that has constant and uniform polarity (flows in one direction). Batteries and small power sources for effects provide a source for DC. See AC.

Depth. A general term often used in describing the intensity of an effect such as reverb, phasing, etc.

Distortion. Also referred to as clipping, distortion is a change in an audio signal resulting in the appearance of frequencies at the output that were not present in the original waveform. Distortion is commonly caused by applying a signal that is too powerful for an amp, speaker, or other electronic device to adequately handle. It is commonly employed as a means of creating sustain.

Distortion effect. A feature that intentionally causes an amp to sound as if it were being overdriven.

Dynamic range. The difference between the minimum and maximum (overload) signal level in audio equipment, often measured in decibels.

E

Effects channel. A channel that includes an effects device (phaser, distortion, flanger, etc.).

Effects loop. Often composed of an output jack and an input jack that allow effects to be connected between the preamp and the power amp (or a successive preamp) in an amplifier. Because the signal level from a preamp is much higher than that derived from most guitars, the signal-to-noise ratio can be greatly increased by using an effect between amp stages rather than between the instrument and the amp.

EQ (equalization). The intentional altering of portions of the audio-frequency spectrum by means of filters or tone controls; often employed to reduce uneven frequency response or feedback.

Extension-speaker jack. A feature usually found on the back of an amp that allows a remote speaker to be used.

F

Feedback. Self-oscillation caused by a regenerating signal loop between the guitar pickup or microphone and the amp and speakers.

FET (field-effect transistor). A kind of solid-state device that is often more stable than standard transistors.

FET distortion. When overdriven, a FET exhibits distortion qualities more like those produced by a tube than most other types of transistors.

FET switching. Circuits containing FETs, which can be used to activate effects or perform channel-switching functions with low noise and low power consumption.

Footswitch. A foot-triggered switch used to activate an amp's reverb, vibrato, or other feature, as well as effects devices.

Frequency response. The range of frequencies over which a device or audio system will perform.

Fuse. A replaceable protective device that breaks a circuit when the current becomes abnormally high. A fast-blow fuse is generally used in delicate circuits, whereas a slow-blow fuse is used in more rugged ones. See Circuit Breaker.

Fuse holder. A socket or metal clip that allows for easy replacement of a fuse. Generally located on the back of an amp or within the chassis.

G

Gain. The amount an amplifier increases the power of a signal, usually expressed in decibels. See Volume.

Gain boost. Increasing the amount of amplification or gain.

Graphic equalizer. A device containing multiple filters with separate, fixed frequency centers, which allows for boosting or cutting particular signal ranges. See Parametric Equalizer.

Ground (also called "earth"). The electrically neutral part of a circuit, often referred to in terms of 0 volts.

Ground switch. Also referred to as a line reverse or polarity switch, this feature allows the polarity of a current to be conveniently reversed, resulting in the elimination of hum.

H

Headroom. A term that expresses the relative difference between the operating and maximum operating points of an audio device.

Heat sink. A metal part with maximized surface areas designed to dissipate heat generated by electronic components.

Hertz (Hz). A unit equal to one cycle per second that measures the frequency of a periodic phenomenon such as an alternating current.

Hiss. A kind of undesireable audio frequency noise. Often called white, pink, or thermal noise.

I

IC (integrated circuit). Also known as a "chip," an IC is a sophisticated, highly miniaturized solid-state circuit that contains the equivalent of many components such as transistors, resistors, capacitors, diodes, etc.

Impedance. Measured in ohms, impedance is the total opposition to the flow of alternating current in a circuit.

Inputs. The entry points where the signal from a guitar or effect may be introduced to an amplifier or other electronic device.

L

LED (light-emitting diode). A small light (often red, green, or yellow) commonly used as an indicator.

Limiter. An electronic circuit that acts much like a compressor, except it keeps the dynamic range of a signal within fixed limits.

Line level. Usually referred to as a signal level of 0dB. Equivalent to a 0.7- to 1-volt signal level into a specified impedance.

M

Master volume. Simultaneously controls the overall volume of one or more channels of an amp. When used in conjunction with a channel's volume control, a master volume enables a guitarist to control the amount of distortion as well as the overall output of the amp.

Matched tubes. Vacuum tubes selected for their similar electrical characteristics. Often employed in amps to produce more efficient operation.

Matching impedance. When the output impedance of a device is compatible with the input impedance of a device to which it is connected, the two are said to match. Mismatched impedances can lead to distortion, signal loss, or poor frequency response.

Microphonic. Sensitivity to vibrations causing noises and ringing. Tubes are especially prone to microphonics and will self-oscillate.

Midrange control. A tone control that affects audio frequencies in the middle range, where the largest concentration of audio energy is usually present.

N

Noise floor. The level at which noise (hiss, hum, etc.) exists in an amplifier. Often used as a reference point in signal-to-noise ratios.

O

Ohm. Symbolized by the Greek letter omega, an ohm is the unit used to measure electrical resistance or impedance.

Open back. A speaker cabinet with no back. The speaker is then unloaded.

Oscillation. Any kind of signal or alternating current including those beyond audibility.

Outputs. Jacks normally situated on the back of an amp that allow one or more auxillary speakers to be attached.

Overdrive level. The level at which distortion begins as a consequence of feeding a device with an overloading signal.

Overload. A load that exceeds an amplifier's capability.

P

Parametric equalizer. An equalizer with one or more center frequencies that are variable over a particular range, in addition to boost and cut capabilities. See Graphic Equalizer.

Passive. Pertaining to electronic circuits that generally subtrack from a signal, and which require no power source. See Active.

Passive tone controls. Tone controls that only attenuate, or cut from, an audio signal. Generally a simple circuit, such as a pot and a capacitor, requiring no external power. See Active Tone Controls.

Peak wattage. Also referred to as peak power, peak wattage is the maximum instantaneous power of a signal. Amplifiers are able to perform at their peak for only short periods of time. See RMS.

Piggyback. Refers to an amp and speaker cabinet combination in which the head (amp circuitry) and speakers are not housed in the same enclosure.

Pilot lamp. A light that indicates whether an amp or other electrical device is turned on.

Potentiometer (pot). A variable resistor used for an amplifier's volume and tone controls.

Power. Working electrical energy measured in watts.

Power amp. An amplifier that has higher-power output capability than a preamp and is designed to drive one or more loudspeakers. Generally contained with the preamp in self-contained or piggyback amps, but also available as a separate unit in some cases.

Power amp in. An input that plugs directly into an amp's power amplifier and bypasses the preamp. This function allows some amps to be used as slaves.

Power attenuator. A device used to soak up power or allow less power transmission between amp and speaker.

Power rating. The maximum power at which an amplifier can operate over a specified period.

Preamp. A stage in an amplifier that raises the signal of a low-level source (such as a guitar) so that it may be further processed.

Preamp out. An output that facilitates taking the preamp's signal and sending it to other power amps, PA mixers, or recording gear.

Push-pull switch. A switch that is operated by a pulling or pushing movement; often combined with a potentiometer.

R

Reverb. The synthetic creation of ambience, or reverberation (echoes spaced so closely together that they are no longer discernible as individual events), most commonly by means of sending a signal through an electronic delay device. In most amps, a module containing metal springs provides the delay.

RMS (root mean square). The true measure of an amp's ability to perform, RMS is based on continuous power at a given number of cycles per second over a period of time not less than 30 seconds. See Peak.

S

Self-contained amp. An amplifier and speaker that are housed in the same cabinet.

Sensitivity. The quantity of input signal level usually specified to allow the amplifier to go to full power with all the controls up.

Slave. A power amplifier that is driven by the preamp of another amp or PA component; often used to provide extra power or to drive cross-stage monitor amps.

Solid state. Refers to electronic components such as diodes and transistors that use semiconductors (crystals) instead of tubes.

Speaker. A device that converts electrical energy into sound waves.

Speaker cone. The cone-shaped part of the speaker that actually works as a piston to cause air motion and consequently sound.

Standby switch. A feature that allows tubes to idle (remain warm) while an amp is not in use; e.g., between sets. This reduces the strain on tubes caused by frequent heating and cooling.

Sustain. The phenomenon in which a sound lasts without appreciable degradation or decay.

T

Toggle switch. A two- or three-position switch operated by flipping (toggling) a protruding lever.

Top (head). An amplifier unit that is separate from any type of speaker enclosure.

Transducer. A device that converts electrical energy into mechanical energy, such as a speaker.

Transformer. Commonly a large, square-shaped or toroidal (doughnut-shaped) component used in the power supply of an amplifier to convert AC main voltage to other suitable voltages. Transformers are sometimes employed as buffers between amps and speakers in order to match their impedances.

Transient response. The ability of an amplifier to handle sudden changes in audio levels without distortion.

Treble boost. Electronic augmentation of high-frequency signals.

Treble control. A tone control that affects high audio frequencies (typically above 5000Hz).

Tremolo. An effect feature on many amps, tremolo is the variance in the *amplitude* (volume) of a sound—generally at a rate between .5 and 20 times per second—achieved by the use of a low-frequency oscillator. Commonly mistaken for vibrato.

Triamping. The utilization of three amplifiers in a given sound system; one each for bass, midrange, and treble frequencies. It utilizes the same basic principles for avoiding distortion as biamping.

Tube. Also referred to as a vacuum tube or valve, a tube is a sealed glass envelope in which the conduction of electrons takes place through a gas or vacuum; most often for amplification or switching applications.

V

Variac. A variable transformer that can change the AC line voltage. It is used to control amplifier power by raising or lowering the AC voltage.

Vibrato. An effect feature that uses an oscillator to cause a regular variation in the frequency (pitch) of a sound. Speed and intensity controls for governing the velocity and depth of the vibrato effect are commonly present on the front panels of amps with this feature.

Voice coil. The central part of the speaker that converts electrical pulses into magnetic pulses. It consists of a wire coil wound around a cylindrical form.

Voltage. Electrical pressure that causes current to flow through a conductor. Its unit of measurement is the volt.

Volume. The overall amount of loudness. See Gain.

W

Wattage. The power capability of an amplifier.

Jim Ferguson and Keith Reinegger

TUBES: MECHANICS & MYSTIQUE

June 1983. Guitarists both today and yesterday are linked in many cases by one piece of equipment: a tube amp. In fact, the tube amp is currently enjoying its greatest popularity with musicians, even though there have been great strides in transistor amp technology over the past 20 years. Some guitarists prefer tube amps, while others are equally fond of transistorized, or solid-state, models. But regardless of how close their sound may be, for many guitarists there remains a certain mystique about tubes.

Why do designs built around tubes sound different from those following the solid-state approach? Simply, tubes work differently. What follows, then, is an explanation of their construction, function, and applications.

Tube construction and operation. A tube is an electronic device consisting of a minimum of four active elements: a heater (filament), a cathode, a grid, and a plate. All of these are sealed in a glass enclosure with its air removed—a vacuum—to prevent the parts from burning. The location of a simple tube's parts is shown in Fig. 1. The filament is heated in order to warm the cathode. Once heated, the cathode begins to emit electrons, which flow from the cathode (which is negatively charged) toward the plate (which is positively charged). The grid's purpose is to control this flow. If the grid were absent, this movement of the electrons would be uncontrolled, much like water rushing from a faucet that's opened all the way.

Theory of operation. When a small signal is applied to the grid, it causes a larger change in the current that flows between the cathode and plate accordingly. In effect, it acts as a valve. A portion of the amp's electronic circuitry, the *grid bias control*, adjusts the proper voltage setting of the grid. The amount of bias varies from tube to tube, depending on its sensitivity, and it acts to keep the tube "idling." When the grid bias is properly set, the tube is balanced to the circuit, and therefore produces a clean, powerful signal (proper biasing also extends the life of the tube).

For optimum performance, the bias setting should be checked whenever power tubes are changed—preferably by a qualified technician using an oscilloscope. A bias adjustment is a relatively simple operation, and can be performed for a minimal bench charge (typically $15.00 to $20.00). Some symptoms of improper bias setting include the amp running too hot, excessive hum after it's been on for a short while, or distortion that just doesn't sound right. The amp doesn't necessarily have to sound bad for its tubes to be incorrectly biased, and these symptoms may indicate other problems. However, if your amp is behaving in an extraordinary manner, a trip to the shop may head off damage to it, regardless of the cause.

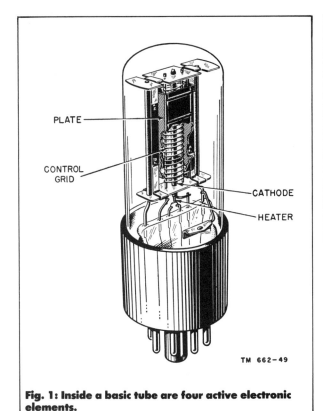

PLATE

CONTROL GRID

CATHODE

HEATER

TM 662-49

Fig. 1: Inside a basic tube are four active electronic elements.

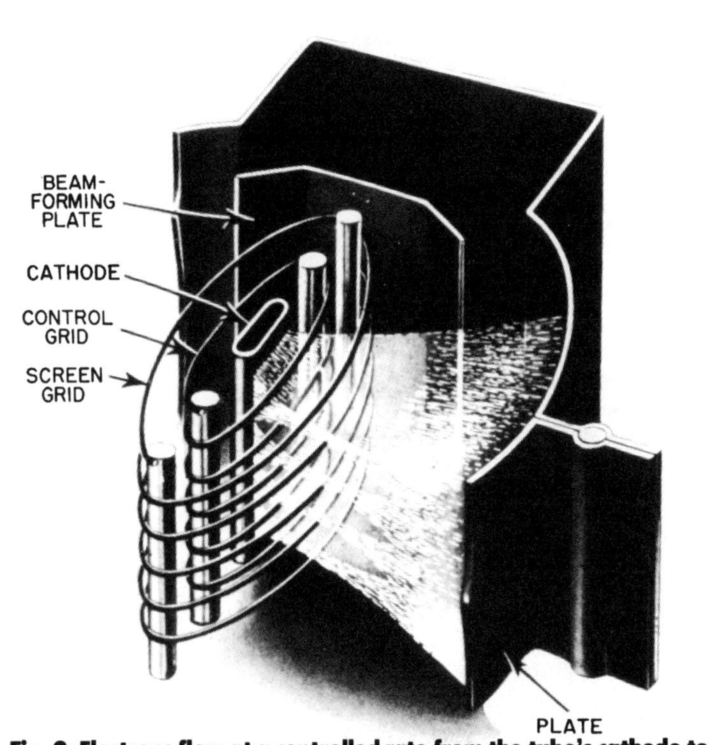

BEAM-FORMING PLATE

CATHODE

CONTROL GRID

SCREEN GRID

PLATE

Fig. 2: Electrons flow at a controlled rate from the tube's cathode to the plate.

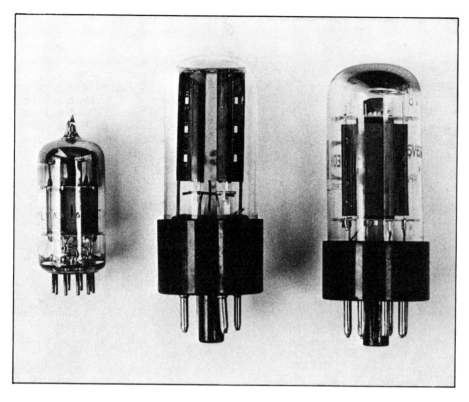

Tubes, transistors, and distortion.

No tube primer would be complete works in an amplifier. Imagine a small guitar amp with no volume or tone controls: just a guitar input, one tube, an output transformer, and a speaker. The guitar's pickup produces a small voltage, the result of the string vibrating in the pickup's magnetic field. In general, this signal is applied to the grid, which in turn causes a large current flow from the cathode to the plate. Thus, a correspondingly large voltage now appears at the plate. This plate is connected to an output transformer, which matches the tube's output impedance to that of the speaker. (Because there is a great disparity between the impedances of the tube amplification circuit and the speaker, the transformer must act as a buffer to interface the two components.) Thus, a small, low-power signal from a guitar's pickup can produce a high-powered signal to drive the speakers.

Naturally, amps don't all sound alike. This is due to variations in the type of tube that is used, the quality of the tubes, and the specific circuit design of the amp. In other words, some tubes amplify more than other tubes under similar conditions. Also, the amount of gain a tube produces varies with the circuit design. This is why different makes of tube amps can sound very different, even though they use the same tube types. In addition, certain amps use completely different types of tubes. A

good example of this is the English-type Marshall using European EL-34 tubes in its power amp section, compared to the U.S. type, which employs American-made 6550 power tubes. The U.S. and English styles sound and play very differently, reflecting the character of their power tubes. That is, the English EL-34 tubes yield more distortion than their American counterparts, although they produce roughly the same amount of volume. With internal bias modification (which mostly involves changing some resistance values), any U.S. Marshall amp can use European EL-34s, and vice versa.

Multi-stage amps.

Larger and more complex amps have many stages of tube amplification: preamp stages, signal-processing stages, and power amp stages.

The Preamp. The preamp stage is much like a mixer in a PA system, which must amplify an incoming mike or guitar signal to *line-level* strength before the signal can be processed with effects for tonal shaping. Likewise, a tube amp must preamplify a guitar's signal so that it can be further processed. This is the first gain stage of the tube amp.

Signal-processing stages. An example of a signal-processing stage is the reverb section, where the signal is diverted through a reverb spring system and then returned by another gain stage, and finally blended with the orig-

inal signal. Tone controls and second gain stages (often employed for an overdrive effect) are other examples of signal-processing stages.

Power-amp stages. The power-amp section takes the preamp's signal and amplifies it many times to a level that can drive the speakers. All tube amps with power ratings of 10 watts or more employ a *push/pull* power amp design. This means that the power tubes work as a team to amplify the signal and drive the speakers. (Practically all transistor amps employ a push/pull configuration as well.) The output tubes all share in the sound, so for maximum efficiency it is desirable to use tubes that operate as similarly as possible. Also, for efficiency, use power tubes of the same make—manufacturer's specifications for tubes bearing the same stock number may vary over a broad range. And, if one power tube is bad, it is advisable to change *all* of them. Having one fresh, powerful tube and three old ones, for example, can create an imbalance in the push/pull effect, resulting in inefficient operation. The power-amp section is only as strong as its weakest link. So, if one tube out of four is faulty or varies from the others in its performance character, the overall sound of the amp will be limited.

The process of output-tube matching dates back almost as far as tube amps. The military began matching certain properties of tubes to produce longer field life and higher performance. Later, top audio companies such as McIntosh developed a system to match power tubes for use in their audio amps, and would guarantee performance specifications only when their matched tube sets were used. Unfortunately, it is impossible to specifically *manufacture* matched power tubes because of the mechanical nature of the device and the extreme operating temperatures that exist within the tube (around 700 degrees F). However, once the tube is made, it can be performance tested for various parameters and matched into sets with identical characteristics.

Limitations.

Since a tube is a mechanical assembly of parts that forms an electronic device, it is subject to some mechanical problems and limitations. Tubes wear out in direct proportion to how hard they are worked (due to the circuit design) and how often and loud you play your amp. Vibration and jarring shorten the useful life of the tube as well. Ideally, a tube could be built so that no vibration existed between its mechanical elements. However, in practice this doesn't happen. So when the tube is vibrated (usually by the speaker), the elements shake, resulting in an additional signal being amplified. This phenomenon is commonly referred to as *microphonics*. The construction methods and materials used in the chassis and cabinet may actually serve to create pleasing microphonics, which give the amp a distinctive desirable sound. However, adverse tube microphonics can be a big problem when the elements of the tube rattle or ring, producing a signal all by itself. A tube with this problem is unsuitable for use in music amps, much like a faulty guitar pickup or a bad microphone is undesirable for most musical purposes.

When to replace tubes. So, when should you change your tubes? Chances are, your *power* tubes are worn out when your amp starts sounding weak, lacks punch, makes funny noises, has its power fading up and down, or loses highs or lows. If your amp squeals, is excessively noisy, loses gain in one channel, hums, lacks sensitivity to touch, or generally feels as if it's working against you, a *preamp* tube could be malfunctioning, and is in need of replacement. In both cases, though, the tubes may not be at fault. Unless you are skilled in specific troubleshooting, regard the high-voltage circuits found in amplifiers as extremely dangerous. Take the amp to a professional for diagnosis and repair.

Unfortunately, you can't simply pull your tubes out and take them to the drugstore or local electronics outlet and evaluate them on one of the tube-test-ing machines designed for TVs. This is because of the high voltage levels at which guitar amplifier tubes are driven. Amp tubes can be powered with 450 volts or more, whereas the testing machine provides only about 150 volts. This difference can completely foul up a diagnosis. Tube-for-tube replacement and a before-and-after comparison is often the most reliable test.

Good-sounding, non-microphonic preamp tubes are the exception, not the rule. Quality preamp tubes along with matched sets of power tubes are a little harder to find, and you may pay more when you do locate them. However, you can expect improved sound and longer life, so there is a payoff. Therefore, if it's at all possible, try several different tubes when replacing worn ones. Some may match better than others, in terms of their output power or distortion characteristics.

Tube functions in the amp. Let's look at a common example of how a tube without an explanation of how tubes distort in a way that is different from transistors. Tubes distort uniquely because as the signal emitting from the plate approaches its maximum potential, the tube gradually begins to react less and less to the original input signal. This results in a type of compression of the signal, and produces a soft clipping. Clipping occurs when the input signal increases but the maximum power has been reached. Thus the signal becomes cut off, or clipped. Transistors, on the other hand, react exactly the same to the input signals right up to their maximum power; then they stop quickly,

creating a sharp clipping. These different types of clipping produce different series of harmonics (overtones). When the transistor amp clips, it produces more odd-order harmonics (and in its worst case can sound hollow and dry), whereas tube distortion produces even-order harmonics. Therefore, in many cases tube distortion sounds warmer. It should be mentioned that various types of transistor and tube distortion are possible, depending on the amp's design.

In the case of a tube amp, preamp and power-amp tubes have different distortion characteristics due to the difference in both their tubes and their circuit design. For example, relying on a master volume-distortion circuit by itself will yield less sensitivity to variations in a player's *touch* than if the amp is attenuated (has its volume limited) after its power stage (that is, with a power attenuator). This is due to the contribution of the output transformer to the sound of the amp and also to the difference in sonic qualities between different power tubes compared to preamp tubes. Leaving some of the distortion to the power-amp section rather than relying mainly on the preamp section gives a broader range of sensitivity. In addition, the nature of the tube allows the player to vary his touch, producing different tonal responses from the amp according to the manner in which he plays.

There are many variables in tube amp designs, and each has its characteristic sounds and quirks. Regardless of what type of amp you use, you will find that like strings on guitars or oil in an automobile, tubes do wear out. Amps are not maintenance free, and as they age, they undergo changes. The tubes are subjected to wear and tear, some of the electronic parts lose their initial properties, and pots and jacks get old. Bad tubes can cause premature failure of other parts, such as the output transformer, speaker, and other vital components. If your amp sounds bad, weak, or otherwise not up to par, don't just hope the problem will go away. Get it fixed. Keep on top of the maintenance, replace the tubes when necessary, and get the most from your amp.
R. Aspen Pittman

A relay is employed to switch tube functions in this amp; five tubes are housed in metal sheaths for extra shielding, while a sixth is left uncovered.

MESA/BOOGIE FACTORY TOUR

May 1983. When Randall Smith built the first Boogie amplifier in his Lagunitas, California, garage in 1971, rock guitarists were filling stages with increasingly larger cabinets and more powerful amps in their hunger to meet the increased volume and tonal demands of large venues. The Marshall stack, standing nearly seven feet tall with a 100-watt top and two cabinets housing a total of eight 12" speakers, reigned supreme.

The Boogie, however, went against the trend. Enclosed in a cabinet no larger than a combo amp (including its single 12" speaker), it stunned guitarists who discovered that the tiny handcrafted beauty was capable of volumes equal to those produced by huge stacks. Moreover, it produced a warm, rich, fat lead tone with a capacity for seemingly infinite sustain at any volume—a formerly unheard-of concept for small amps. If a player wanted a real honking lead tone, he had to push his amp nearly to its maximum output—and that was that.

Smith solved that with a brilliantly conceived master stroke. First, he took an amp circuit with what he felt was an adequate amount of gain, and then increased its abilities by a factor of 50. To control all of the added gain, he devised a unique preamp circuit that utilized a multitude of amplification stages, with input jacks and volume controls between successive stages. Thus, the signal from a guitar plugged into the first stage could be shaped and controlled before being passed on to the second stage for further shaping and amplification.

A third control for master volume gave the player the ability to produce an unprecedented range of sounds from an amp by juggling the various combinations. When Randy placed his amp with an all-tube design (boasting power ratings of 60 or 100 watts) into a cabinet the size of a Fender Princeton, a classic was born. One of the Boogie's earliest champions was Carlos Santana, who first used it on his second album, *Abraxas* [Columbia, PC-30130]. A comparative listening to the sustain and tone on Santana's first LP, *Santana* [Columbia, PC-9781], to *Abraxas* offers dramatic proof of the Boogie's effect on his sound. Guitarists began to get in line for the opportunity to buy one.

The wait, however, was a long one. At one time it stretched up to nine months because Randy was personally fabricating, assembling, testing, and inspecting every single step of each unit. The first person he allowed to help him was his wife, Rayven, who gave up a successful textile design business to take on virtually every step of the operation, including etching the circuit boards and silkscreening the name plates.

Randall Smith is an inveterate tinkerer and inventor. Born 36 years ago in Berkeley, California, he grew up not far away in Orinda, where his intense devotion to craftsmanship was nurtured by two gifted neighbors, Maynard P. Buchler and Stan Stillson. Buchler was the owner and founder of a company that handcrafts some of the world's finest firearms components.

Stillson designed and built industrial control systems and among the many projects that Randy saw laid out in the shop were the complete heating and cooling controls for the Nautilis, America's first nuclear-powered submarine. Stillson's son, who was four years older than Randy, built his own high-power ham radios from scratch. "I guess I was in the sixth or seventh grade when I started getting interested in the projects that Stan's son was doing," says Randy. "He'd design and build a radio and then I'd try to make my own version of it. Then I started getting interested in building state-of-the-art high-fidelity amplifiers. I'd find circuit designs in the tube manuals and just go for it. Tube technology was reaching its peak in those days, and I learned all I could about it."

Hand-oiling hardwood cabinets. The entire finishing process takes a week.

Randy's interest had waned somewhat by the time he went off to college to earn a B.A. in English Literature at U.C. Berkeley. By the time he graduated, however, he was much more interested in playing drums in a rock and roll band than in pursuing a writing career. The year was 1965, and the San Francisco Bay Area was alive with the sound of Big Brother & The Holding Company, the Grateful Dead, Quicksilver Messenger Service, and Country Joe & The Fish. Looking for a way to supplement the meager income he was earning with his band, Randy teamed with the band's organist, Dave Kessner,

to open a music store in Berkeley called Prune Music.

Randy handled the repairs, and his knowledge quickly drew the business of many new bands working in the Bay Area. According to Randy, virtually all of the groups were using Fender amps of one kind or another, and it seldom took longer than ten minutes for him to fix any of them. "Working at Prune really expanded my experience of dealing with guitar players and guitar amps," recalls Randy. "It was easy to see what they were looking for: a wilder, more radical amp, but one that also had better control and a sweeter

tone. Rather than trying to find the *golden tone*, most amplifier manufacturers were busy introducing bigger, more powerful amplifiers—using transistors."

The birth of Boogie started out as a trick Smith wanted to pull on Barry Melton of Country Joe & The Fish. According to Randall, the plan was to take Melton's 12-watt Princeton and soup it up so much that when he turned it on, the volume would blow him off the stage. Drawing on his knowledge of high-powered transmitters, he stripped the Princeton down and rebuilt it somewhat like a souped-up Fender Bassman

1.

Making dovetailed hardwood cabinets in the Mesa/Boogie wood shop: **1.** Roy Hockett and Mike Boles milling a plank to exact thickness. Each cabinet's wood is cut from a single board to ensure a continuous-grain pattern. After drying, the wood is milled, cut, dovetailed, and assembled in a nonstop series of operations in order to avoid warpage and to produce an extremely tight fit. **2.** Dovetails are cut into the ends of the pieces using a router. Selected boards are specially cut to locate the choicest grain patterns in the center of the cabinets' tops. **3.** Tight-fitting dovetails are assembled by Butch Nagayama and Jim Aschow, using a rubber mallet and pipe clamps, which hold the sides together. Placing assembled cabinets in the sun speeds glue curing and heightens the wood's natural color.

2.

3.

circuit with a 60-watt punch and a 12" JBL speaker. The experiment was a success far beyond his own expectations, and he was in immediate demand to perform the same operation for other guitarists, among them Carlos Santana.

After a dozen or so of the Princeton boosts, he decided he wanted to get his name on them because of their increasingly high visibility. He had already decided on the name Boogie, and started silkscreening name plates to put on the amps. The high-gain concept incorporating a series of three volume controls fell into place shortly thereafter while designing a preamp for Lee Michaels to use with his Crown power amps. The final step in the process came when Randall decided that it made little sense to keep buying Fender Princetons to disassemble, and so he started fabricating the Boogies entirely from scratch—including the chassis, cabinet, name plates, circuit boards, and custom transformers. All of this was financed not by bank loans, but rather by rebuilding old Mercedes Benz engines.

These days, Randy no longer has to do every step by himself, although he still personally inspects and tests nearly every unit that leaves the shop, and rides herd over every step of the manufacturing process. The list of Boogie lovers has grown to resemble a guitarist's hall of fame. The Rolling Stones now own 26 units and the Who have 20. Yet, despite its great popularity, the Boogie is still essentially a handcrafted amplifier with a total production over the years now nearing 10,000 units (some manufacturers produce that many in six months). All amplifiers are still made to order, with the waiting list now running from two to eight weeks, depending on the options desired. Prospective customers, however, will soon be able to see, test, and buy a Boogie from a network of a dozen dealers around the country.

In 1980 Randy finally moved the operation out of his Lagunitas home into a small Petaluma, California, complex that allowed him to place all of the manufacturing steps under one roof. The Boogie line now features four products. The Mark II, which combines the features of the original Boogies with several improvements (channel switching, for instance), is the mainstay of the line, with its 60/100-watt rating, single 12" Electro-Voice speaker, and dual-mode footswitching for selection of lead or rhythm settings. Last year Randy reissued the original 60-watt Boogie as the S.O.B. (Son Of Boogie), with the intention of putting a Boogie within the

financial reach of more guitarists. The Series 300 amplifiers are the answer to requests for a higher-powered unit, and while it is rated at only 180 watts RMS, Smith openly invites comparisons to units ranging up to 1,000 watts. The most recent addition to the Boogie line is the D-180 rack-mountable series, a 180-watt bass amp with all the characteristic Boogie features, including a 6-band graphic equalizer.

The adjacent photo essay offers an intimate view of the processes involved in the manufacture of Boogie amps, following their construction from wood and wires to some of the most prestigious amps in rock music.

Jon Sievert

4. The cabinet cutting room: hardwoods are also stored here. **5.** Mike Kane installs matching wood cleats inside a hardwood shell. Meanwhile, wicker cane for grilles is steamed and then stretched during application to the grille frame; it tightens further as it dries. **6.** Roy Hockett and Dave Craig laminate ABS plastic sheets to birch plywood for RoadReady flight case-style bass cabinets. The roller laminating press applies over 3,000 psi (pounds per square inch) of pressure to prevent trapped air pockets that could cause delamination. **7.** The ABS and plywood come out as a single piece.

4.

5.

8.

6.

8. Vinyl covering has been applied to this cabinet, and now Mike Boles uses a power screwdriver to install Sus-4 suspension shock mounts, which isolate the chassis from speaker vibration and other external interference that could affect the unit's performance (the inset photo shows a Sus-4 up close). Also shown are double-grounding braided wires attached to the cabinet's internal foil shield.

7.

9.

10.

11.

12.

9. Sue Warren hand-solders reverb/preamp circuit boards. Each of the several dozen components is installed separately.

10. Primary electronic hardware assembly is performed by Jim Cassero. This chassis for a 60-watt reverb model has been selected and coded as per the customer's order.

11. Installing a Simul-Class power board into a chassis. Tube socket frames are rigidly mounted to chassis (allowing repeated tube changes without damage), while the circuit board is supported by socket pins and foam cushions. The foil traces and components are on the same side of the circuit board in order to simplify parts location and servicing.

12. Final wiring of a "Hun-Ree-Graph" (a nickname for a 100-watt reverb amp with a graphic equalizer) is done by Tina Wood. Each Boogie is signed inside by those who have built and tested it.

13. Every D-180 amp is individually hand wired by Bob Lee. **14.** At the prep bench, Julie McConnell checks hardware, adds the fuse and line-cord strain reliefs, installs preselected tubes, and cleans the chassis. An inspection of the components is made, and the electronics are prepared for technicians to turn the unit on for testing. **15.** Mike Daley, the technician on the left, is firing up a D-180, while Mike Bendinelli is giving a chassis its individual set-up and performance evaluation. Sine and square waves are

13.   **14.**

15.

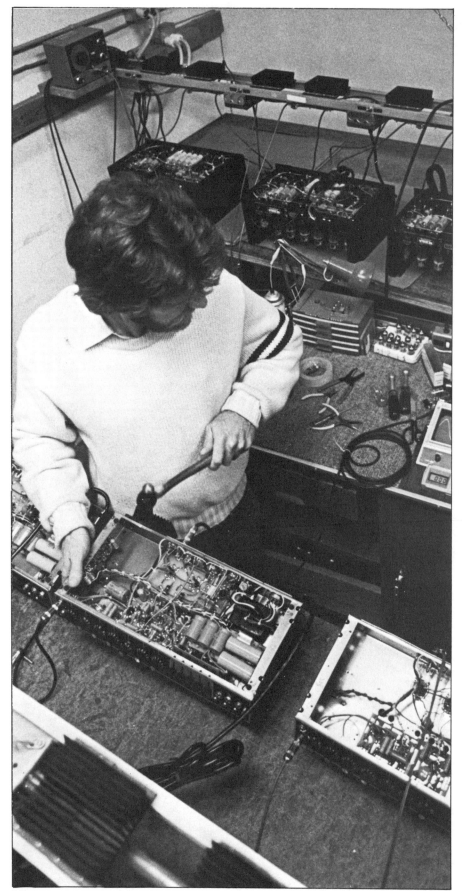

17.

passed through the units to check for noise, stability, and reliability. An important stress test for the amps involves hitting their chassis with a hammer and checking for adverse effects.
16. A second full-performance evaluation after the initial 30-hour burn-in is conducted. Again, hammer blows are applied to the unit while running at full volume. The amp is connected to a speaker and monitored on a mobile lab cart during these tests. **17.** Gary Kephart installs a speaker into a cabinet.
18. The completed amp then receives a serial number and is given a playing test by Randall Smith and Duffy Hoffman. Completed amplifiers are burned-in for 30 more hours prior to final playing to assure optimum performance before shipping.

16.

18.

8.
GUITAR
SYNTHESIZERS

INTRODUCTION

Guitar synthesizers have been on a rocky road since their introduction in the 1970s, but despite the near-collapse of the early market, today's new breed, including the Roland GR-700, Synclavier interface, the JTG, and the Synthaxe have brilliantly harnessed 1980s microelectronics and brought a powerful tool to the player. While still in its infancy, the guitar synth was profiled in *Guitar Player*'s March 1978 A Guided Tour Of The Guitar Synthesizer, at a time when the guitar world was abuzz with talk of "unlimited possibilities." Many of the manufacturers misjudged the market and went out of business, others had products that simply weren't all that their press releases claimed—and guitarists found out very quickly. Nonetheless, the groundwork had been firmly laid. Bob Easton, the president of 360 Systems wrote this revealing look at how the analog synthesizer works, spelling out just how the building blocks of synthesis work. Designs and makers have changed, but the basics remain the same, and this section provides a strong background for today's—and tomorrow's—guitar synthesist. The second part of this chapter is devoted to the guitar synth hardware available in 1980. Again, though, fundamental concepts for synthesists are stressed. The final portion of this chapter is an analysis of the Roland GR-300 and G-808 guitar synthesizers written by Craig Anderton in 1982. These two models proved themselves to be a critical link between the first and second generations of guitar synths, and are still acclaimed in the music industry. Here Craig explains how these two work, how they compare, their possibilities, and their limitations.

A GUIDED TOUR OF THE GUITAR SYNTHESIZER

March 1978. There aren't many old-timers or purists left who would still argue that the electric guitar is not really a guitar at all. On the other hand, few would disagree that the invention of the electric guitar did, in fact, constitute a watershed development, a new instrument that, while retaining much in common with its structural ancestors, nevertheless deserved its own subvocabulary and had to be taken on its own terms. The same is true for the guitar synthesizer.

Aside from innovations in the recording studio and the introduction of mechanical devices such as the hand vibrato, the next advance in the modification of the guitar's sound came in the mid-'50s, with the unveiling of self-contained vibrato or tremolo circuitry in commercial amplifiers such as Fender's Tremolux (introduced in 1955). Except for internal or outboard reverberation kits and a few tape echo units—the latter inaccessible to the average rock and roller on the street due to its expense—few changes in the field occurred until the early '60s, which saw the introduction of Gibson's Maestro Fuzztone—something of a first, in that it provided distortion, a radical alteration of tone, rather than mere embellishment.

The wah-wah brought with it an era in which the alteration of sound was itself an integral component of the musical experience, sometimes equaling, and occasionally surpassing, technique or lyrical content in significance. This was the dawn of the golden age of the external sound modifier, the little magic box with a pedal or footswitch.

All of this was preceded by experiments with electric pianos and organs; electronic music itself gained prominence decades ago in various European quarters through the efforts of the Groupe de Recherche de Musique Concrete, the practice of punched-tape computer synthesis, and other advances.

Voltage-controlled circuitry broke new ground in sonic manipulation; some of the elements associated with keyboard technology were soon adapted by commercial interests to the booming guitar market, resulting in such products as the outboard ring modulator and envelope generator. The plethora of devices entailed unavoidable confusion, since certain effects (e.g., sustain) might be achieved through any number of methods or combinations thereof. The term ''guitar synthesizer'' was inevitably (if not always accurately) adopted by certain advertisers whose commercial intuitions and enthusiasm sometimes exceeded their qualifications as electronics engineers.

Legitimate efforts were made to bring the guitar into the realm of modern technology, and these resulted in products such as EMS's Synthi Hi Fli, Maestro's Universal Synthesizer System, the Syntar, the Condor, Frogg's Spectra-Sound, and others. However, unlike the keyboard, with its inherent suitability as a synthesizer controller, the guitar posed serious physical problems for some of these units. Until recently, there were no commercially available elec-

One of the first-generation guitar synthesizers, the Ampeg Patch 2000.

Pete Townshend tries out an ARP Avatar during a special London preview in the late '70s. Opposite: Roland's GS-500 Synthesizer creates string-like timbres as well as distinctive distortion and filtering.

tronic products that could satisfactorily "read" or faithfully reproduce essential guitar techniques such as hammer-ons, pull-offs, slides, and string bends and convert them into the voltage necessary to trigger a synthesizer. All that has changed, and guitar players now have access to a whole world of sound previously restricted to keyboardists.

What distinguishes a true guitar synthesizer from mere souped-up special effects? For that matter, what *is* a synthesizer in the first place? This question was addressed by Robert Moog, considered by many to be the father of the modern synthesizer. He concluded that, "Any synthesizer worthy of the name will have at least one *audio generator* which produces the raw audio tone, one *filter* which tailors the sound by emphasizing some overtones and cutting down on others, one *amplifier* that shapes the strength of the sound, and one *controller* (such as a keyboard or fingerboard) that translates the musician's 'commands' into sound changes."

One example of a true guitar synthesizer was pioneered by Moog's former associate, Walter Sear of New York. The most visible of the currently available commercial products are those by Roland, Ampeg, ARP, and 360 systems. Like the first electric guitars of thirty years ago, the guitar synthesizer, although a hybrid, is nevertheless another fundamentally new species in

the evolution of instruments, rather than a mere offshoot of existing products. Again, the time has come to establish new criteria, another new sub vocabulary. The following guided tour through a representative guitar synthesizer was written by Robert Easton, president of 360 Systems.

Synthesizers can be mastered as long as they are approached from the proper perspective. As with dogs, teachers, and the Army, it's necessary to get the upper hand in the game. There is a new set of rules and complications here, too. Probably the best way to understand this game is to reduce it all to a set of "building blocks," where each one's job is explained and then they are all hooked together in the proper order. We'll go through a typical synthesizer this way, stopping to read the signposts and observe the sights along the way. We'll also hook up a guitar and its control electronics, so that it's possible to see how the whole system works together. The guitar synthesizer is really a simple picture—but with many pieces; luckily, the relationships among components are very straightforward.

This tour is keyed to the letters on the guitar synthesizer block diagram. To see how any of the pieces fit into the overall picture, match the alphabetical letter alongside the text to the same letter in the drawing.

A good thing to remember about all

synthesizers is that their internal working sometimes have close counterparts in acoustical instruments. In many ways, it's useful to look at them in purely musical and acoustical terms; don't worry about electronic details—this article is an introduction, written in general terms.

A. Much as the strings produce the sound on a guitar, so oscillators are the synthesizer's sound source. But, unlike a string, oscillators can produce a number of different kinds of sounds all at the same time. You can choose which sounds you want and mix several together. This is part of the reason that synthesizers have a bigger vocabulary than other instruments.

One of these sounds is a sawtooth wave, which looks like this on a scope:

Sawteeth can sound brassy or string-like, depending on what you do with them later in the chain of components. All synthesizers have pulse waves, too, but they look like this:

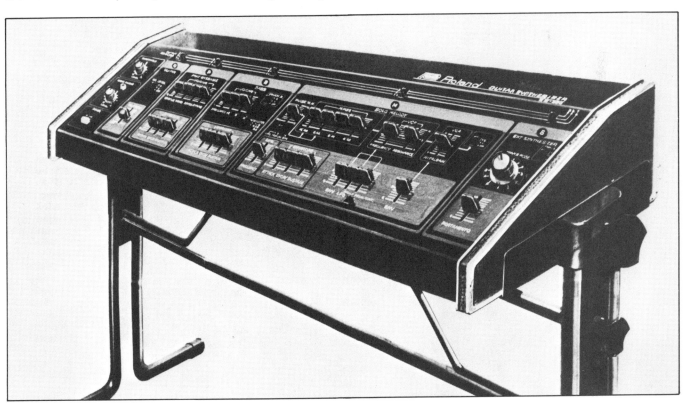

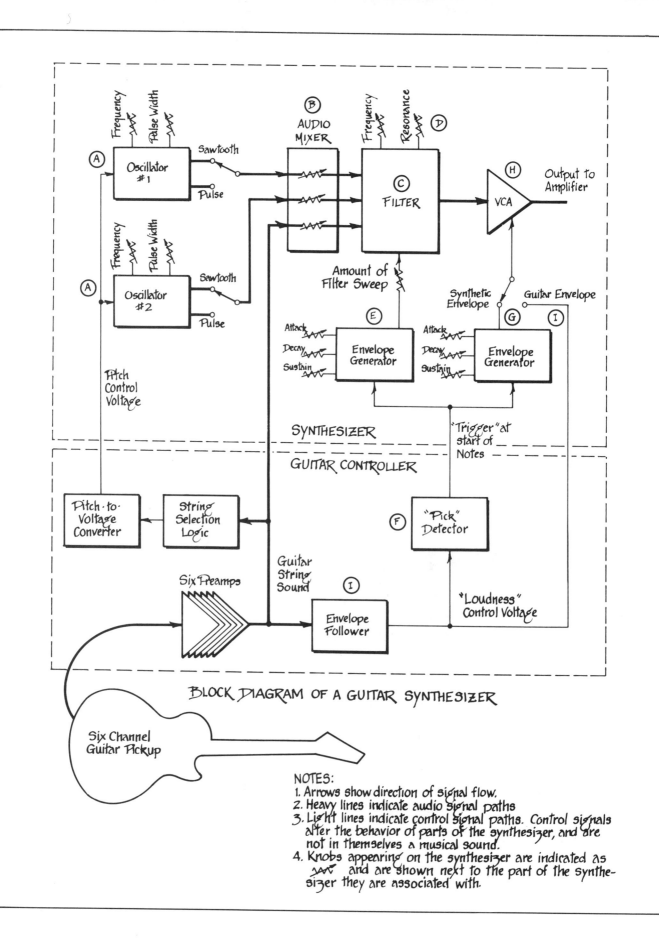

BLOCK DIAGRAM OF A GUITAR SYNTHESIZER

NOTES:
1. Arrows show direction of signal flow.
2. Heavy lines indicate audio signal paths
3. Light lines indicate control signal paths. Control signals alter the behavior of parts of the synthesizer, and are not in themselves a musical sound.
4. Knobs appearing on the synthesizer are indicated as ⌇⌇ and are shown next to the part of the synthesizer they are associated with.

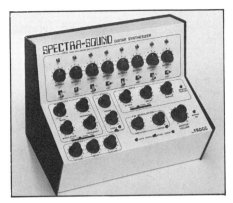

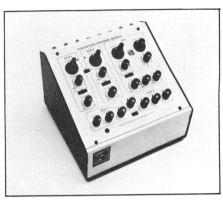

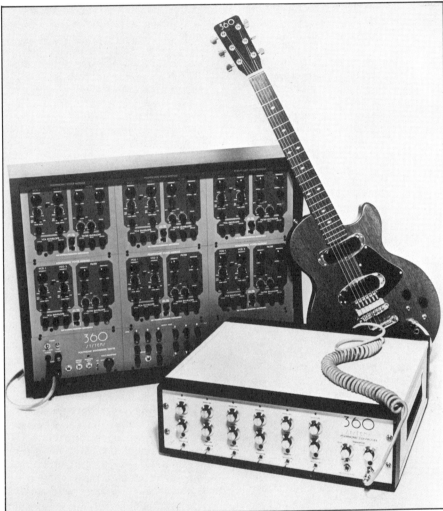

A sampling of '70s guitar synthesis gear (clockwise from top): The Frogg Spectra-Sound, the Oberheim Expander Module (for use with all types of synthesizers), and the 360 Systems Polyphonic Synthesizer.

Pulse waves sound basically reedy but can be changed a lot by adjusting a control called pulse width.

Some versatile synthesizers have two oscillators, both of which can be heard at once. Each can be set to any pitch, so that you can have note clusters (a parallel chord) or a big, thick texture of unisons. Similar effects can be achieved with single-oscillator

units that incorporate suboscillators.

B. Next the sounds from the guitar and both oscillators go to a mixer, which lets you adjust their individual loudnesses. You might want to have, say, a loud bass note, using a sawtooth wave to get a "ripping" sound. Some straight guitar mixed against it would make it a lot fatter. Then a higher-pitched pulse wave could be added just loud enough to make it scream with "bite" or "edge" on the sound. This mix still isn't the final result by any means. We've added up the ingredients, and still it may be pretty rude. However, it may be that this plain and pure mixture is exactly what you want. The rest of the synthesizer *takes things out* in a selective way that shapes each note's sound while you're playing.

C. Our preliminary mix encounters the filter next, and that's were all the really interesting things happen to the sound. Correctly set the filters, and you'll get good press, be acclaimed the New Synthesizer Wizard, and hear people speak your name in reverent tones. Now, let's return to the circuitry. Listen carefully to a synthesizer, or, better yet, a conventional instrument, and notice that notes often start out bright and then darken up a bit; or, in the case of brass instruments, they brighten up a split second after the note starts—a slight "waah." The body of the instrument is responsible for this, and the imaginative synthesizer player will pick up on such details and soon become expert at producing rich and variable textures of his or her own invention—all through skillful counterfeiting of what we've accepted as the best parts of the "real" world's sound.

It's possible to simulate fairly respectable brass instruments; saxophones and violins can come off well, too. Best of all, you can invent your own personal instruments. The biggest part of it lies in your own phrasing, so that you are playing with the same feel and dynamics as that of a saxophonist, violinist, or whatever.

D. Of course, there are many sounds that aren't supposed to resemble real instruments. Increasingly large families of sounds can only be produced on music synthesizers. There's one knob that, when used imaginatively, produces what I call the essence of pure synthesizer. It's called resonance, and it sets the "quackiness" of a sound. It is part of what makes a funky bass funky, and it can also cause arpeggios of overtones to stand out on slow filter sweeps. Great stuff, resonance.

E. But what really determines the true character of a sound more than *anything* else is the length of time these filter sweeps take. Technical people in the early stages of the development of electronic music called this filter sweeper an envelope generator, and since that gibberish is still on everyone's front panels, we'll go along with it. An envelope generator has controls called attack and decay, which set how long it'll take for a sound to brighten and then return again to a darker state. With these controls, the color of a note is made to change in a distinctive way as it sustains. With some experience, these controls are easy to set.

F. In one type of system, a special circuit called a pick detector in the guitar synthesizer locates the start of notes. It's designed so that it can tell the difference between a note hammered on or slid into with the left hand, and a note actually picked with the right hand. When a new note is picked, the envelope generator's attack starts over again, and the synthesizer produces a new filter sweep for each note. But if you just finger a new note with your left hand, only the pitch will change, and the old tone color will continue. Because the electronics can make this distinction between picked and nonpicked notes, it's possible to have the synthesizer articulate your lines in a clear and definite way.

Since the synthesizer's "language" is voltage, an electronic device is employed that converts the pitch of the guitar's note into a corresponding voltage that the synthesizer can "understand." In

a totally different type of synthesizer, components mounted inside the guitar body drive voltage into the strings, creating a magnetic field, so that the strings themselves actually function as the sound source, replacing the VCOs (voltage-controlled oscillators) found in other systems. This approach does not incorporate a pitch-to-voltage converter.

G; H. One thing that cannot be done on regular guitars *can* happen when you're playing a guitar synthesizer: It is possible to have any kind of attack and decay time you want, either on the guitar's own sound or on the synthetic sound. That's because there is still another envelope generator that sets up artificial loudness contours for each note. In much the same way that the first envelope generator makes a filter change in the note's timbre during its duration, this second envelope generator controls a VCA (voltage-controlled amplifier), which is a throttle valve for the synthesizer's loudness. Everytime you pick a new note, your own idea of the appropriate attack/decay time of the loudness will happen. One of the best ways to produce the illusion of many people playing is to have *one* sound start right away (say, the guitar sound), and have the others crescendo in a bit late.

I. If you want, a guitar synthesizer can also copy the dynamics you play on your guitar; play softly, and it'll play softly, too. An intermediate stage known as the guitar interface has a circuit called an envelope follower that hooks up to the synthesizer in order to control loudness, so that synthetic notes only get through in a selected proportion to the loudness of the guitar sound. This kind of control is valuable for certain kinds of solo work where you want the notes to behave exactly as they do on a conventional guitar.

That's the basic synthesizer system. There can be many extras, but they just

assist the main functions. Think of extra features as part of an entourage invited to lend an imposing character to the proceedings. For example, want vibrato? Synthesizers with a low-frequency oscillator can wiggle the pitch of the main oscillators. Need metallic sounds for gongs, percussion, or outer-space work? Ring modulators will get it for you. And white or pink noise can cause thunderstorms, wind shrieks, and even the "spit" on the beginning of brass notes, just for realism.

A true, fully polyphonic (capable of producing more than one note at a time) guitar synthesizer contains everything shown here six times over—once for each string. String-selection logic isn't present at all, because it is only used to decide which one of six strings will run the simpler monophonic synthesizer. The aforementioned alternative approach, in which voltage-driven strings substitute for VCOs, is a different method of achieving polyphonic results.

In large modular synthesizers, each part can be connected to other "modules" with patch cords to assemble an instrument that does a particular thing best. But modular synthesizers are mostly just a bigger collection of the elements shown here and often amount to a number of small synthesizers operating in parallel in order to produce more complex sounds.

Foot controls are handy in live-performance situations and can be made to perform many different tasks. They often produce control voltages that change an operating characteristic, such as how the filter works or the pitch of an oscillator. It's easy to customize these kinds of synthesizers, because many control and sound signals are readily accessible for alteration.

What we have shown here is a general synthesizer that could be used either with a keyboard or guitar controller. Undoubtedly, new synthesizer elements will show up that are particularly useful to guitar players. We are at the beginning of a new age of guitar playing where the guitar is only a controller, and the artist, rather than the manufacturer, will decide what the sound of the moment shall be.

Bob Easton

GUITAR SYNTHESIZER UPDATE

February 1980. For several years now a number of companies, well established and newborn, have been designing and promoting their entries in the still relatively new field of guitar synthesis. Although these instruments have many common factors, the formats vary from self-sufficient units to interfaces (with keyboard synthesizers) and matched sets of guitars and machines. In a field where "state-of-the-art" technology can become passe in a fortnight, guitarists who choose to get into synthesis must be cautious when making an investment. Let's face it: Guitar synthesizers are not inexpensive.

Some serious questions must be raised to help us determine just how much the addition of a synthesizer will broaden our individual performances. Depending on your own musical style or format, one machine might be better suited to you than another. An instrument that is preprogrammable allows the player more latitude inasmuch as punching a single switch will bring in the desired effect, leaving the musician free to concentrate on the other aspects of his or her performance. Still other synthesizers adhere to the "variable" format, which entails patching "from the ground up" and requires some knowledge of synthesis theory to employ effectively. The various machines incorporate a number of components whose technical names tend to scare off quite a few of those interested, but with some homework, understanding how each component works and how they interact can provide opportunities for building sounds that are truly your own.

When seeking product information, owner's manuals are one logical place to start. While every guitar synthesizer on the market includes some explanation of components, the depth of these explanations varies from company to company. Units such as the ARP Avatar, the 360 Spectre/Slavedriver, and the Roland GR/GS 500 provide extremely thorough coverage. Others see fit to merely offer a dictionary approach—brief explanations of functions that leave the experimentation up to you. HEAR, Inc. [1122 University Ave., Berkeley, CA 94702], makers of the Zetaphon, charge an extra $7.50 for the manual to begin with. At any rate, the amount of work you put into learning about (and becoming proficient with) a guitar synthesizer should depend on exactly what can be expected from it and how you intend to use it.

Once you've become familiar with a synthesizer that interests you and have gained a pretty good idea of how it will fit into your equipment, you're then faced with a decision: Whatever type of music you play, there are times when you must play rhythm, and others when stretching out in solo work on a guitar—just a guitar—is the only thing that will do. Does playing a synthesizer, say, 20% of the time, call for a multi-thousand-dollar investment? If you're more adventurous and see yourself as an aspiring synthesist who would use it more often than not, how will the necessary study and practice affect other career-related pursuits?

These are naturally personal questions that only the individual can answer, questions that should be addressed before the actual purchase of a synthesizer. While a multitude of articles concerning guitar synthesis have been published, they have for the most part been aimed at making the player aware of the different models on the market and in providing an education in theory. However, there are other considerations—how reliable are guitar synthesizers, what are their day-to-day operational drawbacks, etc.—that should help the prospective buyer while giving us a better look at the future of guitar synthesis. After all, we ultimately pay the freight.

Among the people interviewed for the technical sections of this article were several product specialists, guitarists employed by the manufacturers who work with these machines long before the public sees them, making changes and suggestions and then becoming extremely proficient in their use for demonstrations. They included Paul Robinson (representing HEAR), Larry DeMarco and Ralph Trimarchi (Electro-Harmonix), Bill Singer (ARP), Cris Briston (Roland), and Bob Easton (360 Systems).

Also queried were retailers from stores who specialize in guitar synthesizers, including E.U. Wurlitzer in Boston, Manny's in New York City, Ward-Brodt in Madison, Wisconsin, Strings & Things in Memphis, Solid Sound in Boulder, Colorado, Hoffman's in Spokane, Washington, Don Wehr's in San Francisco, and Hanich Music in Los Angeles. Finally, retailers and manufacturers provided the names of players who regularly use guitar synthesizers and know what to expect of their performance and reliability, and several of these musicians were interviewed as well.

One of the most distinctive traits of the synthesizer industry is its fluidity. As is the case with so many electronic instruments, manufacturers stand ready at a moment's notice to revamp an existing model or to go to the board and design a new one to compete with the other guy's. As a result, the number of different makes and models of guitar synthesizers has more than tripled in the past three years. The market can only take so much of this before the saturation point is reached and everybody loses.

The companies offering these instruments range in scope from garage/workshop operations to multi-million dollar corporations; while some seem to be gaining ground, a few from both categories are already faltering in the battle to capture and keep the guitar community's attention. This doesn't qualify as the voice of doom, but it's certainly not a good sign. The question arises: Is the guitar synthesizer on the rise, or is it an endangered species?

In my opinion, the most objective replies were from the retailers I interviewed who agreed that there definitely seems to be a future for the guitar synthesizer—but for reasons the rest of us might not expect. In every case, these merchants cited studio players as being the sizable majority of guitar-synthesizer customers, and this makes sense. The competitive session player of today can't just walk into the studio with a guitar, an amp, and reading chops. He has to pack a platoon of goodies as well. When phasers and flangers first popped up, session musicians were the first to run out and buy them. They had to.

Top: The A&F System 1000A employs digital VCOs and is compatible with standard guitar pickups. Bottom: Korg's X-911 has programmable presets and requires no guitar modifications.

The same holds true for guitar synthesizers. When they were new to the market, just owning one practically guaranteed a calendar of dates. Now that these machines are in more hands, mere possession is no longer a competitive edge—it's an outright necessity. The retailers believe that this situation will eventually make synthesizers necessary to guitarists who perform for a living, copping pop tunes laced with guitar-synthesizer riffs.

Electronic devices are fragile to some degree, and as they become more complex, they provide a whole slew of hard-to-pin-down gremlins that are likely to appear in some of them sooner or later. It's the law of averages. If an engineer had to incorporate all of the capabilities of a modern-day guitar synthesizer in one unit without the benefits of microcircuitry, it would probably rival a Buick in size. There's a lot of stuff in there—really *small* stuff. Even if you're careful with your equipment to the point of obsession, something's bound to get knocked around coming out of your trunk at 8:15 for a 9 o'clock gig. If your budget is big and you employ a corps of roadies, well, you know what to expect (sorry, guys, it's often the case).

Words of comfort from the manufacturers promising quick turn-around time on factory repairs are all well and good. They back them up. But what good is a warranty in the middle of a show? (It's fingernails on a blackboard every time I think back to an outdoor concert on a hot Kansas night in '78 when my own first-string and then backup guitar synthesizers blew up in front of a sea of people.)

Guitar synthesizer reliability.

According to the company specialists, their products are as dependable as death and taxes. (Being in the public eye as they are, they don't tend to exaggerate—they have to stand by their words; at the same time, it is understandable why their responses are based on faith and high spirits.) The players I contacted told us that the reliability of guitar synthesizers is roughly equivalent to that of electronic keyboards: Problems do happen; how often depends on how the instruments are handled. These musicians were inclined to complain about the frequency of glitches (misfires) as being the biggest

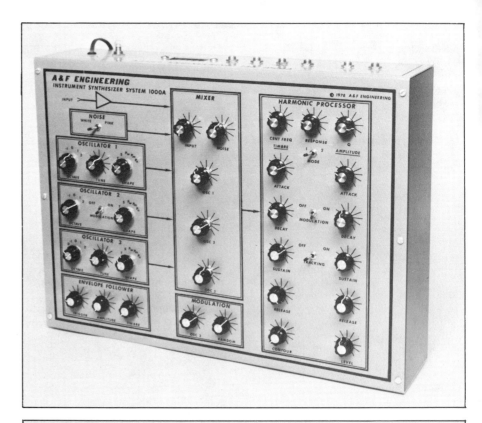

pain in the neck.

The observations of retailers are somewhat more specifically stated. They have found that *all* the guitar synthesizers they sell suffer pretty much the same percentage of malfunctions, a small percentage. But they all stressed the fact that for the most part, synthesizers returned for service are from guitarists who make their living on the road. It would appear, then, that a unit permanently placed in a studio or at least coddled in and out of a session player's car has a far better chance of a trouble-free life than an instrument subjected to the Samsonite test.

With so many different configurations available, it would take several articles to point out the capabilities and limitations of each model, one at a time. But there are some common factors inherent in all of them indicating that they are more limited than their keyboard counterparts.

Operational limitations.

The most visible drawback is the presence of an average of 30 or so dials, buttons, and knobs to be controlled by the guitarist—a two-handed player. One really shouldn't view such a panel array as intimidating. All those fancy component names translate into commonplace, usable, musical terms (e.g., Low Frequency Modulation = vibrato). Learning what each slider does is a simple matter of reading, as well as trial and error. Then, instead of committing a collection of patches or settings to memory, you're free to create sounds by knowing how one control will affect the others. Homework? Yes. Impossible? Definitely not.

Probably the most common limitation found in guitar synthesizers is the fact that most of them are monophonic. (Some can be found in a polyphonic format, such as the Zetaphon. It's available on direct order from HEAR, Inc. for $4,500.00 and employs 12 oscillators, two for each string, as well as a different operative principle—additive synthesis. Most have a "hex guitar/hex fuzz" section, which takes a separate signal from each string (with a six-pole hexaphonic pickup) and delivers the natural polyphonic voice of the guitar. "Hex fuzz" is actually made up of six distortion devices, one for each string; these signals are joined in a summing amp, resulting in what is commonly described as "clean fuzz." Because each string's output is separately overdriven and *then* combined, there is no intermodulation present in the final sound. Some guitar synthesizers offer limited processing possibilities for the hex signal through the synthesizer circuitries—very interesting, but not truly polyphonic synthesis. To produce a synthetic sound, the player must limit himself to lead lines.

Suggest "limitations in guitar synthesis" as the topic for discussion in a room full of guitarists acquainted with them and surer than hell they'll all bring up pitch-to-voltage converters (PVC) within the first five minutes. Everyone has some sort of gripe. A PVC operates by deciphering the incoming note's number of cycles per second (Hz) and then firing the corresponding pitch from the oscillators. First of all, one complete cycle of oscillation must take place for the PVC to do its job accurately. If you're playing in the higher registers, this takes place quickly (the time delay is more noticeable when you're using the lower strings).

Secondly, the average electric guitar has a range of four octaves, and that's a lot of ground for one PVC to cover. Frankly, sometimes it won't "find" you quickly enough. The product specialists I

talked to agreed that *a very clean picking technique is essential to proper triggering*, a technique that every guitarist should want to master anyway. In playing this way, you lessen the chances of losing the PVC in a barrage of muted notes and unintentional harmonics. Fine, this will help, there's no doubt about it. But even if your technique is immaculate, it won't eliminate the problem altogether. This is where the hex section comes into play. By mixing in the hex signal with those from the oscillators, you can mask a misfire more often than not. This is the most common remedy.

There is one other limiting or troublesome factor found in many models, which is unfortunately insurmountable: Any synthesizer employing analog or voltage-controlled oscillators is subject in varying degrees to drifting pitch for a number of reasons. The most simple and understandable cause is jarring the machine—a backstage dropkick, for instance. Heat is another often uncontrollable culprit. If you play outdoor concerts in the bright sun or perform regularly under strong theatrical lighting, you can expect the heat generated in either case to eventually cause the oscillators to drift out of tune, slightly or dramatically, and over the course of time disrupt the overall intonation. Shading the panel from direct light (by hiding it behind something else) will help some. But if the onstage temperature climbs to beach-weather levels, you're more than likely to have problems.

Keyboardists have long enjoyed a wide variety of options in sound available to them. Pianos, organs, harpsichords, clavichords, Clavinets, synthesizers, and so on have given them a wide choice of vehicles all requiring essentially the same skill of keyboard facility. If he chooses, a keyboardist can divide his time between any number of instruments during a night's work. Organ or piano for fills, Clavinet for rhythm parts, synthesizers for lead lines, or whatever the case, the player merely has to shift from one place to another to add diversity.

While a keyboard is technically a *link* to these instruments, it is an integral part of the machine, built right in, and for that reason it makes the response and control of the instrument more readily accessible. With a guitar as the link to a synthesizer, a firm command of nuance and expression is somewhat less tangible. This is due to the fact that most guitar synthesizers are activated by *electronic impulses rather than direct*

physical contacts such as those used with keyboards. (Pitch-to-voltage converters, or frequency followers, all operate by reading the incoming note in number of cycles per second [Hz] and firing its counterpart in the synthesizer bank. In most cases, these instruments are monophonic. Some with two oscillators, others with three, they are triggered by one note with a "higher pitch priority," which means that playing six strings will result in the synthesizer firing the highest note in that chord.)

Another problem that initially hides itself, only to pop up at the worst possible time, is fragile connectors and cords. Some of the manufacturers use rather flimsy materials to make these essential links. A connector with no stress-relief mechanism, on a seven-lead wire no thicker than a Lucky Strike, eventually gets the last laugh unless it's carefully wound for storage in an almost ritualistic fashion.

Another bug to watch for and consider changing is the cord that is permanently attached to the synthesizer panel. Cables are subjected to many accidental tugs, and paying a reputable repairman to install jacks on the machine and the cord will be a lot cheaper in the long run. Shielded seven-lead cable can run you some bucks.

"Down time," or repair time, is something we all have had to deal with at one point or another—nothing is forever. While the average turn-around promised by the manufacturers is about two weeks, 360 Systems and HEAR, Inc., cite same-day service, and Electro-Harmonix warns that their repairs may take up to a month depending on the current volume of returns. So if you can do without your two-thousand-dollar baby for a couple of weeks, sending it back to the factory or to a repair station for a booster shot shouldn't bug you. But suppose the company that sired your machine isn't making them anymore: There's simply not much to say except that the bigger firms will probably stock enough spare parts to perform surgery on their lame ducks for a while (you get nervous), while the smaller companies may already be history (your face breaks out).

There are other minor points that should come under the heading of aggravation rather than limitation. The absence of octave transport devices in some models is just such a thorn. Being able to shift from one sound to another during performance is important to every player, and to the synthesist, being able to change registers quickly provides him with the capability to create some very dynamic contrasts. Many of the guitar synthesizers on the market have octave transports built in, some with up to a five-octave range and footpedal access. Others have omitted the control completely, requiring a rough- and fine-tuning procedure to make the change. Admittedly, the omission isn't enough to make you run home crying if you're a studio player, but the performing guitarist, who needs more latitude, would do well to consider the importance of such a device to his or her onstage capability.

An approach to comparing features. Aside from octave transports, the potential consumer has many things to consider, and it helps to approach them logically, progressing for the most part from the general to the specific. Why spend a lot of time weighing the advantages of a minor feature if you haven't yet chosen between the fundamentally different additive and subtractive processes, or between monophonic and polyphonic synthesizers?

The accompanying table is neither comprehensive nor detailed. It's merely a starting point, suggesting one way to help organize a potential buyer's

thoughts. If one unit in the list has a hex pickup and another doesn't, the reader should conclude *not* that the one synthesizer is more fully equipped but rather that the models operate on different principles. Whether or not a particular feature is worthwhile depends on the extra cost involved and on the personal tastes and professional requirements of the guitarist.

Current roles and uses. With all the technical jargon and vague assertions thrown around concerning guitar synthesizers and their uses, it's not surprising to find a number of players who are a bit confused. A written representation of what synthesizers sound like would be as tough to provide as an explanation of green to a blind man. However, their technical and musical formats are beginning to show a pattern; specifically, the ways in which guitar synthesists are setting up their gear for performance or recording is epitomized by the gadget arrays commonly used by product specialists.

When you see a product specialist demonstrate the guitar synthesizer he represents in a store-sponsored clinic or concert, you're more than likely witness-

ing a performance by one of the better if not the best player on the given instrument. One of his responsibilities is to maintain status. You can cop volumes of tips and information in a single hour of paying close attention to his words, his equipment, and, of course, his playing.

It's only natural that given their allegiances, these people use every additional gizmo and high-end sound-reinforcement component they can lay hands on. (Let's assume that this is done to enhance the instrument's qualities, not to hide deficiencies.) It's common to see a specialist playing through a high-powered stereo setup with a train of volume pedals controlling five or six different signals from the synthesizer band (some split into stereo outputs to begin with), the hex section, and the regular guitar pickups. Any additional signal processing usually falls into the time-based effects category; devices such as phasers, flangers, doublers, and variable delays do a beautiful job when used in tandem with guitar synthesizers.

Explanations in musical terms of the uses of guitar synthesizers are naturally as varied as the people who play them. Still, some general trends are forming in

	Synthesizers						Synthesizer Interfaces			
	ARP Avatar	Electro-Harmonix	HEAR Zetaphon	Roland GR/GS 500	360 Spectre	MCI B-35-S	Polyfusion FF-1	Gentle Electric Model 101	Ampeg Patch 2000	360 Slavedriver
Synthesizer Format	mono	mono	poly	mono	mono	mono	mono	mono	mono	mono
Number of Oscillators	2	3	12(2 per string)	2	2	3	—	—	—	—
Pitch-to-Voltage	yes	yes	yes	yes	yes	no*	yes	yes	no*	yes
Hex Pickup	yes	no	yes	yes	yes	no	no	+	no	yes (bass model is quad)
Hex Fuzz	yes	no	yes	no	yes	no	no	no	no	no
Octave Transport	no	no	yes	yes	yes	no	no	no	no	yes
Footpedal(s)	yes	no	yes	yes	yes	no	yes	yes	yes	yes
Guitar-mounted controls	no	no	no	yes	no	yes	no	no	no	no
Output Provisions	6 stereo, main & separate	1 main	13 main & separate	4 main & separate	2 synth & hex	1 main	1 to synth	4 separate parameter controls	2 synth & guitar	4 guitar & three parameter controls
Interface Provision (with other synth.)	yes	no	yes	yes	yes	no	yes	yes	yes	yes
Programmability	yes (custom)	no	no	no	yes (option)	no	no	no	no	no
Noise Generator	yes	no	no	no	no	yes	no	no	no	no
Options	any feasible factory modification	no	Zeta Modulation Unit	no	Model 700 from Sequential Circuits	no	no	no	no	no

*These machines employ the "fret-contact-voltage-division" principle, a *physical contact* system.
+This unit can be used with a hex pickup (recommended by the company for better performance), specially ordered from the factory.

certain circles: Synthesizer-equipped studio players are now available to record for jingle producers looking for that "hook" bridge or "perking coffee pot"—roles once reserved for "the guy with the Moog satellite," or some such keyboardist. Fusion players and rock and rollers, making up the majority of performing guitar synthesists, generally apply the instrument's ability to add a screaming raunch to solo work and occasionally an unexpected giggle in the midst of mega-powered passages.

Many guitar synthesizers can produce frighteningly accurate reproductions of orchestral instruments. In my own experiences, I have found these capabilities very useful in building entire orchestrations—especially bowed strings—in fully produced studio works, using overdubs, and on occasion in performance with symphony orchestras (I doubt Tchaikovsy meant his oboe part in the *1812 Overture* to be played electronically, but they didn't seem to mind in Wisconsin). The use of a noise generator is widely practiced for simulating environmental sounds. These components produce what is known as pink and/or white noise, a constant static or hiss-like sound shaped with the modifiers into recognizable form. In using the envelope generators to determine attack and release, you can pull off anything from slamming doors to footsteps, hurricanes to helicopters, or just plain scaring the hell out of somebody with a two-ton bomb.

Trends and outlooks. So much for the people who already use a guitar synthesizer. What of the new disciples and prospective customers? Although the idea of guitar synthesis itself is somewhat new, enormous amounts of publicity, advertising funds, designs, counter designs, and related hubbub have long been at work in an effort to make the addition of a guitar synthesizer to your bag of tricks seem a necessary move. "How can you do without one?" was the closing line of one product specialist's mechanical rap at a NAMM (National Association of Music Merchants) convention—a veritable circus of barkers. But how successful is all this promotion turning out to be?

It's very successful for the 360 Systems Spectre, the ARP Avatar, and the Roland GR/GS 500 according to the retailers I contacted (other models available to the public through these retail outlets have not yet formed a readable trend). When asked how many guitar

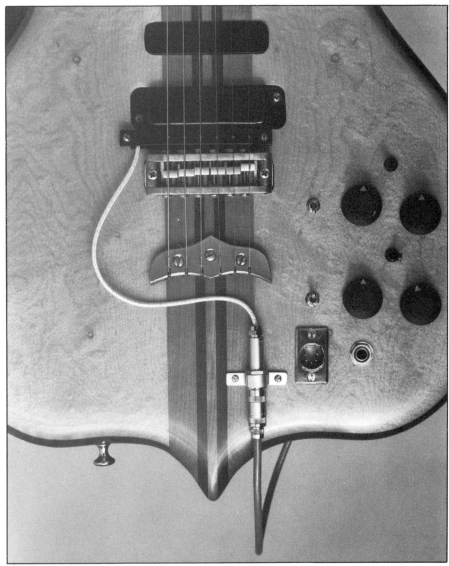

ARP's Avatar pickup installed on an Alembic guitar.

synthesizers they sell in a month—the bottom line in rating success—all of the dealers gave virtually the same response: The consensus is an average of one a month per store . . . not exactly a rage.

The next logical question was aimed at finding out if these sales figures are attributable to the state of the economy in general. The answer, every time, was an enlightening and surprising insight: The music retail business as a whole has always *prospered* in times of financial recession. This has held true since the days of "Tin Pan Alley," and some of the stores quizzed have been around long enough to back that statement with yellowing, dog-eared ledgers. It seems that in such periods the public spends more time and money on temporary forms of escape, especially music. These retailers show an overall

rate of constancy and in some cases a boom in business as the buck gets lighter, day by day. Therefore they can't justify placing the blame for slow-moving guitar synthesizers on inflation or other economic plights.

Why are guitar synthesizers moving so slowly then? Every successful music store can attest to the value of the customer's reactions and desires when measuring the salability of an item. The overall opinion of these merchants, again unanimous, has been formed from such reactions: Guitar synthesizers in their present state, mostly monophonic and with doubted reliability, simply do not strike the majority of electric guitarists in general as being worth the average $2000.00 price tag. As a group they are very interested but prefer to sit out the initial stages, hoping for a polyphonic system to surface in the same price bracket. A multi-oscillator system that would allow *them* to choose either a lead line or chording format, rather than a predetermined design, would apparently not ruffle too many feathers as a four-digit expense. One retailer compared today's guitar synthesizer customer to "the same curiosity seeker who paid $100.00 for a calculator when they first came out."

This attitude may be held by a few people, but there is no denying that guitar synthesis has opened new doors to the ones who chose to get involved in the early years as explorers, both onstage and in the studio. Regardless of their individual proficiencies, it is reasonable to assume that most of them have found new means of expression on many different levels, thereby warranting their investment. There may be some grumbling in the gallery, but "used guitar synthesizer for sale" ads are few and far between. There must be a reason for that.

What's on the horizon? For those who watch and wait, we asked quite a few guitar synthesizer manufacturers if and what they were planning for the future. A few were uncertain of a future at all. Others, more confident, gave stock replies that cited a "continuous effort to design and provide electronic innovations for the musician," giving us a tickle while avoiding a commitment.

There's no doubt that everyone involved would benefit from increased educational efforts; we need more clinics and seminars, and more readable and detailed owner's manuals. Traveling musicians often decry the scarcity of guitar-synthesizer repairmen who have all the mobility, training, equipment, and experience of the technicians who repair guitars, amps, and sound systems.

It looks as if the growth or even the survival of guitar synthesis will depend on the solution of all-too-common electronic engineering problems in the current models, corresponding advances in consumer education and customer service, and the development of fully polyphonic technology at an acceptable cost. The writing on the wall gets easier to read every day.

Steve Ruggere

GUITAR SYNTHESIS: THE ROLAND GR-300 AND G-808

July 1982. Every now and then, a product comes along that seems like a good idea but for one reason or another flops commercially. The world has seen a lot of "Edsels" (like quadraphonic hi-fi), and we musicians have also experienced our share of products that seemed promising but never quite caught on. Witness the guitar synthesizer.

Once hailed as one of the most exciting developments for guitar since the electric pickup, these devices now have failed to make much of an impact—at least the first wave of guitar synths haven't. The ARP Avatar died a slow death along with its parent company; I haven't seen a concerted 360 Systems ad campaign in years; the Patch 2000 is a memory; and while HEAR keeps plugging away at the Zetaphon, they are a small company and currently not a factor in the mass market.

In case you think I'm going to talk about what a shame it is that these devices never caught on, forget it! The units I played had serious flaws that, for me, rendered them useless. One device could only handle one note at a time, and you had to play with an incredibly sterile technique; mute a string, or hit a harmonic, and the whole thing would go crazy. Another one refused to play in tune. Yet another wouldn't allow you to bend strings, and still another was more or less playable (mostly less), but the end result was sonically no better than that achieved by a not very good Minimoog keyboardist. No wonder the units didn't sell and guitar synthesizers acquired a bad reputation.

I did play one, however, that I felt had promise: the GR-500, Roland's first entry into the guitar synth market. Unfortunately, it, too, had flaws—it was complex, difficult to use, and you had to play on a Roland guitar that, to put it charitably, would never be mistaken for a vintage Les Paul.

Then a couple of years ago, Roland—at that point just about the only major company still interested in guitar synthesis—introduced the GR-300, a truly polyphonic device (i.e., you could play full chords and were not limited to single notes). Making its debut at the 1980 NAMM show, the enthusiasm I had for the unit was boundless. Shortly thereafter, I acquired Roland's G-808 guitar and matching GR-300 electronics. After years of using that combination, my initial enthusiasm hasn't diminished one bit. If anything, I think more highly of the unit now than I did upon first handling it, and am still discovering new applications for the device. I consider the GR-300 to be a true watershed product, much like TEAC's first 4-track portable recorder, the Minimoog, or, more recently, the Steinberger bass and Sequential Circuits' Prophet 5 keyboard synth. I am also impressed with Roland's tenacity in trying to put out a good guitar synthesizer, because so far, guitarists in general haven't given *any* of these units a warm welcome. I think, however, it's just a matter of time before the "Electronic Guitar" achieves the recognition it deserves.

Roland offers a number of G-series guitars that are playable as standard electrics, but which also include a hex pickup and a multi-conductor cable that plugs into a box of electronics (the GR series). At first, Roland only produced two Les Paul-style guitars; but now they are branching out, producing a Strat-type instrument, too.

There are two synthesizer packages,

Top: Roland's GR-300 Polyphonic Guitar Synthesizer module has five footswitches and sits on the floor. Bottom: Roland's G-808 guitar.

up or down to a selected pitch, a dual effect that gives a chorus sound, string-select switches that let you engage the synth effect for the strings of your choice (anywhere from just one to all six), a number of footswitches for real-time control, touch-switch vibrato controls, and so on.

Despite these many options, though, the GR-300 electronics package looks simple—deceptively simple, in fact. You might think that the number of possible sounds would be pretty finite, but that just isn't so: There are enough jacks and controls to keep you occupied for a long time. What's more, I was lucky enough to obtain a set of schematics for the GR-300, and it looks like there are a number of simple modifications that can be made that would greatly enhance the machine's possibilities. So, the GR-300 is definitely something you can grow with, especially if you have some do-it-yourself electronics chops.

Okay. so it's technically impressive. Big deal! What *musical* function does it fulfill that you can't get with a guitar? How would you use it live? In the studio? Can you play it like a standard guitar, or do you have to go through a severe attitude change? Is it only for the pros, or can an amateur use it to advantage? And finally, can you overcome some of the unit's built-in deficiencies (the GR-300 may be neat, but it's not perfect)? Read on for the answer to these questions, and more.
Craig Anderton

the basic version GR-100 and the more sophisticated GR-300. Clearly, Roland has made a commitment to the electronic guitar market, despite industry-wide sluggish sales and a less-than-kind consumer eye towards high-ticket items. I should also add that Roland makes a bass synthesizer; however, I have not had a chance to play it. So, here we'll limit our comments to the guitar-oriented devices.

The GR-300 synthesizer module includes three main sections: a hex fuzz, which is the equivalent of putting a separate fuzz on each string; an oscillator bank, which consists of two oscillators that may either track the guitar or be transposed within the range of one octave above or below concert pitch;

and a modifier section, which consists of an envelope follower/inverter with filter and adjustable attack time. The filter is a low-pass filter used on many keyboard synths. The envelope follower varies the cutoff frequency of the filter in response to your dynamics (hitting the strings harder gives a brighter sound, or a "waa" effect; adding the inverter gives an "ow" effect where hitting the strings harder kicks the filter frequency downward, producing a mellow sound that can also be quite percussive when set correctly).

There are several other options, such as compression, a balance control that allows you to balance the mixture of synthesized and straight sounds, "rise" and "fall" controls that let you swoop

GUITAR SYNTHESIZER APPLICATIONS

August 1982. Synth vs. standard guitars. The first thing we need to consider about any guitar synth is the richness of sound brought about by using electronic waveforms. Whereas a standard guitar produces a relatively thin, percussive sound—which guitarists are constantly trying to "fatten up" and "sustain"—synthesizer waveforms are naturally rich and have a tendency to sustain longer. In a polyphonic synthesizer (one that produces a note for each string, thereby allowing chords), you have six extremely rich oscillators at your command. So in many instances, your task with a guitar synthesizer is not to make it fuller, *but to trim out that part of the sound that is overly rich*. Outboard effects can help you with this.

Another difference is in playing options. A standard guitar has tone, volume, maybe a few phase or coil-tap switches, and that's it. A synth guitar lets you mix in varying degrees of fuzz, oscillators, and normal guitar sound—and further lets you alter these sounds by filtering, compressing, selecting synthesized sound only on certain strings,

and so on. As a result, you'll have to do a lot more planning of how you intend to use an electronic guitar, either onstage or in the studio. It's not enough to just pick the thing up and play: You'll need to evolve a strategy for each part you play on a guitar synthesizer, and be familiar enough with the unit to implement the sound you want.

A third difference is the type of rhythm part you'll play with a guitar synthesizer. If you mostly have a straight-guitar sound selected with a little synthetic sound mixed in to give more fullness, you can pretty much play any rhythm part you would play on a normal guitar. However, if you have a rich wash of sound, then playing complex rhythm parts could very well lead to a cluttered, overly busy effect. The key here is to study the background keyboard works of artists such as Tony Banks (Genesis), Roger Powell (Utopia),

Four guitar synthesizer systems (clockwise from top left): Roland's GR-700 programmable polyphonic, GR-500, and GR-338 Bass Guitar Synthesizer; the 360 Systems Slavedriver.

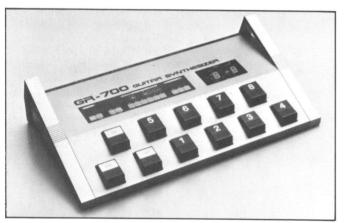

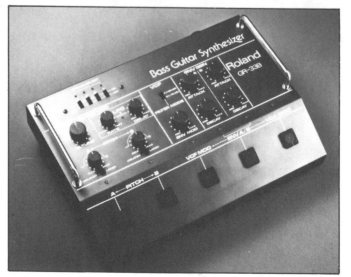

and similar players in bands that use organs, string synthesizers, and other sustaining keyboards for lush parts. Most of these background parts are relatively simple; with a guitar synth, you might find yourself playing one strum and letting the instrument sustain for a measure or two, rather than picking up and down in a continuous manner.

Using effects with polyphonic guitar synthesizers. Many of the effects you traditionally add as outboard units to a traditional guitar are an inherent part of the synth. For example, the GR-300 has a chorus option that imparts a lush chorus effect to each string, as well as an envelope-controlled filter for Mutron effects. The hex fuzz handily replaces outboard fuzz, and there's even a built-in compressor. So, you'll have to decide which outboard effects work best with the synth guitar.

As mentioned previously, many times you need effects to trim the sound down rather than to fatten it up. Since filters selectively remove various components of the sound, my first suggestion would be to add a good graphic or parametric equalizer. These allow you to add midrange peaks for punch, low-frequency boosts for a good bottom end, or pull back the highs if the synth is cutting too much.

Another useful effect with the guitar synthesizer is an echo unit. Since synthesizers tend to have a naturally flat sound that lacks ambience, adding echoes creates the appearance of an acoustical space, which makes the synth sound more "natural."

Lead guitar parts. Several players have told me that guitar synths are useless for lead parts. It ain't so! The problem is that the synthesizer section of the guitar has a little bit of lag in responding to the notes you play (especially with lower notes), so there might be a tiny bit of delay (on the order of a couple dozen milliseconds) between the time you play the note and the time you hear it. The delay is short enough that you probably won't be able to outplay it with respect to speed, but what you *do* lose is that sharp attack so characteristic of many rock lead-guitar parts. As a result, the notes can lack definition. For lead work, I base my sound around the hex fuzz, which, since it doesn't drive an oscillator but rather derives its signal directly from the guitar's strings, preserves the guitar's attack characteristics. You may then add an oscillator sound on top of that for more fullness, and/or boost the response at around 3 to 4kHz with some EQ to create a sound which cuts a little more.

Ensemble work with the guitar synth. Because the sound is so rich, and covers much of the frequency spectrum,

you might run into situations where the guitar synth interferes with vocals, keyboards, and other midrange instruments. You can always pull the synth volume level back to avoid this problem, but that gives a weaker sound. Again, EQ comes to the rescue; pulling back (cutting) in the midrange will make room for other instruments, while leaving a bright top end and solid bottom. This way, you can mix the synth up to a pretty decent level, but still not interfere with other instruments. I generally cut somewhere in the 500Hz to 1kHz range.

But is it for me? The guitar synthesizer is not cheap, so the question of cost effectiveness immediately comes to mind. With a unit like the GR-300, which includes its own guitar, you can of course play the guitar by itself—assuming that you have the right "chemistry" with the guitar. If you do, you can unload a guitar that you might not use as much and use those proceeds towards buying the synthesizer electronics. If you don't like the synth's guitar as much as you like an old favorite, then you have to consider the guitar/synthesizer electronics system as a separate investment.

Admittedly, something like a guitar synthesizer would be a luxury for most guitarists; but if you're ever in situations where you need to get novel textures or a wide range of sounds (studio musician work, for example), it becomes a necessity. On my most recent album project, I played the GR-300 in quite a few places. The two biggest uses were for textural rhythm parts where keyboards were too static sounding, and for extremely smooth, "Boston"-style leads. (When imitating other instruments, I used keyboard synthesizers due to their greater flexibility.) For "power trio" sounds, the GR-300 also proved very useful, since it could fill in a lot of sonic space with just one instrument.

I hope the above tips will put you in the right frame of mind for recognizing that the synthesizer guitar, despite its apparent similarity to the electric guitar, is its own instrument and must be approached in its own way. But once you have it mastered, you'll have a powerful new tool for your sonic arsenal.

Craig Anderton

Left: Andy Summers of the Police using a Roland G-700 guitar with a GR-700 synthesizer. Right, above: 360 Systems guitar synthesizer pickup installed on a Gibson Les Paul Custom. Right, below: The Roland G-707 guitar has an extension between the body and headstock for stable tracking.

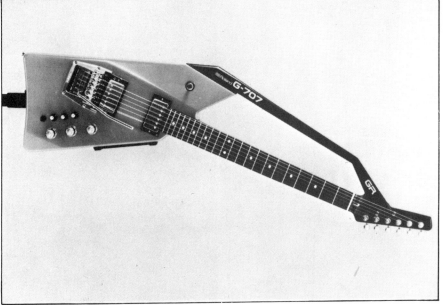

9.
RECENT DEVELOP-
MENTS IN
GUITAR
EQUIPMENT

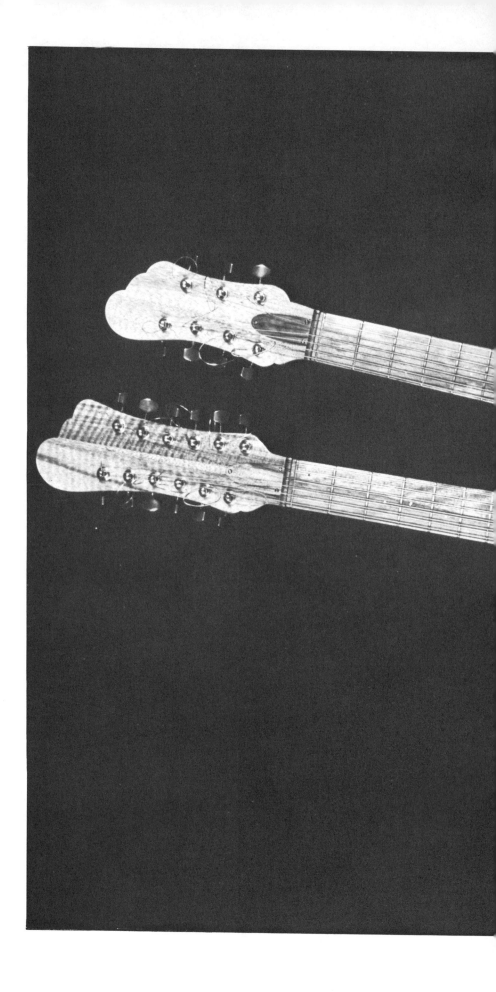

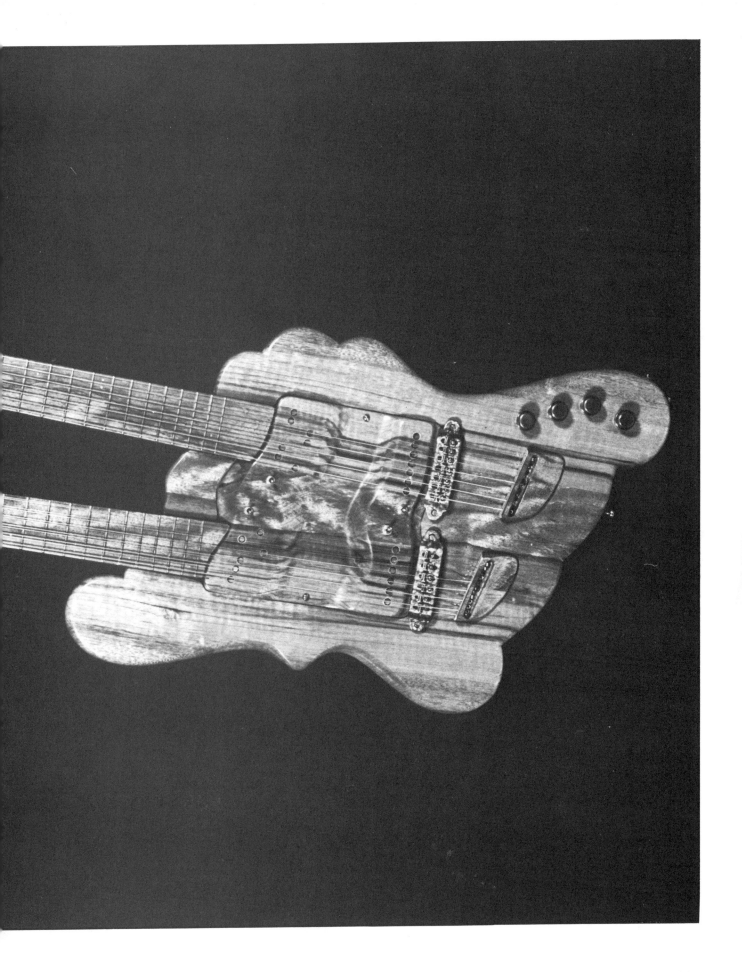

INTRODUCTION

Throughout history, off-beat and sometimes puzzling instruments have been created by dedicated craftsmen, tinkerers, and musicians with special tonal needs. Evolution brought us the kithara, the lute, and the guitar, but along the way were such oddities as the hurdy-gurdy (a string instrument with keys and a crank) and the mando-cello. And while we are familiar with the guitar, the violin, the piano, and the common brass and percussion instruments, there are many talented luthiers creating alternative instruments. This chapter takes a look at some of them and their creations in two parts. First, is Radical Acoustics, a glimpse at some intriguing guitars and near relatives, ranging from 6-strings with mandolin-style bodies to huge, carved birch harp guitars and triple- and quadrupleneck custom acoustics. Multiple soundholes, carved "bubbles" in tops, and collapsible instruments are also surveyed. The Alternative Electrics section is highlighted by a 6-channel stereo guitar, a cast-aluminum high-tech open-frame model, a 27-string clef-shaped instrument, and a folding guitar. Extraordinary? Radical? Perhaps. But so were the creations of Leo Fender, Les Paul, and Ned Steinberger. Today's oddities may be tomorrow's fashion.

RADICAL ACOUSTICS

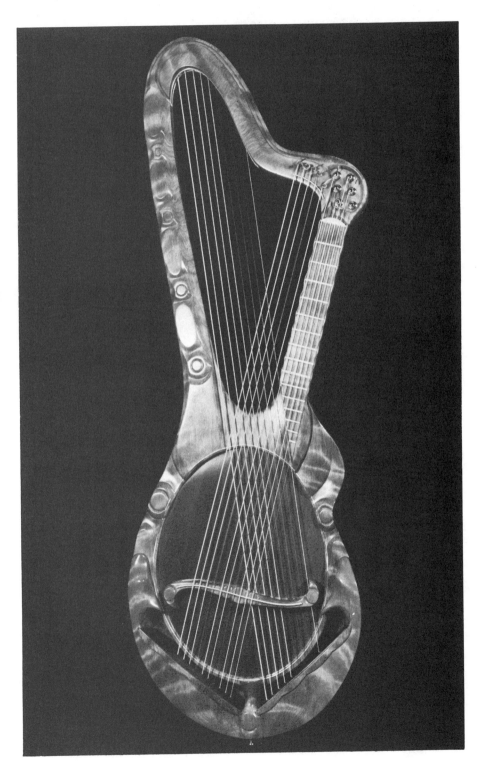

June 1983. Innovation in guitar design may seem to be largely the province of electric instruments these days. The high-voltage birds come in unlimited shapes and colors with bodies built of everything from exotic woods to space-age synthetics, while every month brings out a fresh crop of gadgets and effects. The acoustic instruments appear to change much more slowly by comparison, preserving forms and concepts over decades, even centuries. Where the electric guitar is exuberant and youthful, the acoustic is dignified and traditional. Accurate portrait? Not quite.

Innovation has been as essential—if not as conspicuous—a feature of the history of acoustic instruments as it has been of electrics. Even so eminent a bastion of tradition as C.F. Martin has at times been deemed a radical (when it introduced its X-bracing in the early 1850s, for example, or the Dreadnought body type in 1916). And there have been others—Gibson's arch-top and f-hole designs, Maccaferri's early-'30s cutaways, or the revolutionary steel resonator guitars from National and Dobro. These examples represent only a sampler of the broad range of acoustic experimentation over the years. Not all ideas have been as successful—some, such as a soundboard riddled with dozens of soundholes, have been unceremoniously consigned to what Karl Marx titled the dustbin of history.

So while the acoustic guitar bears considerable tradition and history, it is clear that this by no means precludes innovations, and the desire of luthiers to make something better sounding or better looking (or both) is as strong now as ever before. The prospects for the creative designer actually seem brighter in the current climate, thanks to improved communication, a wealth of historical data, and even the advanced technology that has fostered the growth of electric instruments. Equipped with scientific theories of acoustics and a host of modern testing tools, artisans are now able to subject all the intuitive knowledge of the past to a thorough reexamination.

The experiments are sometimes bold and profound, affecting everything—shape, sound, strings, tunings—and other times subtle, all but undetectable to anyone save the expert. In certain cases exploiting a scientific principle

The curly white birch frame of William Eaton's harp guitar required special chiseling techniques because of its hardness. The four top strings are classical guitar; the others are harp.

Besides its striking appearance, the four-neck guitar by Manson has an unusually rich, full sound. The instrument is constructed from a variety of high-grade woods and features a Swiss pine soundboard (two pieces), Brazilian rosewood sides and back, a Brazilian mahogany neck, and an ebony fingerboard. William Eaton built his 16-string lyre with a burlwood top that he bookmatched to create a natural soundhole. Below the bridge, the strings are an octave higher than they are above it.

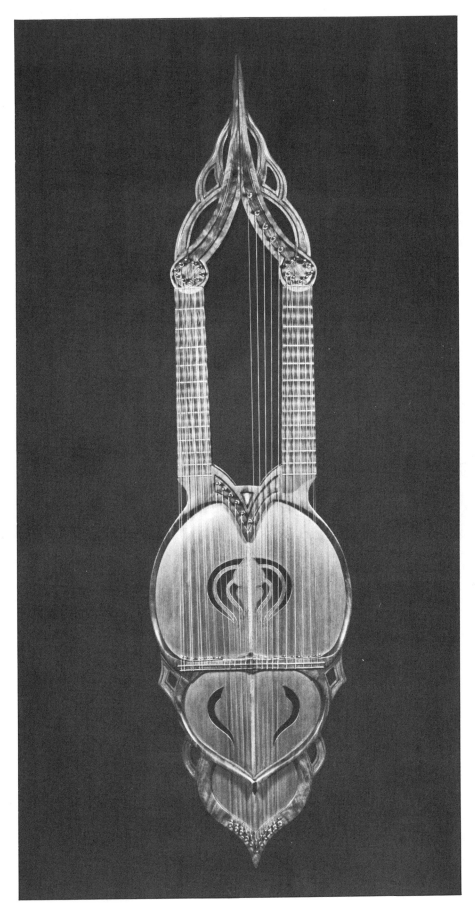

results in a radical departure from an aesthetic one. Such is the case with the Sound Bubble guitar, which achieves its tonal personality through the use of an unlikely looking asymmetrical bulge in the top. At the other end of the spectrum, William Eaton's ethereal masterpieces would be works of art whether or not they were functional.

Each of the unusual works shown here reflects a very different theory or approach to acoustic guitar construction, yet as a whole they give only a glimpse of the sum total of original work being done in the field today. The age-old concept of plucked strings over a hollow soundbox is far from being exhausted, and as these ingenious instruments show, variations on a theme can be as fascinating as they are different from one another.

Stephen Gilchrist is from Warrnambool, Australia, where he gained his first woodworking/handcrafting experience building surfboards. Though he is largely self-taught, a one-year stint as a repairman and builder at the Nashville shop of American stringed-instrument authority George Gruhn helped him to perfect his knowledge and sharpen his skills. Today he is regarded as one of the most capable craftsmen in the field of mandolin construction, and his arch-top guitars command a price of $2,500.

The mandoguitar was an experiment launched by Gruhn and Gilchrist with the idea of extrapolating the design of a Gibson F-5 mandolin to a guitar-sized body, thereby achieving the F-5's noted brilliance, clarity, and volume on a larger scale. The final result differed from expectations, states Gruhn, the mandoguitar being similar in power to a fine traditional arch-top guitar, rather than overpoweringly louder. Gruhn adds that the sound is very well balanced, with excellent sustain and high responsiveness.

The prototype (shown here) was built with its neck set at an angle similar to a mandolin, resulting in an exceptionally high bridge. In theory this should add to the power of the guitar, but to test the idea thoroughly the makers tried out a number of bridges of differing sizes, thicknesses, and materials. The bridge proved to be extremely important—fully as influential as any major structural feature of the body. The only other Gilchrist/Gruhn mandoguitar was built with a shallower neck angle, resulting in a standard-height guitar bridge. This guitar seemed to have better volume and bass response than the prototype.

The mandoguitar features a spruce top, maple back and sides, and ebony

The trio of McPherson triple-soundhole steel-string flat-tops (left to right): an electric 6-string with built-in pickup, and acoustic 12-string, and an acoustic 6-string. Mathew McPherson says his search for a better soundhole pattern was inaugurated the day he realized that in an acoustic guitar "the sound that goes into the large area of the lower bout rolls around and dies before the rich sustaining tones can get out." Interestingly enough, the prototype for this design was achieved through creative mutilation of a $65.00 instrument, the last in a long line of such sacrifices by the persevering inventor.

fingerboard. Its body is 17" wide, 3½" deep; the scale length is 24¾".

Mathew McPherson of Edina, Minnesota, was not satisfied with the sound of the acoustic guitar; thinking it to be too muddy, he sought to brighten it up. His experiments resulted in a radically revised soundboard with three strategically placed soundholes, none of them in the conventional location.

What makes this story unique is that the inventor is not a luthier. McPherson has been playing guitar for 35 years—since the age of 14—performing steadily in the U.S., Canada, and abroad, and writing songs. His design innovation was achieved by intuitive leap, as well as an ambitious experimental program implemented by hacksaw. McPherson now holds two U.S. patents on the triple-soundhole acoustic and imports a

line of the instruments from Japan, ranging in price from approximately $335.00 to $490.00.

English luthier Andrew Manson built his first acoustic guitar in 1967. It incorporated a radical, if questionable, feature: an oak soundboard (replaced by plywood after a car wreck, with considerable improvement in tone). Subsequently, under the tutelage of well-known craftsman Stephen Delft, Manson made great strides forward and now operates one of England's most flourishing and highly regarded guitar building and repair companies. Though the staff of five also manufactures a line of electric instruments, acoustic guitars remain the province of the company founder.

Manson Guitars Limited has a way of building reputations without conscious effort. For example, they have never actively sought the patronage or endorsement of name players, yet among those who use their instruments are Mike Oldfield and John Paul Jones, former Led Zeppelin bassist.

Another reputation is for the radical nature of some of their acoustic designs. The first was a tripleneck for John Paul Jones. The idea came to Manson as he observed Jones scrambling to change guitars during a concert. The luthier quietly built the instrument on his own initiative and showed it to the surprised rock performer. Jones was pleased, but kept the tripleneck a secret until he could bring it onstage during a show—as Manson relates, "just to see Jimmy Page's face when he sees it." Reportedly, the ploy was a success, and Page was duly astounded.

Pat Roberts, a London guitarist, saw the tripleneck and contacted Manson to propose a quadrupleneck. The unparalleled guitar, which took two years of on-and-off work to complete, combines 6- and 12-string, mandolin, and tiple necks. (A tiple is a four-course, medium-scale instrument of Argentinian origin.)

Another experimental guitar that contributed to Manson's reputation for adventurousness was a collapsible model. This was first executed as a special order for John Paul Jones, who desired a high-quality acoustic that could be dismantled and packed into a small hardshell case for ease of transport on aircraft. Several others have been built since the prototype.

Manson estimates a $1,824.00 price tag for a tripleneck without inlays or pickups; to duplicate Roberts' quadru-

The predecessor of the quadrupleneck: John Paul Jones' tripleneck, combining 6-string, 12-string, and mandolin. Although novel in appearance, the instrument was built with a practical aim in mind—putting a variety of sounds within hand's reach. The neck is made of Brazilian mahogany and ebony; the back and sides are maple; the soundboard is spruce. Special features include string dampers (hinged metal plates backed with firm rubber at the string nuts), and internal Barcus—Berry transducers (hence the volume control knob at the mandolin's upper bouts). The cloverleaf shape of the soundholes is ornamental—part of the Celtic motif of inlays and rosette.

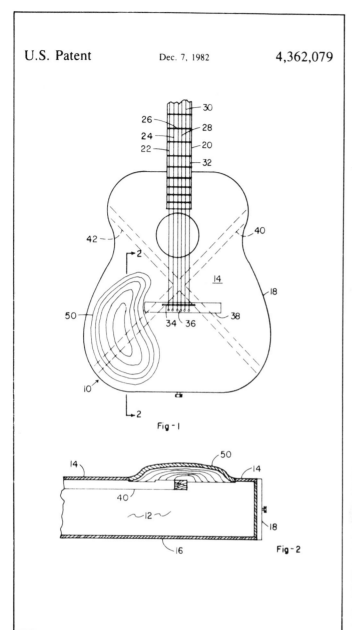

U.S. Patent Dec. 7, 1982 4,362,079

Fig - 1

Fig - 2

Above left: Diagram from U.S. Patent for "Accentuator Plate For Vibrating Soundboard In Stringed Musical Instruments"—Sound Bubble, for short. A patent application has also been filed on the guitar's unique bracing system. **Right:** The collapsible shown here belongs to Canadian guitarist Mike Mathews, who designed the inlays, bridgeplate, and soundhole. The neck/body joint is a dovetail fan and socket arrangement, while the headstock/neck joint is augmented with a spring-loaded catch. Humidity changes can wreak havoc on the fitting of wooden joints, a problem Manson overcame by applying an ebony veneer to the neck's fan joint, and a leather lining in the body's dovetail socket. Ebony is relatively stable under humidity shifts,

while flexible leather adapts to minor expansions or contractions. **Opposite left:** William Eaton built his 16-string lyre with a burlwood top that he bookmatched to create a natural soundhole. Below the bridge, the strings are an octave higher than they are above it.

pleneck would cost the buyer approximately $4,500.00. The price of custom work varies considerably, depending upon the specifications.

"It's not just something a little bit different—it's a radically different approach to the acoustic instrument," says inventor/artisan Charles Kelly. What is it? The Sound Bubble—U.S. Patent 4,362,079.

The Sound Bubble may be described as a slightly domed, kidney-shaped area on the bass side of the lower bout. It is an unlikely looking innovation, but according to Kelly, the Sound Bubble dramatically increases acoustic efficiency, or the guitar's ability to translate the energy of the strings into sound. The

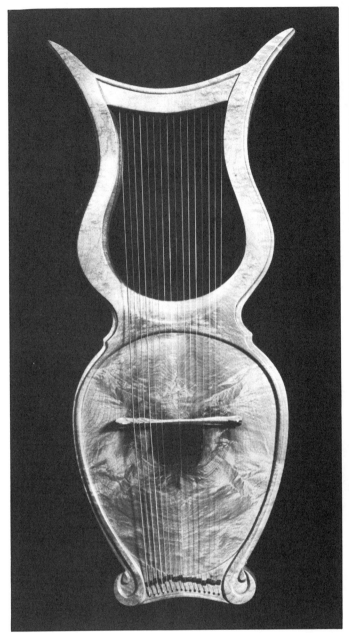

top of a regular guitar is pumped in a fairly uniform motion by the bridge. According to Kelly, the Sound Bubble creates a different stiffness ratio between the left and right halves of the guitar, thereby inducing a laminar (streamlined) air flow within the sound-box. This in turn decreases energy loss from friction, resulting in a gain in acoustic efficiency.

The Sound Bubble guitar is built by R & K Engineering of San Francisco, California. The Sound Bubble guitar costs approximately $1,500.00; the price of fitting a standard guitar with a Sound Bubble top depends upon the instrument.

Cosmic coincidence seemed to be

operating the day a student of Phoenix luthier John Roberts came knocking at the door of William Eaton's Tempe, Arizona, home in 1971. The student was offering to sell a guitar he had made. Eaton was so intrigued that he paid a visit to Roberts' shop in the city. One thing led to another, and today Eaton has risen to instructor's status at the Roberto-Venn School of Lutherie (formed by Roberts and associate Bob Venn).

Though one can tell at a glance that his instruments are out of the ordinary, Eaton seems surprised to hear the term "radical" used in conjunction with them. "I don't consider them radical," he says. "It's been said that there's nothing new

under the sun, and when you study all the different kinds of instruments, you find that almost every kind of concept is already out there. By the same token, my instruments are variations on themes that have existed throughout eternity, and for me they do include the present, and past, and future."

Eaton's first experimental guitar,

which followed a half-dozen conventional acoustics, was the 26-string guitar shown here. The auxiliary strings (two sets of seven) do more than vibrate sympathetically; they are tuned diatonically to the key of the composition being played and may be plucked or strummed. A flattened string bridge gives two of the auxiliaries a sitar-like buzz. The six pairs of strings at center are tuned E-E, A-A, D-E, G-G, B-C, and D-E. The enormous string tension is kept from buckling the top by an inner reinforcing frame of basswood that follows the contour of the sides.

The harp guitar is not unprecedented in concept, though its crossed-strings design may well be unique. The range of the instrument is from three octaves below Middle C to B♭ above it. Curly white birch proved to be ideal for the frame because of its lightness and dense-grained sturdiness.

The magnificent doubleneck creation known as O'ele'n Strings (pronounced o-ay-lin) took nearly a year and a half to complete. Its name derives from the 11 drone strings between the two necks. Though its baroque form and decoration seem to echo a lute or theorbo, the original inspiration for this instrument was an engraved design on a large wardrobe closet.

The instruments shown here are one-of-a-kind creations, making it difficult to fix prices; however, Eaton is willing to consider commissions on a custom-order basis.

David Alzofon

Two views of William Eaton's 26-string guitar, which features "male and female" shaped soundholes in the upper left and right bouts. Their conception began as a meditation on Indian musical notation.

ALTERNATIVE ELECTRICS

June 1983. Many common features on automobiles such as fuel injection and independent suspension were originally the ideas of mechanics and designers involved with building custom racing machines. Often, innovations in guitar design have evolved in much the same way, with specialized or custom items gradually working their way into manu-

facturers' lists of standard features. While large companies strive to build instruments having wide appeal, it is often the individual luthier who leads the field in design creativity.

Although the instruments featured in the following article differ radically, one thing they have in common is that each was built by an experienced

guitarist. While it remains to be seen if these designs can succeed in a highly competitive marketplace, they nevertheless serve valid functions not filled by conventional guitars.

Steve Ripley's 6-Channel Stereo Guitar. Four years ago 33-year-old recording engineer/guitarist Steve Ripley, who's worked with Leon Russell and Bob Dylan, among others, decided to build an electric guitar that could be recorded in true stereo. "It occurred to me that I could record almost any instrument in stereo except for the electric guitar—its sound comes from one

Ripley's Guitar has pan pots for placing each string at a different point in the stereo spectrum.

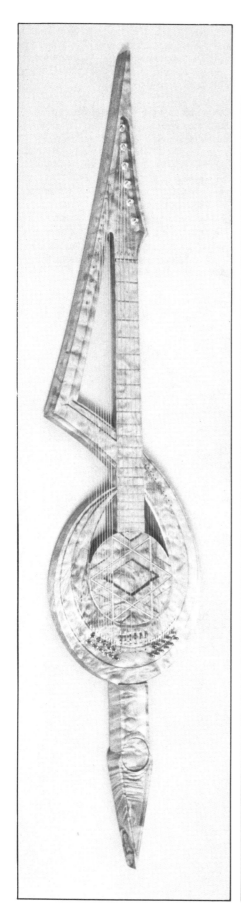

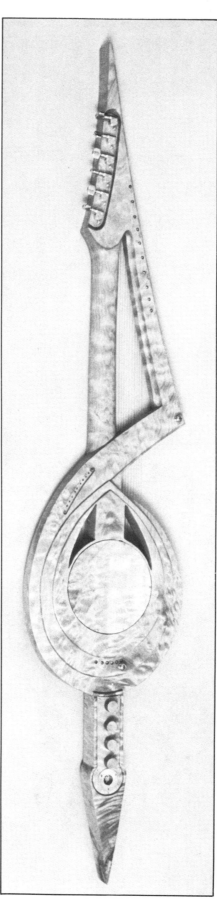

speaker," he explains. "Our ears want to hear stereo. In recording, about 90% of the time a producer wants the rhythm guitar tracks at least doubled so that they can be put left and right. With my instrument, an infinitely variable stereo mix can be achieved onboard. Any combination of strings can be directed through any channel. This creates a much fuller sound than regular instruments and gives a guitarist versatility of sound he never had."

Ripley worked with pickup designer Bill Bartolini on the guitar's specially wound 6-channel humbucking pickups. Special circuitry tunes each pickup's response to that of standard humbuckers (because its bobbins are cylindrical as opposed to oblong, the pickups operate at a much higher frequency than usual), and each coil has its own preamp—12 in all. "While I've always been a fan of passive electronics, it took a certain amount of circuitry to create a stereo guitar that sounds like conventional instruments," Steve says.

Six 3-position toggle switches located near the tailpiece allow for separate selection of either front, back, or both pickups for each string. And all six channels have pan pots that enable the final signals to be mixed for stereo output. A mode switch cuts out the six toggles, bypassing the instrument's 6-channel capabilities. Other features include tone and volume controls, Gotoh tuners, and a brass bridge. Steve Ripley's 6-channel stereo guitar costs $2,000.00.

William Eaton's Spiral Clef Guitar. "If I were to put a price tag on this instrument based on the number of hours worked, it would have a value of between $1,000.00 and $2,000.00. But if you factor in its magic, design, creativity, and other intangibles, maybe its worth a lot more," William Eaton explains about his 27-string electric, which was inspired by a musical tone.

Carved from a single piece of quilted maple, Eaton's guitar features a conventional 6-string neck and two groups of sympathetic strings (10 strings are positioned to the left of the neck, and 11 to the right). Autoharp tuners are used for the drone strings, while gold-plated Schaller Mini tuners adjust the center six strings.

William's instrument is quadraphonic and uses four bar-type pickups, which he built by hand (two are used on

Front and back views of Eaton's Spiral Clef Guitar: Note four volume knobs on the instrument's back.

the 6-string neck, while one is employed for each group of sympathetic strings). The pickups are integrated into the star design on the main body of the instrument and are controlled by four volume pots located on the back of the tail section. A female Cannon (4-pin) connector enables the unit to be used with a custom speaker system. All strings attach from the back of the body, and the specially designed tuneable bridge (6-string neck) uses six triangle-shaped pieces which slide in a track.

Although Eaton's instruments were built with his own classical and folk-influenced music in mind, he does accept commissions: "I tailor an instrument to a person's essence and their perception of music."

Dave Petschulat's Doubleneck Guitar.

Luthier Dave Petschulat has made instruments for Mick Jones, Nancy Wilson, Steve Morse, Dave Hlubek, Jackson Browne, and Eddie Van Halen, although the detachable doubleneck was intended for his own use: "I came up with the interlocking system because I wanted to have more versatility with my own sound by being able to change quickly to another guitar." But besides the fact that its bodies separate, what really qualifies Dave's instrument as an alternative electric is that it's probably the first time a solidbody has been joined to an *acoustic* guitar.

The acoustic upper guitar features a spruce top, mahogany back and sides, and an ebony fingerboard and bridge. A transducer (pickup) and small preamp are located under a back panel. The electric neck features a mahogany back, a maple top, and an ebony fingerboard, and two Seymour Duncan JB H-4 pickups. Because a pan pedal with a center-tap pot is used to switch between necks, two cords are necessary. All equalization is achieved offboard, so the solidbody has only a volume control. Straplok connectors enable the two bodies to be separated quickly.

Petschulat's doubleneck is equipped with a vibrato system of his own design: "I make all of the parts by hand. I'm currently working on a system that will eliminate clamps. And I'm developing a concept that could revolutionize the way necks are fretted." About the shape of the instrument, Dave says: "I've always liked the aggressiveness of the Gibson Explorer; there's an obvious sim-

Eaton's quadraphonic Cloud guitar has 10 pickups arranged in four groups.

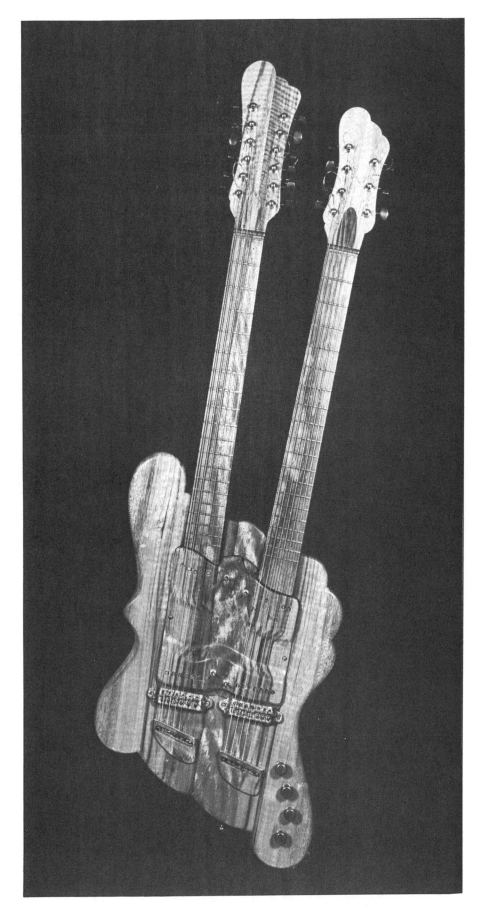

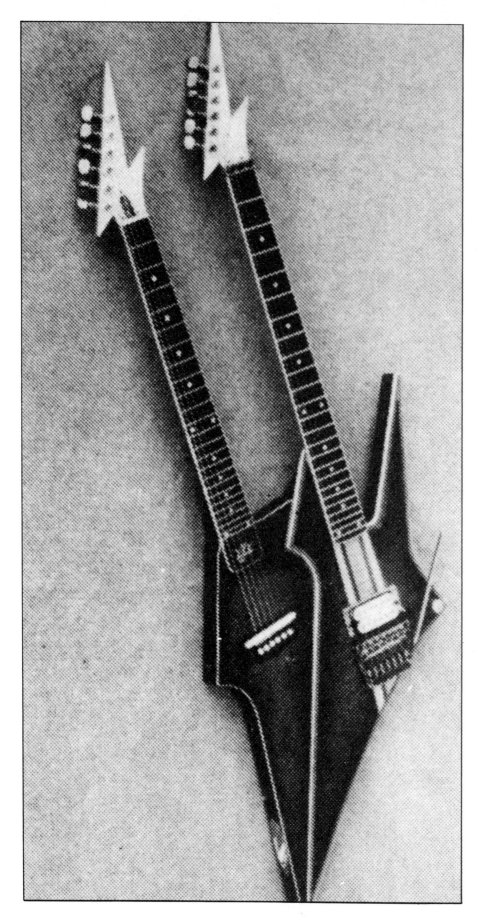

ilarity. I was trying to build a guitar that looked as if it could be ridden as well as played." Dave Petschulat's doublenecks cost about $3,000.00.

Gary Ejen's Flutar. While Gary Ejen is working on designs for a new kind of drum synthesizer and a gyro-elevation anti-gravity car, the Flutar is his first actual prototype. Built expressly for two-handed technique, the Flutar features a 30-fret, 31" scale length and an extra-wide fingerboard. "The name Flutar was used because two-handed technique playing often results in melodies that are very flute-like. I wanted the electric guitar to be known as an instrument of beauty, as well as power," says Gary.

In addition to providing more playing room, the Flutar's extended neck enhances its ability to feed back and makes fretting easier because the longer scale length results in reduced string tension. Both the neck and body are made of ash, and the instrument is equipped with Ibanez pickups and circuitry. Gary builds on a custom basis and offers the Flutar for about $900.00.

After considering several body shapes, Ejen finally settled on the one he considered to be the most futuristic looking. Although Ejen's second prototype will be the same shape as the first, it will employ several new features: "My next guitar is going to be made of polymer resin, and will use a new, patented photographic finish that will rival some of the most beautiful woods. The new process results in a very high gloss and gives the impression of a distorted, highly altered wood grain."

Dave Bunker's Touch Guitar/Organ. Dave Bunker is no stranger to innovative guitar design: In the mid-'60s he developed a headless electric that included separate pickups for each string. His latest concept, the Bunker Touch Guitar/Organ, combines the touch capabilities of a Chapman Stick, the familiarity of standard guitar fingerboards, and the high-tech features of an electric organ.

Although the lower fingerboard can be played with conventional technique, both necks use sensitive, specially designed electronics that are touch activated (electronic muting ensures

Left: Dave Petschulat's doubleneck comes apart, allowing the guitarist to use either half separately. Right: Gary Ejen's Flutar features a 30-fret fingerboard and is designed expressly for two-handed fretting technique.

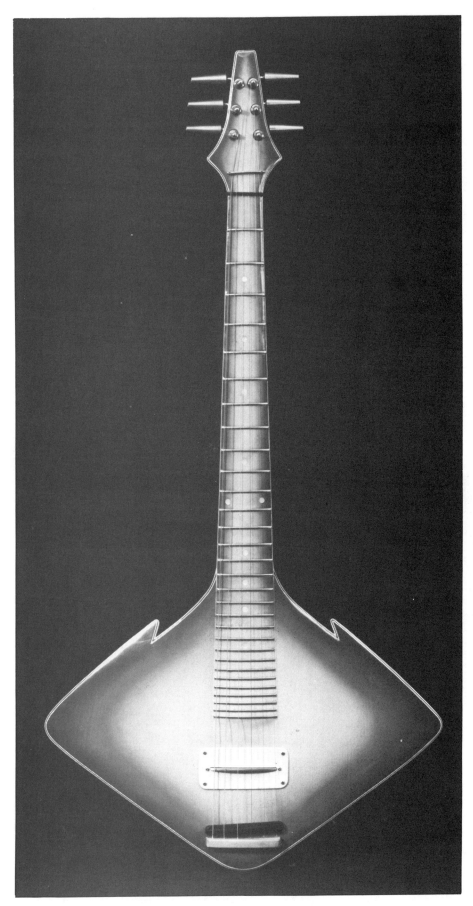

that the strings are totally silent unless pressed). The 8-string neck (the high *E* and *B* strings are tuned in pairs) is played by the right hand reaching over the fretboard, while the 4-string neck is played from a conventional left-hand position. Each string has two pickups (front and back), which can be individually balanced. Both maple necks are headless and use Bunker-designed tuners located at the base of the walnut body.

While the Bunker Touch Guitar/ Organ is compatible with a standard guitar amplifier, it is designed to be used with a special microprocessor system similar to that of an electronic organ. A control panel mounted on top of the instrument's case enables up to 16 different programs to be preselected. (In addition to various organ stops, programming options include a choice of pickups, filters, and the musical range desired.) Each program is conveniently activated by a memory piston (push button) located next to the 6-string fingerboard. Multiple channels are available at the output.

Regarding the time it takes for a guitarist to get used to his instrument, Dave says, "You can play simple stuff in about two months, but it takes from six months to a year to become proficient." The Touch Guitar/Organ alone (without memory pistons) sells for $2,500.00. A ten-piston model costs from $4,800.00 to $5,200.00, while the 16-piston instrument goes for around $9,000.00.

Keith Bell's Bellform E-3 Guitar. "I couldn't buy the kind of guitar I wanted, so I built one myself," explains Keith Bell, who has worked as a model builder for several major auto companies, including Chrysler, Ford, and General Motors.

The E-3's neck/tailstock assembly is a single piece of carbon fiber and epoxy casting (a previous prototype was aluminum), which is light but strong. A quick-release tailpiece (using levers to take up string slack) and special built-in tuning machines with an 18:1 gear ratio enable the guitar's strings to be changed in less than 30 seconds.

A 3-position toggle switch controlling the selection of pickups is recessed near the cutaway to eliminate accidental tripping. A 9-position sliding switch enables a variety of effects to be selected at the guitar, rather than with footpedals. In addition, the instrument uses two 3-coil pickups of Bell's own design; one is built into the fingerboard, while the other is near the bridge. A slot

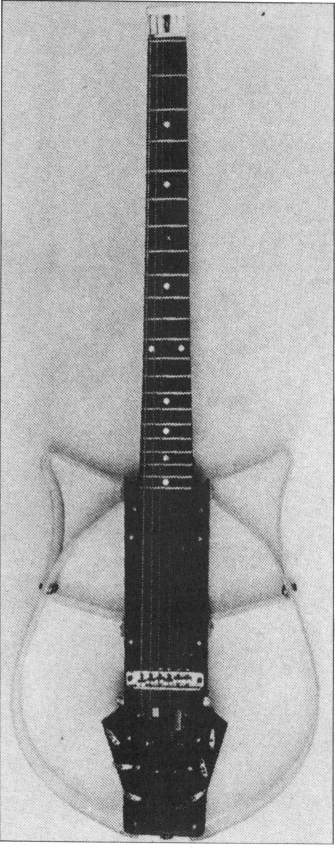

between the two pickups allows for the quick installation of additional units (note position of Seymour Duncan pickup in photo).

Modulus' Folding Guitar. Geoff Gould's Modulus company has produced necks and guitars made of graphite and epoxy since 1977. Molded single pieces of graphite, the necks of his instruments are extremely strong, yet lightweight. But Gould isn't the only innovator at Modulus. Larry Robinson, one of Geoff's employees, has recently combined several ideas into a unique design: an extremely light, folding guitar.

Robinson's instrument uses a patented folding mechanism designed by Leigh Copeland, and folds where the headless neck joins the approximately 4½"-wide body (both the body and neck are graphite). Like the tuning machines, the release/locking mechanism is part of the guitar's tailpiece assembly.

Notably, the perimeter of the body (rounded portion) is formed by flexible polypropylene straps, which collapse close to the body for compact carrying or storage; the instrument has a total length of 19" when folded. Other features include two EMG mini humbucking pickups, and sliding volume and tone controls. Production of the guitar is contingent upon a legal agreement between Robinson, Copeland, and Modulus.

Jim Ferguson

Although Bell has built approximately 15 acoustic and electric prototypes, the E-3 is the first to go into production. He expects the guitar's price to range from $2,600.00 to $3,000.00.

Far left: Dave Bunker's Touch Guitar/Organ combines touch capability with organ design. Left: Modulus' Folding Guitar has a body perimeter consisting of flexible polypropylene straps.

ABOUT THE AUTHORS

David Alzofon is a freelance writer and author of the instruction manual *Mastering Guitar* (Simon & Shuster, '81).

Craig Anderton is widely known as an expert writer on musical electronics. He is the author of *Electronic Projects For Musicians* and *Home Recording For Musicians*, the former editor of *Polyphony Magazine*, and a long-time contributor to *Guitar Player*.

John Brosh is a freelance writer and editor who's work has appeared in *Guitar Player* and other music publications.

John Carruthers is a Southern California luthier/repairman who has designed, built, and modified guitars for scores of well known rock and studio players.

Jim Ferguson is an assistant editor for *Guitar Player* and an accomplished jazz and classical guitarist. As a freelance writer, his work has appeared in many publications. He has also written notes for albums by Jim Hall, Tal Farlow, and Charlie Byrd.

George Gruhn, head of Nashville's Gruhn Guitars, is one of America's most highly respected collectors, historians, and rare guitar dealers. He has been a regular columnist for *Guitar Player* since 1976.

Richard Honeycutt is a freelance writer with an expertise in the electrical engineering of amplifiers.

Whitey Morrison is Gibson's plant manager at their Nashville facility.

Tom Mulhern is associate editor for *Guitar Player* and has been with GPI Publications since 1977.

Jas Obrecht is an assistant editor for *Guitar Player* and an accomplished blues guitarist, writer and editor, who's work has appeared in many publications.

Aspen Pittman is an audio equipment designer, consultant, and long-time guitar player.

Keith Reinegger is an electrical engineer with extensive experience in amplifier design, as well as repairs and modifications.

Jim Schwartz is a former assistant editor for *Guitar Player* who is now a Professor of English at South Dakota School of Mines and Technology.

Jon Sievert is the staff photographer for GPI Publications and has authored numerous articles for *Guitar Player, Frets,* and *Keyboard,* and other music magazines.

Tom Wheeler is the editor for *Guitar Player* and author of *The Guitar Book* ('76) and *American Guitars* ('83, both published by Harper & Row).

Read these other distinguished music books compiled by the editors of Guitar Player, Keyboard, and Frets magazines.**

▶ MASTERS OF HEAVY METAL
Edited by Jas Obrecht
"Goes to the eye of the hurricane," (Portland, Oregonian). "Fascinating!" (Newark Star Ledger). For fans and players of the immensely powerful, hugely popular, hard-core rock and roll style: intense, high-energy, guitar-dominated. Including serious, informative interviews with Jimi Hendrix, Eddie Van Halen, Jimmy Page, Randy Rhoads, Judas Priest, the Scorpions, and others. Profusely illustrated.
Paperback/$8.95 0-688-02937-X

▦ ROCK KEYBOARD
Edited by Bob Doerschuk   Foreword by Keith Emerson
The first major book to document and celebrate thirty years of rock and roll keyboard history: the creative genius, the incredible personalities, the technical development. From boogie-woogie ancestry to the most sophisticated electronic synthesizers. Including exclusive interviews, true history, and astute analysis of Fats Domino, Little Richard, Jerry Lee Lewis, Al Kooper, Leon Russell, Booker T. Jones, Elton John, Billy Joel, Michael McDonald, David Paich & Steve Porcaro, Brian Eno, Thomas Dolby, and others. Photos throughout.
Paperback/$12.95/0-688-02961-2

▦ THE BIG BOOK OF BLUEGRASS
Edited by Marilyn Kochman   Foreword by Earl Scruggs
Bill Monroe, Lester Flatt, Earl Scruggs, David Grisman, Ricky Skaggs, and other popular bluegrass artists offer practical tips on playing, with note-by-note musical examples, plus valuable advice on technique and performance. The history, the greatest players, the genuine art of this authentic American commercial country folk music, more pupular than ever today. Over 100 rare photos and over 50 favorite songs.
Hardcover/$24.95/0-688-02940-X
Paperback/$12.95/0-688-02942-X

▦ THE ART OF ELECTRONIC MUSIC
Edited by Greg Armbruster & Tom Darter   Foreword by Dr. Robert A. Moog
The first definitive book: the creative and technical development of an authentic musical revolution. From the Theremin Electrical Symphony to today's most advanced synthesizers. Scientific origins, the evolution of hardware, the greatest artists—in stories, interviews, illustrations, analysis, and practical musical technique. From the pages of Keyboard Magazine.
Hardcover/0-688-03105-6
Paperback/0-688-03106-4

From your bookstores or directly from the publisher.

QUILL
A Division of William Morrow & Company
105 Madison Avenue
New York, NY 10016

**To subscribe, write GPI, 20085 Stevens Creek, Cupertino, CA 95014.